GCSE
Combined Science
Chemistry

The Complete Course for Edexcel

How to get your free Online Edition

Go to **cgpbooks.co.uk/extras** and enter this code...

0851 6287 7301 3995

This code will only work once. If someone has used this book before you, they may have already claimed the Online Edition.

Published by CGP

From original material by Paddy Gannon.

Editors:
Alex Billings, Katie Burton, Mary Falkner, Robin Flello, Sarah Pattison, Sophie Scott, Hayley Thompson.

Contributor:
Mike Bossart

ISBN: 978 1 78294 815 5

With thanks to Katherine Faudemer and Rachel Kordan for the proofreading.
With thanks to Ana Pungartnik for the copyright research.

Edexcel specification reference points reproduced by permission of Edexcel and Pearson Education.

Page 28 contains public sector information published by the Health and Safety Executive
and licensed under the Open Government Licence.
http://www.nationalarchives.gov.uk/doc/open-government-licence/version/3/

Graph to show trend in atmospheric carbon dioxide level and global temperature on page 235
based on data by EPICA community members 2004 and Siegenthaler et al 2005.

Printed by Elanders Ltd, Newcastle upon Tyne.
Clipart from Corel®

Contents

Introduction

Working Scientifically

Topic 1 — Key Concepts in Chemistry

Topic 1a — Formulae, Equations and Hazards

Topic 1b — Atomic Structure and the Periodic Table

Topic 1c — Bonding and Types of Substance

Topic 1d — Calculations Involving Masses

Topic 2 — States of Matter and Mixtures

Topic 3 — Chemical Changes

Topic 4 — Extracting Metals and Equilibria

Topic 4a — Obtaining and Using Metals

Topic 4b — Reversible Reactions and Equilibria

Topic 6 — Groups in the Periodic Table

We've missed out Topic 5 because, for GCSE Combined Science, you don't need to learn it — it's only for students who are taking the GCSE Chemistry qualification.

Topic 7 — Rates of Reaction and Energy Changes

Topic 7a — Rates of Reaction

Topic 7b — Energy Changes in Reactions

Topic 8 — Fuels and Earth Science

Practical Skills

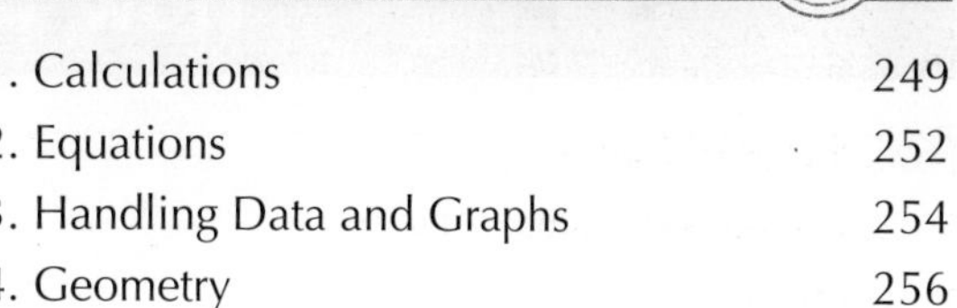

Maths Skills

Exam Help

Reference

How to use this book

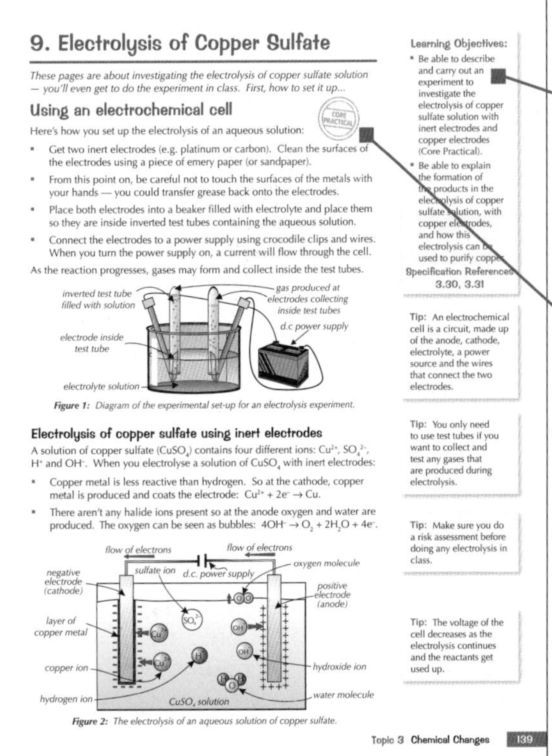

9. Electrolysis of Copper Sulfate

These pages are about investigating the electrolysis of copper sulfate solution — you'll even get to do the experiment in class. First, how to set it up...

Using an electrochemical cell

CORE PRACTICAL

Here's how you set up the electrolysis of an aqueous solution:

- Get two inert electrodes (e.g. platinum or carbon). Clean the surfaces of the electrodes using a piece of emery paper (or sandpaper).
- From this point on, be careful not to touch the surfaces of the metals with your hands — you could transfer grease back onto the electrodes.
- Place both electrodes into a beaker filled with electrolyte and place them so they are inside inverted test tubes containing the aqueous solution.
- Connect the electrodes to a power supply using crocodile clips and wires. When you turn the power supply on, a current will flow through the cell.

As the reaction progresses, gases may form and collect inside the test tubes.

Figure 1: Diagram of the experimental set-up for an electrolysis experiment.

Electrolysis of copper sulfate using inert electrodes

A solution of copper sulfate ($CuSO_4$) contains four different ions: Cu^{2+}, SO_4^{2-}, H^+ and OH^-. When you electrolyse a solution of $CuSO_4$ with inert electrodes:

- Copper metal is less reactive than hydrogen. So at the cathode, copper metal is produced and coats the electrode: $Cu^{2+} + 2e^- \rightarrow Cu$.
- There aren't any halide ions present so at the anode oxygen and water are produced. The oxygen can be seen as bubbles: $4OH^- \rightarrow O_2 + 2H_2O + 4e^-$.

Figure 2: The electrolysis of an aqueous solution of copper sulfate.

Learning Objectives:

- Be able to describe and carry out an experiment to investigate the electrolysis of copper sulfate solution with inert electrodes and copper electrodes (Core Practical).
- Be able to explain the formation of the products in the electrolysis of copper sulfate solution, with copper electrodes, and how this electrolysis can be used to purify copper.

Specification Reference 3.30, 3.31

Tip: An electrochemical cell is a circuit, made up of the anode, cathode, electrolyte, a power source and the wires that connect the two electrodes.

Tip: You only need to use test tubes if you want to collect and test any gases that are produced during electrolysis.

Tip: Make sure you do a risk assessment before doing any electrolysis in class.

Tip: The voltage of the cell decreases as the electrolysis continues and the reactants get used up.

Topic 3 **Chemical Changes** 139

Learning Objectives

- These tell you exactly what you need to learn, or be able to do, for the exam.
- There's a specification reference at the bottom that links to the Edexcel specification.

Core Practicals

There are some Core Practicals that you'll be expected to do throughout your course. You need to know all about them for the exams. They're all marked up with this symbol:

CORE PRACTICAL

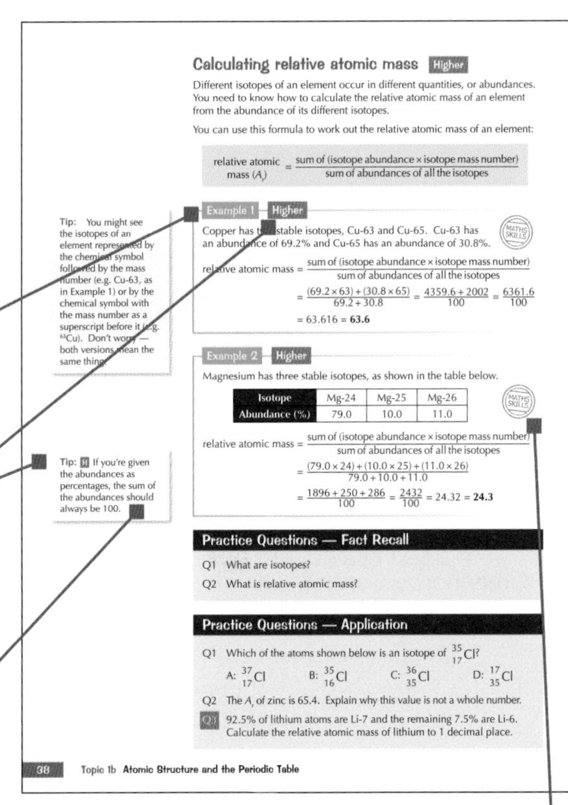

Calculating relative atomic mass Higher

Different isotopes of an element occur in different quantities, or abundances. You need to know how to calculate the relative atomic mass of an element from the abundance of its different isotopes.

You can use this formula to work out the relative atomic mass of an element:

$$\text{relative atomic mass } (A_r) = \frac{\text{sum of (isotope abundance} \times \text{isotope mass number)}}{\text{sum of abundances of all the isotopes}}$$

Example 1 Higher

Copper has two stable isotopes, Cu-63 and Cu-65. Cu-63 has an abundance of 69.2% and Cu-65 has an abundance of 30.8%.

MATHS SKILLS

$$\text{relative atomic mass} = \frac{\text{sum of (isotope abundance} \times \text{isotope mass number)}}{\text{sum of abundances of all the isotopes}}$$

$$= \frac{(69.2 \times 63) + (30.8 \times 65)}{69.2 + 30.8} = \frac{4359.6 + 2002}{100} = \frac{6361.6}{100}$$

$$= 63.616 = \mathbf{63.6}$$

Example 2 Higher

Magnesium has three stable isotopes, as shown in the table below.

MATHS SKILLS

Isotope	Mg-24	Mg-25	Mg-26
Abundance (%)	79.0	10.0	11.0

$$\text{relative atomic mass} = \frac{\text{sum of (isotope abundance} \times \text{isotope mass number)}}{\text{sum of abundances of all the isotopes}}$$

$$= \frac{(79.0 \times 24) + (10.0 \times 25) + (11.0 \times 26)}{79.0 + 10.0 + 11.0}$$

$$= \frac{1896 + 250 + 286}{100} = \frac{2432}{100} = 24.32 = \mathbf{24.3}$$

Tip: You might see the isotopes of an element represented by the chemical symbol followed by the mass number (e.g. Cu-63, as in Example 1) or by the chemical symbol with the mass number as a superscript before it (e.g. ^{63}Cu). Don't worry — both versions mean the same thing.

Tip: H If you're given the abundances as percentages, the sum of the abundances should always be 100.

Practice Questions — Fact Recall

Q1 What are isotopes?

Q2 What is relative atomic mass?

Practice Questions — Application

Q1 Which of the atoms shown below is an isotope of $^{35}_{17}Cl$?

A: $^{37}_{17}Cl$ B: $^{35}_{16}Cl$ C: $^{36}_{35}Cl$ D: $^{17}_{35}Cl$

Q2 The A_r of zinc is 65.4. Explain why this value is not a whole number.

Q3 92.5% of lithium atoms are Li-7 and the remaining 7.5% are Li-6. Calculate the relative atomic mass of lithium to 1 decimal place.

38 Topic 1b **Atomic Structure and the Periodic Table**

Examples

These are here to help you understand the theory.

Higher Exam Material

- Some of the material in the book will only come up in the exam if you're sitting the higher exam papers.
- This material is clearly marked with boxes that look like this:

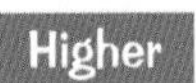

Tips and Exam Tips

- There are tips throughout the book to help you understand the theory.
- There are also exam tips to help you with answering exam questions.

Maths Skills

- There's a range of maths skills you could be expected to apply in your exams. The section on pages 249-256 is packed with plenty of maths that you'll need to be familiar with.
- Examples that show these maths skills in action are marked up with this symbol:

MATHS SKILLS

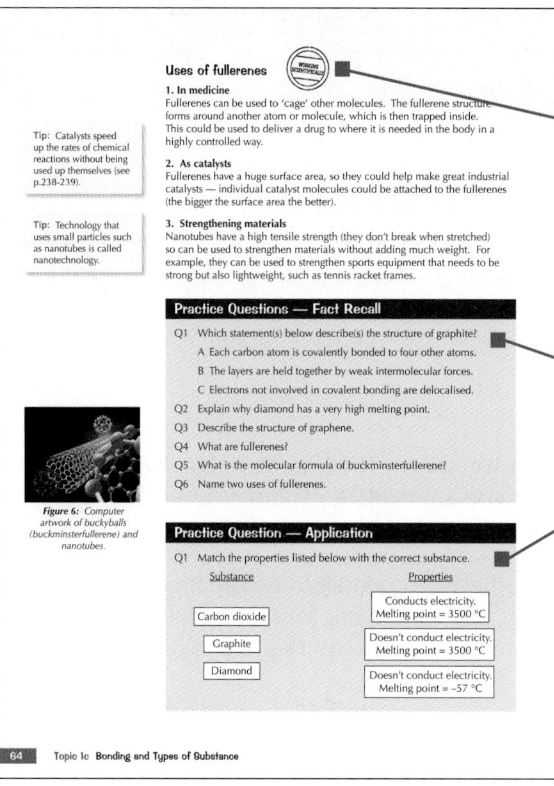

Uses of fullerenes

1. In medicine
Fullerenes can be used to 'cage' other molecules. The fullerene structure forms around another atom or molecule, which is then trapped inside. This could be used to deliver a drug to where it is needed in the body in a highly controlled way.

Tip: Catalysts speed up the rates of chemical reactions without being used up themselves (see p.238-239).

2. As catalysts
Fullerenes have a huge surface area, so they could help make great industrial catalysts — individual catalyst molecules could be attached to the fullerenes (the bigger the surface area the better).

Tip: Technology that uses small particles such as nanotubes is called nanotechnology.

3. Strengthening materials
Nanotubes have a high tensile strength (they don't break when stretched) so can be used to strengthen materials without adding much weight. For example, they can be used to strengthen sports equipment that needs to be strong but also lightweight, such as tennis racket frames.

Practice Questions — Fact Recall

Q1 Which statement(s) below describe(s) the structure of graphite?
A Each carbon atom is covalently bonded to four other atoms.
B The layers are held together by weak intermolecular forces.
C Electrons not involved in covalent bonding are delocalised.
Q2 Explain why diamond has a very high melting point.
Q3 Describe the structure of graphene.
Q4 What are fullerenes?
Q5 What is the molecular formula of buckminsterfullerene?
Q6 Name two uses of fullerenes.

Figure 6: Computer artwork of buckyballs (buckminsterfullerene) and nanotubes.

Practice Question — Application

Q1 Match the properties listed below with the correct substance.

Substance	Properties
Carbon dioxide	Conducts electricity. Melting point = 3500 °C
Graphite	Doesn't conduct electricity. Melting point = 3500 °C
Diamond	Doesn't conduct electricity. Melting point = –57 °C

64 Topic 1c Bonding and Types of Substance

Working Scientifically

- Working Scientifically is a big part of GCSE Combined Science. There's a whole section on it at the front of the book.
- Working Scientifically is also covered throughout the book wherever you see this symbol:

Practice Questions

- Fact recall questions test that you know the facts needed for your chemistry exams.
- Annoyingly, the examiners also expect you to be able to apply your knowledge to new situations — application questions give you plenty of practice at doing this.
- All the answers are in the back of the book.

Practical Skills

There's also a whole section on pages 241-248 with extra details on practical skills you'll be expected to use in the Core Practicals, and apply knowledge of in the exams.

Exam-style Questions

- Practising exam-style questions is really important — this book has some at the end of every topic to test you.
- They're the same style as the ones you'll get in the real exams.
- All the answers are in the back of the book, along with a mark scheme to show you how you get the marks.
- Higher-only questions are marked like this: 

Topic Checklist

Each topic has a checklist at the end with boxes that let you tick off what you've learnt.

Glossary

There's a glossary at the back of the book full of definitions you need to know for the exams, plus loads of other useful words.

Exam Help

There's a section at the back of the book stuffed full of things to help you with the exams.

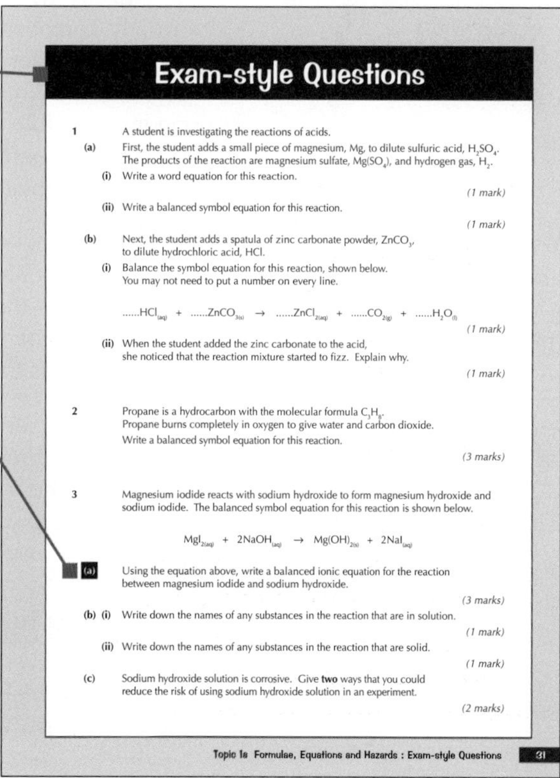

Exam-style Questions

1 A student is investigating the reactions of acids.
(a) First, the student adds a small piece of magnesium, Mg, to dilute sulfuric acid, H_2SO_4. The products of the reaction are magnesium sulfate, $Mg(SO_4)$, and hydrogen gas, H_2.
(i) Write a word equation for this reaction. *(1 mark)*
(ii) Write a balanced symbol equation for this reaction. *(1 mark)*
(b) Next, the student adds a spatula of zinc carbonate powder, $ZnCO_3$, to dilute hydrochloric acid, HCl.
(i) Balance the symbol equation for this reaction, shown below. You may not need to put a number on every line.
$$......HCl_{(aq)} + ...ZnCO_{3(s)} \rightarrow ......ZnCl_{2(aq)} + ...CO_{2(g)} + ...H_2O_{(l)}$$
(1 mark)
(ii) When the student added the zinc carbonate to the acid, she noticed that the reaction mixture started to fizz. Explain why. *(1 mark)*

2 Propane is a hydrocarbon with the molecular formula C_3H_8. Propane burns completely in oxygen to give water and carbon dioxide. Write a balanced symbol equation for this reaction. *(3 marks)*

3 Magnesium iodide reacts with sodium hydroxide to form magnesium hydroxide and sodium iodide. The balanced symbol equation for this reaction is shown below.
$$MgI_{2(aq)} + 2NaOH_{(aq)} \rightarrow Mg(OH)_{2(s)} + 2NaI_{(aq)}$$
(a) Using the equation above, write a balanced ionic equation for the reaction between magnesium iodide and sodium hydroxide. *(3 marks)*
(b) (i) Write down the names of any substances in the reaction that are in solution. *(1 mark)*
(ii) Write down the names of any substances in the reaction that are solid. *(1 mark)*
(c) Sodium hydroxide solution is corrosive. Give **two** ways that you could reduce the risk of using sodium hydroxide solution in an experiment. *(2 marks)*

Topic 1a Formulae, Equations and Hazards : Exam-style Questions 31

1. The Scientific Method

Science is all about finding things out and learning things about the world we live in. This topic is all about the scientific process — how a scientist's initial idea turns into a theory that is accepted by the wider scientific community.

Hypotheses

Scientists try to explain things. Everything. They start by observing something they don't understand — it could be anything, e.g. planets in the sky, a person suffering from an illness, what matter is made of... anything.

Then, they come up with a **hypothesis** — a possible explanation for what they've observed. (Scientists can also sometimes form a model too — a simplified description or a representation of what's physically going on — see next page).

The next step is to test whether the hypothesis might be right or not. This involves making a **prediction** based on the hypothesis and testing it by gathering evidence (i.e. data) from investigations. If evidence from experiments backs up a prediction, you're a step closer to figuring out if the hypothesis is true.

Testing a hypothesis

Normally, scientists share their findings in peer-reviewed journals, or at conferences. **Peer-review** is where other scientists check results and scientific explanations to make sure they're 'scientific' (e.g. that experiments have been done in a sensible way) before they're published. It helps to detect false claims, but it doesn't mean that findings are correct — just that they're not wrong in any obvious way.

Tip: Investigations include lab experiments and studies.

Once other scientists have found out about a hypothesis, they'll start basing their own predictions on it and carry out their own experiments. They'll also try to reproduce the original experiments to check the results — and if all the experiments in the world back up the hypothesis, then scientists start to think the hypothesis is true.

Tip: Sometimes it can take a really long time for a hypothesis to be accepted.

However, if a scientist somewhere in the world does an experiment that doesn't fit with the hypothesis (and other scientists can reproduce these results), then the hypothesis is in trouble. When this happens, scientists have to come up with a new hypothesis (maybe a modification of the old hypothesis, or maybe a completely new one).

Accepting a hypothesis

If pretty much every scientist in the world believes a hypothesis to be true because experiments back it up, then it usually goes in the textbooks for students to learn. Accepted hypotheses are often referred to as **theories**.

Our currently accepted theories are the ones that have survived this 'trial by evidence' — they've been tested many, many times over the years and survived (while the less good ones have been ditched). However... they never, never become hard and fast, totally indisputable fact. You can never know... it'd only take one odd, totally inexplicable result, and the hypothesising and testing would start all over again.

Example

Over time, scientists have come up with different hypotheses about the structure of the atom.

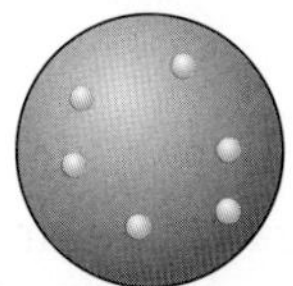

About 100 years ago we thought atoms looked like this.

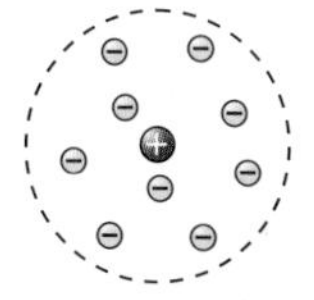

Then we thought they looked like this.

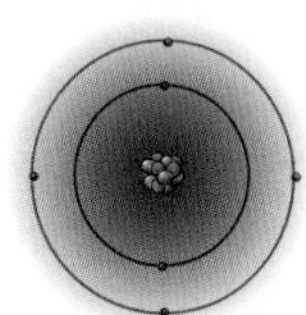

And then we thought they looked like this.

Tip: There's lots more about the structure of the atom on pages 32-36.

Models

Models are used to describe or display how an object or system behaves in reality. They're often based on evidence collected from experiments, and should be able to accurately predict what will happen in other, similar experiments. There are different types of models that scientists can use to describe the world around them. Here are just a few:

- A **descriptive model** shows what's happening in a certain situation, without explaining why. It won't necessarily include details that could be used to predict the outcome of a different scenario. For example, a graph showing the rate of a reaction at different temperatures (see p.194) would be a descriptive model.
- A **representational model** is a simplified description or picture of what's going on in real life. It can be used to explain observations and make predictions. E.g. particle theory is a simplified way of explaining how particles behave in different states of matter (see p.95-96). It can be used to explain how changes of state occur.
- **Spatial models** are used to summarise how data is arranged within space. For example, a three-dimensional model of a covalent molecule would be a spatial model.
- **Computational models** use computers to make simulations of complex real-life processes, such as climate change. They're used when there are a lot of different variables (factors that change) to consider, and because you can easily change their design to take into account new data.
- **Mathematical models** can be used to describe the relationship between variables in numerical form (e.g. as an equation), and therefore predict outcomes of a scenario. For example, an equation can be written to predict how the pH of a solution will change if the concentration of H^+ ions in the solution changes.

Tip: Like hypotheses, models have to be tested before they're accepted by other scientists. You can test models by using them to make a prediction, and then carrying out an investigation to see whether the results match the prediction.

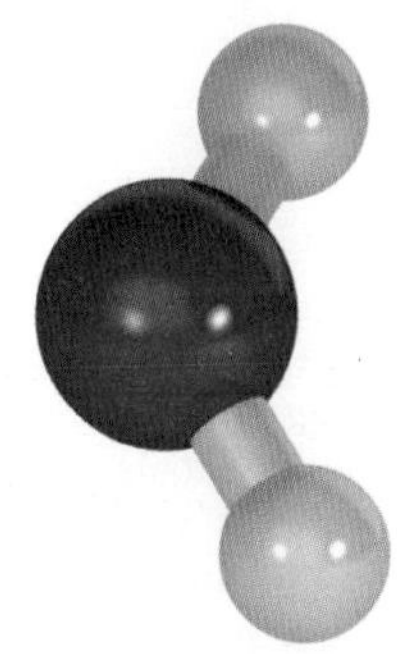

Figure 1: *A spatial model showing how the atoms are arranged in a water molecule.*

Tip: Mathematical models are made using patterns found in data and also using information about known relationships between variables.

All models have limitations on what they can explain or predict. Climate change models have several limitations — for example, it's hard to take into account all the biological and chemical processes that influence climate. It can also be difficult to include regional variations in climate.

Communicating results

Tip: New scientific discoveries are usually communicated to the public in the news or via the internet. They might be communicated to governments and large organisations via reports or meetings.

Some scientific discoveries show that people should change their habits, or they might provide ideas that could be developed into new technology. So scientists need to tell the world about their discoveries.

Example

Several technologies are being developed that make use of fullerenes (see p.63). These include drug delivery systems for use in medicine. Information about these systems needs to be communicated to doctors so they can make use of them, and to patients, so they can make informed decisions about their treatment.

Tip: If you're reading an article about a new scientific discovery, always think about how the study was carried out. It may be that the sample size was very small, and so the results aren't representative (see page 10 for more on sample sizes).

Reports about scientific discoveries in the media (e.g. newspapers or television) aren't peer-reviewed. This means that, even though news stories are often based on data that has been peer-reviewed, the data might be presented in a way that is over-simplified or inaccurate, leaving it open to misinterpretation.

It's important that the evidence isn't presented in a **biased** way. This can sometimes happen when people want to make a point, e.g. they overemphasise a relationship in the data. (Sometimes without knowing they're doing it.) There are all sorts of reasons why people might do this.

Examples

- They want to keep the organisation or company that's funding the research happy. (If the results aren't what they'd like they might not give them any more money to fund further research.)
- Governments might want to persuade voters, other governments or journalists to agree with their policies about a certain issue.
- Companies might want to 'big up' their products, or make impressive safety claims.
- Environmental campaigners might want to persuade people to behave differently.

Tip: An example of bias is a newspaper article describing details of data supporting an idea without giving any of the evidence against it.

There's also a risk that if an investigation is done by a team of highly-regarded scientists it'll be taken more seriously than evidence from less well known scientists. But having experience, authority or a fancy qualification doesn't necessarily mean the evidence is good — the only way to tell is to look at the evidence scientifically (e.g. is it repeatable, valid, etc.).

2. Scientific Applications and Issues

New scientific discoveries can lead to lots of exciting new ways of using science in our everyday lives. Unfortunately, these developments may also come with social, economic or moral problems that need to be considered.

Using scientific developments

Lots of scientific developments go on to have useful applications.

Examples

- The discovery that argon, like all noble gases, is unreactive, has lead to its use in lightbulbs. Unlike oxygen in the air it doesn't react with the filament, so the bulb lasts longer.
- The discovery that crude oil can be cracked (broken down) into smaller, more useful parts has allowed us to match the supply of different fuels to demand.

Tip: There's lots more about the properties of noble gases on page 186, and there's more about cracking crude oil on pages 229-230.

Issues created by science

Scientific knowledge is increased by doing experiments. And this knowledge leads to scientific developments, e.g. new technologies or new advice. These developments can create issues though. For example, they could create political issues, which could lead to developments being ignored, or governments being slow to act if they think responding to the developments could affect their popularity with voters.

Example

Some governments were pretty slow to accept the fact that human activities are causing climate change, despite all the evidence. This is because accepting it means they've got to do something about it, which costs money and could hurt their economy. This could lose them a lot of votes.

Tip: See pages 235-236 for more on climate change.

Scientific developments can cause a whole host of other issues too.

Examples

- **Economic issues:** Society can't always afford to do things scientists recommend (e.g. investing heavily in alternative energy sources) without cutting back elsewhere.
- **Social issues:** Decisions based on scientific evidence affect people — e.g. should fossil fuels be taxed more highly (to invest in alternative energy)? Would the effect on people's lifestyles be acceptable?
- **Environmental issues:** Human activity often affects the environment. For example, building a dam to produce electricity will change the local habitat so some species might be displaced. But it will also reduce our need for fossil fuels, so will help to reduce climate change.
- **Personal issues:** Some decisions will affect individuals. For example, someone might support alternative energy, but object if a wind farm is built next to their house.

Figure 1: *A dam used to produce electricity. This could be a potential alternative to fossil fuels, but some people have concerns about how it could affect the surrounding habitat.*

3. Limitations of Science

Science has taught us an awful lot about the world we live in and how things work — but science doesn't have the answer for everything.

Questions science hasn't answered yet

We don't understand everything. And we never will. We'll find out more, for sure — as more hypotheses are suggested, and more experiments are done. But there'll always be stuff we don't know.

Examples

- Today we don't know as much as we'd like about the impacts of climate change. How much will sea levels rise? And to what extent will weather patterns change?
- We also don't know anywhere near as much as we'd like about the universe. Are there other life forms out there? And what is the universe made of?

Figure 1: *Global warming could cause weather patterns to change — which may result in longer, hotter droughts in some areas.*

In order to answer scientific questions, scientists need data to provide evidence for their hypotheses. Some questions can't be answered yet because the data can't currently be collected, or because there's not enough data to support a theory. But eventually, as we get more evidence, we probably will be able to answer these questions. By then, there'll be loads of new questions to answer though.

Questions science can't answer

There are some questions that all the experiments in the world won't help us answer — for example, the "should we be doing this at all?" type questions.

Example

Think about new drugs which can be taken to boost your 'brain power'.

- Some people think they're good as they could improve concentration or memory. New drugs could let people think in ways beyond the powers of normal brains.
- Other people say they're bad — they could give you an unfair advantage in exams. And people might be pressured into taking them so that they could work more effectively, and for longer hours.

Tip: Some experiments have to be approved by ethics committees before scientists are allowed to carry them out. This stops scientists from getting wrapped up in whether they <u>can</u> do something before anyone stops to think about whether they <u>should</u> do it.

The question of whether something is morally or ethically right or wrong can't be answered by more experiments — there is no "right" or "wrong" answer. The best we can do is get a consensus from society — a judgement that most people are more or less happy to live by. Science can provide more information to help people make this judgement, and the judgement might change over time. But in the end it's up to people and their conscience.

4. Risks and Hazards

A lot of things we do could cause us harm. But some things are more hazardous than they at first seem, whereas other things are less hazardous than they at first seem. This may sound confusing, but it'll all become clear...

What are risks and hazards?

A **hazard** is something that could potentially cause harm. All hazards have a **risk** attached to them — this is the chance that the hazard will cause harm.

The risks of some things seem pretty obvious, or we've known about them for a while, like the risk of causing acid rain by polluting the atmosphere, or of having a car accident when you're travelling in a car.

New technology arising from scientific advances can bring new risks. These risks need to be thought about alongside the potential benefits of the technology, in order to make a decision about whether it should be made available to the general public.

Example

Sun creams have been developed that use tiny particles called nanoparticles. These sun creams are better at protecting skin from UV rays. They also cover the skin better and don't leave white marks.

However, the full effects of nanoparticles on the body aren't known. They're so small that it's possible that they could pass through the skin and end up in cells within the body, where they could have dangerous side effects. It's also unknown how they could affect the environment if they get washed away into rivers or the sea.

So people need to weigh up the risks against the benefits of using these new sun creams.

Estimating risk

You can estimate the risk based on how many times something happens in a big sample (e.g. 100 000 people) over a given period (e.g. a year). For example, you could assess the risk of a driver crashing by recording how many people in a group of 100 000 drivers crashed their cars over a year.

To make a decision about an activity that involves a hazardous event, we don't just need to take into account the chance of the event causing harm, but also how serious the consequences would be if it did.

The general rule is that, if an activity involves a hazard that's very likely to cause harm, with serious consequences if it does, that activity is considered high-risk.

Example 1

If you go for a run, you may sprain an ankle. But most sprains recover within a few days if they're rested, so going for a run would be considered a low-risk activity.

Example 2

If you go skiing, you may fall and break a bone. This would take many weeks to heal, and may cause further complications later on in life. So skiing would be considered higher risk than running.

Perceptions of risk

Not all risks have the same consequences, e.g. if you chop veg with a sharp knife you risk cutting your finger, but if you go scuba-diving you risk death. You're much more likely to cut your finger during half an hour of chopping than to die during half an hour of scuba-diving. But most people are happier to accept a higher probability of an accident if the consequences are short-lived and fairly minor.

Tip: Risks people choose to take are called 'voluntary risks'. Risks that people are forced to take are called 'imposed risks'.

People tend to be more willing to accept a risk if they choose to do something (e.g. go scuba diving), compared to having the risk imposed on them (e.g. having a nuclear power station built next door).

People's perception of risk (how risky they think something is) isn't always accurate. They tend to view familiar activities as low-risk and unfamiliar activities as high-risk — even if that's not the case. For example, cycling on roads is often high-risk, but many people are happy to do it because it's a familiar activity. Air travel is actually pretty safe, but a lot of people perceive it as high-risk. People may over-estimate the risk of things with long-term or invisible effects, e.g. ionising radiation.

Reducing risk in investigations

Part of planning an investigation is making sure that it's safe. To make sure your experiment is safe you must identify all the **hazards**. Hazards include:

Tip: You can find out about potential hazards by looking in textbooks, doing some internet research, or asking your teacher.

- Microorganisms: e.g. some bacteria can make you ill.
- Chemicals: e.g. sulfuric acid can burn your skin and alcohols catch fire easily.
- Fire: e.g. an unattended Bunsen burner is a fire hazard.
- Electricity: e.g. faulty electrical equipment could give you a shock.

Once you've identified the hazards you might encounter, you should think of ways of reducing the risks from the hazards.

Figure 1: *Scientists wearing safety goggles to protect their eyes during an experiment.*

Examples

- If you're working with sulfuric acid, always wear gloves and safety goggles. This will reduce the risk of the acid coming into contact with your skin and eyes.
- If you're using a Bunsen burner, stand it on a heatproof mat. This will reduce the risk of starting a fire.

5. Designing Investigations

To be a good scientist you need to know how to design a good experiment, including how to make sure you get good quality results.

Making predictions from a hypothesis

Scientists observe things and come up with hypotheses to explain them. To decide whether a **hypothesis** might be correct you need to do an investigation to gather evidence, which will help support or disprove the hypothesis. The first step is to use the hypothesis to come up with a **prediction** — a statement about what you think will happen that you can test.

Example

If your hypothesis is 'increasing temperature causes reactions to go faster', then your prediction might be 'a reaction carried out at a high temperature will finish faster than the same reaction carried out at a low temperature'.

Once a scientist has come up with a prediction, they'll design an investigation to see if there are patterns or relationships between two variables. For example, to see if there's a pattern or relationship between the variables 'temperature of reaction' and 'time taken for reaction to finish'.

Tip: A variable is just something in the experiment that can change.

Repeatable and reproducible results

Results need to be **repeatable** and **reproducible**. Repeatable means that if the same person does an experiment again using the same methods and equipment, they'll get similar results. Reproducible means that if someone else does the experiment, or a different method or piece of equipment is used, the results will be similar.

Tip: Data that's repeatable and reproducible is reliable and scientists are more likely to have confidence in it.

Example

In 1998, a scientist claimed to have found a link between the MMR vaccine (for measles, mumps and rubella) and autism. This meant many parents stopped their children from being vaccinated, leading to a rise in the number of children catching measles. However, the results have never been reproduced. Health authorities have now decided that the vaccine is safe.

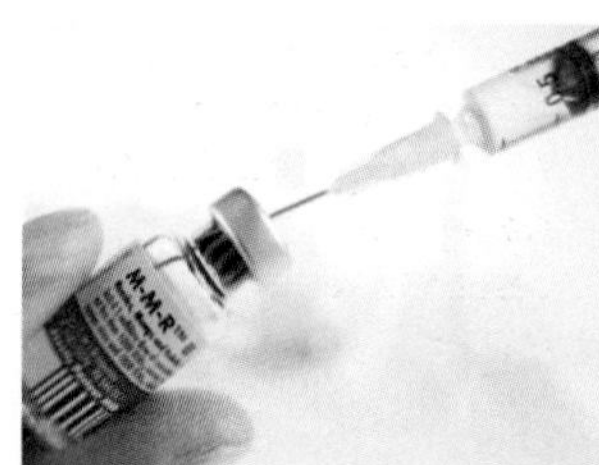

Figure 1: *The MMR vaccine.*

Ensuring the test is valid

Valid results are repeatable, reproducible and answer the original question.

Example

Do power lines cause cancer?

Some studies have found that children who live near overhead power lines are more likely to develop cancer. What they'd actually found was a **correlation** (relationship) between the variables "presence of power lines" and "incidence of cancer". They found that as one changed, so did the other.

But this data isn't enough to say that the power lines cause cancer, as there might be other explanations. For example, power lines are often near busy roads, so the areas tested could contain different levels of pollution. As the studies don't show a definite link they don't answer the original question.

Tip: Peer review (see page 2) is used to make sure that results are valid before they're published.

Tip: See pages 20-21 for more on correlation.

Ensuring it's a fair test

Tip: For the results of an investigation to be valid the investigation must be a fair test.

In a lab experiment you usually change one variable and measure how it affects another variable. To make it a fair test, everything else that could affect the results should stay the same (otherwise you can't tell if the thing you're changing is causing the results or not — the data won't be valid).

Tip: You'd also need to keep other factors the same for this to be a fair test, such as the volumes of reactants and the surface area of any solid reactants.

Example

You might change only the temperature of a chemical reaction and measure how this affects the rate of reaction. You need to keep, for example, the concentration of the reactants the same, otherwise you won't know if any change in the rate of reaction is caused by the change in temperature, or a difference in reactant concentration.

The variable you change is called the **independent variable**. The variable you measure when you change the independent variable is called the **dependent variable**. The variables that you keep the same are called **control variables**.

Example

In the rate of reaction example, temperature is the independent variable, the rate of the reaction is the dependent variable and the concentrations of reactants, the volumes of reactants etc. are control variables.

Controlling variables in a study

A study is an investigation that doesn't take place in the lab. It's important that a study is a fair test, just like a lab experiment. It's a lot trickier to control the variables in a study than it is in a lab experiment though. Sometimes you can't control them all, but you can use a **control group** to help. This is a group of whatever you're studying (people, crops, animals, etc.) that's kept under the same conditions as the group in the experiment, but doesn't have anything done to it.

Tip: A pesticide is a chemical that can be used to kill insects and other pests.

Example

If you're studying the effect of pesticides on crop growth, pesticide is applied to one field but not to another field (the control field). Both fields are planted with the same crop, and are in the same area (so they get the same weather conditions).

The control field is there to try and account for variables like the weather, which don't stay the same all the time, but could affect the results.

Sample size

Data based on small samples isn't as good as data based on large samples. A sample should be representative of the whole population (i.e. it should share as many of the various characteristics in the population as possible) — a small sample can't do that as well.

The bigger the sample size the better, but scientists have to be realistic when choosing how big.

Example

If you were studying the effects of a chemical used to sterilise water on the people drinking it, it'd be great to study everyone who was drinking the water (a huge sample), but it'd take ages and cost a bomb. It's more realistic to study a thousand people, with a mixture of ages, gender, and race.

Tip: It's hard to spot anomalies if your sample size is too small.

Trial runs

It's a good idea to do a **trial run** (a quick version of your experiment) before you do the proper experiment. Trial runs are used to figure out the range (the upper and lower limits) of independent variable values used in the proper experiment. If there was no change in the dependent variable between your upper and lower values in the trial run, then you might increase the range until there was an observable change. Or if there was a large change, you might want to make your higher and lower values closer together.

Tip: If you don't have time to do a trial run, you could always look at the data other people have got doing a similar experiment and use a range and interval values similar to theirs.

Example

For a rate of reaction experiment, you might do a trial run with a temperature range of 10-50 °C. If there was no reaction at the lower end (e.g. 10-20 °C), you might narrow the range to 20-50 °C for the proper experiment.

Trial runs can be used to figure out appropriate intervals (gaps) between the values too. The intervals can't be too small (otherwise the experiment would take ages), or too big (otherwise you might miss something).

Example

If using 1 °C intervals doesn't give you much change in the rate of reaction each time you might decide to use 5 °C intervals, e.g 20, 25, 30, 35, 40, 45, 50 °C...

Trial runs can also help you figure out whether or not your experiment is repeatable.

Tip: Consistently repeating the results is crucial for checking that your results are repeatable.

Example

If you repeat it three times and the results are all similar, the experiment is repeatable.

6. Collecting Data

Once you've designed your experiment, you need to get on and do it. Here's a guide to making sure the results you collect are good.

Getting good quality results

When you do an experiment you want your results to be **repeatable**, **reproducible** and as **accurate** and **precise** as possible.

To check repeatability you need to repeat the readings and check that the results are similar — you should repeat each reading at least three times. To make sure your results are reproducible you can cross check them by taking a second set of readings with another instrument (or a different observer).

Tip: For more on means see page 14.

Your data also needs to be accurate. Really accurate results are those that are really close to the true answer. The accuracy of your results usually depends on your method — you need to make sure you're measuring the right thing and that you don't miss anything that should be included in the measurements. For example, estimating the amount of gas released from a reaction by counting the bubbles isn't very accurate because you might miss some of the bubbles and they might have different volumes. It's more accurate to measure the volume of gas released using a gas syringe.

Tip: Sometimes, you can work out what result you should get at the end of an experiment (the theoretical result) by doing a bit of maths. If your experiment is accurate there shouldn't be much difference between the theoretical result and the result you actually get.

Your data also needs to be precise. Precise results are ones where the data is all really close to the mean (average) of your repeated results (i.e. not spread out).

Example

Look at the data in this table. Data set 1 is more precise than data set 2 because all the data in set 1 is really close to the mean, whereas the data in set 2 is more spread out.

Repeated measurement	Data set 1	Data set 2
1	12	11
2	14	17
3	13	14
Mean	13	14

Choosing the right equipment

When doing an experiment, you need to make sure you're using the right equipment for the job. The measuring equipment you use has to be sensitive enough to measure the changes you're looking for.

Example

If you need to measure changes of 1 cm^3 you need to use a measuring cylinder that can measure in 1 cm^3 steps — it'd be no good trying with one that only measures 10 cm^3 steps, it wouldn't be sensitive enough.

Figure 1: *Different types of measuring cylinder and glassware — make sure you choose the right one before you start an experiment.*

The smallest change a measuring instrument can detect is called its **resolution**. For example, some mass balances have a resolution of 1 g, some have a resolution of 0.1 g, and some are even more sensitive.

Also, equipment needs to be **calibrated** by measuring a known value. If there's a difference between the measured and known value, you can use this to correct the inaccuracy of the equipment.

Example

If a known mass is put on a mass balance, but the reading is a different value, you know that the mass balance has not been calibrated properly.

Tip: Calibration is a way of making sure that a measuring device is measuring things accurately — you get it to measure something you know has a certain value and set the device to say that amount.

Errors

Random errors

The results of an experiment will always vary a bit due to **random errors** — unpredictable differences caused by things like human errors in measuring.

Example

Errors made when reading from a measuring cylinder are random. You have to estimate or round the level when it's between two marks — so sometimes your figure will be a bit above the real one, and sometimes a bit below.

You can reduce the effect of random errors by taking repeat readings and finding the mean. This will give you a more precise result.

Tip: Repeating the experiment in the exact same way and calculating a mean won't correct a systematic error.

Systematic errors

If a measurement is wrong by the same amount every time, it's called a **systematic error**.

Example

If you measured from the very end of your ruler instead of from the 0 cm mark every time, all your measurements would be a bit small.

Tip: If there's no systematic error, then doing repeats and calculating a mean can make your results more accurate.

Just to make things more complicated, if a systematic error is caused by using equipment that isn't zeroed properly it's called a **zero error**. You can compensate for some of these errors if you know about them though.

Example

If a mass balance always reads 1 gram before you put anything on it, all your measurements will be 1 gram too heavy. This is a zero error. You can compensate for this by subtracting 1 gram from all your results.

Figure 2: A mass balance that has been set to zero.

Tip: A zero error is a specific type of systematic error.

Anomalous results

Sometimes you get a result that doesn't seem to fit in with the rest at all. These results are called **anomalous results** (or outliers).

Example

The entry in the table that's circled is an anomalous result because it's much larger than any of the other data values.

Experiment	A	B	C	D	E	F
Rate of reaction (cm^3/s)	10.5	11.2	10.8	(85.4)	10.6	11.1

You should investigate anomalous results and try to work out what happened. If you can work out what happened (e.g. you measured something totally wrong) you can ignore them when processing your results.

Tip: There are lots of reasons why you might get an anomalous result, but usually they're due to human error rather than anything crazy happening in the experiment.

7. Processing Data

Once you've collected some data, you might need to process it.

Tip: If you're recording your data as decimals, make sure you give each value to the same number of decimal places.

Organising data

It's really important that your data is organised. Tables are dead useful for organising data. When you draw a table, use a ruler, make sure each column has a heading (including the units) and keep it neat and tidy.

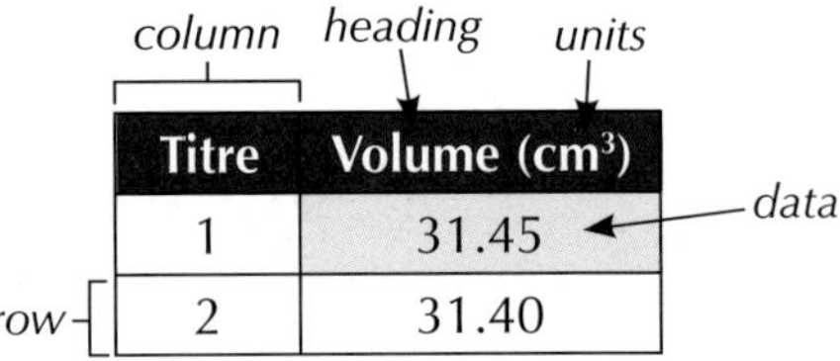

Titre	Volume (cm^3)
1	31.45
2	31.40

Figure 1: *Table showing the volume of acid needed to neutralise an alkali.*

Processing your data

When you've collected data from a number of repeats of an experiment, it's useful to summarise it using a few handy-to-use figures.

Mean and range

When you've done repeats of an experiment, you should always calculate the **mean** (a type of average). To do this, add together all the data values and divide by the total number of values in the sample.

You might also need to calculate the **range** (how spread out the data is). To do this, find the largest number and subtract the smallest number from it.

Tip: You should ignore anomalous results when calculating the mean or the range — see the previous page for more on anomalous results.

Example

Look at the data in the table below. The mean and range of the data for each test tube has been calculated.

Test tube	Repeat (g)			Mean (g)	Range (g)
	1	2	3		
A	28	37	31	$(28 + 37 + 31) \div 3 = 32$	$37 - 28 = 9$
B	47	51	61	$(47 + 51 + 61) \div 3 = 53$	$61 - 47 = 14$

Uncertainty

As you can see from the table above, when you repeat a measurement, you often get a slightly different figure each time you do it, leading to a range in results. These variations are due to random errors which mean that each result has some **uncertainty** to it. The measurements you make will also have some uncertainty in them due to limits in the resolution of the equipment you use. This all means that the mean of a set of results will also have some uncertainty to it. Here's how to calculate the uncertainty of a mean result:

$$\text{uncertainty} = \frac{\text{range}}{2}$$

Tip: There's more about errors on the previous page.

The larger the range, the less precise your results are and the more uncertainty there will be in your results. Uncertainties are shown using the '±' symbol.

Example

The table below shows the results of a titration experiment to determine the volume of 0.5 mol/dm^3 sodium hydroxide solution needed to neutralise 25 cm^3 of a solution of hydrochloric acid with unknown concentration. Calculate the uncertainty of the mean.

Repeat	1	2	3	mean
Volume of sodium hydroxide (cm^3)	20.2	19.8	20.0	20.0

1. The range is: 20.2 – 19.8 = 0.400 cm^3
2. So the uncertainty of the mean is: range ÷ 2 = 0.400 ÷ 2 = 0.200 cm^3. You'd write this as **20.00 ± 0.2 cm^3**

Tip: Since uncertainty affects precision, you'll need to think about it when you come to evaluating your results (see page 21).

Measuring a greater amount of something helps to reduce uncertainty. For example, in a rate of reaction experiment, measuring the amount of product formed over a longer period compared to a shorter period will reduce the percentage uncertainty in your results.

Exam Tip
If a question asks you to give your answer to a certain number of significant figures, make sure you do this, or you might not get all the marks.

Rounding to significant figures

The first **significant figure** (s.f.) of a number is the first digit that isn't a zero. The second, third and fourth significant figures follow on immediately after the first (even if they're zeros). When you're processing your data you may well want to round any really long numbers to a certain number of significant figures.

Example

0.6874976 rounds to **0.69** to **2 s.f.** and to **0.687** to **3 s.f.**

Tip: When rounding a number, if the next digit after the last significant figure you're using is less than 5 you should round it down, and if it's 5 or more you should round it up.

When you're doing calculations using measurements given to a certain number of significant figures, you should give your answer to the lowest number of significant figures that was used in the calculation. If your calculation has multiple steps, only round the final answer, or it won't be as accurate.

Example

For the calculation: 1.2 ÷ 1.85 = 0.648648648...

1.2 is given to 2 significant figures. 1.85 is given to 3 significant figures. So the answer should be given to 2 significant figures.

Round the final significant figure (0.648) up to 5: 1.2 ÷ 1.85 = **0.65 (2 s.f.)**

The lowest number of significant figures in the calculation is used because the fewer digits a measurement has, the less accurate it is. Your answer can only be as accurate as the least accurate measurement in the calculation.

8. Graphs and Charts

It can often be easier to see trends in data by plotting a graph or chart of your results, rather than by looking at numbers in a table.

Tip: Categoric data is data that comes in distinct categories, such as 'type of material' (e.g. wood, metal, paper) and 'state of matter' (e.g. solid, liquid, gas). Discrete data can only take certain values, because there are no in-between values, e.g. 'number of people' (because you can't have half a person). Continuous data is numerical data that can have any value within a range, e.g. length, volume, temperature.

Plotting your data on a graph or chart

One of the best ways to present your data after you've processed it is to plot your results on a graph or chart. The type of graph or chart you use depends on the type of data you've collected.

Bar charts and histograms

You can use a bar chart to display the data if the independent variable is **categoric**, **discrete**, or **continuous**. If the data is categoric or discrete you need to include gaps between the bars (see Figure 1). If it's continuous then the bars should be touching. If the independent variable is **continuous**, the frequency data can be shown on a histogram. Histograms may look like bar charts, but it's the area of the bars that represents the frequency (rather than the height). The height of each bar is called the **frequency density** and is found by dividing the frequency by the class width. (The class width is just the width of the bar on the histogram, see Figure 1.)

Tip: Frequency is just the number of times that something occurs. It's often shown in a frequency table.

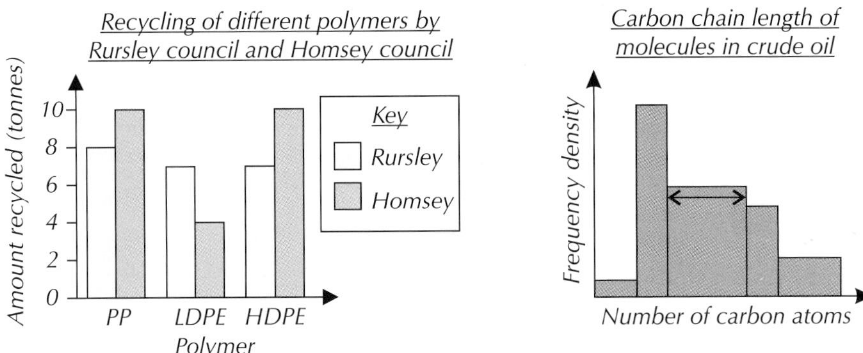

Figure 1: *An example of a bar chart (left) and a histogram (right).*

Tip: A frequency diagram is a histogram where the width of all the bars are the same and frequency is plotted on the *y*-axis, rather than frequency density.

Graphs

If both the independent and the dependent variables are **continuous** you should use a graph to display the data. Here are the golden rules for drawing graphs:

- Draw it nice and big (covering at least two thirds of the graph paper).
- Put the independent variable (the thing you change) on the *x*-axis (the horizontal one).
- Put the dependent variable (the thing you measure) on the *y*-axis (the vertical one).
- Label both axes and remember to include the units.
- To plot the points, use a sharp pencil and make a neat little cross.

Tip: If you're not in an exam, you can use a computer to plot your graph and draw your line of best fit for you.

- Don't join the dots up. You need to draw a line of best fit (or a curve of best fit if your points make a curve). When drawing a line (or curve), try to draw the line through or as near to as many points as possible, ignoring anomalous results.
- If you've got more than one set of data, include a key.
- Give your graph a title explaining what it is showing.

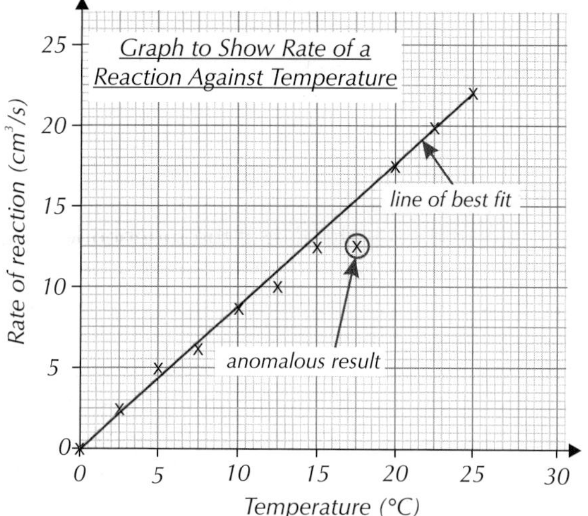

Figure 2: *An example of a graph.*

Tip: Use the biggest data values you've got to draw a sensible scale on your axes. Here, the highest rate of reaction is 22 cm^3/s, so it makes sense to label the *y*-axis up to 25 cm^3/s.

Correlations

Graphs are used to show the relationship between two variables. Data can show three different types of **correlation** (relationship):

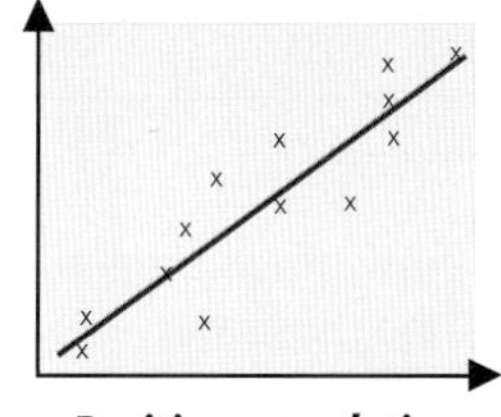

Positive correlation
As one variable increases the other increases.

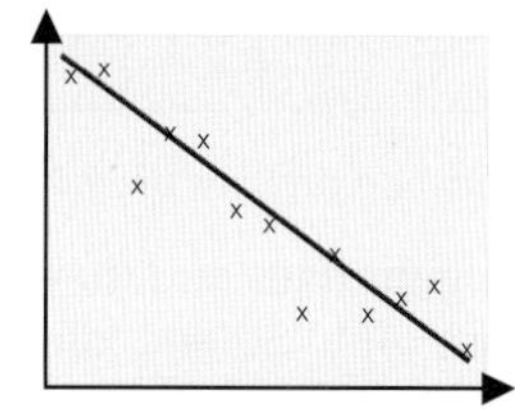

Negative correlation
As one variable increases the other decreases.

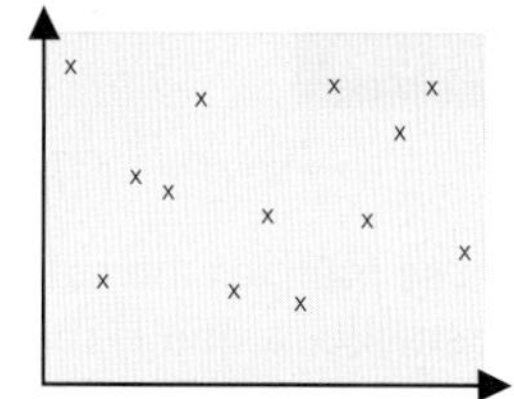

No correlation
There's no relationship between the two variables.

Tip: Just because two variables are correlated doesn't mean that the change in one is causing the change in the other. There might be other factors involved — see pages 20-21 for more.

9. Units

Using the correct units is important when you're drawing graphs or calculating values with an equation. Without them, your numbers don't mean anything.

S.I. units

Lots of different units can be used to describe the same quantity. For example, volume can given in terms of cubic feet, cubic metres or pints. It would be confusing if different scientists used different units to define quantities, as it would be hard to compare people's data. To stop this happening, scientists have come up with a set of standard units, called **S.I. units**, that all scientists use to measure their data. Here are some S.I. units you'll see in chemistry:

Tip: S.I. stands for 'Système International', which is French for 'international system'.

Quantity	S.I. Base Unit
mass	kilogram, kg
length	metre, m
time	second, s
amount of substance	mole, mol

Figure 1: *Some common S.I. units used in chemistry.*

Scaling prefixes

Quantities come in a huge range of sizes. For example, the volume of a swimming pool might be around 2 000 000 000 cm^3, while the volume of a cup is around 250 cm^3. To make the size of numbers more manageable, larger or smaller units are used. There are prefixes that can be used in front of units to make them bigger or smaller:

prefix	tera (T)	giga (G)	mega (M)	kilo (k)	deci (d)	centi (c)	milli (m)	micro (μ)	nano (n)
multiple of unit	10^{12}	10^{9}	1 000 000 (10^{6})	1000	0.1	0.01	0.001	0.000001 (10^{-6})	10^{-9}

Figure 2: *Scaling prefixes used with units.*

These prefixes are called **scaling prefixes** and they tell you how much bigger or smaller a unit is than the base unit. So one kilometre is one thousand metres.

Converting between units

To swap from one unit to another, all you need to know is what number you have to divide or multiply by to get from the original unit to the new unit — this is called the **conversion factor** and is equal to the number of times the smaller unit goes into the larger unit.

- To go from a bigger unit to a smaller unit, you multiply by the conversion factor.
- To go from a smaller unit to a bigger unit, you divide by the conversion factor.

Exam Tip
If you're going from a smaller unit to a larger unit, your number should get smaller.
If you're going from a larger unit to a smaller unit, your number should get larger.
This is a handy way to check you've done the conversion correctly.

There are some conversions that'll be particularly useful for the chemistry content in GCSE Combined Science. Here they are...

Mass can have units of kg and g.

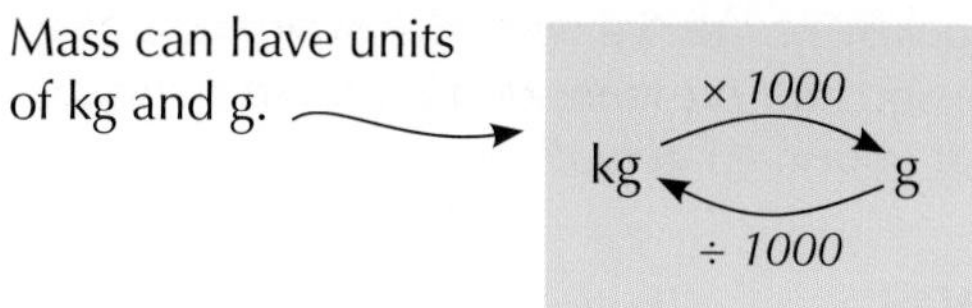

Energy can have units of J and kJ.

× 1000
kJ
J
÷ 1000

Exam Tip
Before you put values into an equation, you need to make sure they have the right units.

Time can have units of min and s.

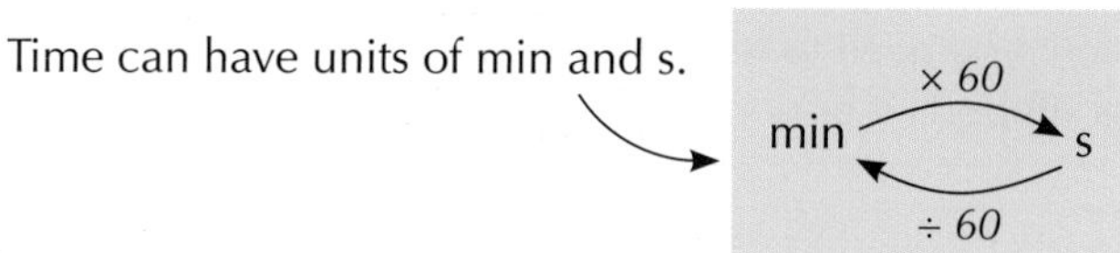

Volume can have units of m^3, dm^3 and cm^3.

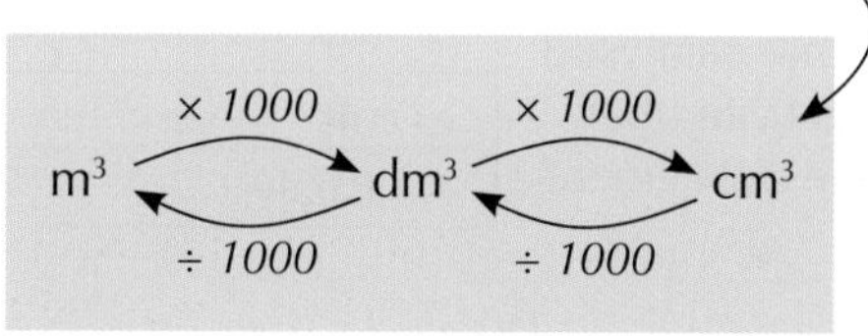

Exam Tip
Being familiar with these common conversions could save you time when it comes to doing calculations in the exam.

Concentration can have units of mol/dm^3 and mol/cm^3.

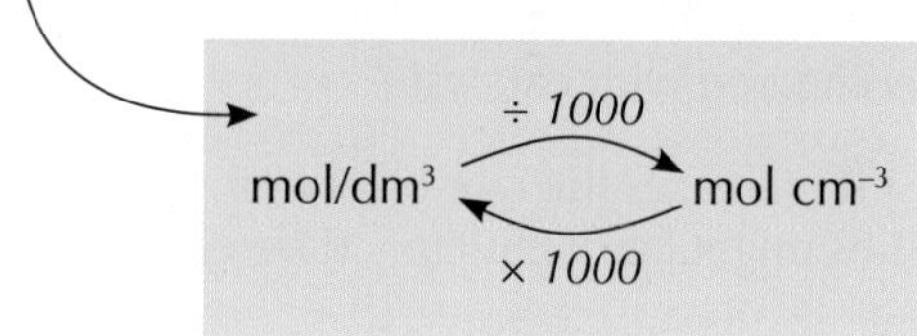

Tip: mol cm^{-3} is the same as mol/cm^3. It's just a different way of writing it.

Examples

- To go from dm^3 to cm^3, you'd multiply by 1000.

  2 dm^3 is equal to 2 × 1000 = **2000 cm^3**

- To go from grams to kilograms, you'd divide by 1000.

  3400 g is equal to 3400 ÷ 1000 = **3.4 kg**

10. Conclusions and Evaluations

So... you've planned an amazing experiment, you've done the experiment, collected some data and have processed and presented your data in a sensible way. Now it's time to figure out what your data actually tells you.

How to draw conclusions

Drawing conclusions might seem pretty straightforward — you just look at your data and say what pattern or relationship you see between the dependent and independent variables.

But you've got to be really careful that your conclusion matches the data you've got and doesn't go any further. You also need to be able to use your results to justify your conclusion (i.e. back up your conclusion with some specific data).

When writing a conclusion, you need to refer back to the original hypothesis and say whether the data supports it or not.

Example

A scientist carried out an experiment to determine which of two catalysts increased the rate of a reaction more. The scientist hypothesised that catalyst B would make the reaction go faster than catalyst A. The results of the experiment are shown in the table.

Catalyst	Rate of reaction ($cm^3\ s^{-1}$)
A	13.5
B	19.5
No catalyst	5.5

The conclusion of this experiment would be that catalyst B makes this reaction go faster than catalyst A, so the data supports the hypothesis.

The justification for this conclusion is that the rate of this reaction was 6 cm^3/s faster using catalyst B compared with catalyst A.

You can't conclude that catalyst B increases the rate of any other reaction more than catalyst A — the results might be completely different.

Tip: Graphs are useful for seeing whether two variables are correlated (see page 17).

Correlation and causation

If two things are correlated (i.e. there's a relationship between them) it doesn't necessarily mean that a change in one variable is causing the change in the other — this is really important, don't forget it. There are three possible reasons for a correlation:

Tip: Causation just means one thing is causing another.

1. Chance

Even though it might seem a bit weird, it's possible that two things show a correlation in a study purely because of chance.

Example

One study might find a correlation between the number of people with breathing problems and the distance they live from a cement factory. But other scientists don't get a correlation when they investigate it — the results of the first study are just a fluke.

2. They're linked by a third variable

A lot of the time it may look as if a change in one variable is causing a change in the other, but it isn't — a third variable links the two things.

> **Example**
>
> There's a correlation between water temperature and shark attacks. This isn't because warm water makes sharks crazy. Instead, they're linked by a third variable — the number of people swimming (more people swim when the water's hotter, and with more people in the water shark attacks increase).

Tip: Lots of things are correlated without being directly related. E.g. the level of carbon dioxide (CO_2) in the atmosphere and the amount of obesity have both increased over the last 100 years, but that doesn't mean increased atmospheric CO_2 is causing people to become obese.

3. Causation

Sometimes a change in one variable does cause a change in the other.

> **Example**
>
> There's a correlation between smoking and lung cancer.
> This is because chemicals in tobacco smoke cause lung cancer.

You can only conclude that a correlation is due to cause if you've controlled all the variables that could be affecting the result. (For the smoking example, this would include age and exposure to other things that cause cancer.)

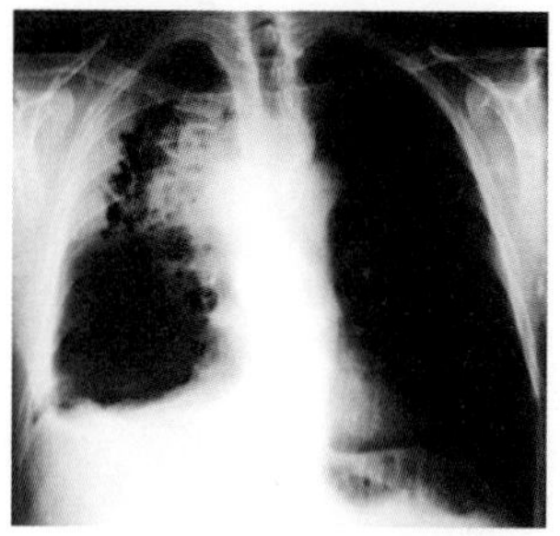

Figure 1: *A coloured chest X-ray of a smoker who has lung cancer.*

Evaluation

This is the final part of an investigation. Here you need to evaluate (assess) the following things about your experiment and the data you gathered.

- **The method**: Was it valid? Did you control all the other variables to make it a fair test?
- **The quality of your results:** Was there enough evidence to reach a valid conclusion? Were the results repeatable, reproducible, accurate and precise?
- **Anomalous results**: Were any of the results anomalous? If there were none then say so. If there were any, try to explain them — were they caused by errors in measurement? Were there any other variables that could have affected the results? You should comment on the level of uncertainty in your results too.

Once you've thought about these points you can decide how much confidence you have in your conclusion. For example, if your results are repeatable, reproducible and valid and they back up your conclusion then you can have a high degree of confidence in your conclusion.

You can also suggest any changes to the method that would improve the quality of the results, so that you could have more confidence in your conclusion. For example, you might suggest changing the way you controlled a variable, or increasing the number of measurements you took. Taking more measurements at narrower intervals could give you a more accurate result.

You could also make more predictions based on your conclusion, then further experiments could be carried out to test them.

Tip: When suggesting improvements to the investigation, always make sure that you say why you think this would make the results better.

1. Chemical Equations

Learning Objectives:
- Be able to write word equations for chemical reactions.
- Be able to write balanced chemical equations.

Specification References
0.2, 0.3

Chemical equations crop up again and again in chemistry. You need to know what they show and how to write them.

Chemical reactions

During a chemical reaction, bonds between atoms break and the atoms change places — the atoms from the substances you start off with (the reactants) rearrange themselves to form different chemicals. These new chemicals are called the products. You can show what happens in a chemical reaction using equations.

Word equations

Word equations show what happens in a chemical reaction using the full names of the substances involved. They show the **reactants** (the substances that react together) and the **products** (the substances that are made in a reaction).

Example

Magnesium and oxygen react to form magnesium oxide.
This can be represented by a word equation:

magnesium + oxygen → magnesium oxide

Magnesium and oxygen are the reactants in this reaction.
Magnesium oxide is the product.

Tip: The reactants are on the left-hand side of an equation and the products are on the right-hand side.

Symbol equations

A symbol equation can be used to show the same reaction as a word equation, but using chemical symbols and formulae. When balanced correctly, they also show the ratio of the amounts of substances involved in the reaction.

Examples

The balanced symbol equation for the reaction of magnesium (Mg) and oxygen (O_2) to form magnesium oxide (MgO) is:

$$2Mg + O_2 \rightarrow 2MgO$$

The balanced symbol equation for the reaction of sodium (Na) and chlorine (Cl_2) to form sodium chloride (NaCl) is:

$$2Na + Cl_2 \rightarrow 2NaCl$$

The '2's in front of Na, Mg, MgO and NaCl are there to balance the equations — there's more on this coming up.

Balancing equations

There must always be the same number of atoms of each element on both sides of an equation — they can't just disappear. If there aren't the same number on each side then the equation isn't balanced.

Tip: Equations must be balanced because mass doesn't disappear during a reaction — there are always the same atoms present at the end of a reaction as there are at the start. This is known as the law of conservation of mass (there's more on this on page 74).

Example

Sulfuric acid (H_2SO_4) reacts with sodium hydroxide (NaOH) to give sodium sulfate (Na_2SO_4) and water (H_2O). To write the symbol equation start by writing out all of the formulas in an equation:

$$H_2SO_4 + NaOH \rightarrow Na_2SO_4 + H_2O$$

The formulae are all correct but the numbers of some atoms don't match up on both sides (e.g. there are three Hs on the left, but only two on the right). So the equation isn't balanced.

Exam Tip
If you're asked to write a symbol equation, you always have to make sure it's balanced. If it's not balanced, it's not a correct equation.

Method for balancing equations

You balance an equation by putting numbers in front of formulae where needed. All you do is this:

1. Find an element that doesn't balance and pencil in a number to try and sort it out.
2. See where it gets you. It may create another imbalance — if so, just pencil in another number and see where that gets you.
3. Carry on chasing unbalanced elements and it'll sort itself out pretty quickly.

Figure 1: A titration can be used to make sodium sulfate using the reaction in Example 1.

Example 1

In the equation above, you're short of H atoms on the right-hand side — there are three H atoms on the left and only two on the right.

$$H_2SO_4 + NaOH \rightarrow Na_2SO_4 + H_2O$$

The only thing you can do about it is add more H_2O. Try making it $2H_2O$.

$$H_2SO_4 + NaOH \rightarrow Na_2SO_4 + 2H_2O$$

But now you have too many H atoms and O atoms on the right-hand side. To balance that, you could try putting 2NaOH on the left-hand side.

$$H_2SO_4 + 2NaOH \rightarrow Na_2SO_4 + 2H_2O$$

And suddenly there it is — everything balances. There are four H, one S, six O and two Na on each side of the equation.

Tip: You can't change the small numbers inside formulae (like changing H_2O to H_3O). You can only put numbers in front of formulae (like changing H_2O to $3H_2O$).

Example 2

The equation below is short of Cl atoms on the left-hand side:

$$Al + Cl_2 \rightarrow AlCl_3$$

Try making it $3Cl_2$ instead of just Cl_2.

$$Al + 3Cl_2 \rightarrow AlCl_3$$

Now there are too many Cl atoms on the left-hand side.
Balance up the Cl atoms by putting 2 before the $AlCl_3$.

$$Al + 3Cl_2 \rightarrow 2AlCl_3$$

Now you can balance the Al atoms by adding a 2 in front of the Al.

$$2Al + 3Cl_2 \rightarrow 2AlCl_3$$

Everything is now balanced. There are two Al atoms on each side and six Cl atoms on each side.

Tip: If you made it '$2Cl_2$', you'd have four Cl on the left-hand side. There isn't a whole number that you could put in front of $AlCl_3$ to also give you four Cl on the right-hand side. So it's best to try $3Cl_2$.

Symbol equations show how many atoms of one element there are compared to the number of atoms of other elements. So it's fine to double, or triple, or quadruple the number of atoms in a balanced equation, as long as you do the same to every term in the equation.

Example

Balanced equation to show the reaction of aluminium and chlorine. → $2Al + 3Cl_2 \rightarrow 2AlCl_3$

The numbers added to the equation to balance it have all been doubled. The equation is still balanced. → $4Al + 6Cl_2 \rightarrow 4AlCl_3$

Tip: You don't have to use whole numbers to balance an equation. For example: $2Mg + O_2 \rightarrow 2MgO$ can also be shown as $Mg + \frac{1}{2}O_2 \rightarrow MgO$. However, it's usually easiest to use whole numbers.

Practice Questions — Application

Q1 Copper sulfate and iron react to form iron sulfate and copper.

a) What substances are the products in this reaction?

b) What substances are the reactants in this reaction?

c) Write a word equation for the reaction of copper sulfate and iron.

Q2 Sodium hydroxide reacts with hydrochloric acid to give sodium chloride and water. Write a word equation for this reaction.

Q3 Balance the following equations:

a) $Cl_2 + KBr \rightarrow Br_2 + KCl$

b) $HCl + Mg \rightarrow MgCl_2 + H_2$

c) $C_3H_8 + O_2 \rightarrow CO_2 + H_2O$

d) $Fe_2O_3 + CO \rightarrow Fe + CO_2$

Tip: The more you practise balancing equations, the quicker you'll get...

2. More on Equations

There's a bit more to learn about symbol equations — so prepare yourself for some information about what state symbols and ionic equations are...

Learning Objectives:
- Be able to correctly use the state symbols (s), (l), (g) and (aq).
- Be able to recall the formulae of elements, simple compounds and ions.
- H Be able to write balanced ionic equations.

Specification References
0.1, 0.3, 0.4

State symbols

A chemical reaction can be shown using a word equation or a symbol equation. Symbol equations can include state symbols next to each substance — they tell you what physical state the reactants and products are in:

(s) — solid	(l) — liquid	(g) — gas	(aq) — aqueous

Example 1

Aqueous hydrochloric acid reacts with solid calcium carbonate to form aqueous calcium chloride, liquid water and carbon dioxide gas.

$$2HCl_{(aq)} + CaCO_{3(s)} \rightarrow CaCl_{2(aq)} + H_2O_{(l)} + CO_{2(g)}$$

Example 2

Ions are often dissolved in water when they react. For example, aqueous calcium ions will react with aqueous hydroxide ions to form a white precipitate of calcium hydroxide.

$$Ca^{2+}{}_{(aq)} + 2OH^-{}_{(aq)} \rightarrow Ca(OH)_{2(s)}$$

Tip: If a compound is described as aqueous, that means it's dissolved in water.

Exam Tip
When you learn an equation for a reaction, it might help to learn the state symbols as well. Most are common sense, e.g. oxygen is pretty much always a gas, but it can be tricky to know if something is aqueous or not.

Formulae of common molecules and ions

It's a good idea to learn the chemical formulae of these common molecules — you'll come across them a lot:

Water — H_2O	Hydrogen — H_2
Ammonia — NH_3	Chlorine — Cl_2
Carbon dioxide — CO_2	Oxygen — O_2

Tip: The plural of formula is formulae.

You also need to be able to recall the formulae of certain **ions**. For single atoms, you can use the periodic table to work out what charges their ions will have (see page 49). For ions made up of groups of atoms, it's not so simple. You just have to learn these ones:

Ammonium — NH_4^+	Carbonate — CO_3^{2-}
Hydroxide — OH^-	Sulfate — SO_4^{2-}
Nitrate — NO_3^-	

Tip: Ions form when atoms, or groups of atoms, gain or lose electrons to form charged particles (see page 48).

Ionic equations Higher

> **Exam Tip H**
> The examiners might be kind and give you the balanced equation — if they do, you can skip straight to step 2.

You can write an **ionic equation** for any reaction involving ions that happens in solution. In ionic equations, only the reacting particles (and the products they form) are included. Here's how to write an ionic equation:

1. Start by writing out a full, balanced equation for the reaction.
2. Split any dissolved ionic compounds up into ions.
3. Finally, take out any ions that appear on both sides of the equation.

> **Tip: H** The state symbols tell you that HNO_3, NaOH and $NaNO_3$ are in solution, but the water is a liquid.

> **Tip: H** Leave anything that isn't an ion in solution (like the water) as it is.

Example 1 Higher

Write an ionic equation for the reaction between sodium hydroxide and nitric acid: $HNO_{3(aq)} + NaOH_{(aq)} \rightarrow NaNO_{3(aq)} + H_2O_{(l)}$

1. Check the full equation is balanced (see page 23). This one is — there is the same number of each type of atom on each side.
2. The ionic substances from the equation will dissolve, breaking up into ions in solution. So next you rewrite the equation to show all of the ions that are in the reaction mixture:

$$H^+_{(aq)} + NO_3^-{}_{(aq)} + Na^+_{(aq)} + OH^-_{(aq)} \rightarrow Na^+_{(aq)} + NO_3^-{}_{(aq)} + H_2O_{(l)}$$

3. To get from this to the ionic equation, just cross out any ions that appear on both sides — that's the sodium ions and the nitrate ions.

$$H^+_{(aq)} + \cancel{NO_3^-}_{(aq)} + \cancel{Na^+}_{(aq)} + OH^-_{(aq)} \rightarrow \cancel{Na^+}_{(aq)} + \cancel{NO_3^-}_{(aq)} + H_2O_{(l)}$$

So the ionic equation for this reaction is: $\mathbf{H^+_{(aq)} + OH^-_{(aq)} \rightarrow H_2O_{(l)}}$

The charges on each side of an ionic equation should balance out too. In this example, the total charge on the left-hand side is +1 + (–1) = 0, and the total charge on the right-hand side is 0 — so the charges do balance.

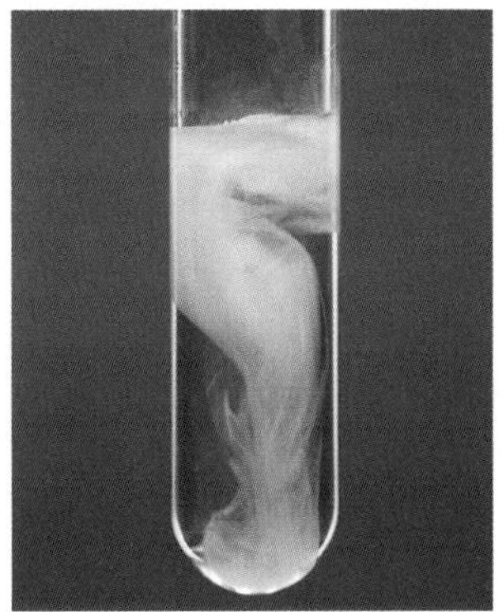

Figure 1: Calcium chloride reacting with sodium hydroxide to form solid, white calcium hydroxide.

> **Tip: H** The state symbols in the full equation show that the $Ca(OH)_2$ is a solid. You don't split it up into ions, because it isn't in solution.

Example 2 Higher

Write an ionic equation for the reaction between calcium chloride and sodium hydroxide: $CaCl_{2(aq)} + 2NaOH_{(aq)} \rightarrow Ca(OH)_{2(s)} + 2NaCl_{(aq)}$

1. The equation is already balanced.
2. Rewrite the equation to show all of the ions in the reaction mixture:

$$Ca^{2+}_{(aq)} + 2Cl^-_{(aq)} + 2Na^+_{(aq)} + 2OH^-_{(aq)} \rightarrow Ca(OH)_{2(s)} + 2Na^+_{(aq)} + 2Cl^-_{(aq)}$$

3. To get from this to the ionic equation, just cross out any ions that appear on both sides — in this case, that's the Na^+ and Cl^- ions.

$$Ca^{2+}_{(aq)} + \cancel{2Cl^-}_{(aq)} + \cancel{2Na^+}_{(aq)} + 2OH^-_{(aq)} \rightarrow Ca(OH)_{2(s)} + \cancel{2Na^+}_{(aq)} + \cancel{2Cl^-}_{(aq)}$$

So the ionic equation for this reaction is: $\mathbf{Ca^{2+}_{(aq)} + 2OH^-_{(aq)} \rightarrow Ca(OH)_{2(s)}}$

This time, the total charge on the left-hand side is +2 + (2 × –1) = 0, and the total charge on the right-hand side is 0 — so the charges do balance.

Practice Questions — Fact Recall

Q1 List the four state symbols and what they stand for.

Q2 Give the formulae of the following common molecules or ions:

a) water b) carbon dioxide

c) carbonate ion d) sulfate ion

Q3 Give the names of the following common molecules or ions:

a) NH_3 b) NO_3^-

c) Cl_2 d) O_2

e) NH_4^+

Practice Questions — Application

Q1 Give the state symbols for the following substances:

a) A piece of magnesium metal.

b) Ammonia gas.

c) Calcium nitrate dissolved in water.

Q2 Iron is a solid at room temperature. It can react with dilute hydrochloric acid to form iron(II) chloride, which is soluble in water, and hydrogen gas. The equation for this reaction is shown below.

$$Fe + 2HCl \rightarrow FeCl_2 + H_2$$

Rewrite the equation so that it includes state symbols.

Q3 The full, balanced equations for three reactions that take place in solution are shown below. Write ionic equations for these reactions.

a) $Mg_{(s)} + ZnCl_{2\,(aq)} \rightarrow MgCl_{2(aq)} + Zn_{(s)}$

b) $BaCl_{2\,(aq)} + Na_2SO_{4(aq)} \rightarrow 2NaCl_{(aq)} + BaSO_{4\,(s)}$

c) $Na_2CO_{3\,(aq)} + 2HNO_{3\,(aq)} \rightarrow 2NaNO_{3\,(aq)} + H_2O_{(l)} + CO_{2\,(g)}$

Tip: H Use the table below to help you answer Q3.

Metal	Ion formed
Mg	Mg^{2+}
Zn	Zn^{2+}
Ba	Ba^{2+}
Na	Na^+

Tip: H For Q3, if you can't remember the charges on any of the compound ions you need, have a quick look back at page 25.

Learning Objectives:

- Be able to describe the use of hazard symbols on containers to indicate the dangers associated with the contents.
- Be able to describe the use of hazard symbols on containers to inform people about safe-working precautions with these substances in the laboratory.
- Be able to evaluate the risks in a practical procedure and suggest suitable precautions for a range of practicals.

Specification References
0.5, 0.6

3. Hazards and Risk

Carrying out chemistry experiments can be a risky business. Thankfully, there are plenty of things you can do to help keep you safe in the lab.

What is a hazard?

A **hazard** is anything that has the potential to cause harm or damage. The **risk** associated with that hazard is the probability of someone (or something) being harmed if they are exposed to the hazard.

WORKING SCIENTIFICALLY

Hazard symbols

Lots of the chemicals you meet in chemistry can be bad for you or dangerous in some way. Their containers will have symbols on them to tell you what the dangers are. Understanding these symbols will help you work safely in the lab. Here are some hazard symbols that you'll need to know about:

Oxidising

Provides oxygen, which allows other materials to catch fire more easily and burn more fiercely. Example: Liquid oxygen.

Keep oxidising substances away from flammable substances, clothing and skin.

Highly Flammable

Catches fire easily.
Example: Petrol.

Keep flammable substances away from open flames.
Don't let them come into contact with your skin or clothing.

Tip: Chemicals can have more than one hazard associated with them.

Environmental Hazard

Harmful to organisms and to the environment.
Example: Mercury.

You must dispose of a chemical like this properly and never release it into the environment (e.g. don't tip it down a sink).

Corrosive

Destroys materials, including living tissues (e.g. eyes and skin). Example: Concentrated sulfuric acid.

Never let corrosive substances come into contact with your eyes, skin or clothing.

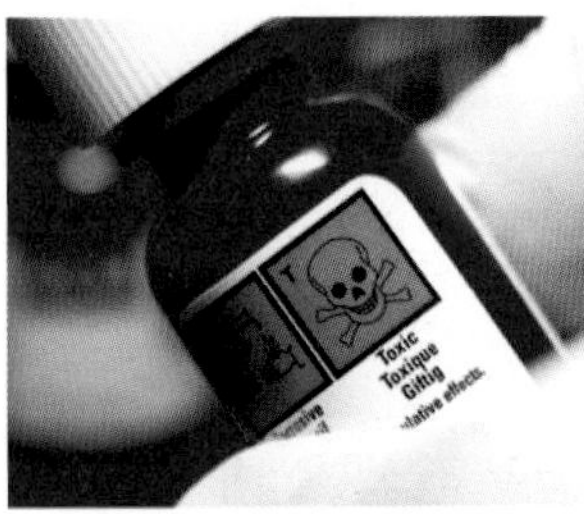

Figure 1: A hazard label on a chemical bottle. This chemical is both corrosive and toxic.

Toxic

Can cause death by, e.g. swallowing, breathing in, absorption through skin. Example: Hydrogen cyanide.

Never let toxic substances come into contact with the skin. Never breathe them in.

Harmful

Can cause irritation, reddening or blistering of the skin. Example: Bleach.

Keep harmful substances away from skin, eyes and clothing.

Identifying hazards and risks

Many chemistry experiments have risks associated with them. These can include risks associated with the equipment you're using (e.g. the risk of burning from an electric heater) as well as risks associated with chemicals (see previous page).

When you plan an experiment, you need to identify all the hazards and what the risk is from each hazard. This includes working out how likely it is that something could go wrong, and how serious it would be if it did. You then need to think of ways to reduce these risks. This procedure is called a risk assessment.

Example

A student is going to react a solution of sodium hydroxide with hydrochloric acid to form a metal salt and water. Identify any hazards in this experiment, and suggest how they could reduce the risk.

Sodium hydroxide and hydrochloric acid are harmful at low concentrations and corrosive at high concentrations. Harmful substances can cause blistering or reddening of the skin, but corrosive substances are much more dangerous if they come into contact with your skin or eyes.

To reduce the risks posed by these hazards, the student should try to use low concentrations of the substances if possible, and wear gloves, a lab coat and goggles when handling the chemicals.

Figure 2: *A scientist wearing safety goggles to protect his eyes during an experiment.*

Practice Questions — Fact Recall

Q1 Explain what is meant by the following terms, with respect to chemical experiments:

a) hazard

b) risk

Q2 Explain what is meant by each of the following chemical hazards:

a) oxidising

b) corrosive

c) highly flammable

Practice Question — Application

Q1 A scientist is carrying out an experiment that involves using potassium permanganate. Potassium permanganate is oxidising, harmful and an environmental hazard.

Suggest appropriate safety precautions the scientist could take to minimise the risk associated with using potassium permanganate.

Exam Tip

Whenever you're handling any hazardous chemicals, it's sensible to wear gloves, a lab coat and goggles to stop anything getting on to your skin or clothes or into your eyes. If you're stuck on a question about a risk assessment, that's a good way to start.

Topic 1a Checklist — Make sure you know...

Chemical Equations

- [ ] That the reactants in a chemical reaction are on the left-hand side of a chemical equation.
- [ ] That the products of a chemical reaction are on the right-hand side of a chemical equation.
- [ ] That word and symbol equations are used to show the reactants and products of a chemical reaction.
- [ ] How to write word equations for reactions.
- [ ] How to write balanced symbol equations for reactions.

More on Equations

- [ ] What the state symbols (s), (l), (g) and (aq) mean and how to use them in equations.
- [ ] The formulae of the following common molecules: water, ammonia, carbon dioxide, hydrogen, chlorine and oxygen.
- [ ] The formulae of the following common ions: ammonium ion, hydroxide ion, nitrate ion, carbonate ion and sulfate ion.
- [ ] H That an ionic equation can be written for any reaction involving ions that happens in solution.
- [ ] H That an ionic equation only shows the reacting particles and the products that they form.
- [ ] H How to write an ionic equation from a full, balanced equation.

Hazards and Risk

- [ ] What the terms hazard and risk mean in the context of chemical experiments.
- [ ] Why hazard symbols are placed on the side of chemical containers.
- [ ] How to determine the hazards and risks in a practical procedure.
- [ ] How to safely carry out an experiment by taking precautions to minimise the hazards and risks.

Exam-style Questions

1 A student is investigating the reactions of acids.

(a) First, the student adds a small piece of magnesium, Mg, to dilute sulfuric acid, H_2SO_4. The products of the reaction are magnesium sulfate, $Mg(SO_4)$, and hydrogen gas, H_2.

(i) Write a word equation for this reaction.

(1 mark)

(ii) Write a balanced symbol equation for this reaction.

(1 mark)

(b) Next, the student adds a spatula of zinc carbonate powder, $ZnCO_3$, to dilute hydrochloric acid, HCl.

(i) Balance the symbol equation for this reaction, shown below. You may not need to put a number on every line.

$$......HCl_{(aq)} + ...ZnCO_{3(s)} \rightarrow ......ZnCl_{2(aq)} + ...CO_{2(g)} + ...H_2O_{(l)}$$

(1 mark)

(ii) When the student added the zinc carbonate to the acid, she noticed that the reaction mixture started to fizz. Explain why.

(1 mark)

2 Propane is a hydrocarbon with the molecular formula C_3H_8. Propane burns completely in oxygen to give water and carbon dioxide.

Write a balanced symbol equation for this reaction.

(3 marks)

3 Magnesium iodide reacts with sodium hydroxide to form magnesium hydroxide and sodium iodide. The balanced symbol equation for this reaction is shown below.

$$MgI_{2(aq)} + 2NaOH_{(aq)} \rightarrow Mg(OH)_{2(s)} + 2NaI_{(aq)}$$

(a) Using the equation above, write a balanced ionic equation for the reaction between magnesium iodide and sodium hydroxide.

(3 marks)

(b) (i) Write down the names of any substances in the reaction that are in solution.

(1 mark)

(ii) Write down the names of any substances in the reaction that are solid.

(1 mark)

(c) Sodium hydroxide solution is corrosive. Give **two** ways that you could reduce the risk of using sodium hydroxide solution in an experiment.

(2 marks)

Learning Objective:
- Be able to describe how the Dalton model of an atom has changed over time because of the discovery of subatomic particles.

Specification Reference
1.1

1. The History of the Atom

Our current idea of the structure of the atom didn't just materialise out of thin air — theories have been built upon over time to get to where we are now.

The plum pudding model

At the start of the 19th century John Dalton described atoms as solid spheres, and said that different spheres made up the different elements.

In 1897, J J Thomson concluded from his experiments that atoms weren't solid spheres. His measurements of charge and mass showed that an atom must contain even smaller, negatively charged particles — **electrons**. So the 'solid sphere' idea of atomic structure had to be changed. The new theory was known as the '**plum pudding model**' — see Figure 1. This showed the atom as a ball of positive charge with electrons stuck in it.

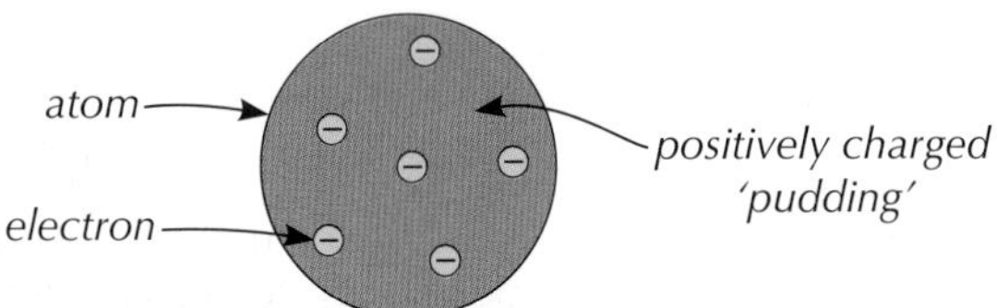

Figure 1: *The plum pudding model.*

Rutherford's nuclear model

In 1909 Ernest Rutherford and his students Hans Geiger and Ernest Marsden conducted the famous gold foil experiment. They fired positively charged alpha particles at an extremely thin sheet of gold.

From the plum pudding model, they were expecting the particles to pass through the sheet or be slightly deflected at most. This was because the positive charge of each atom was thought to be spread out through the 'pudding' of the atom. But, whilst most of the particles did go straight through the gold sheet, some were deflected more than expected, and a small number were deflected backwards. So the plum pudding model couldn't be right.

Rutherford came up with an idea that could explain this new evidence — the nuclear model of the atom. In this, there's a tiny, positively charged **nucleus** at the centre, where most of the mass is concentrated. A 'cloud' of negative electrons surrounds this nucleus. Most of the atom is empty space.

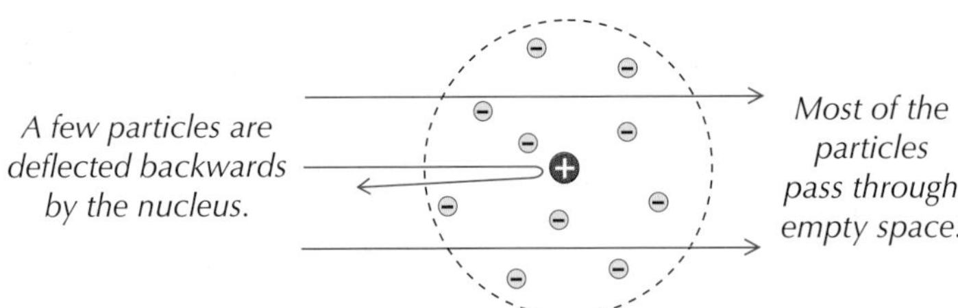

Figure 2: *The gold foil experiment.*

Tip: Models are used to predict the outcome of experiments. If the prediction is proved wrong, the model may need to change. WORKING SCIENTIFICALLY

Exam Tip
Questions on these pages may focus on the development of scientific models and theories over time. Remember, theories are built upon previous work and new evidence which has come to light. WORKING SCIENTIFICALLY

Bohr's nuclear model

Scientists realised that electrons in a 'cloud' around the nucleus of an atom, as Rutherford had described, would be attracted to the nucleus, causing the atom to collapse.

Niels Bohr proposed a new nuclear model of the atom to solve this problem (see Figure 3). He suggested that the electrons can only orbit the nucleus in fixed **shells** and aren't found anywhere in between. Each shell has a fixed energy. Bohr's theory of atomic structure was supported by many experiments and it helped to explain lots of other scientists' observations at the time.

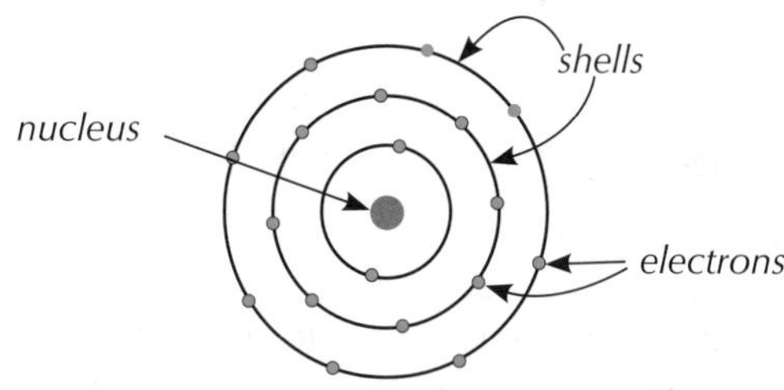

Figure 3: *Bohr's model of the atom proposes that electrons orbit the nucleus at fixed distances.*

Tip: For a theory to be accepted there must be experimental evidence to support it. WORKING SCIENTIFICALLY

Figure 4: *Niels Bohr (1885-1962) suggested that electrons were contained in shells of fixed energies.*

The discovery of protons and neutrons

Further experiments by Rutherford and others showed that the nucleus could be divided into smaller particles, each of which has the same charge as a single hydrogen nucleus. By the late 1920's, scientists were referring to these particles as **protons**.

About 20 years after scientists had accepted that atoms have nuclei, James Chadwick carried out an experiment which provided evidence for neutral particles in the nucleus. These became known as **neutrons**. The discovery of neutrons resulted in a model of the atom which was pretty close to the modern day version.

Tip: As scientists did more experiments, new evidence was found and the nuclear model was modified to fit it. This is how most scientific knowledge develops — new evidence prompts people to come up with new ideas. These ideas are used to make predictions. People can then do experiments to test these predictions.

Practice Questions — Fact Recall

Q1 Describe John Dalton's model of the atom.

Q2 Give the name of the subatomic particle discovered by J J Thomson.

Q3 Ernest Rutherford developed the first nuclear model of the atom based on the results of the gold foil experiment.

a) Describe the gold foil experiment and its results.

b) Explain how evidence from this experiment disproved the plum pudding model.

Q4 Bohr built upon the work of Ernest Rutherford by developing a new nuclear model of the atom.

Describe Bohr's suggestion for how the electrons were arranged within an atom.

2. The Atom

Atoms are the basis of all of chemistry. So you really need to know what they are. Luckily, these pages are here to help out with that...

Learning Objectives:
- Know the relative charge and relative mass of protons, neutrons and electrons.
- Be able to describe the structure of an atom as a nucleus containing protons and neutrons, surrounded by electrons in shells.
- Know that most of the mass of an atom is concentrated in the nucleus.
- Be able to describe the nucleus of an atom as very small compared to the overall size of the atom.
- Be able to explain why atoms contain equal numbers of protons and electrons.
- Be able to describe atoms of a given element as having the same number of protons in the nucleus and that this number is unique to that element.
- Know the meaning of the term 'mass number' of an atom.
- Be able to calculate the numbers of protons, neutrons and electrons in atoms given the atomic number and mass number.

Specification References
1.2-1.8, 1.10

Protons, neutrons and electrons

The atom is made up of three subatomic particles — **protons**, **neutrons** and **electrons**. Protons are heavy and positively charged. Neutrons are heavy and neutral. Electrons have hardly any mass and are negatively charged.

Particle	Proton	Neutron	Electron
Relative charge	+1	0	–1
Relative mass	1	1	0.0005

Figure 1: *The relative charges and masses of protons, neutrons and electrons. Relative mass (measured in atomic mass units) measures mass on a scale where the mass of a proton or neutron is 1.*

The structure of the atom

Atoms are the tiny particles that everything is made up of — they have a radius of about 1×10^{-10} metres. Atoms are so tiny that a 50p piece contains about 77 400 000 000 000 000 000 000 of them. There are quite a few different (and equally useful) models of the atom — but chemists tend to like the nuclear model best. The nuclear model shows atoms as having a small **nucleus** surrounded by **electrons** (see Figure 2).

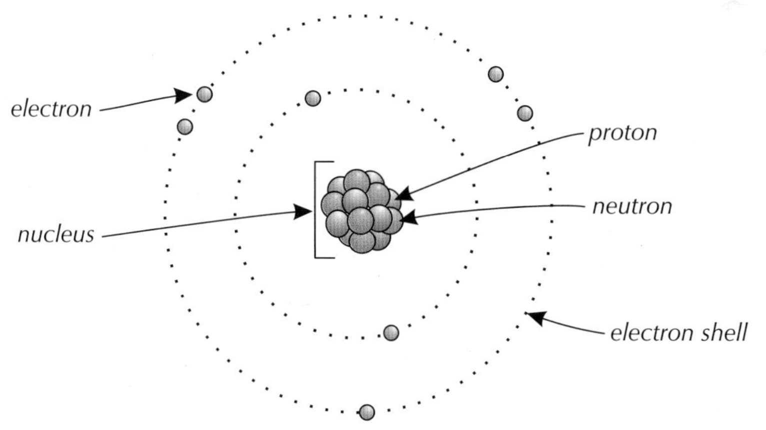

Figure 2: *The nuclear model of the atom.*

The nucleus

The nucleus is in the middle of the atom. It contains **protons** and **neutrons**. The nucleus has a positive charge overall because of the protons (see above).

Almost all of the mass of an atom is concentrated in the nucleus. But size-wise it's tiny compared to the rest of the atom. The radius is 1×10^{-14} m, about 1/10 000 of the size of the atom.

Tip: The measurements 1×10^{-10} m and 1×10^{-14} m are written in standard form. Standard form is used for showing very <u>large</u> or very <u>small</u> numbers. There's more on standard form in the Maths Skills section.

The electrons

The electrons are negatively charged. They move around the nucleus in **electron shells**. Electrons are tiny, but their orbitals (shells) cover a lot of space. The size of their shells determines the size of the atom.

Electrons have a tiny mass. Their relative mass is 0.0005 — that means they have a mass two thousand times smaller than a proton or neutron.

Tip: A shell is just an area where electrons are found. At GCSE you'll usually see them drawn as circles around the nucleus. Shells are sometimes called energy levels.

Electrical charge

The number of protons always equals the number of electrons in an atom. The charge on the electrons (–1) is the same size as the charge on the protons (+1) — but opposite. This means atoms have no charge overall — they are neutral.

Tip: The relative mass of an electron is so tiny compared to a proton or neutron that it's sometimes given as 0.

Example

This atom has 7 protons and 7 electrons. Each proton has a charge of +1, so the total charge of the nucleus is +7. (Neutrons have no charge, remember.)

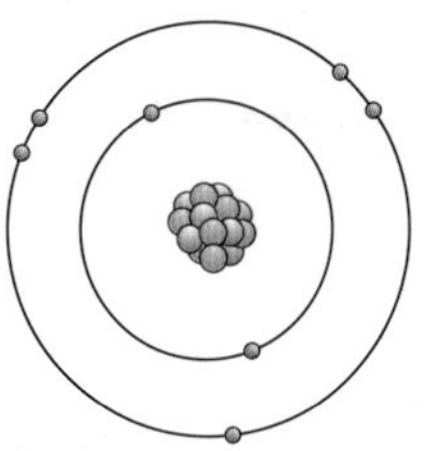

As there are 7 electrons and each electron has a charge of –1, the charge of the nucleus is cancelled out. The atom doesn't have a charge overall.

Tip: Protons, neutrons and electrons are all types of subatomic particle.

If some electrons are added or removed, the atom becomes charged and is then an **ion**. In an ion, the number of protons doesn't equal the number of electrons. For example, an ion with a 2– charge has two more electrons than protons (see page 48 for more on ions).

Tip: An ion is an atom or group of atoms that has lost or gained electrons.

Atomic number and mass number

The nuclear symbol of an atom tells you its **atomic number** and **mass number**.

The atomic number of an atom tells you how many protons it contains. Every atom of an element has the same number of protons. In a neutral atom the number of protons is equal to the number of electrons, so a neutral atom will also have a number of electrons equal to its atomic number.

The mass number of an atom tells you the total number of protons and neutrons that it contains.

Example

Here's the nuclear symbol for an atom of magnesium:

The mass number is 24. This tells you that the total number of protons and neutrons in the atom is 24.

$$^{24}_{12}\text{Mg}$$

The chemical symbol tells you that the atom is magnesium.

The atomic number is 12. This tells you that there are 12 protons in an atom of magnesium.

To work out the number of neutrons in an atom, you just subtract the atomic number from the mass number.

Exam Tip
You could be asked to calculate the number of protons, neutrons or electrons in an atom from its atomic number and mass number. So make sure you know how to do it.

Example 1

Here's the nuclear symbol for an atom of titanium:

mass number ⟶ 48
atomic number ⟶ 22

$$^{48}_{22}\text{Ti}$$

Number of protons in the atom = atomic number = 22.

The total number of protons and neutrons in the atom is 48.
So the number of neutrons in the atom = 48 – 22 = 26.

(The number of electrons in a neutral atom is equal to the number of protons, so the number of electrons in the atom will be 22.)

Example 2

An atom of sodium has a mass number of 23 and the atomic number 11. How many neutrons does this atom have in its nucleus?

Number of protons = atomic number = 11
Total number of protons and neutrons = mass number = 23
Number of neutrons = 23 – 11 = **12**

Practice Questions — Fact Recall

Q1 What is the relative charge of:
a) a proton? b) a neutron? c) an electron?

Q2 What is the relative mass of a proton?

Q3 Briefly describe the structure of an atom. Use the terms 'proton', 'neutron', 'electron', 'nucleus' and 'shell' in your answer.

Q4 Atoms are uncharged particles. Explain why.

Q5 a) What does the atomic number tell you about an atom?
b) What does the mass number tell you about an atom?

Practice Questions — Application

Q1 An atom of fluorine has an atomic number of 9 and a mass number of 19. How many neutrons does the atom have in its nucleus?

Q2 An atom of gold has the atomic number 79 and a mass number of 197. Calculate how many protons, neutrons and electrons it contains.

Q3 An atom of copper (Cu) has 29 protons and 34 neutrons. Draw the nuclear symbol for this atom.

Q4 Find the number of protons and neutrons in each of these atoms:
a) $^{16}_{8}\text{O}$ b) $^{27}_{13}\text{Al}$ c) $^{51}_{23}\text{V}$ d) $^{108}_{47}\text{Ag}$

3. Isotopes and Relative Atomic Mass

Atoms of the same element always have the same number of protons, but the number of neutrons can change. And that's where isotopes come in.

What are isotopes?

Isotopes are different forms of the same element, which have the same number of protons but a different number of neutrons. This means they have the same atomic number but a different mass number.

Example

Carbon-12 and carbon-13 are a well known pair of isotopes. They each have 6 protons, as carbon has an atomic number of 6. But carbon-12 has 6 neutrons (giving it a mass number of 12), while carbon-13 has 7 neutrons (giving it a mass number of 13).

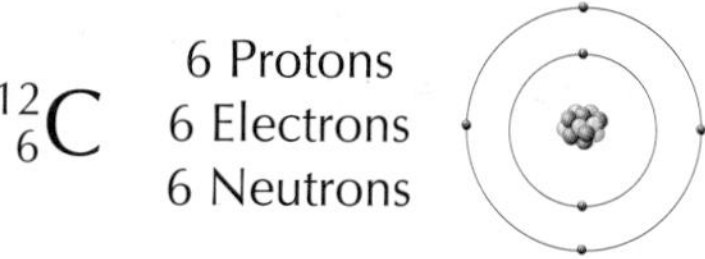

$^{13}_{6}C$ 6 Protons 6 Electrons 7 Neutrons

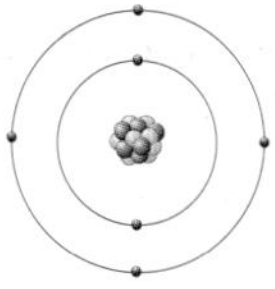

Relative atomic mass

In the periodic table, the elements all have two numbers next to them, as shown in Figure 1. The smaller one is the atomic number of the element. The bigger one is the **relative atomic mass** (A_r) of the element.

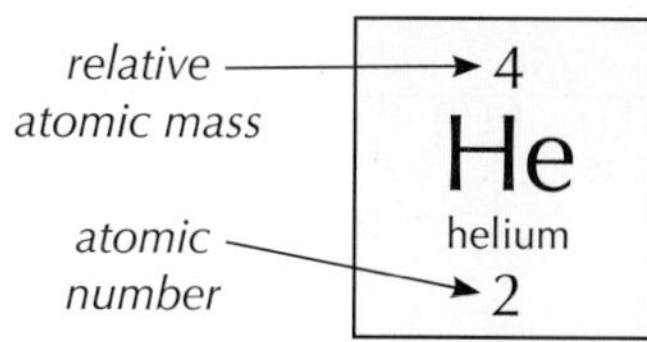

Figure 1: *Helium and carbon, as shown in the periodic table.*

The relative atomic mass of an element is the average mass of one atom of the element, compared to $^{1}/_{12}$ of the mass of one atom of carbon-12.

If an element only has one isotope, its A_r will be the same as the mass number (see p.35) of that isotope. But if an element has more than one isotope, its A_r is the average of the mass numbers of all the different isotopes, taking into account how much there is of each one — so it might not be a whole number.

Example

Chlorine has two stable isotopes, chlorine-35 and chlorine-37. There's quite a lot of chlorine-35 around and not so much chlorine-37 — so chlorine's A_r works out as 35.5 (much closer to 35 than to 37).

Learning Objectives:

- Know that isotopes are different atoms of the same element containing the same number of protons but different numbers of neutrons in their nuclei.
- Be able to explain how the existence of isotopes results in relative atomic masses of some elements not being whole numbers.
- **H** Be able to calculate the relative atomic mass of an element from the relative masses and abundance of its isotopes.

Specification References
1.9, 1.11, 1.12

Tip: The name of an isotope tells you what its mass number is. So carbon-12 has a mass number of 12, and carbon-13 has a mass number of 13. (All the atoms of an element have the same atomic number, so you don't need to be told what the atomic number is.)

Calculating relative atomic mass Higher

Different isotopes of an element occur in different quantities, or abundances. You need to know how to calculate the relative atomic mass of an element from the abundance of its different isotopes.

You can use this formula to work out the relative atomic mass of an element:

$$\text{relative atomic mass } (A_r) = \frac{\text{sum of (isotope abundance} \times \text{isotope mass number)}}{\text{sum of abundances of all the isotopes}}$$

Tip: You might see the isotopes of an element represented by the chemical symbol followed by the mass number (e.g. Cu-63, as in Example 1) or by the chemical symbol with the mass number as a superscript before it (e.g. ^{63}Cu). Don't worry — both versions mean the same thing.

Example 1 Higher

Copper has two stable isotopes, Cu-63 and Cu-65. Cu-63 has an abundance of 69.2% and Cu-65 has an abundance of 30.8%.

$$\text{relative atomic mass} = \frac{\text{sum of (isotope abundance} \times \text{isotope mass number)}}{\text{sum of abundances of all the isotopes}}$$

$$= \frac{(69.2 \times 63) + (30.8 \times 65)}{69.2 + 30.8} = \frac{4359.6 + 2002}{100} = \frac{6361.6}{100}$$

$$= 63.616 = \mathbf{63.6}$$

Example 2 Higher

Magnesium has three stable isotopes, as shown in the table below.

Isotope	Mg-24	Mg-25	Mg-26
Abundance (%)	79.0	10.0	11.0

$$\text{relative atomic mass} = \frac{\text{sum of (isotope abundance} \times \text{isotope mass number)}}{\text{sum of abundances of all the isotopes}}$$

$$= \frac{(79.0 \times 24) + (10.0 \times 25) + (11.0 \times 26)}{79.0 + 10.0 + 11.0}$$

$$= \frac{1896 + 250 + 286}{100} = \frac{2432}{100} = 24.32 = \mathbf{24.3}$$

Tip: H If you're given the abundances as percentages, the sum of the abundances should always be 100.

Practice Questions — Fact Recall

Q1 What are isotopes?

Q2 What is relative atomic mass?

Practice Questions — Application

Q1 Which of the atoms shown below is an isotope of $^{35}_{17}Cl$?

A: $^{37}_{17}Cl$ B: $^{35}_{16}Cl$ C: $^{36}_{35}Cl$ D: $^{17}_{35}Cl$

Q2 The A_r of zinc is 65.4. Explain why this value is not a whole number.

Q3 92.5% of lithium atoms are Li-7 and the remaining 7.5% are Li-6. Calculate the relative atomic mass of lithium to 1 decimal place.

4. Development of the Periodic Table

Early chemists tried to understand patterns in the properties of the elements by sorting them into tables — that's how the Periodic Table was developed.

Learning Objectives:

- Be able to describe how Mendeleev arranged the known elements into a periodic table by using the properties of these elements and their compounds.
- Be able to explain that Mendeleev thought he had arranged elements in order of increasing relative atomic mass, but this was not always true because of the relative abundance of isotopes of some pairs of elements in the periodic table.
- Be able to describe how Mendeleev used his table to predict the existence and properties of some elements not then discovered.

Specification References
1.13-1.15

Mendeleev's periodic table

WORKING SCIENTIFICALLY

In 1869, Dmitri Mendeleev arranged the 50 or so elements known at the time into a Table of Elements. He began by sorting the elements into groups, based on their properties (and the properties of their compounds).

As he did this, he realised that if he put the elements in order of atomic mass, a pattern appeared — he could put elements with similar chemical properties in columns.

Mendeleev's Table of Elements

H																
Li	Be											B	C	N	O	F
Na	Mg											Al	Si	P	S	Cl
K	Ca	*	Ti	V	Cr	Mn	Fe	Co	Ni	Cu	Zn	*	*	As	Se	Br
Rb	Sr	Y	Zr	Nb	Mo	*	Ru	Rh	Pd	Ag	Cd	In	Sn	Sb	Te	I
Cs	Ba	*	*	Ta	W	*	Os	Ir	Pt	Au	Hg	Tl	Pb	Bi		

Figure 1: *Mendeleev's Table of Elements*

A few elements, however, seemed to end up in the wrong columns. In some cases this was because the atomic mass Mendeleev had was wrong (due to the presence of isotopes) — but some elements just didn't quite fit the pattern. Wherever this happened, he switched the order of the elements to keep those with the same properties in the same columns.

To keep elements with similar properties together, Mendeleev also had to leave some gaps (shown by the *s in the table above). He used the properties of the other elements in the columns with the gaps to predict the properties of these undiscovered elements. When they were found and they fitted the pattern, it helped to confirm his ideas. For example, Mendeleev predicted the chemical and physical properties of an element he called ekasilicon, which we know today as germanium.

Figure 2: *Dmitri Mendeleev (1834-1907)*

Practice Questions — Fact Recall

Q1 Briefly describe how Mendeleev arranged the elements in his version of the Periodic Table.

Q2 Mendeleev left gaps in his Periodic Table. He used the properties of the other elements in the columns with the gaps to predict the properties of these undiscovered elements.

Explain how this later helped to confirm that his ideas were correct.

5. The Modern Periodic Table

The periodic table is a chemist's best friend. At first glance it might seem a bit intimidating but it's got loads of useful information in it.

Learning Objectives:

- Be able to describe that in the periodic table, elements with similar properties are placed in the same vertical columns called groups.
- Be able to describe that in the periodic table, elements are arranged in order of increasing atomic number, in rows called periods.
- Be able to explain the meaning of the atomic number of an element in terms of position in the periodic table and number of protons in the nucleus.
- Be able to explain how the electronic configuration of an element is related to its position in the periodic table.
- Be able to identify elements as metals or non-metals according to their position in the periodic table, explaining this division in terms of the atomic structure of the elements.

Specification References 1.16-1.18, 1.20

What is the periodic table?

Once protons and electrons were discovered, the **atomic number** (see p.35) of each element could be found, based on the number of protons in its nucleus. The modern periodic table shows the elements in order of ascending atomic number — and they fit the same patterns that Mendeleev worked out.

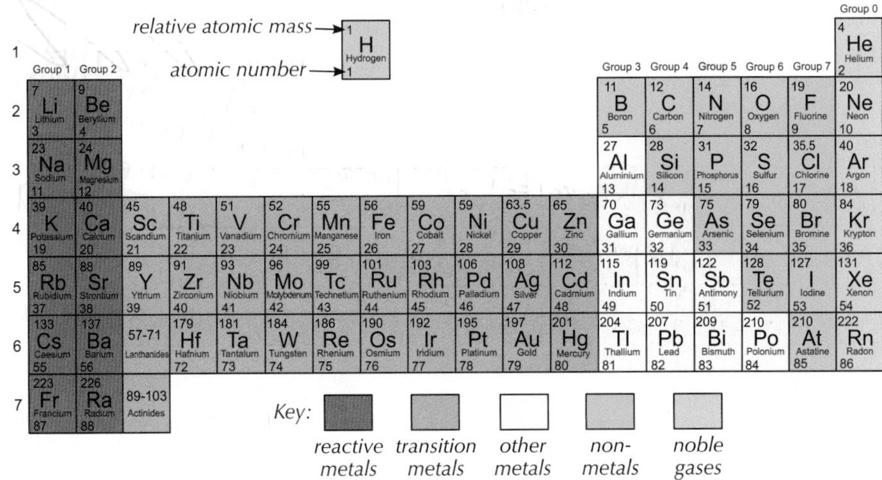

Figure 1: *The periodic table of the elements.*

The periodic table is laid out so elements with similar chemical properties form columns called groups. The rows are called periods. Each new period represents another full shell of electrons (see p.42 for more on electron shells).

Electronic structure and the periodic table

The period number of an element tells you how many electron shells it has.

Examples

Nitrogen is a period 2 element. Nitrogen atoms have two electron shells.

Bromine is a period 4 element. Bromine atoms have four electron shells.

The group number of an element tells you how many electrons there are in its outer shell.

Examples

Group 1 elements, like lithium, sodium and potassium, all have one electron in their outer electron shell.

Group 7 elements, like chlorine, bromine and iodine, all have seven electrons in their outer electron shell.

Figure 2: *Lithium, sodium and potassium are all in group 1, so they have similar properties. For example, they are all soft metals that are shiny when cut.*

The exception to the rule is the elements in Group 0. These elements all have full outer shells of 8 electrons (or 2 in the case of helium).

If you know the position of an element in the periodic table, you can work out its electronic configuration — see page 43 for more on how to do this.

Metals and non-metals

The elements in the periodic table can be classified as **metals** or **non-metals**. The non-metals are found in the top right of the periodic table (with the exception of hydrogen). The metals make up the rest of table, and are separated from the non-metals by a zig-zag line running from boron to astatine (see Figure 4).

Figure 3: *Copper (top) is a metal and sulfur (bottom) is a non-metal.*

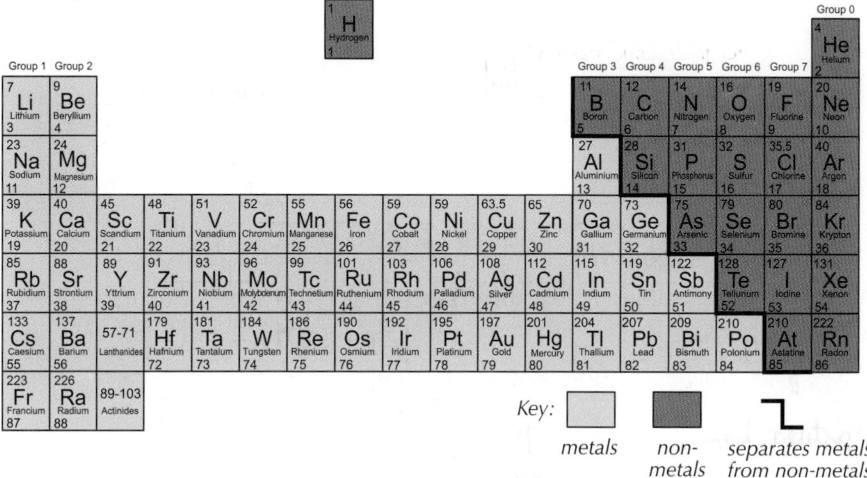

Figure 4: *The division between metals and non-metals in the periodic table.*

Metals tend to form positive ions (by losing electrons) and non-metals tend to form negative ions (by gaining electrons).

Practice Questions — Fact Recall

Q1 What does an element's period number tell you about its electronic configuration?

Q2 What does an element's group number tell you about it's electronic configuration?

Q3 How many electrons do Group 1 elements have in their outer shell?

Practice Questions — Application

Q1 Using a periodic table, state how many electrons boron has in its outer shell.

Q2 Name any three elements from the periodic table that have three electron shells.

6. Electronic Configurations

Learning Objectives:
- Be able to predict the electronic configuration of the first 20 elements in the periodic table using diagrams and numbers (e.g. 2.8.1).
- Be able to explain how the electronic configuration of an element is related to its position in the periodic table.

Specification References
1.19, 1.20

Electronic configurations might sound like a bit of a mouthful, but it's actually just about knowing how the electrons are arranged inside atoms.

How are the electrons arranged in atoms?

Electrons always occupy **shells** (sometimes called **energy levels**). The electron shells with the lowest energy are always filled first — these are the ones closest to the nucleus. Only a certain number of electrons are allowed in each shell — see Figure 1.

Shell	Maximum number of electrons
1st	2
2nd	8
3rd	8

Figure 1: *Table showing how many electrons each electron shell can hold.*

Atoms are much happier when they have full electron shells — like the **noble gases** in Group 0. In most atoms the outer shell is not full and this makes the atom react to fill it.

Tip: There's more on noble gases (Group 0 elements) on p.186-187.

Electronic configurations

The **electronic configuration** of an element is how the electrons are arranged in an atom of that element. You need to know the electronic configurations for the first 20 elements (things get a bit more complicated after that). But they're not hard to work out. You just need to follow these steps:

1. Find the number of electrons in an atom of the element (you can find this from the atomic number of the element, which is on the periodic table).
2. Draw the first electron shell and add up to two electrons to it.
3. Draw the second electron shell and add up to eight electrons to it.
4. If you need to, draw the third electron shell and add up to eight electrons.
5. As soon as you've added enough electrons, stop.

Tip: Representing 3D objects, such as atoms, using 2D diagrams is an important maths skill.

Tip: Sometimes you'll see electrons drawn as dots and other times as crosses. For these diagrams, it doesn't matter which you use.

Example

Draw the electronic configuration of nitrogen.

1. The atomic number of nitrogen is seven, so it has seven protons and therefore seven electrons.
2. Draw the first electron shell and add 2 electrons.
3. Draw the second shell and add the remaining five electrons.
4. Nitrogen only has seven electrons so you don't need to draw a third shell.

1st shell

2nd shell

MATHS SKILLS

Tip: You'd usually draw the first four electrons in each shell spread out around the shell. Then the next four electrons are drawn next to them to make pairs of electrons. But you don't need to worry about this for GCSE — just make sure you've got the right number of electrons in each shell.

Drawing an atom is one way of showing its electronic configuration, but you can also write out the electronic structure using numbers.

Tip: An electronic configuration is sometimes called an <u>electronic structure</u>.

Examples

1. You can show the electronic configuration of nitrogen using a diagram like this...

   ...or you can write it out like this:

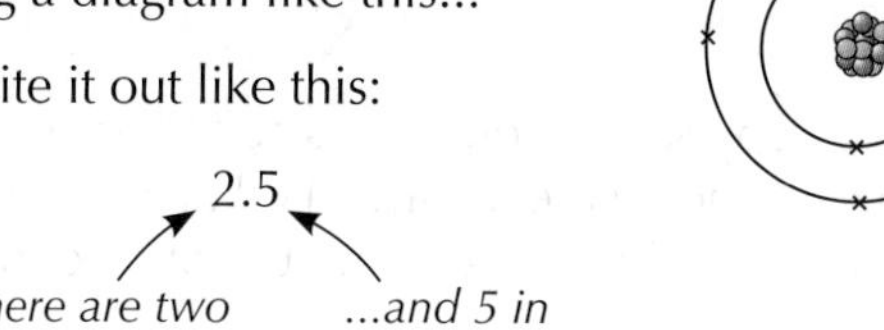

2.5

This shows that there are two electrons in the 1st shell... *...and 5 in the 2nd.*

MATHS SKILLS

2. Argon has 18 electrons. Two can go in the first shell and eight can go in the second. That leaves eight to go into the third electron shell. So the electronic configuration of argon is 2.8.8.

3. Aluminium has 13 electrons. Two electrons can go in the first shell, and eight can go in the second shell. This leaves 13 – (2 + 8) = 3 electrons to go in the third shell. So aluminium has an electronic configuration of 2.8.3.

Exam Tip
You need to be able to <u>draw</u> and <u>write</u> electronic configurations for the first 20 elements of the periodic table. So make sure you know how to do it both ways.

After the 3rd shell is filled things get more complicated. Luckily, the only electronic configurations with electrons in the 4th shell that you need to know are potassium (2.8.8.1) and calcium (2.8.8.2).

Electronic configurations and the periodic table

You can also work out the electronic configuration of an element from its period number and group number in the periodic table. The period number is the same as the number of electron shells the element has. The group number tells you how many electrons are in the outer shell of the element.

Examples

Oxygen is in Period 2 of the periodic table, so it has 2 electron shells. The first shell must be full (2). Oxygen is in Group 6, so it must have 6 electrons in its outer shell. So its electronic configuration is 2.6.

Sodium is in Period 3, so it has 3 electron shells. The first two shells must be full (2.8). Sodium is in Group 1, so it must have 1 electron in its outer shell. So its electronic configuration is 2.8.1.

Tip: Remember, the first electron shell contains a maximum of two electrons and the second and third electron shells contain a maximum of eight electrons each.

Practice Questions — Fact Recall

Q1 In an atom, which shell fills with electrons first?

Q2 Copy and complete the table on the right to show the maximum number of electrons that can go in each of the first three electron shells.

Shell	Maximum number of electrons
1st	
2nd	
3rd	

Tip: You'll need a periodic table to answer some of these questions so that you can find the atomic numbers of the elements. You'll find one on the inside of the back cover.

Tip: You don't need to draw the protons and neutrons when you're drawing the electronic configuration of an element. You can just draw a circle to represent the nucleus instead (as in Q1).

Practice Questions — Application

Q1 This diagram shows the electronic configuration of an element. Which element is it?

Q2 Which element has the electronic configuration 2,4?

Q3 Which element has the electronic configuration 2,8,6?

Q4 Which element has the electronic configuration 2,8,8,2?

Q5 Draw the electronic configuration of oxygen.

Q6 Draw the electronic configuration of boron.

Q7 Draw the electronic configuration of chlorine.

Q8 Write out the electronic configuration of phosphorus.

Q9 Write out the electronic configuration of magnesium.

Q10 Write out the electronic configuration of silicon.

Topic 1b Checklist — Make sure you know...

The History of The Atom

- ☐ That, before the discovery of the electron, scientists thought that atoms were solid spheres. This was known as the Dalton model, after the scientist John Dalton.
- ☐ What the plum pudding model is and why this model was proposed.
- ☐ How the work of Rutherford, Geiger and Marsden disproved the plum pudding model.
- ☐ What Bohr proposed about the arrangement of the electrons in the atom and how the nuclear model was adapted as a result of this.
- ☐ How the discovery of protons and neutrons changed the accepted model of the atom.

The Atom

- ☐ The relative masses and charges of protons, neutrons and electrons.
- ☐ That the radius of an atom is very small (around 1×10^{-10} m).
- ☐ The structure of the atom, including the arrangement of protons, neutrons and electrons.
- ☐ That most of the mass of the atom is found in the nucleus.
- ☐ That the size of the nucleus is tiny compared to the size of the atom.
- ☐ That atoms are neutral (have no overall charge) because they contain equal numbers of protons and electrons.
- ☐ That the atomic number of an atom tells you the total number of protons in the nucleus.
- ☐ That atoms of the same element have the same number of protons and atoms of different elements have different numbers of protons.

cont...

- ☐ That the mass number of an atom tells you the total number of protons and neutrons in the nucleus.
- ☐ How to calculate the numbers of protons, neutrons and electrons in an atom from the atomic number and mass number.

Isotopes and Relative Atomic Mass

- ☐ That isotopes are atoms with the same number of protons but a different number of neutrons.
- ☐ That the relative atomic mass of an element is the average mass of all the isotopes of the element. This results in the relative atomic masses of some elements not being whole numbers.
- ☐ H How to calculate the relative atomic mass of an element using the mass numbers of its isotopes and their abundances.

Development of the Periodic Table

- ☐ That Mendeleev ordered the elements in his early version of the periodic table using their properties and the properties of their compounds.
- ☐ That in Mendeleev's table, the elements were arranged in order of increasing atomic mass.
- ☐ That to keep elements with similar properties in the same group, Mendeleev sometimes had to swap elements around or leave gaps.
- ☐ That Mendeleev predicted the properties of the undiscovered elements that would fit in the gaps.
- ☐ That the discovery of elements that fitted Mendeleev's predictions provided evidence that supported his system of ordering the elements.

The Modern Periodic Table

- ☐ That elements in the periodic table are arranged in order of atomic number.
- ☐ That, in the periodic table, elements with similar properties are placed in vertical columns, called groups.
- ☐ That the horizontal rows in the periodic table are called periods.
- ☐ How the position of an element in the periodic table relates to its electronic configuration.
- ☐ That most elements are metals and can be found towards the bottom left of the periodic table. Non-metals can be found towards the top right of the periodic table.

Electronic Configurations

- ☐ That electrons will fill the shells closest to the nucleus of an atom first.
- ☐ That the first three electron shells can hold 2, 8 and 8 electrons respectively.
- ☐ How to work out the electronic configurations of the first 20 elements of the periodic table.
- ☐ How to work out the electronic configuration of an element from its position in the periodic table.

Exam-style Questions

1 (a) Complete this diagram so that it shows the electronic configuration of carbon.

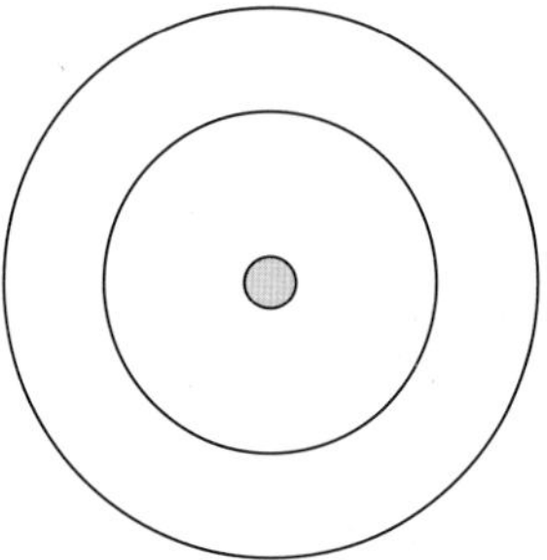

(2 marks)

(b) What is the overall charge of the nucleus of an atom of carbon?
Explain your answer.

(2 marks)

2 Dmitri Mendeleev created one of the earliest versions of the periodic table.
The elements in his table were arranged in order of relative atomic mass.

(a) Mendeleev left some gaps in his table.
Explain why.

(1 mark)

(b) How are the elements ordered in the modern periodic table?

(1 mark)

3 A neutral atom of a mystery element, **X**, contains 16 protons,
18 neutrons and 16 electrons.

(a) The atom has the electronic configuration 2.8.6.

(i) What group of the periodic table does element **X** belong to?

(1 mark)

(ii) Which period of the periodic table would you find element **X** in?

(1 mark)

(b) The nucleus of another atom contains 17 protons and 18 neutrons.
Is this also an atom of the element **X**? Explain your answer.

(1 mark)

4 Through their experiments using alpha particles, Rutherford, Geiger and Marsden proposed a new structure for the atom known as the nuclear model.

(a) Describe Rutherford's nuclear model of the atom.

(2 marks)

(b) In nuclear models of the atom, most of the mass of the atom is found in the nucleus. Explain why, using ideas about the relative masses of the particles that make up an atom.

(2 marks)

5 Chlorine is a non-metallic element.
A particular atom of chlorine has the nuclear symbol $^{37}_{17}Cl$.

(a) Complete **Figure 1** by filling in the missing information about the atomic structure of this atom of chlorine.

Atomic number	
Mass number	37
Number of protons	17
Number of electrons	
Number of neutrons	

Figure 1

(3 marks)

(b) (i) Another atom of chlorine has the nuclear symbol $^{35}_{17}Cl$.
Its nucleus contains fewer neutrons than an atom of $^{37}_{17}Cl$.
What is the term for atoms of the same element that contain different numbers of neutrons?

(1 mark)

(ii) 25% of chlorine atoms are $^{37}_{17}Cl$. The other 75% of chlorine atoms are $^{35}_{17}Cl$.
Use this information to calculate the relative atomic mass (A_r) of chlorine.
Give your answer to 3 significant figures.

(2 marks)

(c) Give the electronic configuration of chlorine in number form.

(1 mark)

(d) Sodium is a Group 1 element that readily reacts with chlorine.
Complete the diagram below to show the electronic configuration of sodium.

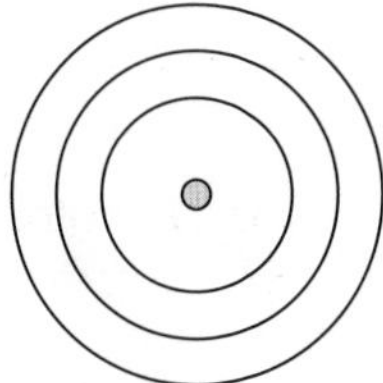

(2 marks)

Topic 1c Bonding and Types of Substance

Learning Objectives:
- Know that an ion is an atom or group of atoms with a positive or negative charge.
- Be able to calculate the numbers of protons, neutrons and electrons in simple ions, given the atomic number and mass number.
- Be able to explain the formation of ions in ionic compounds from their atoms, limited to compounds of elements in groups 1, 2, 6 and 7.
- Be able to deduce the formulae of ionic compounds (including oxides, hydroxides, halides, nitrates, carbonates and sulfates) given the formulae of the constituent ions.
- Be able to explain the use of the endings -ide and -ate in the names of compounds.

Specification References 1.22-1.26

1. Ions

Ions crop up all over the place in chemistry. These next few pages will give you the lowdown on what ions are, how to name them and how they form.

Formation of ions

Ions are charged particles. They can be single atoms (e.g. Na^{+}) or groups of atoms (e.g. NO_3^{-}). Ions form when atoms lose or gain electrons.

- Positive ions (**cations**) form when atoms lose electrons — they have more protons than electrons.
- Negative ions (**anions**) form when atoms gain electrons — they have more electrons than protons.

The number of electrons lost or gained is the same as the charge on the ion.

Examples

- If 2 electrons are lost from an atom, the ion will have a charge of 2+. The ion contains 2 more protons than electrons.
- If an atom gains 3 electrons, it will have a charge of 3–. The ion now contains 3 more electrons than protons.

When atoms lose or gain electrons to form ions, they end up with full outer shells — this makes the ions very stable.

Protons, neutrons and electrons in ions

On pages 35-36, you saw how to use the atomic number and mass number of an atom to work out how many protons, neutrons and electrons it contains. For ions, you can find the number of protons and neutrons in the same way. But to find the number of electrons, you'll need to think about how many electrons the atom lost or gained to form the ion. Here are some examples:

Example 1

An atom of fluorine has the nuclear symbol $^{19}_{9}F$. Calculate the number of protons, neutrons and electrons in an F^{-} ion formed from this atom.

The atomic number of the atom is 9, so the F^{-} ion must contain **9 protons**.

The mass number of the atom is 19. To work out the number of neutrons in the F^{-} ion, subtract the number of protons from the mass number: 19 – 9 = **10 neutrons**.

F^{-} has a charge of 1–, so it must have one more electron than protons. So the F^{-} ion must contain 9 + 1 = **10 electrons**.

Tip: The atomic number tells you the number of protons in an atom. The mass number tells you the total number of protons and neutrons in an atom.

Example 2

An atom of iron has the nuclear symbol $^{56}_{26}Fe$. Calculate the number of protons, neutrons and electrons in a Fe^{2+} ion formed from this atom.

The atomic number of the atom is 26, so the Fe^{2+} ion contains **26 protons**.

The mass number is 56, so the Fe^{2+} ion contains 56 – 26 = **30 neutrons**.

Fe^{2+} has a charge of 2+, so it must have two more protons than electrons. So the Fe^{2+} ion must contain 26 – 2 = **24 electrons**.

Ionic charge and group number

You don't have to remember what ions most elements form — you can just look at the periodic table. Elements in the same **group** all have the same number of outer electrons. So they have to lose or gain the same number to get a full outer shell. And this means that they form ions with the same charges.

Exam Tip
You'll be given a periodic table in the exam so don't worry about trying to memorise it.

The elements that most readily form ions are those in Groups 1, 2, 6 and 7. Group 1 and Group 2 elements are metals. They lose electrons to form positive ions. Group 6 and Group 7 elements are non-metals. They gain electrons to form negative ions.

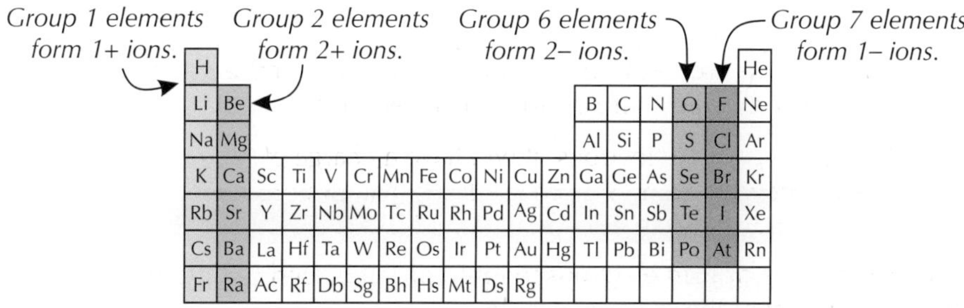

Figure 1: *Periodic table group number and ionic charge.*

Working out the formula of an ionic compound

Ionic compounds (see p.54-55) are made up of a positively charged part and a negatively charged part. The overall charge on an ionic compound is zero, so the negative charges in the compound must balance the positive charges.

You can use this information, along with the charges on the individual ions present, to work out the formula of an ionic compound.

Tip: Calcium is in Group 2 of the periodic table, so you know it forms 2+ ions. The nitrate ion, NO_3^-, is just one of those common compound ions (see p.25) whose formula and charge you might be expected to recall.

Example 1

What is the chemical formula of the ionic compound calcium nitrate?

The formula of a calcium ion is Ca^{2+}. The formula of a nitrate ion is NO_3^-.

The compound must be neutral, so work out the ratio of Ca : NO_3 that gives an overall charge of zero.

To balance the 2+ charge on Ca^{2+}, you need two NO_3^- ions: (+2) + (2 x –1) = 0. So, the formula must be $Ca(NO_3)_2$.

Tip: The brackets in $Ca(NO_3)_2$ show that there are two lots of the nitrate ion (NO_3) in the molecule.

Tip: Sodium is in Group 1 of the periodic table, so it forms 1+ ions. The sulfate ion, SO_4^{2-}, is another common compound ion (see p.25) you need to know.

Example 2

What is the chemical formula of sodium sulfate?

MATHS SKILLS

The formulae of the sodium and sulfate ions are Na^+ and SO_4^{2-}.

To make the compound neutral, you need 2 Na^+ ions to balance the 2– charge on the SO_4^{2-} ion: $(2 \times +1) + (-2) = 0$. So the formula is Na_2SO_4.

Naming ions

There are a couple of rules you need to know when it comes to naming ions.

- Ions with names ending in -ate are negative ions containing oxygen and at least one other element.

Tip: The naming of positive ions is easier than for negative ions. For example, it's fine to refer to Na^+ as a 'sodium ion' or 'sodium cation'. The only positive ion you're likely to come across that has a special name is the ammonium ion (NH_4^+).

Examples

Nitrate, NO_3^- — a negative ion containing nitrogen and oxygen.

Carbonate, CO_3^{2-} — a negative ion containing carbon and oxygen.

- Ions with names ending in -ide are negative ions containing only one element (apart from hydroxide ions which are OH^-).

Examples

Chloride, Cl^- — a negative ion containing only chlorine.

Oxide, O^{2-} — a negative ion containing only oxygen.

Practice Questions — Fact Recall

Q1 Briefly describe how a positive ion is formed from an atom.

Q2 What charge do ions formed from Group 2 elements have?

Q3 If the name of an ion ends in -ate, what does this tell you about it?

Q4 If the name of an ion ends in -ide, what does this tell you about it?

Practice Questions — Application

Q1 Calculate the number of protons, neutrons and electrons in the following ions:

a) Br^- (formed from $^{80}_{35}Br$) b) Ca^{2+} (formed from $^{40}_{20}Ca$)

c) Na^+ (formed from $^{23}_{11}Na$) d) Se^{2-} (formed from $^{79}_{34}Se$)

Q2 Write down the chemical formulas of the following ionic compounds:

a) sodium chloride b) magnesium iodide

c) calcium oxide d) potassium oxide

Q3 Ammonium ions have the formula NH_4^+. Carbonate ions have the formula CO_3^{2-}. Write down the formula of ammonium carbonate.

Tip: Remember, you can use the periodic table to find the charges on ions formed from elements in Groups 1, 2, 6 and 7.

2. Ionic Bonding

There's plenty to know about ionic bonding — what it is, how it works, how to represent it... So best crack on...

Learning Objectives:
- Be able to explain how ionic bonds are formed by the transfer of electrons between atoms to produce cations and anions.
- Be able to draw dot and cross diagrams to represent ionic bonding.

Specification Reference
1.21

What is ionic bonding?

When metals react with non-metals, electrons are transferred from the metal atoms to the non-metal atoms. The metal atoms lose electrons to become positively charged ions (cations) with a full outer shell of electrons. The non-metal atoms gain electrons and become negatively charged ions (anions) with a full outer shell of electrons.

The oppositely charged ions are strongly attracted to each other, and this strong electrostatic attraction holds the ions together in the ionic compound. This is known as **ionic bonding**.

Representing ionic bonding

Dot and cross diagrams are used to show what happens during ionic bonding. The electrons in one type of atom are represented by dots, and the electrons in the other type of atom are represented by crosses. This means you can tell which atom the electrons in an ion originally came from. To show the charge on each ion, you use a big square bracket and a + or –.

Tip: In reality, all electrons are identical. You just use different symbols (dots and crosses) so that it's clear which atom each electron came from.

Example

- A potassium atom has one electron in its outer shell.
- A chlorine atom has seven electrons in its outer shell.
- Potassium and chlorine react to form the compound potassium chloride, which is held together by ionic bonding.
- The potassium ion and the chloride ion both have full outer shells.

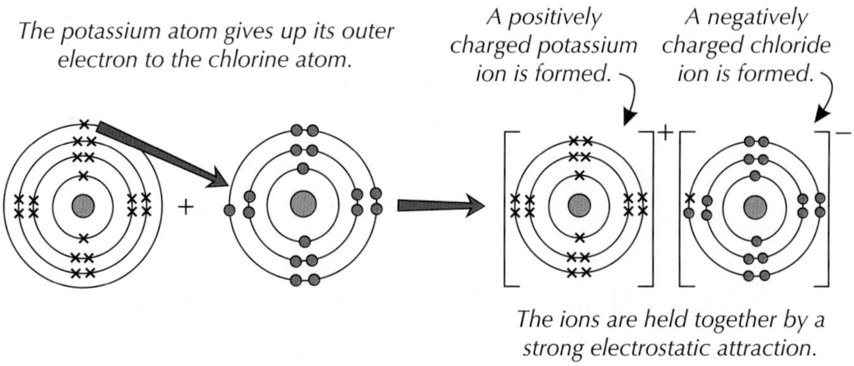

The potassium atom gives up its outer electron to the chlorine atom.

A positively charged potassium ion is formed.

A negatively charged chloride ion is formed.

The ions are held together by a strong electrostatic attraction.

Figure 1: *The formation of potassium chloride.*

Tip: Being able to interpret and draw diagrams to represent scientific ideas and models is an important skill. WORKING SCIENTIFICALLY

Tip: Most metals only have a few electrons in their outer shells. To get a full outer shell, it's easier for them to lose these than to gain enough to fill their outer shells up. The opposite is true for non-metals. It's easier for them to gain a few electrons than to lose all the electrons in their outer shells.

More dot and cross diagrams of ionic structures

The potassium chloride example on the previous page showed the bonding between a Group 1 metal and a Group 7 non-metal, where one electron was transferred. Sometimes, more than one electron is transferred during ionic bonding. The examples below show cases where two electrons are transferred.

Tip: Remember, you can work out how many electrons an atom will gain or lose from its group number. See page 49.

Example 1

A Group 2 metal and a Group 6 non-metal — magnesium oxide

The magnesium atom gives up its two outer electrons, becoming an Mg^{2+} ion. The oxygen atom picks up the electrons, becoming an O^{2-} (oxide) ion.

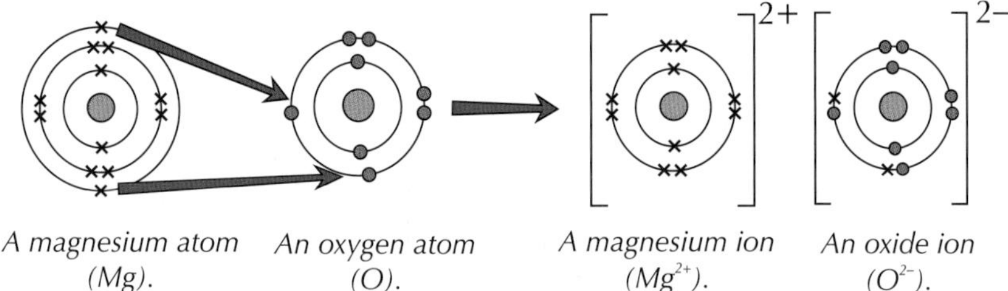

Figure 2: *The formation of magnesium oxide.*

Example 2

A Group 2 metal and a Group 7 non-metal — calcium chloride

The calcium atom gives up its two outer electrons, becoming a Ca^{2+} ion. The two chlorine atoms pick up one electron each, becoming two Cl^- (chloride) ions.

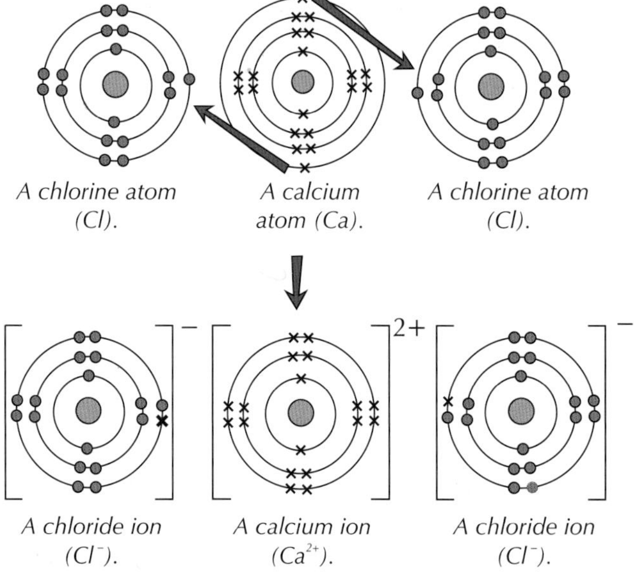

Figure 3: *The formation of calcium chloride.*

Exam Tip

Don't forget to include the charge when you're drawing the electronic configurations of ions — you won't get all the marks without it.

Example 3

A Group 1 metal and a Group 6 non-metal — sodium oxide

Two sodium atoms each give up their single outer electron, becoming two Na^+ ions. The oxygen atom picks up the two electrons, becoming an O^{2-} ion.

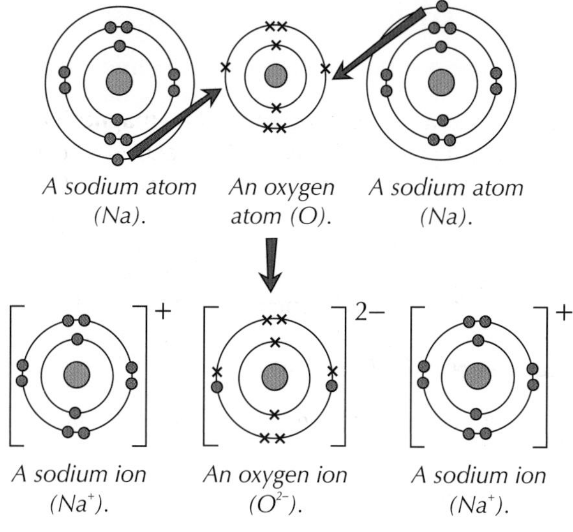

Figure 4: *The formation of sodium oxide.*

Tip: Sometimes only the outer, incomplete electron shells are shown in dot and cross diagrams. This can make it clearer to see what's going on. So, for example, a sodium atom could be shown as:

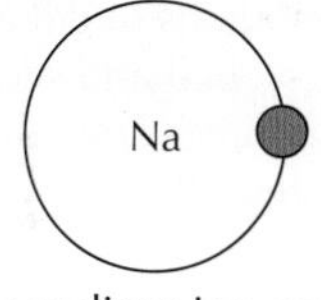

and a sodium ion as:

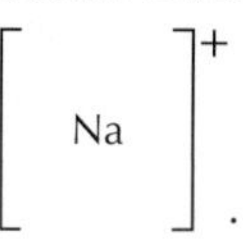

Practice Questions — Fact Recall

Q1 What is ionic bonding?

Q2 What types of elements do ionic bonds form between?

Q3 Draw dot and cross diagrams to show the electron transfer when the following compounds are formed:

a) potassium chloride

b) magnesium oxide

c) sodium oxide

Practice Questions — Application

Q1 Potassium reacts with iodine to form potassium iodide.

a) Describe, in terms of electrons and electron transfer, the reaction between potassium and iodine.

b) Explain why the electron transfer will be the same in the reaction between potassium and fluorine.

Q2 Draw a dot and cross diagram to show the formation of lithium oxide from lithium and oxygen.

Exam Tip
Sometimes, an exam question about a dot and cross diagram will tell you whether to draw all the electron shells or just the outer shell. Make sure you read the question carefully and follow any instructions like this.

3. Ionic Compounds

Ionic compounds actually form giant structures containing many, many ions. Of course, in the world of chemistry, a grain of salt counts as 'giant'...

Learning Objectives:

- Know that ionic compounds have lattice structures consisting of a regular arrangement of ions held together by strong electrostatic forces (ionic bonds) between oppositely charged ions.
- Be able to explain why elements and compounds can be classified as ionic.
- Be able to describe the limitations of dot and cross, ball and stick and three-dimensional representations of compounds.
- Be able to explain how the structure and bonding of ionic substances results in their physical properties.
- Be able to explain the high melting and boiling points of ionic compounds, in terms of forces between ions.
- Be able to explain whether or not ionic compounds conduct electricity as solids, when molten and in aqueous solution.

Specification References
1.27, 1.32, 1.33, 1.41

Tip: The ability to use 2D representations of 3D objects is an important maths skill. MATHS SKILLS

The structure of ionic compounds

Ionic compounds have a structure called a giant **ionic lattice** (a closely-packed regular arrangement of ions). There are very strong **electrostatic forces** of attraction between oppositely charged ions which act in all directions. Ionic compounds can be represented in different ways:

WORKING SCIENTIFICALLY

1. Dot and cross diagrams

These were covered on pages 51-53. They are useful for showing how ionic compounds are formed and where the electrons in the ions come from. But they don't show the structure of the compound, the relative sizes of the ions or how they're arranged.

2. 3D models

3D models show the relative sizes of the ions, as well as the regular pattern of ions in an ionic crystal. However, they only let you see the outer layer of the compound.

Example

Here's a picture of a 3D model of a tiny part of a sodium chloride (salt) crystal. A whole crystal (see Figure 2) would consist of billions of ions. The Na^+ and Cl^- ions are held together in a regular, cube-shaped lattice.

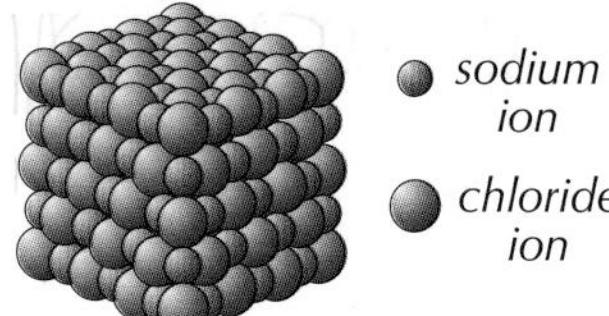

3. Ball and stick models

Like 3D models, ball and stick models show the regular pattern of ions in an ionic lattice, as well as how all the ions are arranged (see Figure 2). In addition, they show that the crystal extends beyond what is shown in the diagram. They may show the relative sizes of the ions, but sometimes the ions are not shown to scale. Ball and stick models of ionic compounds also suggest that there are gaps between the ions, when in reality there aren't.

Figure 1: *Crystals of salt.*

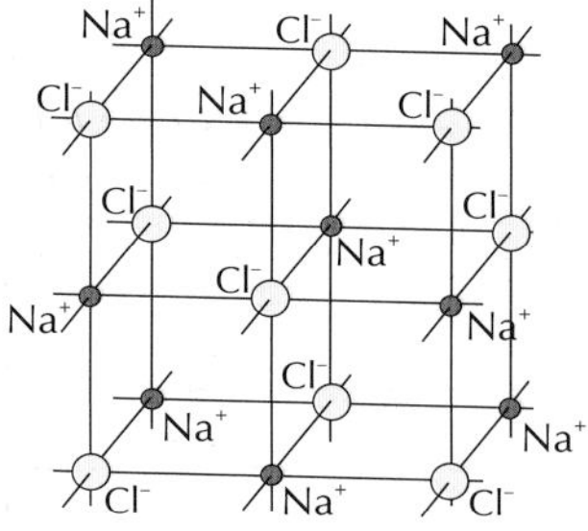

Figure 2: *Ball and stick model of sodium chloride.*

Properties of ionic compounds

Melting and boiling point

Ionic compounds all have high melting points and high boiling points due to the strong electrostatic attraction between the ions. It takes a large amount of energy to overcome this attraction and break the many strong bonds.

Solubility

Most ionic compounds dissolve easily in water.

Electrical conductivity

Ionic compounds don't conduct electricity when solid because the ions are all held in fixed positions and can't move. However, when they're melted or dissolved, the ions are free to move and they'll carry electric charge.

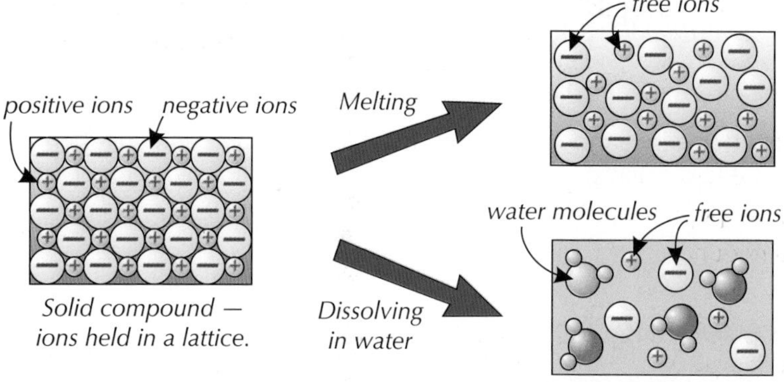

Figure 3: *Particle diagrams of an ionic compound when solid, melted and dissolved.*

Tip: It might seem odd that you need a lot of energy to melt ionic compounds, but they dissolve really easily in water. This is because parts of water molecules are slightly charged, which helps to pull the charged ions away from the lattice.

Tip: An electric current is a flow of charged particles, which can either be ions or free electrons.

Figure 4: *The ionic compound potassium chloride conducts electricity when it's dissolved in water. It completes the circuit so the bulb lights up.*

Practice Questions — Fact Recall

Q1 What type of structure do ionic compounds have?

Q2 Give one advantage and one disadvantage of using each of the following representations to show ionic bonding:

a) dot and cross diagrams b) ball and stick models

Q3 Sketch a ball and stick model of part of a sodium chloride lattice.

Q4 Describe the properties of a typical ionic compound, including melting point, solubility and conductivity.

Practice Question — Application

Q1 Which of the substances shown in the table below is most likely to be potassium chloride? Explain your answer.

Substance	Melting point	Soluble in water	Conducts electricity when solid
A	38	No	No
B	770	Yes	No
C	962	No	Yes

Exam Tip
If you're asked to describe the electrical conductivity of a substance, make sure you consider its conductivity in different states, including what happens when the substance is in solution.

4. Covalent Bonding

Learning Objectives:

- Be able to explain how a covalent bond is formed when a pair of electrons is shared between two atoms.
- Be able to describe the limitations of dot and cross, ball and stick and two- and three-dimensional representations of molecules.

Specification References
1.28, 1.41

Ionic bonding — done. Next up is covalent bonding, which is all about atoms sharing their electrons.

What is covalent bonding?

A **covalent bond** is formed when a pair of electrons is shared between two atoms. Atoms share electrons with each other to get full outer shells. They only share electrons in their outer shells and both atoms involved in the bond end up with one extra electron in their outer shell. The positively charged nuclei of the bonded atoms are attracted to the shared pair of electrons by electrostatic forces, making covalent bonds very strong.

Each single covalent bond provides one extra shared electron for each atom. Each atom involved has to make enough covalent bonds to fill up its outer shell (which makes the atom very stable). See Figure 1 for a reminder of how many electrons the first three shells can hold.

Shell	Max. number of electrons
1st	2
2nd	8
3rd	8

***Figure 1:** Table showing the number of electrons each shell (energy level) can hold.*

Covalent bonds occur between non-metal atoms. This can either be in non-metallic elements, e.g. Cl_2 or O_2, or in compounds of non-metals, e.g. H_2O or CH_4.

Representing covalent bonding

There are a few different ways of representing covalent bonding. They each have their advantages and disadvantages.

1. Dot and cross diagrams

In dot and cross diagrams, the shared electrons can be drawn in the overlap between the outer orbitals of the two atoms.

Tip: Just the outer electron shells are shown in these diagrams.

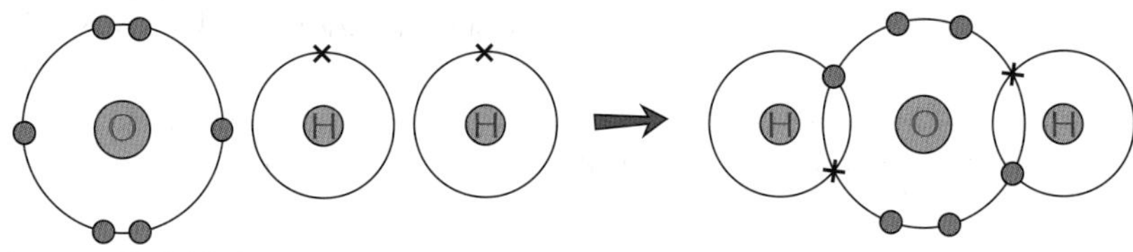

***Figure 2:** Dot and cross diagrams showing covalent bonding in water.*

Sometimes the orbitals aren't shown.

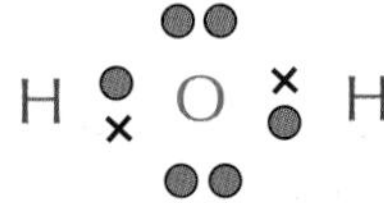

***Figure 3:** Dot and cross diagram without orbitals.*

Dot and cross diagrams are useful for showing which atoms the electrons in a covalent bond come from, but they don't show the relative sizes of the atoms, or how the atoms are arranged in space.

2. Displayed formulas

A displayed formula is a two-dimensional representation of a molecule that shows the covalent bonds as single lines between atoms.

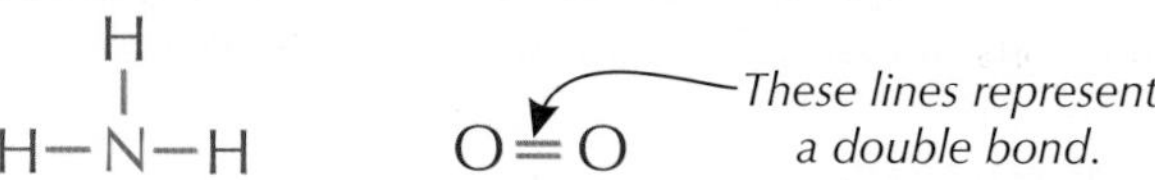

Figure 4: *Displayed formulas of ammonia and oxygen.*

This is a great way of showing what atoms something contains, as well as how they are connected in large molecules. However, they don't show the 3D structure (shape) of the molecule, which atoms the electrons in the covalent bond have come from or the correct scales of the atoms.

Exam Tip
When drawing displayed formulas make sure you show every bond in the molecule.

3. 3D models and ball and stick models

3D models show the atoms in a molecule and how they are arranged in space — so they show you the shape of the molecule. Ball and stick models show the bonds as well as the atoms. Other types of 3D model usually don't.

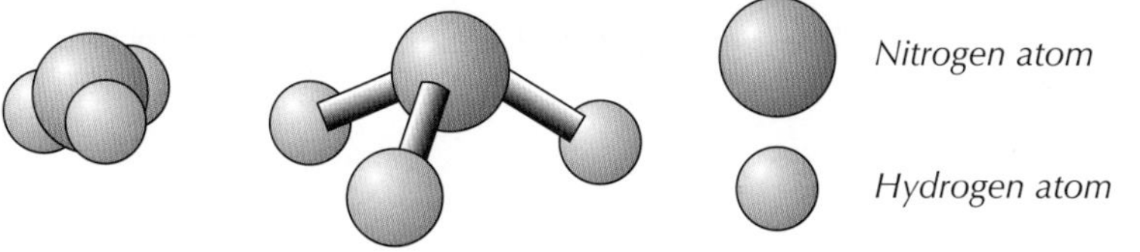

Figure 5: *3D models of ammonia. The second is a ball and stick model showing bonds.*

Figure 6: *A ball and stick model of methane.*

Ball and stick models can show double bonds clearly too.

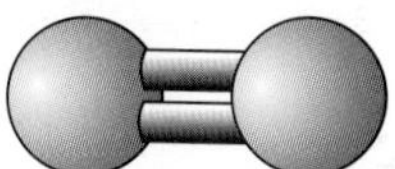

Figure 7: *Ball and stick model showing an oxygen molecule.*

A disadvantage of 3D models is that they can get confusing for large molecules that contain lots of atoms. Ball and stick models make it look like there are big gaps between the atoms — in reality this is where the electron clouds interact. They also don't show where the electrons in the bonds have come from, and sometimes the atoms are not shown to scale.

Practice Questions — Fact Recall

Q1 Why do atoms share electrons with each other in covalent bonding?

Q2 How many extra electrons does a single covalent bond provide to an atom?

Q3 a) Give one advantage of representing covalent bonding using:

i) Dot and cross diagrams.

ii) Ball and stick models.

b) Give one disadvantage of representing covalent bonding using:

i) Ball and stick models.

ii) Displayed formulas.

5. Simple Molecular Substances

There are two very different types of covalent substances — simple molecules and giant covalent substances. First, the simple molecules...

Simple molecules

Simple molecules are made up of only a few atoms joined by **covalent bonds**. Hydrogen, hydrogen chloride, methane, water, oxygen and carbon dioxide are all examples of simple molecules, and you need to know about the bonding in them all.

Simple molecules are tiny. They generally have sizes around 10^{-10} m — they're not much bigger than individual atoms. The bonds that form between atoms in these molecules are generally about 10^{-10} m too.

1. Hydrogen (H_2)

Hydrogen atoms have just one electron. They only need one more to complete the first shell, so they often form **single covalent bonds** to achieve this (see Figure 1).

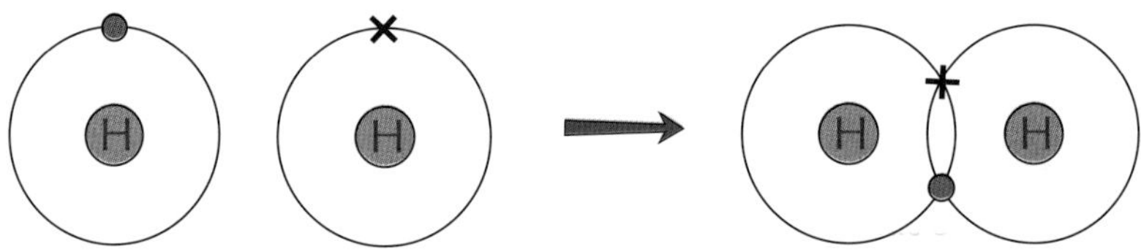

Two hydrogen atoms.

The hydrogen atoms share one pair of electrons to form one covalent bond. Both atoms now have full outer shells.

Figure 1: *The formation of a covalent bond between hydrogen atoms.*

As mentioned on pages 56-57, you can also represent the bonding as a dot and cross diagram without the orbitals, or as a displayed formula.

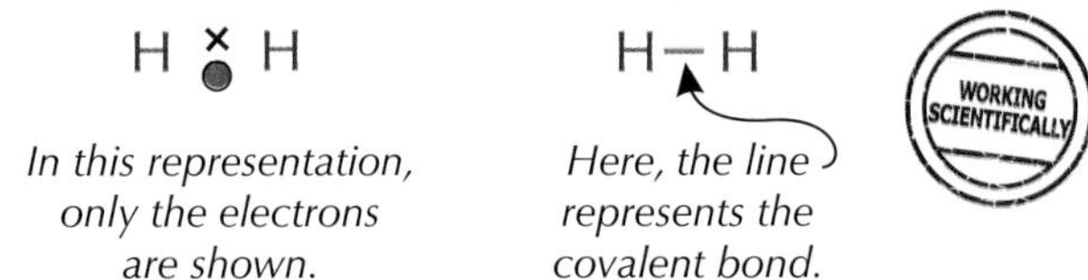

In this representation, only the electrons are shown.

Here, the line represents the covalent bond.

Figure 2: *Alternative representations of the bonding in hydrogen molecules.*

2. Hydrogen chloride (HCl)

The bonding in hydrogen chloride is very similar to that in hydrogen (H_2). Again, both atoms only need one more electron to complete their outer shells, so they share one pair of electrons and one single covalent bond is formed.

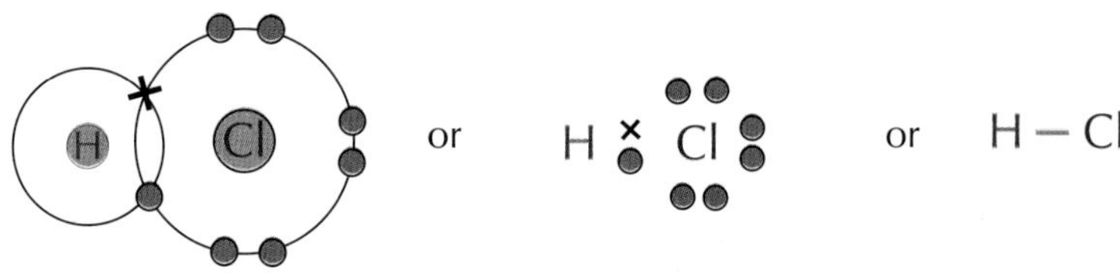

Figure 3: *Representations of covalent bonding in hydrogen chloride.*

Learning Objectives:

- Know that covalent bonding results in the formation of molecules.
- Be able to explain why elements and compounds can be classified as simple molecular.
- Know the typical size of atoms and small molecules.
- Be able to explain the formation of simple molecular substances using dot and cross diagrams, including hydrogen, hydrogen chloride, water, methane, oxygen and carbon dioxide.
- Be able to explain how the structure and bonding of simple covalent substances results in their physical properties.
- Be able to explain the low melting and boiling points of simple molecular compounds.
- Be able to explain the poor electrical conductivity of simple molecular compounds.
- Be able to describe, using poly(ethene) as an example, that simple polymers consist of large molecules containing chains of carbon atoms.

Specification References
1.29-1.32, 1.34, 1.39

Tip: Hydrogen chloride dissolves in water to form hydrochloric acid.

3. Methane (CH_4)

Carbon has four outer electrons, which is half a full shell. So it forms four covalent bonds to make up its outer shell. Hydrogen atoms only need to form one covalent bond to achieve a full outer shell. So a carbon atom will form covalent bonds with four hydrogen atoms to form a CH_4 molecule (methane).

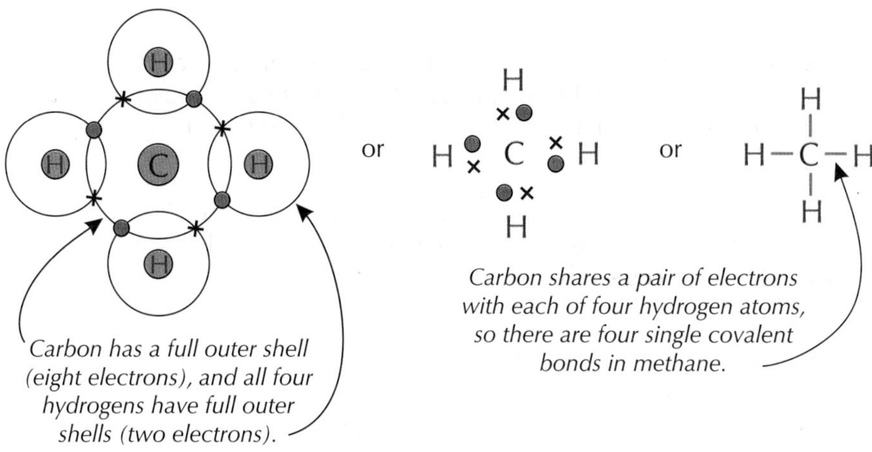

Figure 4: *Representations of covalent bonding in methane.*

Tip: It's easy to think that methane molecules are flat when you see diagrams like this. They're actually tetrahedral shapes (imagine one hydrogen at each corner of a triangular-based pyramid and the carbon atom in the centre of it). This is one of the disadvantages of dot and cross diagrams and displayed formulas — you can't see the shape of the molecule.

4. Water (H_2O)

Oxygen atoms have six outer electrons. They need two more electrons to fill up their outer shells. In water molecules, the oxygen shares electrons with two hydrogen atoms to form two single covalent bonds. You've already met the dot and cross diagram for water — it's on page 56.

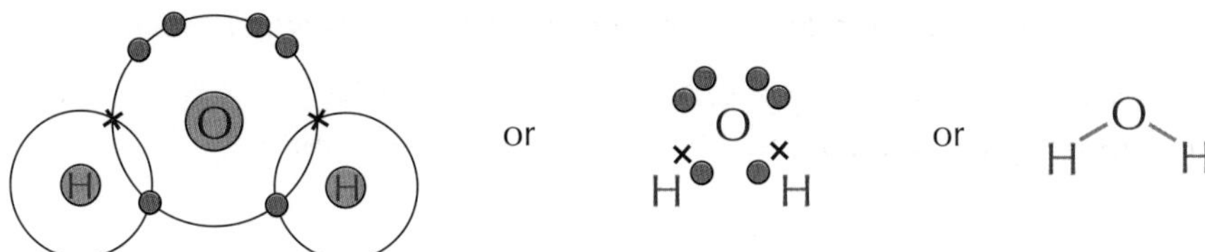

Figure 5: *Representations of covalent bonding in water.*

Exam Tip
Always check you've got the bonding right by counting the number of electrons each atom has in its outer shell. If any of the atoms haven't got a full outer shell you've gone wrong somewhere.

5. Oxygen (O_2)

As you saw above, oxygen atoms have six outer electrons. In order to fill their outer shells, each oxygen atom in O_2 can share two electrons with another oxygen atom. Two pairs of electrons are shared between the pair of oxygen atoms — this is known as a **double covalent bond**.

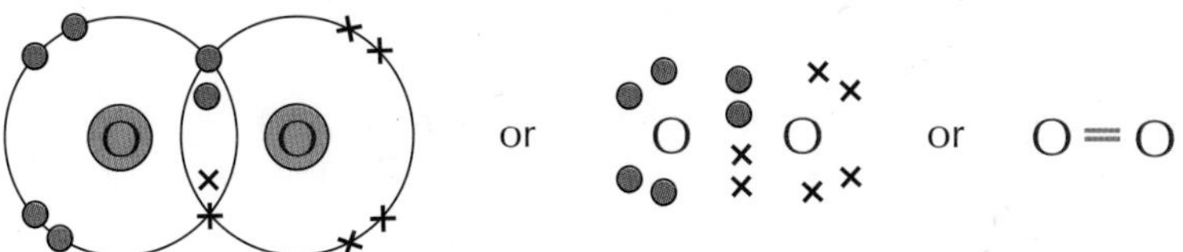

Figure 6: *Representations of covalent bonding in oxygen.*

6. Carbon dioxide (CO_2)

Carbon has four outer electrons, which is half a full shell. It needs four more electrons to complete its outer shell. Oxygen atoms have six outer shell electrons, so need two more to achieve a full shell. In carbon dioxide, a carbon atom shares two pairs of electrons with two oxygen atoms to form two double covalent bonds.

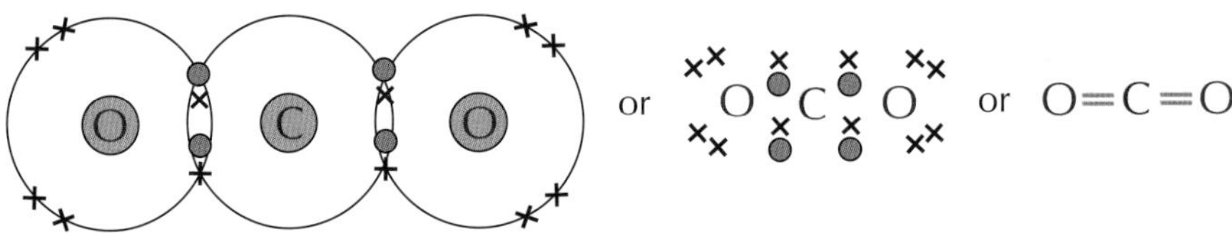

Figure 7: *Representations of covalent bonding in carbon dioxide.*

Properties of simple molecules

Tip: There's no easy rule about solubility in water for simple molecules. Some are soluble and some aren't.

Electrical conductivity

Covalent substances made up of simple molecules don't conduct electricity in any state — there are no ions or free electrons so there's nothing to carry an electrical charge.

Melting and boiling points

Simple molecular substances have low melting and boiling points, so they are mostly gases or liquids at room temperature (but they can be solids).

The reason for the low melting and boiling points is that, although the atoms within the small molecules form very strong covalent bonds with each other, the forces of attraction between the molecules (**intermolecular forces**) are very weak (see Figure 9). It's only the weak intermolecular forces that need to be overcome to melt or boil a simple molecular substance — not the much stronger covalent bonds. Overcoming these weak intermolecular forces doesn't take much energy, so the melting and boiling points are low.

Figure 8: *Water is a simple molecular compound. Not much energy is needed to break the intermolecular forces and melt it so it's a liquid at room temperature.*

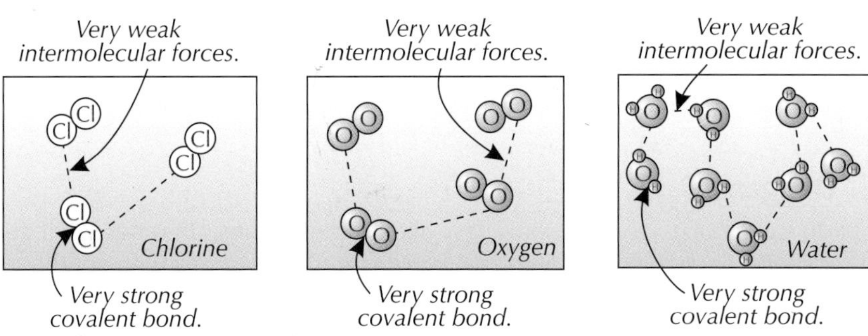

Figure 9: *The bonding within and between simple molecules.*

As molecules get bigger, the strength of the intermolecular forces increases, so more energy is needed to break them, and the melting points and boiling points increase.

Tip: The larger the molecules that a substance is made up of, the more likely it is to be solid at room temperature.

Polymers

Polymers are molecules made up of long chains of covalently bonded carbon atoms. They're formed when lots of small molecules called monomers join together. A famous example is poly(ethene).

Figure 10: *Poly(ethene) can be used to make plastic film for wrapping and packaging.*

Example

Many ethene molecules can be joined up to produce poly(ethene).

Many ethene molecules

A section of poly(ethene)

Here's the short way of drawing a poly(ethene) molecule.

The bonds through the brackets join up to the next repeating unit.

n is a large number. It tells you that the unit is repeated lots of times.

Poly(ethene)

Tip: You might also see poly(ethene) being called 'polythene' or 'polyethylene' — they're both just old names for the same polymer.

Practice Questions — Fact Recall

Q1 What is a simple molecule?

Q2 Name the molecules shown by the dot and cross diagrams below.

a)

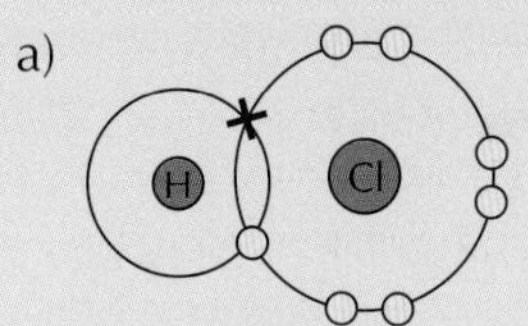

b)

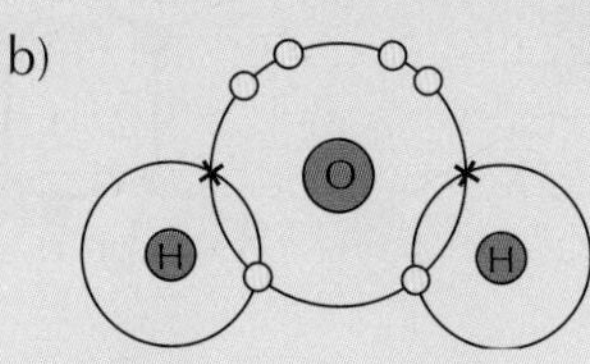

Q3 Draw dot and cross diagrams to represent the following molecules.

a) hydrogen b) carbon dioxide c) methane

Q4 Simple molecular substances have low melting points. Explain why.

Q5 Do simple molecules conduct electricity? Explain your answer.

Q6 Name the polymer that is made by joining lots of ethene molecules.

Practice Question — Application

Q1 A nitrogen atom has two shells of electrons. Its second shell contains five electrons. Nitrogen can form covalent bonds with hydrogen atoms. Describe and explain the bonding in the molecule that is formed.

6. Giant Covalent Structures

The last few pages have covered small covalent substances. Now it's time to look at the large ones, and some examples of giant structures based on carbon.

Learning Objectives:

- Be able to explain why elements and compounds can be classified as giant covalent.
- Be able to explain how the structure and bonding of giant covalent substances results in their physical properties.
- Know that graphite and diamond are different forms of carbon and that they are examples of giant covalent substances.
- Be able to describe the structures of graphite and diamond.
- Be able to explain, in terms of structure and bonding, why graphite is used to make electrodes and as a lubricant, whereas diamond is used in cutting tools.
- Be able to explain the properties of fullerenes including C_{60} and graphene in terms of their structures and bonding.

Specification References 1.32, 1.35-1.38

What are giant covalent structures?

Giant covalent structures are made up of lots of atoms that are all bonded to each other by strong covalent bonds. They have very high melting and boiling points as lots of energy is needed to break the covalent bonds. They generally don't contain charged particles, so they don't conduct electricity (apart from graphite and graphene, which do conduct electricity). Giant covalent structures aren't soluble in water, either.

Diamond and graphite are both carbon-based giant covalent structures.

Diamond

In diamond, each carbon atom forms four covalent bonds with other carbon atoms. This forms a very rigid structure, making diamond very hard, so it's used to strengthen cutting tools (e.g. saw teeth and drill bits). Diamond also has a very high melting point because the strong covalent bonds take a lot of energy to overcome. It doesn't conduct electricity because it has no free electrons or ions.

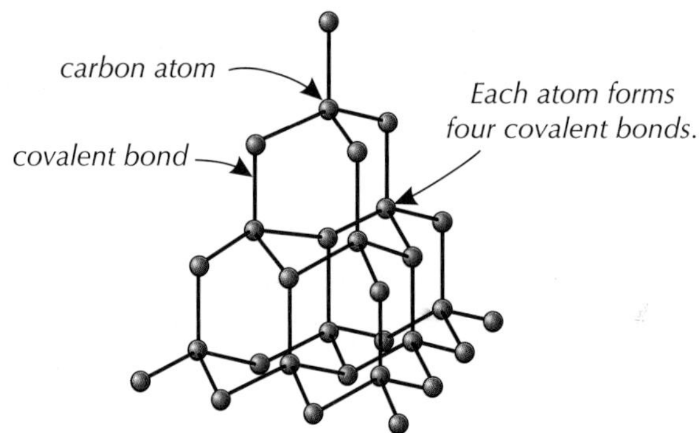

Figure 1: *The structure of diamond.*

Figure 2: *A cut, polished and sparkly diamond.*

Graphite

In graphite, each carbon atom only forms three covalent bonds. This creates sheets of carbon atoms arranged in hexagons. There aren't any covalent bonds between the layers — they're only held together by weak **intermolecular forces**, so they're free to move over each other. This makes graphite soft and slippery, so it's ideal as a lubricating material.

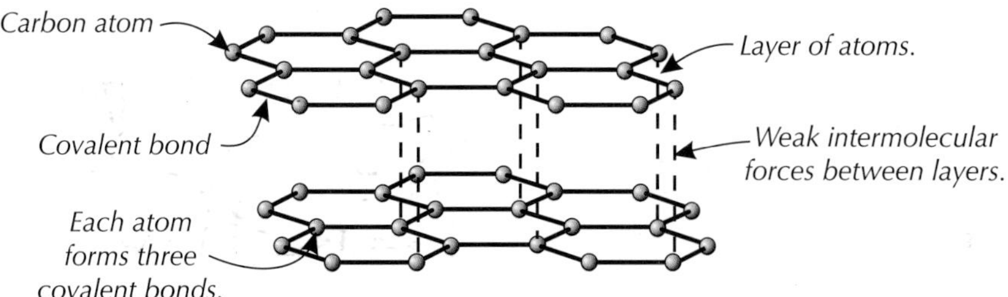

Figure 3: *The structure of graphite.*

Graphite has a high melting point because the covalent bonds in the layers need a lot of energy to break.

In graphite, only three out of each carbon's four outer electrons are used in bonds, so each carbon atom has one electron that's delocalised (free) and can move. This means that graphite conducts electricity, so can be used to make electrodes (see page 133).

Tip: A substance needs charged particles (ions or electrons) which are free to move in order to conduct electricity.

Graphene

Graphene is a sheet of carbon atoms joined together in hexagons. It's basically a single layer of graphite. The sheet is just one atom thick, making it a two-dimensional compound.

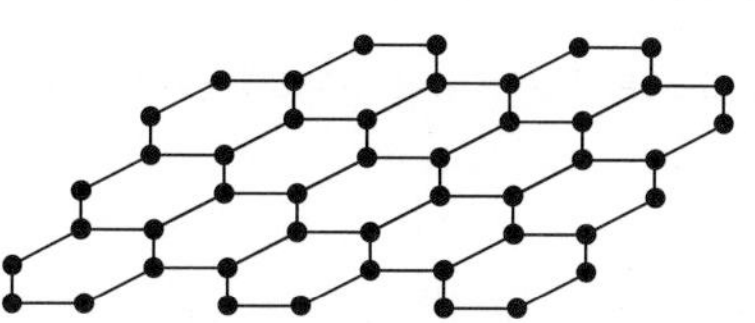

Figure 5: *The structure of graphene.*

Figure 4: *Graphite. Not as pretty as diamond :(*

The network of covalent bonds makes graphene very strong. It's also incredibly light, so can be added to composite materials to improve their strength without adding much weight.

Like graphite, graphene contains delocalised electrons, so it can conduct electricity through the whole structure. This means it has the potential to be used in electronics.

Fullerenes

Fullerenes are hollow molecules of carbon, shaped like tubes or balls. They're mainly made up of carbon atoms arranged in hexagons, but can also contain pentagons (rings of five carbon atoms) or heptagons (rings of seven carbon atoms).

Examples

Buckminsterfullerene

Buckminsterfullerene was the first fullerene to be discovered. It's got the molecular formula C_{60} and forms a hollow sphere containing 20 hexagons and 12 pentagons. It's a stable molecule that forms soft brownish-black crystals.

Nanotubes

Nanotubes are fullerenes which are tiny carbon cylinders. The ratio between the length and the diameter of nanotubes is very high. They're good conductors of heat and electricity.

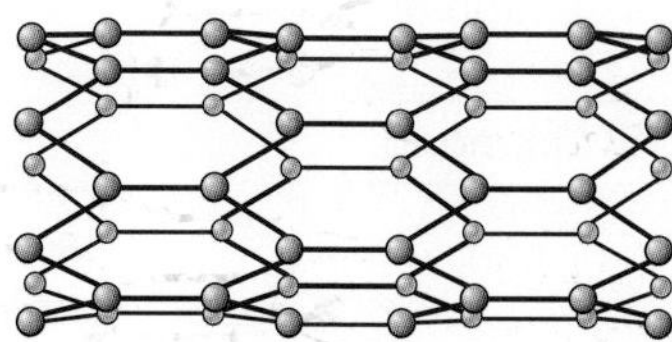

Tip: Other balls of carbon atoms have since been made, e.g. C_{70}.

Tip: This is the basic nanotube structure, but there are loads of interesting variations, such as tubes within tubes.

Uses of fullerenes

1. In medicine

Fullerenes can be used to 'cage' other molecules. The fullerene structure forms around another atom or molecule, which is then trapped inside. This could be used to deliver a drug to where it is needed in the body in a highly controlled way.

Tip: Catalysts speed up the rates of chemical reactions without being used up themselves (see p.205-206).

2. As catalysts

Fullerenes have a huge surface area, so they could help make great industrial catalysts — individual catalyst molecules could be attached to the fullerenes (the bigger the surface area the better).

Tip: Technology that uses small particles such as nanotubes is called nanotechnology.

3. Strengthening materials

Nanotubes have a high tensile strength (they don't break when stretched) so can be used to strengthen materials without adding much weight. For example, they can be used to strengthen sports equipment that needs to be strong but also lightweight, such as tennis racket frames.

Practice Questions — Fact Recall

Q1 Which statement(s) below describe(s) the structure of graphite?

A Each carbon atom is covalently bonded to four other atoms.

B The layers are held together by weak intermolecular forces.

C Electrons not involved in covalent bonding are delocalised.

Q2 Explain why diamond has a very high melting point.

Q3 Describe the structure of graphene.

Q4 What are fullerenes?

Q5 What is the molecular formula of buckminsterfullerene?

Q6 Name two uses of fullerenes.

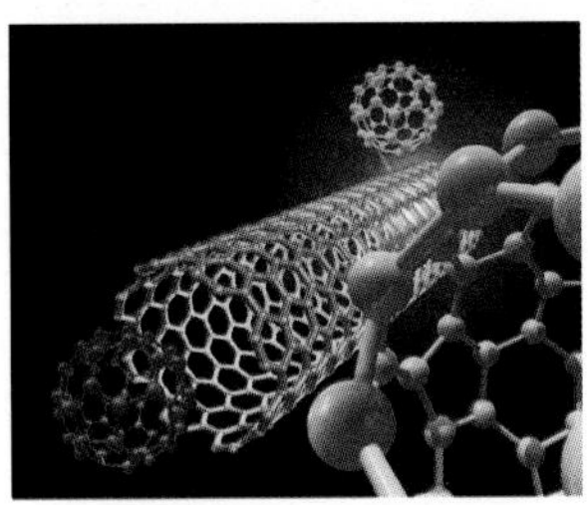

Figure 6: *Computer artwork of buckyballs (buckminsterfullerene) and nanotubes.*

Practice Question — Application

Q1 Match the properties listed below with the correct substance.

Substance	Properties
Carbon dioxide	Conducts electricity. Melting point = 3500 °C
Graphite	Doesn't conduct electricity. Melting point = 3500 °C
Diamond	Doesn't conduct electricity. Melting point = –57 °C

7. Metallic Bonding

Metallic bonding is the final type of bonding in this section. Metals have lots of interesting properties and that's all down to their structure and bonding...

Learning Objectives:

- Be able to explain why elements and compounds can be classified as metallic.
- Be able to explain how the structure and bonding of metallic substances results in their physical properties.
- Be able to explain the properties of metals, including malleability and the ability to conduct electricity.
- Be able to describe most metals as shiny solids, which have high melting points, high density and are good conductors of electricity.
- Be able to compare the relative boiling points and electrical conductivity of metals and non-metals.

Specification References
1.32, 1.40, 1.42

The structure of metals

Metals consist of a giant structure. The atoms in a metal are arranged in a regular pattern (see Figure 1). Metals are said to have giant structures because they have lots of atoms. Exactly how many depends on how big the piece of metal is.

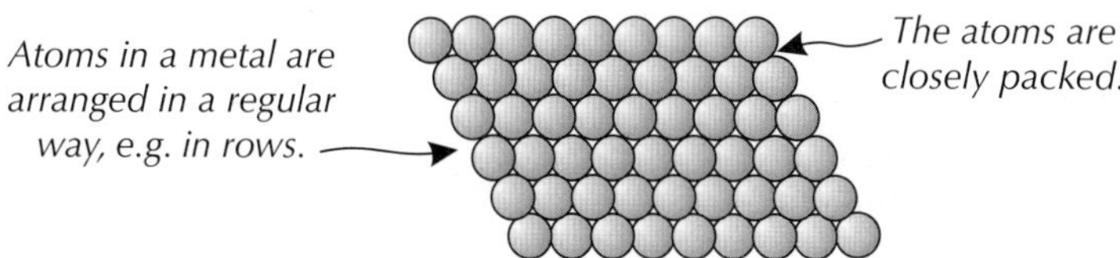

Figure 1: *The structure of a metal.*

Bonding in metals

In metals, the electrons in the outer shells of the atoms are **delocalised**. This means that they aren't associated with a particular atom or bond — they're free to move through the whole structure (see Figure 2). There are strong forces of electrostatic attraction between the positive metal ions and the negative electrons and these forces, known as metallic bonding, hold the metal structure together.

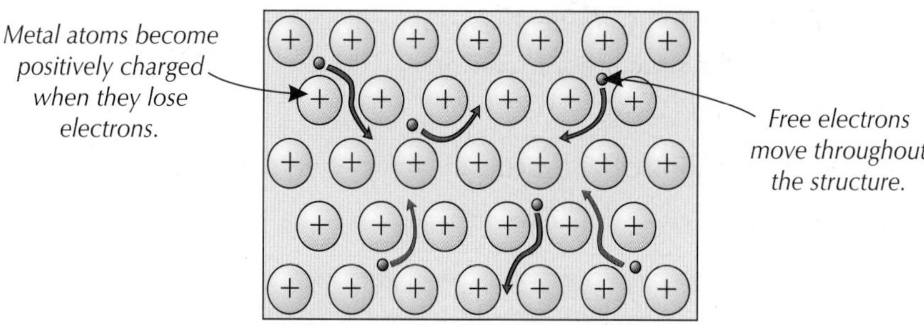

Figure 2: *Delocalised electrons within a giant metallic structure.*

Properties of metals

High melting and boiling points

The electrostatic forces between the metal atoms and the delocalised sea of electrons are very strong, so need lots of energy to be broken. This means that most compounds with metallic bonds have very high melting and boiling points, so they're generally shiny solids at room temperature.

Tip: Not only are metals hard to melt and boil, they aren't soluble in water either. This is also due to the fact that large amounts of energy are required to break the metallic bonds between the ions.

Conductivity

Metals have delocalised electrons that are free to move through the whole structure. Because of this, they are much better conductors of thermal energy and electricity than most non-metals. The electrons carry the current or the thermal energy through the structure.

Malleability

Metals consist of atoms held together in a regular structure. The atoms form layers that are able to slide over each other — see Figure 3. This means they are **malleable** — they can be hammered or rolled into flat sheets.

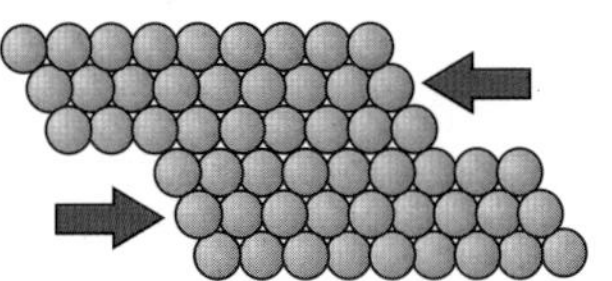
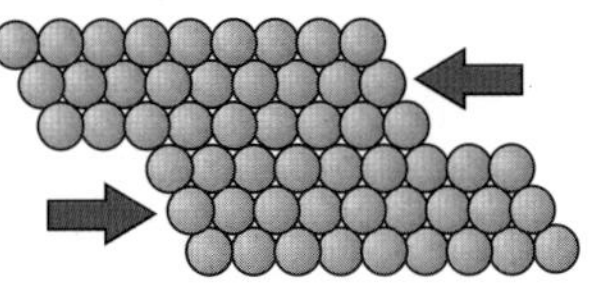

Figure 3: *Layers of atoms in a metal sliding over each other.*

Figure 4: *Lead lining on a roof pressed into shape.*

Density

The densities of metals are generally higher than those of non-metals. The ions in the metallic structure are packed close together, so there aren't as many gaps in the structure as in non-metals.

Physical properties of metals and non-metals

All metals undergo metallic bonding, which causes them to have similar basic physical properties. Non-metals tend to form covalent bonds, so they don't tend to exhibit the same properties as metals.

Non-metals form a variety of different structures, so have a wide range of chemical and physical properties. They tend to be dull looking, more brittle, have lower boiling points (they're not generally solids at room temperature), don't generally conduct electricity and often have a lower density than metals.

Tip: Head to page 41 for more about the position of metals and non-metals in the periodic table.

Metals and non-metals also have different chemical properties. Non-metals can be found on the top and right-hand side of the periodic table, so their outer shells are generally over half-filled and they tend to gain electrons to form full outer shells. Metals are found at the bottom and left-hand side of the periodic table, so their shells are generally under half-filled. They tend to lose electrons to gain full outer shells.

Practice Questions — Fact Recall

Q1 Describe the structure of a metal.

Q2 What type of forces hold the particles in a metal together?

Q3 Explain why metals can be easily shaped.

Q4 Metals are good conductors of heat. Explain why.

Q5 Why do metals generally have higher densities than non-metals?

Q6 Compare the following properties in metals and non-metals:

a) electrical conductivity

b) boiling point

Topic 1c Checklist — Make sure you know...

Ions

- [ ] That any atom or molecule that carries a positive or negative charge is known as an ion.
- [ ] That negative ions are known as anions, and that positive ions are called cations.
- [ ] That positive ions are formed when an atom or molecule loses electrons, and that negative ions are formed when an atom or molecule gains electrons.
- [ ] How to use atomic number and mass number to calculate the number of protons, neutrons and electrons in a simple ion.
- [ ] What the charges are on ions of elements from Groups 1, 2, 6 and 7 and that they have these charges because the atoms lose or gain enough electrons to obtain full outer shells.
- [ ] How to work out the formula of an ionic compound from the formulae of the ions it contains.
- [ ] What the endings -ide and -ate mean, in terms of the names of ions.

Ionic Bonding

- [ ] That ionic bonding involves the transfer of electrons between atoms to form ions.
- [ ] That ions usually have full outer shells of electrons.
- [ ] How to represent the electron transfer in ionic bonding using dot and cross diagrams.

Ionic Compounds

- [ ] That ions in ionic compounds are held together in a giant lattice by electrostatic forces.
- [ ] The different ways of representing ionic compounds, and the pros and cons of each representation.
- [ ] That ionic compounds have high melting and boiling points because a lot of energy is needed to overcome the strong electrostatic forces that hold the ions together.
- [ ] That most ionic compounds dissolve easily in water.
- [ ] That solid ionic compounds cannot conduct electricity as the ions are held in fixed positions.
- [ ] That melted or dissolved ionic compounds can conduct electricity as the ions are free to move.

Covalent Bonding

- [ ] That a covalent bond is a pair of electrons shared between two atoms.
- [ ] That non-metal atoms form covalent bonds by sharing electrons to fill their outer electron shells.
- [ ] The different ways of representing molecules, and the pros and cons of each representation.

cont...

Simple Molecular Substances

- [ ] That simple molecules form when atoms join together through covalent bonds.
- [ ] That simple molecules are not much bigger than atoms, having dimensions in the region of 10^{-10} m.
- [ ] How to use dot and cross diagrams to show the bonding in simple molecules, including hydrogen, hydrogen chloride, methane, water, oxygen and carbon dioxide.
- [ ] That simple molecular substances tend to have low melting and boiling points because the forces between molecules (intermolecular forces) are weak, so not much energy is needed to overcome them.
- [ ] That simple molecules have no free ions or electrons so they don't conduct electricity.
- [ ] That polymers are large covalent molecules made up of repeating carbon-based units. Poly(ethene) is an example of a polymer.

Giant Covalent Structures

- [ ] That giant covalent structures are made up of lots of atoms that are all bonded to each other by strong covalent bonds.
- [ ] That giant covalent substances typically do not dissolve in water and most do not conduct electricity.
- [ ] That giant covalent substances have very high melting and boiling points because large amounts of energy are needed to break all the strong covalent bonds that hold the atoms together.
- [ ] That diamond and graphite are forms of carbon that have giant covalent structures.
- [ ] The structure of diamond and why it means that diamond is hard and doesn't conduct electricity.
- [ ] How the properties of diamond make it suitable for use in cutting tools.
- [ ] The structure of graphite and why it means that graphite is soft and slippery and a good conductor.
- [ ] That graphite is an ideal lubricant and is also used to make electrodes.
- [ ] The structure and properties of graphene.
- [ ] The structure and properties of fullerenes (including buckminsterfullerene).

Metallic Bonding

- [ ] That metals consist of giant structures in which the atoms are held together by delocalised electrons.
- [ ] That most metals have high melting and boiling points because large amounts of energy are needed to break the strong electrostatic forces between the metal atoms and the delocalised electrons.
- [ ] That most metals are shiny solids at room temperature and pressure.
- [ ] That the delocalised electrons mean that metals conduct electricity and heat.
- [ ] That metals are malleable (can be hammered, rolled into flat sheets and easily shaped) because in a metal the atoms are arranged in layers that can slide over each other.
- [ ] That most metals have high densities.
- [ ] The main differences between the general properties of metals and non-metals.

Exam-style Questions

1 The structure of a substance affects its properties. The melting point, boiling point and electrical conductivity of four substances were tested. The results are shown in the table below.

Substance	Melting point (°C)	Boiling point (°C)	Conducts electricity?
A	–218.4	–182.96	no
B	1535	2750	yes
C	1410	2355	no
D	801	1413	no if solid, yes if molten

Use the words from the box to complete the sentences below.
You can use each term once, more than once or not at all.

ionic	simple molecular	giant covalent	metallic

The structure of substance A is ....

The structure of substance B is ....

The structure of substance C is ....

The structure of substance D is ....

(4 marks)

2 Oxygen is found in group 6 of the periodic table. It has the atomic number 8.

(a) An oxide ion, O^{2-}, can be formed from an oxygen atom.

(i) How many electrons are present in an oxide ion?

(2 marks)

(ii) Sodium oxide is composed of sodium ions (Na^+) and oxide ions.
Give the formula of the compound sodium oxide.

(1 mark)

(b) Two oxygen atoms can bond together covalently to form an oxygen molecule, O_2.
Draw a dot and cross diagram to represent an oxygen molecule.
You only need to show the outer electrons in the oxygen atoms.

(2 marks)

3 Lithium chloride is formed from lithium and chlorine.
The diagrams below show the electronic structures of lithium and chlorine atoms.

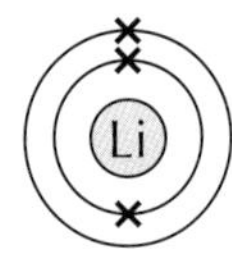

Lithium atom

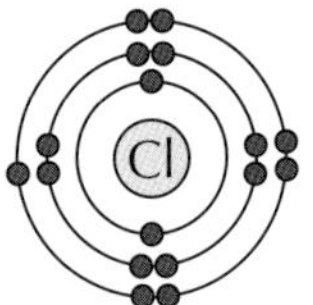

Chlorine atom

(a) Two chlorine atoms can react together to form a molecule of chlorine gas, Cl_2.

(i) Name the type of bond formed between the two atoms in chlorine gas.

(1 mark)

(ii) Explain, as fully as you can, why chlorine is a gas at room temperature.

(4 marks)

(b) Lithium and chlorine can react together to form lithium chloride.

(i) Complete the dot and cross diagram below to show the electronic structures of the particles formed during the reaction of lithium and chlorine.

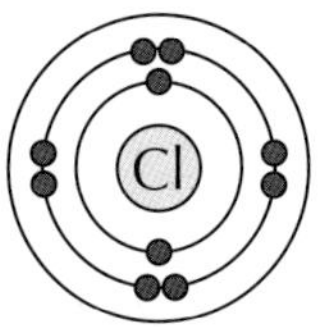

(3 marks)

(ii) Lithium chloride has a high melting point. Explain why.

(2 marks)

4 Carbon can exist in different forms. How the atoms are arranged and the bonding between the atoms determines which form of carbon is made.

(a)* Diamond and graphite are giant covalent forms of carbon.
Diamond is very hard, but graphite is soft and slippery.
Explain why this is. Your answer should include details of the arrangements of atoms and the bonding in the structures.

(6 marks)

(b) Name the two-dimensional form of carbon shown below.

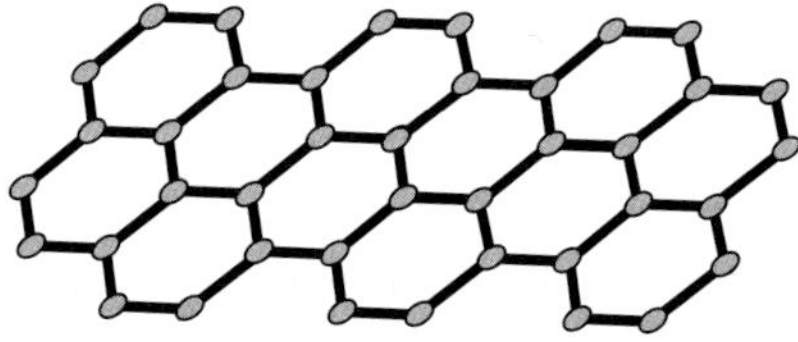

(1 mark)

(c) Explain why the structure shown in part b) can conduct electricity.

(3 marks)

1. Relative Mass

Calculations involving mass sound a lot scarier than they actually are. Give these pages a read and you should get to grips with them in no time...

Learning Objectives:
- Be able to calculate relative formula mass using relative atomic masses.
- Be able to deduce the empirical formula of a compound from the formula of its molecule.
- Be able to deduce the molecular formula of a compound from its empirical formula and its relative molecular mass.

Specification References
1.43, 1.45

Calculating relative formula mass

The **relative formula mass** (M_r) of a compound is just all the relative atomic masses (A_r) of the atoms in that compound added together.

Examples

- Magnesium chloride ($MgCl_2$) contains one atom of magnesium and two atoms of chlorine. Magnesium has a relative atomic mass of 24 and chlorine has a relative atomic mass of 35.5, so the relative formula mass of magnesium chloride is 24 + (2 × 35.5) = 95.
- Calcium hydroxide has the formula $Ca(OH)_2$. The small number 2 after the bracket means that there's two lots of everything that's inside the brackets. So, $Ca(OH)_2$ contains one atom of calcium, two atoms of oxygen and two atoms of hydrogen. Calcium has an A_r of 40, oxygen has an A_r of 16 and hydrogen has an A_r of 1. So, the relative formula mass of calcium hydroxide is 40 + (2 × 16) + (2 × 1) = 74.

MATHS SKILLS

Finding the empirical formula

The **empirical formula** of a compound gives the simplest possible whole number ratio of atoms of each element within that compound. It's slightly different to the **molecular formula** of a compound, which gives you the actual number of atoms of each element within the compound. Often, the empirical and molecular formulae of a compound will be the same.

Tip: Remember — relative atomic mass is the average mass of an element, taking into account the different masses of isotopes that make up the element (see p.37). You can find the relative atomic masses of elements in the periodic table.

Example

The molecular formula of hydrogen bromide is HBr.
This can't be simplified so HBr is also the empirical formula.

But occasionally they're different.

Example 1

Find the empirical formula of glucose, $C_6H_{12}O_6$.

- The numbers in the molecular formula of glucose are 6, 12 and 6.
- To simplify the ratio, divide them by the largest number that goes into 6, 12 and 6 exactly — that's 6:
  C: 6 ÷ 6 = 1 H: 12 ÷ 6 = 2 O: 6 ÷ 6 = 1
- The empirical formula of glucose is CH_2O.

MATHS SKILLS

Tip: The little numbers to the right of the elements in an empirical formula must be integers (whole numbers) — you can't have half an atom.

Example 2

Find the empirical formula of diaminobenzene, $C_6H_4(NH_2)_2$.

- Start by simplifying the molecular formula by getting rid of the brackets around NH_2. Multiply the number of each atom inside the brackets by the small number outside: N: $1 \times 2 = 2$ H: $2 \times 2 = 4$
- Write out the molecular formula with the total numbers of N and H: $C_6H_8N_2$.
- The numbers in the simplified molecular formula are 6, 8 and 2.
- The largest number that goes into those numbers is 2.

  C: $6 \div 2 = 3$ H: $8 \div 2 = 4$ N: $2 \div 2 = 1$
- The empirical formula of diaminobenzene is C_3H_4N.

Finding the molecular formula

You can use the empirical formula of a compound, together with its M_r, to find its molecular formula. Here are the steps you need to follow:

1. Find the M_r of the empirical formula using the A_r values of the elements that make up the compound.
2. Divide the M_r of the compound by the M_r of the empirical formula.
3. Multiply everything in the empirical formula by the result of step 2.

Example 1

Compound X has the empirical formula C_2H_6N. The M_r of compound X is 88. Find the molecular formula of compound X.

1. Start by finding the M_r of C_2H_6N. The A_r of carbon is 12, the A_r of hydrogen is 1 and the A_r of nitrogen is 14.

Tip: You can find the A_r of every single element in the periodic table — there's one at the back of the book.

$$
\begin{aligned}
M_r(C_2H_6N) &= (2 \times A_r(C)) + (6 \times A_r(H)) + A_r(N) \\
&= (2 \times 12) + (6 \times 1) + 14 \\
&= 24 + 6 + 14 = 44
\end{aligned}
$$

2. Now that you've got the M_r of the empirical formula, you can divide the M_r of compound X by it.

$$88 \div 44 = 2$$

3. To get the molecular formula of compound X, multiply the numbers of atoms in the empirical formula by 2.

C: $2 \times 2 = 4$ H: $6 \times 2 = 12$ N: $1 \times 2 = 2$

So the molecular formula of compound X is $C_4H_{12}N_2$.

Example 2

Compound Y has the empirical formula CH_2O. The M_r of compound Y is 90. Find the molecular formula of compound Y.

1. Start by finding the M_r of CH_2O. The A_r of carbon is 12, the A_r of hydrogen is 1 and the A_r of oxygen is 16.

$$M_r(CH_2O) = A_r(C) + (2 \times A_r(H)) + A_r(O)$$
$$= 12 + (2 \times 1) + 16$$
$$= 12 + 2 + 16 = 30$$

2. Now that you've got the M_r of the empirical formula, you can divide the M_r of compound Y by it.

$$90 \div 30 = 3$$

3. To get the molecular formula of compound Y, multiply the numbers of atoms in the empirical formula by 3.

C: $1 \times 3 = 3$ H: $2 \times 3 = 6$ O: $1 \times 3 = 3$

So the molecular formula of compound Y is $C_3H_6O_3$.

Practice Questions — Fact Recall

Q1 Describe how you would work out the relative formula mass (M_r) of a compound.

Q2 Define the term 'empirical formula'.

Practice Questions — Application

Use the periodic table at the back of the book to answer these questions.

Q1 What is the relative formula mass of:

a) oxygen (O_2)?

b) potassium hydroxide (KOH)?

c) nitric acid (HNO_3)?

d) calcium carbonate ($CaCO_3$)?

Q2 Write down the empirical formula of:

a) aluminium oxide (Al_2O_3)

b) pentacosene ($C_{25}H_{50}$)

c) benzenetriol ($C_6H_6O_3$)

Q3 Find the molecular formula of:

a) a compound with the empirical formula C_4H_9 and M_r of 114.

b) a compound with the empirical formula $C_3H_5O_2$ and M_r of 146.

c) a compound with the empirical formula $C_4H_6Cl_2O$ and M_r 423.

Exam Tip
The A_r for any elements you need might be given to you in the question. If not, you can look them up in the periodic table.

2. Conservation of Mass

Learning Objectives:
- Be able to explain the law of conservation of mass applied to a closed system including a precipitation reaction in a closed flask.
- Be able to explain the law of conservation of mass applied to a non-enclosed system including a reaction in an open flask that takes in or gives out a gas.

Specification Reference 1.47

Conservation of mass isn't too tricky to get your head round. You need to know how to use this idea to work out masses and balance equations.

Mass conservation in chemical reactions

During chemical reactions, things don't appear out of nowhere and things don't just disappear. You still have the same atoms at the end of a chemical reaction as you had at the start. They're just arranged in different ways. Because of this, no mass is lost or gained — we say that mass is conserved during a reaction. This is summarised by the law of **conservation of mass**:

> During a chemical reaction, no atoms are destroyed and no atoms are created. This means there are the same number and types of atoms on each side of a reaction equation.

Mass conservation in a closed system

You can see the conservation of mass in action if you do a reaction in a closed system (this is a system where nothing can get in or out). The total mass of the system before and after doesn't change. A good way of showing this is to do a precipitation reaction.

Tip: A precipitation reaction happens when two solutions react and an insoluble solid, called a precipitate, forms in the solution.

Example

Copper sulfate solution reacts with sodium hydroxide to form insoluble copper hydroxide and soluble sodium sulfate:

$$CuSO_{4(aq)} + 2NaOH_{(aq)} \rightarrow Cu(OH)_{2(s)} + Na_2SO_{4(aq)}$$

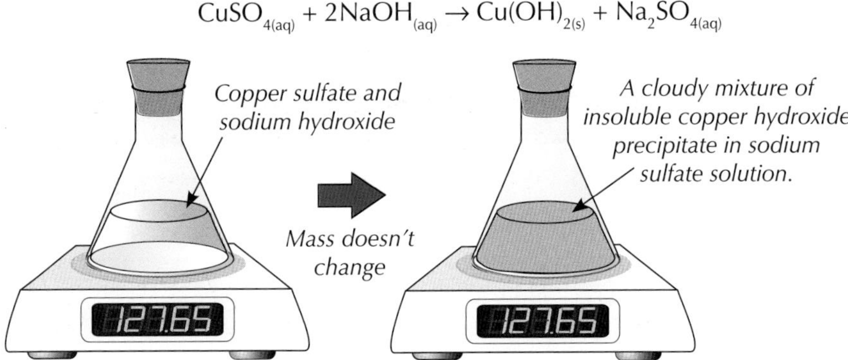

Figure 1: *Precipitation reaction between copper sulfate solution and sodium hydroxide.*

As no reactants or products can escape, the scales will read the same throughout the experiment.

Conservation of mass and M_r

By adding up the relative formula masses of the substances on each side of a balanced symbol equation, you can see that mass is conserved. The total M_r of the reactants equals the total M_r of the products.

Example

The balanced equation for the reaction between lithium and fluorine is: $2Li + F_2 \rightarrow 2LiF$.
Relative atomic masses, A_r: Li = 7, F = 19

Total M_r of reactants = (2 × 7) + (2 × 19) = 14 + 38 = 52

Total M_r of products = 2 × (7 + 19) = 2 × 26 = 52

The total M_r on the left-hand side of the equation is equal to the total M_r on the right-hand side, so mass is conserved.

Calculating reacting masses

You can use the idea of conservation of mass to work out the mass of individual reactants and products in a reaction.

Example

6 g of magnesium completely reacts with 4 g of oxygen. What mass of magnesium oxide is formed?

The total mass of the reactants is 4 + 6 = 10 g, so the mass of the product (magnesium oxide) must be 10 g.

Exam Tip
You could be asked to work out the mass of a product formed, or the mass of a reactant used. Just remember — the total mass of the products is exactly the same as the total mass of the reactants.

Reactions where mass seems to change

For some types of reaction, if you carry them out in a container that isn't sealed, you might find that the mass of stuff inside the reaction container has either increased or decreased during the reaction.

Reactions where the mass seems to increase

If the mass increases, it's probably because one or more of the reactants is a gas that's found in air (e.g. oxygen) and all the products are solids, liquids or aqueous.

- The particles in a gas move around and fill the space they're in. So before the reaction, the gas is floating around in the air. It's there, but it's not contained in the reaction vessel, so you can't account for its mass.
- When the gas reacts to form part of the product, the particles become contained inside the reaction vessel — so the total mass of the stuff inside the reaction vessel increases.

Tip: If the reaction vessel is sealed, then no particles can get in or out, so the mass of the reaction vessel won't change.

Example

When a metal reacts with oxygen in an unsealed container, the mass in the container increases. This is because the mass of the metal oxide produced equals the total mass of the metal and the oxygen that reacted from the air, but the mass of the stuff inside the container at the beginning of the reaction was just the mass of the metal, and not the oxygen.

$$\text{metal}_{(s)} + \text{oxygen}_{(g)} \rightarrow \text{metal oxide}_{(s)}$$

Figure 2: *When magnesium is heated in a crucible, it forms magnesium oxide. During the reaction, the mass of substance inside the crucible will increase.*

Tip: A gas will expand to fill any container it's in. So if a reaction vessel isn't sealed, the gas expands out of the vessel and escapes into the air around. There's more about this on p.96.

Reactions where the mass seems to decrease

If the mass decreases, it's probably because one of the products is a gas and all the reactants are solids, liquids or aqueous.

- Before the reaction, all the reactants are contained in the reaction vessel.
- If the vessel isn't enclosed, then the gas that's produced can escape from the reaction vessel as it's formed. It's no longer contained in the reaction vessel, so you can't account for its mass — the total mass of the stuff inside the reaction vessel decreases.

Example

When a metal carbonate thermally decomposes to form a metal oxide and carbon dioxide gas, the mass in the reaction vessel will decrease if it isn't sealed, as the carbon dioxide will escape from the vessel and its mass won't be measured. But in reality, the mass of the metal oxide and the carbon dioxide produced will equal the mass of the metal carbonate that decomposed.

$$\text{metal carbonate}_{(s)} \rightarrow \text{metal oxide}_{(s)} + \text{carbon dioxide}_{(g)}$$

Figure 3: When copper carbonate (green) is heated, it thermally decomposes to form copper oxide (black) and carbon dioxide gas.

Practice Questions — Fact Recall

Q1 State the law of conservation of mass.

Q2 State the relationship between the sum of the relative formula masses of the products and the sum of the relative formula masses of the reactants in a reaction.

Q3 Give an example of a reaction where the mass of the products in the reaction container would be greater than the mass of the reactants.

Practice Questions — Application

Q1 Calculate the mass of copper oxide formed when 127 g of copper reacts with 32 g of oxygen to form copper oxide.

Q2 During a reaction, 56 g of nitrogen reacts with hydrogen to form 68 g of ammonia (NH_3). What is the mass of hydrogen that reacts?

Q3 Predict what will happen to the mass in an unsealed reaction vessel if zinc carbonate is heated inside it so that it thermally decomposes.

Q4 Chlorine reacts with sodium bromide according to the following equation: $Cl_2 + 2NaBr \rightarrow Br_2 + 2NaCl$.
Use the relative formula masses of the reactants and products to show that mass is conserved in this reaction.

Q5 A student heated 5 g of calcium in an unsealed test tube so that it reacted with oxygen. At the end of the reaction, the mass of the product inside the test tube was 7 g. Explain this observation.

Tip: For Q4, you can use the periodic table inside the back cover to find the relative atomic masses of the elements.

3. Calculating Empirical Formulae

You first met empirical formulae on page 71, but now they're back and they mean business...

Learning Objectives:
- Be able to calculate the formulae of simple compounds from reacting masses.
- Understand that the formulae calculated from reacting masses are empirical formulae.
- Be able to describe an experiment to determine the empirical formula of a simple compound such as magnesium oxide.

Specification References 1.44, 1.46

Calculating empirical formulae from masses

You can work out the empirical formula of a compound from the masses of the elements it contains. Here are the steps you need to follow to do this:

1. Use the periodic table to find the A_r of all the elements in the compound.
2. Divide the mass of each element in the compound by its relative atomic mass (A_r). This is to find the relative amount of each element.
3. Write the relative amount of each element as a ratio.
4. Find the smallest whole number ratio between the elements in the compound. To do this, divide each number in the ratio by the smallest number.
5. Use the smallest whole number ratio to write the empirical formula.

Tip: See page 250 for more on writing ratios.

Example

A sample of a hydrocarbon contains 36 g of carbon and 6 g of hydrogen. Calculate the empirical formula of the hydrocarbon.

MATHS SKILLS

1. Carbon has an A_r of 12, and hydrogen has an A_r of 1.
2. Find the relative amount of each element in the hydrocarbon by dividing the mass of each element by its A_r.

   A_r(C) = 12 relative amount of C = 36 ÷ 12 = 3
   A_r(H) = 1 relative amount of H = 6 ÷ 1 = 6

3. The ratio is currently C : H = 3 : 6.
4. To find the smallest ratio, divide by the smallest number — here it's 3.

   C: 3 ÷ 3 = 1
   H: 6 ÷ 3 = 2

5. The smallest whole number ratio is C : H = 1 : 2.
   So, the empirical formula is CH_2.

Tip: For more on using the periodic table to find the A_r of an element, see page 40.

Tip: Make sure you keep the ratio the right way round between steps 3 to 5.

Using experiments to find empirical formulae

You need to be able to describe how you'd go about finding the empirical formula of a compound using an experiment. There's an example on the next page of how you'd do it for magnesium oxide.

> **Tip:** Heating the crucible will make sure it's clean and there are no traces of oil or water lying around from a previous experiment.

Example

1. Get a crucible and heat it until it's red hot.
2. Leave the crucible to cool, then weigh it, along with its lid.
3. Add some clean magnesium ribbon to the crucible. Reweigh the crucible, lid and magnesium ribbon. The mass of magnesium you're using is this reading minus the initial reading for the mass of the crucible and lid.
4. Heat the crucible containing the magnesium. Put the lid on the crucible so as to stop any bits of solid from escaping, but leave a small gap to allow oxygen to enter the crucible.
5. Keep heating the crucible strongly for around 10 minutes, or until all the magnesium ribbon has turned white.
6. Allow the crucible to cool and reweigh the crucible with the lid and its contents. The mass of magnesium oxide you have is this reading, minus the initial reading for the mass of the crucible and lid.

> **Tip:** Make sure that all of the magnesium in the crucible has reacted or else your results won't be accurate.

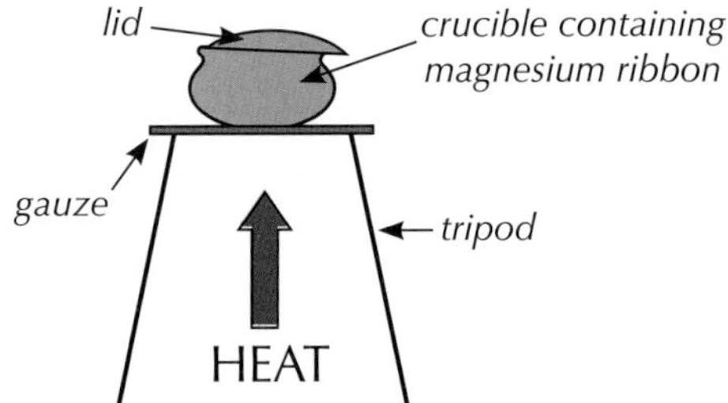

Figure 1: *Heating magnesium ribbon in a crucible.*

Figure 2: *Students heating magnesium in a crucible to form magnesium oxide.*

You can use the results of the experiment to work out the empirical formula.

Example

A student heats 1.08 g of magnesium ribbon in a crucible so it completely reacts to form magnesium oxide. The total mass of magnesium oxide formed was 1.80 g. Calculate the empirical formula of magnesium oxide.

The extra mass in the magnesium oxide must have come from oxygen, so you can work out the mass of oxygen:

MATHS SKILLS

$$\text{mass of O} = 1.80 - 1.08 = 0.72 \text{ g}$$

Work out the relative amount of magnesium and oxygen atoms involved in the reaction by dividing the mass of each one by its relative atomic mass:

$A_r(\text{Mg}) = 24$ $1.08 \div 24 = 0.045$
$A_r(\text{O}) = 16$ $0.72 \div 16 = 0.045$

Work out the lowest whole number ratio between Mg and O by dividing the relative amounts of both by the smallest number.

$$\text{Mg} = 0.045 \div 0.045 = 1$$
$$\text{O} = 0.045 \div 0.045 = 1$$

This shows that the ratio between O and Mg in the formula is 1 : 1, so the empirical formula of the magnesium oxide must be MgO.

> **Tip:** You know the extra mass must have come from oxygen because of the law of conservation of mass (see page 74) — the mass of magnesium present is the same before and after the reaction.

Practice Questions — Application

Q1 Calculate the empirical formula of a compound containing:

a) 72 g of carbon (C) and 6 g of hydrogen (H).

b) 96 g of carbon, 16 g of hydrogen and 142 g of chlorine (Cl).

c) 192 g of carbon, 10 g of hydrogen, 28 g of nitrogen (N) and 64 g of oxygen (O).

Q2 A scientist carried out some experiments where she reacted some metals with oxygen to give their metal oxides. She carried out the experiments in a crucible. Her results are shown in the table below. Assume that the only product formed in each reaction is metal oxide.

Metal reacted	Mass of crucible / g	Mass of crucible and metal / g	Mass of crucible and oxide / g
Magnesium	24.898	26.650	27.818
Beryllium	23.491	24.616	26.616
Lithium	25.230	25.552	25.920

a) Calculate the mass of oxygen that reacted with magnesium.

b) Using the data in the table, show that the empirical formula of beryllium oxide is BeO.

c) Using the data in the table, calculate the empirical formula of lithium oxide.

Learning Objective:

- Be able to calculate the concentration of solutions in g dm^{-3}.

Specification Reference 1.49

4. Concentration

Solutions are mixtures that contain one substance (the solute) dissolved in another substance (the solvent). The easiest way to describe the amount of solute in a solvent is by its concentration.

What is concentration?

Lots of reactions in chemistry take place between substances that are dissolved in a solvent to form a solution. The amount of a substance (e.g. the mass) in a certain volume of a solution is called its **concentration**. The more solute (the substance that's dissolved) there is in a given volume, the more concentrated the solution.

Tip: The state symbol for a substance in solution is 'aq'.

Calculating concentration in terms of mass

Concentration can be measured in grams per dm^3 (g dm^{-3}) — so 1 gram of stuff dissolved in 1 dm^3 of solution has a concentration of 1 g dm^{-3}. Here's the formula for finding concentration from the mass of solute:

$$\text{concentration (g dm}^{-3}\text{)} = \frac{\text{mass of solute (g)}}{\text{volume of solution (dm}^3\text{)}}$$

Tip: 1 dm^3 is the same as 1 litre or 1000 cm^3.

Example 1

What's the concentration in g dm^{-3} of a solution of sodium chloride where 30 g of sodium chloride is dissolved in 0.20 dm^3 of water?

$$\text{concentration} = \frac{30}{0.20} = 150 \text{ g dm}^{-3}$$

Example 2

What's the concentration in g dm^{-3} of iron chloride solution where 10 g of iron chloride is dissolved in 25 cm^3 of water?

First, change the units of volume from cm^3 to dm^3.

volume = 25 ÷ 1000 = 0.025 dm^3

Then use the equation to find the concentration of the solution.

$$\text{concentration} = \frac{10}{0.025} = 400 \text{ g dm}^{-3}$$

Tip: There's more information about how to convert between units on pages 18-19.

Finding the mass of solute in a solution

You can rearrange the equation above in order to calculate the mass of solute in a given volume of solution if you know the concentration.

Tip: A solute is a substance that is dissolved in a liquid (the solvent). When a solute is dissolved in a solvent they form a solution.

Example

What's the mass of copper chloride in 20 cm³ of an 80 g dm^{-3} solution of copper chloride?

MATHS SKILLS

First, change the units of volume from cm³ to dm³.

volume = 20 ÷ 1000 = 0.020 dm³

Rearrange the equation to make mass the subject by multiplying each side by volume:

mass = concentration × volume = 80 × 0.020 = 1.6 g

Exam Tip
Always double check the units of any data you're given before you use it in a calculation, in case you need to convert them first.

Practice Questions — Fact Recall

Q1 What is concentration?

Q2 State the equation that links the concentration of a solution in g dm^{-3} with the mass of the solute and the volume of the solution.

Tip: This handy formula triangle might help when rearranging the equation for concentration:

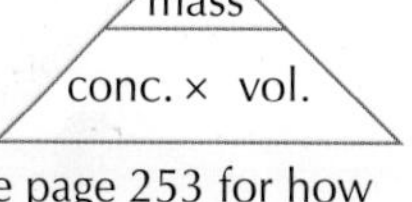

(See page 253 for how to use formula triangles.)

Practice Questions — Application

Q1 Calculate the concentrations of the following solutions, in g dm^{-3}.

a) A solution containing 150 g of iron chloride in 3 dm³ of solvent.

b) A solution containing 48 g of hydrochloric acid in 0.4 dm³ of solvent.

Q2 Calculate the concentrations of the following solutions, in g dm^{-3}.

a) A solution containing 60 g of sodium hydroxide in 120 cm³ of solvent.

b) A solution containing 2.4 g of sodium chloride in 8 cm³ of solvent.

Q3 Calculate the mass of solute in the following solutions.

a) The mass of sodium carbonate in 2.5 dm³ of a 32 g dm^{-3} solution of sodium carbonate.

b) The mass of copper sulfate in 0.35 dm³ of a 60 g dm^{-3} solution of copper sulfate.

Q4 Calculate the mass of solute in the following solutions.

a) The mass of sulfuric acid in 80 cm³ of a 200 g dm^{-3} solution of sulfuric acid.

b) The mass of magnesium chloride in 15 cm³ of a 120 g dm^{-3} solution of magnesium chloride.

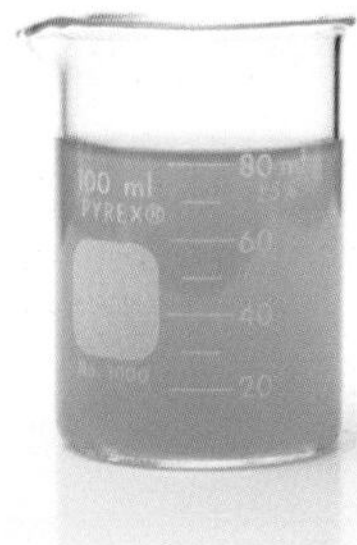

Figure 1: Copper sulfate solution.

5. Calculating Masses from Equations

If you know the balanced equation for a reaction and the M_r values of the substances involved, you're most of the way to working out their masses...

Learning Objectives:

- Be able to calculate the masses of reactants and products from balanced equations, given the mass of one substance.
- H Be able to explain why the mass of product formed during a reaction is controlled by the mass of the reactant which is not in excess.

Specification References
1.48, 1.52

Calculating the mass of a product

If you know the balanced equation for a reaction and the mass of one of the substances, you can work out the mass of any other substance in the reaction. Here are the steps you need to follow:

1. Write out the balanced equation.
2. Work out the relative formula masses (M_r) of the reactants and products that you're interested in.
3. For the substance that you know the mass of, work out the relative amount of it in the reaction. To do this, divide its mass by its relative formula mass.
4. Use the balanced equation to work out the relative amount of the other substance.
5. Then multiply the relative amount of the substance you don't know the mass of by its relative formula mass. This gives the mass of that substance in the reaction.

Tip: To make sure that a particular reactant fully reacts, another reactant might be 'in excess'. This means that there is more of it than is necessary for the reactant of interest to be completely used up. At the end of the reaction, some of the reactant that was in excess will be left over.

Exam Tip
In the exam, you might be expected to know the equation for a reaction (if it's one you've studied), or you might be given the balanced symbol equation in the question.

Example 1

What mass of calcium chloride ($CaCl_2$) is produced when 3.7 g of calcium hydroxide ($Ca(OH)_2$) reacts with an excess of hydrochloric acid (HCl)?

1. The balanced symbol equation for this reaction is:

$$Ca(OH)_2 + 2HCl \rightarrow CaCl_2 + 2H_2O$$

2. The substances you're interested in are $Ca(OH)_2$ and $CaCl_2$. Their relative formula masses (M_r) are:

$$M_r \text{ of } Ca(OH)_2 = 40 + (2 \times (16 + 1)) = 74$$
$$M_r \text{ of } CaCl_2 = 40 + (2 \times 35.5) = 111$$

3. Calculate the relative amount of calcium hydroxide in the reaction.

relative amount of $Ca(OH)_2$ = mass ÷ M_r = 3.7 ÷ 74 = 0.050

4. Look at the balanced equation to work out the relative amount of calcium chloride that will be formed:

The ratio of $Ca(OH)_2$ to $CaCl_2$ in the equation is 1:1. This means that 1 molecule of $Ca(OH)_2$ will react to produce 1 molecule of $CaCl_2$. So the relative amount of $CaCl_2$ produced will also be 0.050.

5. Calculate the mass of $CaCl_2$ produced.

mass = relative amount of substance × M_r = 0.050 × 111 = 5.6 g

Example 2

What mass of aluminium oxide is produced when 135 g of aluminium is burned in air?

MATHS SKILLS

1. The balanced symbol equation for this reaction is:

$$4Al + 3O_2 \rightarrow 2Al_2O_3$$

2. You know the mass of Al. The product you want is Al_2O_3.

A_r of Al = 27
M_r of $Al_2O_3 = (2 \times 27) + (3 \times 16) = 102$

3. Calculate the relative amount of aluminium in the reaction.

Relative amount of Al = mass ÷ M_r = 135 ÷ 27 = 5

4. Look at the ratio of Al to Al_2O_3 in the balanced equation to work out how much aluminium oxide will be formed:

The ratio of Al to Al_2O_3 is 4 : 2. This means that 4 molecules of Al react to produce 2 molecules of Al_2O_3. The relative amount of Al_2O_3 is half that of Al, so the relative amount of Al_2O_3 is 2.5.

5. Calculate the mass of Al_2O_3 produced.

mass = relative amount of substance × M_r = 2.5 × 102 = 255 g

Tip: If a reaction is said to be carried out 'in air', then any gases in the reaction that are found in air (e.g. oxygen) will be in excess (unless you're told otherwise).

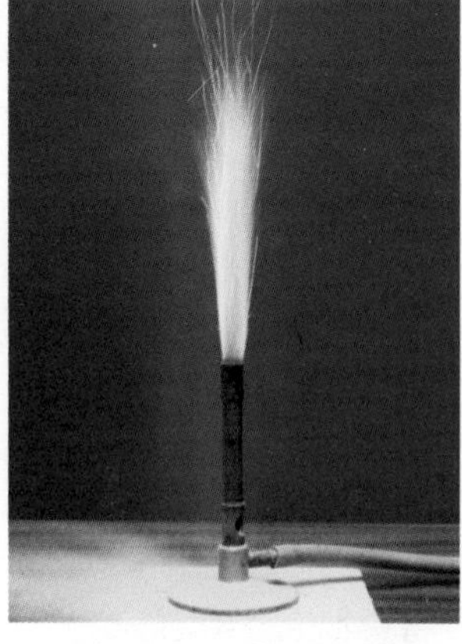

Figure 1: *Aluminium powder burning in air.*

Calculating the mass of a reactant

You can use the same basic method as on the previous page to find how much reactant you'd need to use to make a certain mass of product.

Example

How much zinc carbonate ($ZnCO_3$) would need to decompose to form 24.3 g of zinc oxide (ZnO)?

MATHS SKILLS

1. The balanced symbol equation for this reaction is:

$$ZnCO_3 \rightarrow ZnO + CO_2$$

2. The reactant is $ZnCO_3$. The product you know the mass of is ZnO.

M_r of $ZnCO_3 = 65 + 12 + (3 \times 16) = 125$
M_r of $ZnO = 65 + 16 = 81$

3. Calculate the relative amount of zinc oxide in the reaction.

relative amount of ZnO = mass ÷ M_r = 24.3 ÷ 81 = 0.30

4. Look at the ratio of reactants and products in the equation to work out how much zinc carbonate is needed to produce this amount of ZnO:

The ratio of $ZnCO_3$ to ZnO is 1 : 1. So 1 molecule of $ZnCO_3$ decomposes to produce 1 molecule of ZnO — the same number of molecules are produced. So the relative amount of $ZnCO_3$ will be 0.30.

5. Calculate the mass of $ZnCO_3$ that reacts.

mass = relative amount of substance × M_r = 0.30 × 125 = 38 g

Tip: It's useful to know how to calculate the amount of reactant needed to make a set amount of product when you're planning experiments. If you know how much product you want to end up with, you can then work out the minimum amount of reactant needed to make this quantity.

Tip: This time it's the amount of product you know, so in step 3 you have to find the relative amount of product rather than reactant.

Limiting reactants Higher

Tip: H Being able to use scientific vocabulary such as 'in excess' and 'limiting reactant' is an important part of working scientifically.

WORKING SCIENTIFICALLY

A reaction stops when all of one of the reactants is used up. Any other reactants are in excess. The reactant that's used up is called the **limiting reactant** (because it limits the amount of product that's formed).

The amount of product formed is directly proportional to the amount of the limiting reactant used. This is because if you add more of the limiting reactant there will be more reactant particles to take part in the reaction, which means more product particles are made (as long as the other reactants are in excess).

Tip: H If you know the mass of the limiting reactant in a reaction, you can use the method on page 82 to work out how much product will be formed during the reaction.

Example Higher

When 2.24 g of iron were reacted with an excess of copper sulfate solution, 2.54 g of copper were produced. How much copper would be produced if 6.72 g of iron were reacted in an excess of copper sulfate solution?

6.72 ÷ 2.24 = 3, so three times as much iron was used in the second reaction. As iron is the limiting reactant, three times as much copper will be produced. 3 × 2.54 = 7.62 g.

Practice Question — Fact Recall

Q1 What is a limiting reactant?

Practice Questions — Application

Q1 During an experiment, a small piece of sodium was added to a bowl of water. The sodium reacted with the water until the entire piece disappeared. Identify:

a) the limiting reactant.

b) the reactant(s) in excess.

Tip: H You don't need to work out the symbol equation for the reaction in Q2 — you just have to work out how the relative amounts of products and reactants will change.

Q2 3.25 g of zinc reacts with an excess of hydrochloric acid to form 6.80 g of zinc chloride.

a) Describe what would happen to the amount of zinc chloride produced if the amount of zinc that reacted was doubled and the amount of hydrochloric acid remained in excess.

b) How much zinc would react in an excess of hydrochloric acid to produce 1.36 g of zinc chloride?

Tip: Use the periodic table inside the back cover to answer questions 3-4.

Q3 Calculate the mass of potassium chloride (KCl) that will be formed if 36.2 g of aqueous potassium bromide (KBr) reacts with an excess of chlorine. The balanced symbol equation for this reaction is:

$$2KBr + Cl_2 \rightarrow 2KCl + Br_2$$

Q4 Calculate the mass of aluminium chloride ($AlCl_3$) that will be made if 15.4 g of hydrochloric acid (HCl) reacts with an excess of aluminium. The balanced symbol equation for this reaction is:

$$6HCl + 2Al \rightarrow 2AlCl_3 + 3H_2$$

6. The Mole 

Don't worry, you haven't accidentally opened a book about lawn maintenance. Moles are used in chemistry to measure amounts of substances.

Learning Objectives:

- H Know that one mole of particles of a substance is defined as a mass of 'relative particle mass' in grams.
- H Know that one mole of particles of a substance is defined as the Avogadro constant number of particles (6.02×10^{23} atoms, molecules, formulae or ions) of that substance.
- H Be able to calculate the number of particles of a substance in a given number of moles of that substance and vice versa.
- H Be able to calculate the number of moles of particles of a substance in a given mass of that substance and vice versa.
- H Be able to calculate the number of particles of a substance in a given mass of that substance and vice versa.

Specification References
1.50, 1.51

The Avogadro constant

Just like 'a million' is this many: 1 000 000; or 'a billion' is this many: 1 000 000 000, so 'the **Avogadro constant**' is this many: 602 000 000 000 000 000 000 000 or 6.02×10^{23}. And that's all it is. Just a number.

What is a mole?

In chemistry, amounts of substances are measured in **moles**. One mole of any substance is just the amount of that substance that contains an Avogadro number of particles — so 6.02×10^{23} particles. The particles could be atoms, molecules or ions.

The mass of one mole of atoms or molecules of any substance is exactly the same number of grams as the **relative atomic mass** (A_r) or **relative formula mass** (M_r) of the element or compound. In other words, one mole of atoms or molecules of any substance will have a mass in grams equal to the value of the relative particle mass (A_r or M_r) for that substance. Here are some examples:

Examples — Higher

- Carbon (C) has an A_r of 12.
  So one mole of iron weighs exactly 12 g.
- Nitrogen gas (N_2) has an M_r of $2 \times 14 = 28$.
  So one mole of nitrogen weighs exactly 28 g.
- Hexane (C_6H_{14}) has an M_r of $(6 \times 12) + (14 \times 1) = 86$.
  So one mole of hexane weighs exactly 86 g.

This means that 12 g of carbon, or 28 g of N_2, or 86 g of hexane all contain the same number of particles, namely one mole (6.02×10^{23}).

Calculations involving the number of particles

The mole is simply a measure of how many particles there are of a substance. You need to be able to work out the number of molecules, atoms or ions in a certain number of moles.

Example — Higher

How many atoms are there in 5 moles of oxygen gas?

1. To find the number of particles, multiply Avogadro's constant by the number of moles you have: $6.02 \times 10^{23} \times 5 = 3.01 \times 10^{24}$
2. There are two atoms in each molecule of oxygen, so multiply your answer by 2 to get the number of atoms: $3.01 \times 10^{24} \times 2 = 6.02 \times 10^{24}$

Tip: Giving your answer in standard form saves you having to write out lots of 0's. Standard form is where your number is written as '(a number between 1 and 10) $\times 10^{x}$'. There's more about this on pages 250-251.

You also need to be able to work out the number of moles of a substance there are in a certain number of particles.

Example — Higher

How many moles of carbon are there in 3.25×10^{24} particles of propane?

1. There are three carbon atoms in a molecule of propane, so begin by multiplying the number of particles by 3: $3.25 \times 10^{24} \times 3 = 9.75 \times 10^{24}$
2. To convert from particles to moles, divide the number of particles by Avogadro's constant: $9.75 \times 10^{24} \div 6.02 \times 10^{23} = 16.2$ moles

Calculating amounts of substances

You can find the number of moles in a given mass of a substance using this formula:

$$\text{Number of moles} = \frac{\text{Mass in g (of element or compound)}}{M_r \text{ (of element or compound) or } A_r \text{ (of element)}}$$

Example 1 — Higher

How many moles are there in 42 g of carbon?

The A_r of carbon is 12, so the number of moles in 42 g of carbon is:

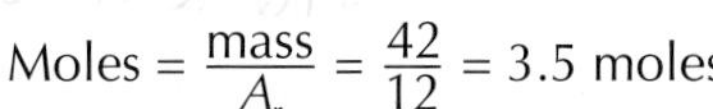

$$\text{Moles} = \frac{\text{mass}}{A_r} = \frac{42}{12} = 3.5 \text{ moles}$$

Tip: H An easy way to rearrange the equation is to use the formula triangle below — just cover up the thing you want to find with your finger and write down what's left showing.

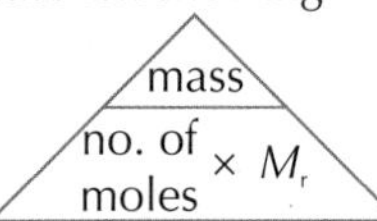

Example 2 — Higher

How many moles are there in 66 g of carbon dioxide (CO_2)?

M_r of CO_2 = 12 + (16 × 2) = 44

$$\text{No. of moles} = \frac{\text{mass}}{M_r} = \frac{66}{44} = 1.5 \text{ mol}$$

You can also rearrange the equation above to find the mass of a known number of moles of a substance, or to find the M_r of a substance from the mass and the number of moles.

Example — Higher

What is the mass in g of 0.80 moles of sulfuric acid (H_2SO_4)?

The M_r of sulfuric acid is (2 × 1) + 32 + (4 × 16) = 98.

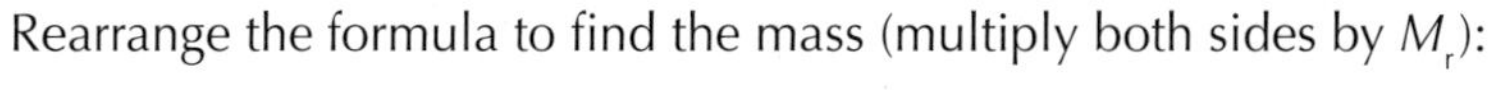

Rearrange the formula to find the mass (multiply both sides by M_r):

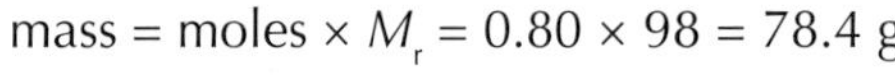

mass = moles × M_r = 0.80 × 98 = 78.4 g

So 0.80 moles of sulfuric acid would weigh 78 g.

Exam Tip
Unless told otherwise, the number of significant figures you give your answer to should be the same as the piece of data in the question with the smallest number of significant figures.

Converting between number of atoms and mass

In the exam you may be asked to calculate how many atoms there are in a given mass of substance (or vice versa).

Tip: H If you need to get from a number of particles to a mass, start by dividing by Avogadro's constant. Then, use the equation on the previous page to work out the mass from the number of moles.

Example — Higher

How many magnesium atoms are there in 60 g of Mg? (A_r of Mg = 24)

1. Start by converting the mass into moles using the equation:

$$\text{moles} = \text{mass} \div A_r$$
$$= 60 \div 24 = 2.5 \text{ moles}$$

2. Multiply the number of moles by Avogadro's constant to find the number of atoms:

$$2.5 \times 6.02 \times 10^{23} = 1.5 \times 10^{24} \text{ atoms}$$

Practice Questions — Fact Recall

Q1 What is the value of the Avogadro constant? Give your answer in standard form.

Q2 What is a mole?

Q3 What equation can you use to convert between moles and grams?

Exam Tip
You could be expected to rearrange equations in the exam. There's more on how to rearrange equations on pages 252-253.

Practice Questions — Application

Use the periodic table at the back of the book to answer these questions.

Q1 What is the mass of one mole of each of the following?

a) Sodium (Na) b) Helium (He)

c) Bromine (Br_2) d) Potassium oxide (K_2O)

Q2 How many moles are there in each of the following?

a) 19.5 g of potassium (K)

b) 76.8 g of sulfur dioxide (SO_2)

Q3 How much would the following weigh in grams?

a) 0.50 moles of magnesium oxide (MgO)

b) 1.40 moles of calcium hydroxide ($Ca(OH)_2$)

Q4 How many atoms are there in each of the following?

a) 0.80 moles of nickel (Ni)

b) 2.0 moles of sodium chloride (NaCl)

Q5 How many molecules are there in 27.2 g of ammonia (NH_3)?

Figure 1: One mole of a variety of compounds.

7. The Mole and Equations 

You learnt how to balance equations back on page 23. But you also need to be able to write balanced equations from the masses of reactants and products involved in the reaction. And that's what these pages are all about.

Learning Objective:

- H Be able to deduce the stoichiometry of a reaction from the masses of the reactants and products.

Specification Reference 1.53

Understanding chemical equations

In a balanced equation, the big numbers in front of the chemical formulas tell you the relative number of **moles** of each reactant that take part in the reaction, and the relative number of moles of each product that are formed. The little numbers within the chemical formulas tell you how many atoms of each element there are in the smallest unit of the substance.

Tip: H Remember that a mole is just the amount of a substance that contains 6.02×10^{23} particles. See page 85 for more.

Example — Higher

$$Mg_{(s)} + 2HCl_{(aq)} \rightarrow MgCl_{2(aq)} + H_{2(g)}$$

In this reaction, 1 mole of magnesium and 2 moles of hydrochloric acid react to form 1 mole of magnesium chloride and 1 mole of hydrogen gas.

Tip: H The ratio of the moles of substances in a reaction is called the stoichiometry.

The ratio of moles of reactants and products in a reaction always stays the same. You can use this fact to work out how many moles of a reactant or product is involved in a reaction, if you're given information about one of the other substances in the reaction.

Example 1 — Higher

How many moles of water are formed if 2 moles of methane combust completely in oxygen? The balanced equation for this reaction is: $CH_4 + 2O_2 \rightarrow CO_2 + 2H_2O$

From the balanced equation, you can see that 1 mole of methane reacts to form 2 moles of water, so the molar ratio is 1:2. So 2 moles of methane will react to form $(2 \times 2) = 4$ moles of water.

Example 2 — Higher

How many moles of oxygen will react if 3 moles of magnesium react completely to form magnesium oxide? The balanced equation for this reaction is: $2Mg + O_2 \rightarrow 2MgO$

From the balanced equation, you can see that 2 moles of magnesium react with 1 mole of oxygen, so the molar ratio is 2:1. So 3 moles of magnesium will react with $(3 \div 2) = 1.5$ moles of oxygen.

Tip: H You can also see from the reaction equation that the molar ratio of magnesium to magnesium oxide is 1:1, so in this experiment 3 moles of magnesium oxide will form.

Balancing equations using reacting masses

If you know the masses of the reactants and products that took part in a reaction, you can work out the balanced symbol equation for the reaction. Here are the steps you should take:

1. Divide the mass of each substance by its relative formula mass to find the number of moles.
2. Divide the number of moles of each substance by the smallest number of moles in the reaction.
3. If any of the numbers aren't whole numbers, multiply all the numbers by the same amount so that they all become whole numbers.
4. Write the balanced symbol equation for the reaction by putting these numbers in front of the chemical formulas.

Tip: H The equation 'number of moles = mass ÷ M_r' will be really helpful in these calculations. Have a look back at page 86 for a reminder.

Example 1 **Higher**

8.1 g of zinc oxide (ZnO) reacts completely with 0.60 g of carbon to form 2.2 g of carbon dioxide and 6.5 g of zinc. Write a balanced symbol equation for this reaction. Relative atomic masses, A_r: C = 12, O = 16, Zn = 65.

1. First work out the M_r (or A_r) for each of the substances in the reaction:

   ZnO: 65 + 16 = 81 C: 12 CO_2: 12 + (2 × 16) = 44 Zn: 65

   Then divide the mass of each substance by its M_r to calculate how many moles of each substance reacted or were produced:

   ZnO: $\frac{8.1}{81}$ = 0.10 mol C: $\frac{0.60}{12}$ = 0.050 mol

   CO_2: $\frac{2.2}{44}$ = 0.050 mol Zn: $\frac{6.5}{65}$ = 0.10 mol

2. Divide by the smallest number of moles, which is 0.050:

   ZnO: $\frac{0.10}{0.050}$ = 2.0 C: $\frac{0.050}{0.050}$ = 1.0

   CO_2: $\frac{0.050}{0.050}$ = 1.0 Zn: $\frac{0.10}{0.050}$ = 2.0

3. The numbers are all whole numbers, so you can write out the balanced symbol equation straight away.
4. So the balanced equation is: $2ZnO + C \rightarrow CO_2 + 2Zn$

Exam Tip H
These calculations have several steps, so always write down your working to stop you getting in a muddle in the exam.

Tip: H Dividing by the smallest number of moles gives the ratio of the amounts of each substance in the reaction.

Example 2 **Higher**

2.7 g of an element, X, reacts completely with 2.4 g of oxygen to form 5.1 g of an oxide, X oxide. Write a balanced symbol equation for this reaction.
A_r(X) = 27, $M_r(O_2)$ = 32, M_r(X oxide) = 102

MATHS SKILLS

1. First divide the mass of each substance by its M_r (or A_r) to find how many moles of each substance reacted or were produced:

   X: $\frac{2.7}{27} = 0.10$ mol O_2: $\frac{2.4}{32} = 0.075$ mol   X oxide: $\frac{5.1}{102} = 0.050$ mol

2. Divide by the smallest number of moles, which is 0.050:

   X: $\frac{0.10}{0.050} = 2.0$ O_2: $\frac{0.075}{0.050} = 1.5$ X oxide: $\frac{0.050}{0.050} = 1.0$

3. Multiply all the values by two so the number of moles of oxygen becomes a whole number:

   X: $2.0 \times 2 = 4$ O_2: $1.5 \times 2 = 3$ X oxide: $1.0 \times 2 = 2$

4. So the balanced equation is: $4X + 3O_2 \rightarrow 2(\text{X oxide})$

   You can see from the reaction equation that 2 units of X oxide contain 4 atoms of X and 6 atoms of O. So one unit of X oxide contains 2 atoms of X and 3 atoms of O, making the formula of X oxide X_2O_3.

   So the balanced equation is: $4X + 3O_2 \rightarrow 2X_2O_3$

Exam Tip H
Always check that the final equation is balanced. If your answer is correct, the number of atoms of each element on the left-hand side should be the same as the number of atoms of each element on the right-hand side.

Tip: H You should multiply all the values you get in step 2 by the smallest possible number that will make them all whole numbers.

Practice Questions — Application

Q1 What is the relative number of moles of water in each of the following reactions?

a) $Ca + 2H_2O \rightarrow Ca(OH_2) + H_2$ b) $HCl + NaOH \rightarrow NaCl + H_2O$

Q2 The balanced equation for the reaction between magnesium and oxygen is: $2Mg + O_2 \rightarrow 2MgO$.
How many moles of magnesium would react to form 3 moles of magnesium oxide?

Q3 The balanced equation for the reaction between chlorine and sodium bromide is: $Cl_2 + 2NaBr \rightarrow Br_2 + 2NaCl$.
How many moles of bromine (Br_2) would form from 0.4 moles of sodium bromide?

Tip: H For Q2 and Q3, start by using the reaction equation to work out the molar ratios of the substances you're interested in.

Q4 4.6 g of sodium reacted with 1.6 g of oxygen to form 6.2 g of sodium oxide (Na_2O). Use the reacting masses to write a balanced symbol equation for this reaction.
Relative atomic masses (A_r): O = 16, Na = 23

Q5 2.34 g of potassium reacted with 2.19 g of hydrochloric acid (HCl) to form 4.47 g of potassium chloride (KCl) and 0.06 g of hydrogen. Use the reacting masses to write a balanced symbol equation for this reaction. Relative atomic masses (A_r): H = 1, Cl = 35.5, K = 39

Q6 1.20 g of a hydrocarbon, Z, combusts completely in 4.48 g of oxygen to form 3.52 g of carbon dioxide (CO_2) and 2.16 g of water (H_2O). Write a balanced symbol equation for this reaction.
(A_r): Z = 30   (M_r): O_2 = 32, H_2O = 18, CO_2 = 44

Topic 1d Checklist — Make sure you know...

Relative Mass

- [ ] How to calculate the relative formula mass (M_r) of a substance by adding up the relative atomic masses (A_r) of all the atoms in the formula.
- [ ] How to work out the empirical formula of a molecule by finding the smallest whole number ratio between the atoms in its molecular formula.
- [ ] How to use the M_r and empirical formula of a compound to calculate its molecular formula.

Conservation of Mass

- [ ] What the law of conservation of mass is.
- [ ] That the mass of a closed system, such as a precipitation reaction occurring in a stoppered conical flask, does not change during a reaction.
- [ ] That the mass of the products in a reaction is equal to the mass of the reactants.
- [ ] How to calculate the masses of substances in a reaction using balanced symbol equations.
- [ ] That if the mass of the substances in a reaction seems to increase, it's usually because at least one of the reactants is a gas, and all the products are solids, liquids or solutions.
- [ ] That if the mass of the substances in a reaction seems to decrease, it's usually because at least one of the products is a gas, and all the reactants are solids, liquids or solutions.

Calculating Empirical Formulae

- [ ] How to work out the empirical formula of a compound from the mass of the elements that it contains.
- [ ] How to carry out an experiment to determine the empirical formulae of a compound e.g. by heating a metal in a pre-weighed crucible exposed to the air.
- [ ] How to calculate the empirical formula of a compound from the results of an experiment, by using the mass of the reactants and the mass of the products.

Concentration

- [ ] That the concentration of a solution is determined by the amount of dissolved substance and the volume of the solution.
- [ ] How to calculate the concentration of a solution in g dm^{-3}.
- [ ] How to calculate the mass of solute in a volume of solution from the concentration in g dm^{-3}.

Calculating Masses from Equations

- [ ] How to calculate the mass of product formed in a reaction from the balanced symbol equation and the mass of one reactant.

cont...

- [ ] How to calculate the mass of reactant needed to make a given amount of product from the balanced symbol equation.
- [ ] H That the reactant that gets used up first in a chemical reaction is known as the limiting reactant.
- [ ] H How the limiting reactant controls how much product is formed.

The Mole

- [ ] H That the Avogadro constant has the value 6.02×10^{23}.
- [ ] H That amounts in chemistry can be measured in moles.
- [ ] H That the number of particles (atoms, ions or molecules) in one mole of any substance is equal to the Avogadro constant.
- [ ] H That the relative formula mass of a substance is the same as the mass, in grams, of one mole of that substance.
- [ ] H How to convert number of particles to moles and vice versa.
- [ ] H How to convert mass to moles and vice versa using the formula: moles = mass ÷ M_r.
- [ ] H How to convert number of particles to mass and vice versa, via the formula: moles = mass ÷ M_r.

The Mole and Equations

- [ ] H That symbol equations give you the ratio of the number of moles of each substance in a reaction (the stoichiometry).
- [ ] H How to balance a chemical equation using the masses of the reactants and products.

Exam-style Questions

1 A scientist carries out an experiment to react copper with oxygen to form copper oxide. The balanced equation for the reaction is:

$$2Cu_{(s)} + O_{2(g)} \rightarrow 2CuO_{(s)}$$

The scientist measures 2.54 g of copper into an unsealed reaction container and heats it to start the reaction. Once all the copper has reacted, the scientist finds that the mass of the reaction container has increased by 0.64 g.

(a) Calculate the relative formula mass of copper oxide.
Relative atomic masses (A_r): O = 16, Cu = 63.5

(1 mark)

(b) Explain how the balanced symbol equation follows the law of conservation of mass.

(1 mark)

(c) What mass of oxygen reacts with the copper in this experiment?

(1 mark)

(d) Explain why the mass inside the reaction vessel increases during this experiment.

(2 marks)

2 Calcium carbonate decomposes when it's heated to form calcium oxide and carbon dioxide. The balanced equation for the reaction is:

$$CaCO_{3(s)} \rightarrow CaO_{(s)} + CO_{2(g)}$$

During an experiment, 7.0 g of calcium oxide and 5.5 g of carbon dioxide are formed.

(a) What mass of calcium carbonate was there at the beginning of the reaction?

(1 mark)

(b) Predict the mass of calcium oxide that would be produced if the same reaction was carried out using three times as much calcium carbonate.

(1 mark)

(c) Calculate the relative formula masses of each of the substances in the reaction.
Relative atomic masses (A_r): C = 12, O = 16, Ca = 40

(3 marks)

(d) Use your answer to part (c) to show that mass is conserved in this reaction.

(2 marks)

3 A student wants to prepare a 150 g dm^{-3} solution of magnesium chloride ($MgCl_2$).

(a) What mass of magnesium chloride should the student dissolve in order to make 30 cm^3 of this solution?

(2 marks)

(b) The student adds 60 cm^3 of water to the 30 cm^3 of 150 g dm^{-3} solution. What is the concentration of the diluted solution in g dm^{-3}?

(2 marks)

4 In a reaction, 0.50 g of hydrogen and 4.0 g of oxygen react to form 4.5 g of water.

(a) Use the data to write a balanced symbol equation for this reaction.

(4 marks)

(b) The reaction is carried out again using 0.20 g of hydrogen and the same mass of oxygen. Explain why hydrogen will be a limiting reactant in this reaction.

(1 mark)

5 4.8 g of magnesium reacts in an excess of zinc chloride solution to form magnesium chloride and zinc. The equation for this reaction is:

$$Mg + ZnCl_2 \rightarrow MgCl_2 + Zn$$

(a) How many moles of magnesium react?

(1 mark)

(b) What mass of magnesium chloride is produced by this reaction?

(3 marks)

(c) At the start of the reaction, the solution contained 35 g of zinc chloride. What mass of zinc chloride will be left in the solution after the reaction has taken place?

(4 marks)

(d) The reaction is repeated using the same amount of magnesium, but this time a volume of zinc chloride solution that contains 20 g of zinc chloride. State, with reasoning, whether the zinc chloride is still in excess.

(2 marks)

6 A mixture is being made that will contain 8% bromine by mass.

(a) What mass of calcium bromide, $CaBr_2$, is needed to provide enough bromine to make 30 g of this mixture?

(4 marks)

(b) Another mixture is made using 1.5 g of calcium bromide. How many atoms of Br are in 1.5 g of $CaBr_2$?

(3 marks)

1. States of Matter

You've probably learnt about solids, liquids and gases many times before. But make sure you know how the particle model can be used to explain the three different states.

Learning Objective:
- Be able to describe the arrangement, movement and the relative energy of particles in each of the three states of matter: solid, liquid and gas.

Specification Reference 2.1

The three states of matter

Materials come in three different forms — **solid**, **liquid** and **gas**. These are three states of matter. Which state a material is in depends on how strong the forces of attraction are between the particles of the material (the atoms, ions or molecules). The strength of forces between particles is determined by:

- the material (the structure of the substance and the type of bonds holding the particles together),
- the temperature,
- the pressure.

You can use a model called the particle model to explain how the particles in a material behave in each of the three states of matter. In the particle model, each particle is considered to be a small, solid, inelastic sphere.

Tip: The properties of each state of matter depend on the strength of the forces between the particles.

Tip: In the particle model, each particle could be a molecule, an ion or an atom.

Solids

In solids, there are strong forces of attraction between particles. These forces hold the particles close together in fixed positions to form a very regular lattice arrangement.

The particles in a solid don't have much energy, so they don't move from their positions. Because of this, all solids keep a definite shape and volume. The particles vibrate about their positions, and as the temperature increases, the particles vibrate more. This is why solids expand slightly when heated.

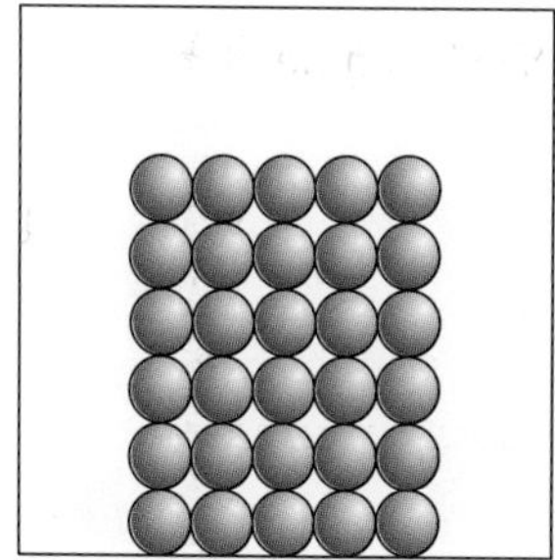

Figure 1: *Particle model of a solid.*

Tip: A model is a representation of a theory which can be used to explain observations from experiments. See p.3 for more on models. WORKING SCIENTIFICALLY

Figure 2: Various elements in different states of matter.

Liquids

In liquids, there are weak forces of attraction between the particles. The particles are randomly arranged and are free to move past each other, but they tend to stick closely together. Liquids have a definite volume but don't keep a definite shape, and will flow to fill the bottom of a container — see Figure 3.

The particles in a liquid are constantly moving with random motion. The hotter the liquid gets, the faster the particles move. This causes liquids to expand slightly when heated. The particles of a substance in the liquid state will have more energy than when the substance is in the solid state, but less energy than when the substance is in the gas state.

Tip: The models of the states of matter represent 3D objects (particles) in a 2D form.

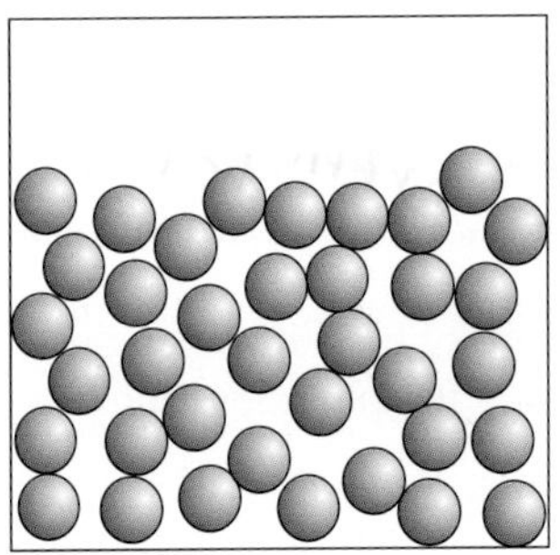

Figure 3: *Particle model of a liquid.*

Gases

In gases, the forces of attraction between the particles are very weak. The gas particles are free to move, and do so constantly with random motion. They travel in straight lines, until they collide with another particle or with the walls of the container. When a gas molecule hits the walls of the container, it exerts a pressure on the walls.

The particles are very far apart, so much so that most of a gas is actually empty space. Gases don't keep a definite shape or volume and will always fill any container. The hotter a gas gets, the faster the particles move and the harder and more frequently they hit the walls of the container. This causes the pressure of the gas to increase, or, if the container isn't sealed the volume of the gas will increase. For any given substance, in the gas state its particles will have more energy than in the solid state or the liquid state.

Tip: Gases will expand to fill any container they're in. This means that if they're in an unsealed flask they'll escape out into the atmosphere.

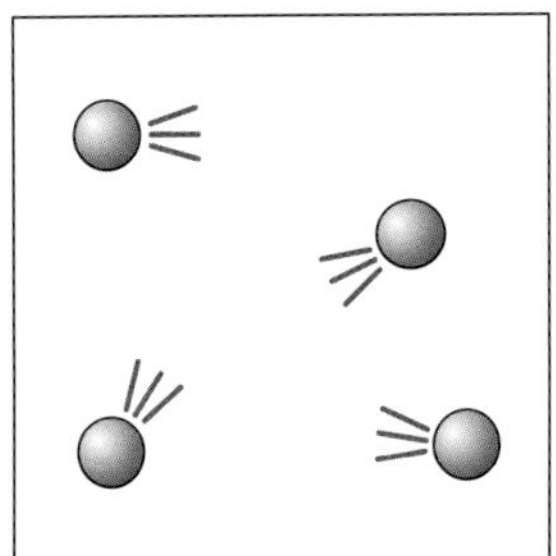

Figure 4: *Particle model of a gas.*

Practice Questions — Fact Recall

Q1 Name the three states of matter.

Q2 In which state(s) do substances have a:

a) definite volume?

b) definite shape?

Q3 Explain why a solid expands when it is heated.

Q4 Use the particle model to explain how the particles in a gas behave in a container.

Q5 Compare the energy of the particles in a substance in the solid state, liquid state and gas state.

Practice Question — Application

Q1 A scientist has a sample of solid menthol in a beaker. He gently heats the menthol, and it turns into a liquid. He notices that the liquid menthol has flowed to fill the bottom of the beaker, whereas when the menthol was solid it kept its shape.
Explain this difference, using ideas about the forces of attraction between particles.

2. Changes of State

Substances aren't stuck in one state forever. Heating them up or cooling them down changes them from one state to another.

Learning Objectives:

- Be able to recall the names used for the interconversions between the three states of matter, recognising that these are physical changes (contrasted with chemical reactions that result in chemical changes).
- Be able to explain the changes in arrangement, movement and energy of particles during the interconversions between the three states of matter.
- Be able to predict the physical state of a substance under specified conditions, given suitable data.

Specification References 2.2-2.4

What happens when a substance changes state?

Changes of state are **physical changes** — only the arrangement or the energy of the particles changes, not the particles themselves. Physical changes can often be undone by heating or cooling the substance.

From solid to liquid — melting

When a solid is heated, its particles gain energy and they vibrate more. This weakens the forces that hold the solid together and makes the solid expand. At a certain temperature, called the melting point, the particles have enough energy to break free from their positions. This change is called **melting** and the solid becomes a liquid.

From liquid to gas — boiling

When a liquid is heated, the particles get more energy. This energy makes them move faster, which weakens the attractive forces holding them together. At a certain temperature (known as the boiling point) the particles have enough energy to overcome the forces between them. This change is called **boiling** and the liquid becomes a gas.

Tip: Evaporation is also a change of state from liquid to gas. It can happen a long way below the boiling point though. The particles in a liquid have a variety of energies, so some at the surface can have enough energy from the surroundings to escape the pull of their neighbours.

From gas to liquid — condensing

As a gas cools, the particles no longer have enough energy to overcome the forces of attraction between them. Below a certain temperature, the forces between the gas particles are strong enough that the gas becomes a liquid. This change is called **condensing**.

From liquid to solid — freezing

When a liquid cools, there isn't enough energy to overcome the attractions between the particles, so the particles are less free to move. At the melting point, the forces between the particles become strong enough that the particles are held in place. The liquid becomes a solid. This change is called **freezing**.

Tip: The red arrows in Figure 2 show heat being added. The blue arrows show heat being given out.

Figure 1: *Ice melting to turn into liquid water.*

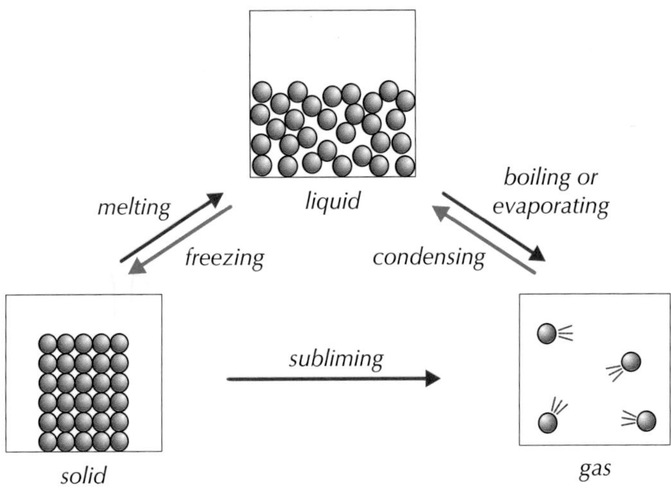

Figure 2: *Particle model showing changes of state.*

Chemical changes

Chemical changes are different to physical changes. Chemical changes happen during chemical reactions, when bonds between atoms break and the atoms change places. The atoms from the substances you start off with (the reactants) are rearranged to form different substances (the products). Compared to physical changes, chemical changes are often hard to reverse.

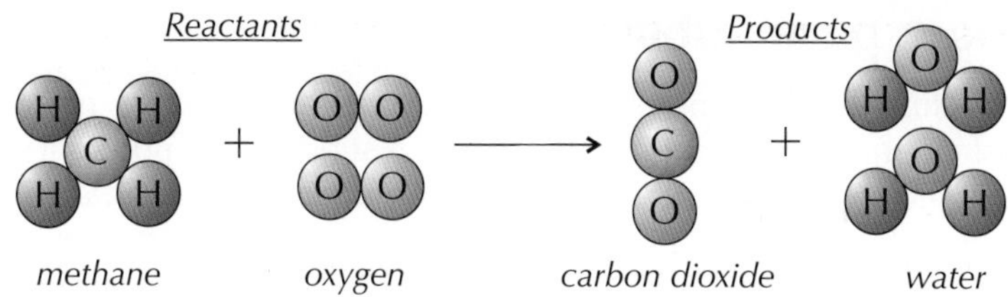

Figure 3: *Diagram showing the chemical reaction of methane with oxygen.*

Predicting the state of a substance

You might be asked to predict what state a substance is in at a certain temperature. If the temperature is below the melting point of substance, it'll be a solid. If it is above the boiling point, it'll be a gas. If it's in between the two points, then it's a liquid.

Example

Which of the substances in the table is a liquid at room temperature (25 °C)?

	melting point	boiling point
oxygen	–219 °C	–183 °C
nitrogen	–210 °C	–196 °C
bromine	–7 °C	59 °C

Oxygen and nitrogen have boiling points below 25 °C, so will both be gases at room temperature.

Bromine melts at –7 °C and boils at 59 °C.
So, it's a liquid at room temperature.

Tip: The melting and boiling points of a material are bulk properties. They depend on how lots of particles interact together. A single particle, such as an atom, doesn't have a melting or a boiling point.

Practice Questions — Fact Recall

Q1 What is it called when a substance changes from solid to liquid?

Q2 Use the particle model to describe the process of:

a) melting, b) condensing.

Practice Question — Application

Q1 Ethanol melts at –114 °C and boils at 78 °C.
Predict the state of ethanol at:

a) –150 °C, c) 0 °C,

b) 25 °C, d) 100 °C.

3. Purity

Purity is really important in chemistry. Chemists are always trying to find new ways to produce products which are as pure as possible, but it can be tricky.

Learning Objectives:

- Be able to explain the difference between the use of 'pure' in chemistry compared with its everyday use, and the differences in chemistry between a pure substance and a mixture.
- Be able to interpret melting point data to distinguish between pure substances which have a sharp melting point and mixtures which melt over a range of temperatures.

Specification References
2.5, 2.6

What is a pure substance?

In everyday life, the word 'pure' is often used to mean 'clean' or 'natural'. In chemistry, it has a more specific meaning. A substance is **pure** if it's completely made up of a single element or compound. If a substance contains more than one compound, or different elements that aren't all part of a single compound, then the substance is described as a **mixture**.

Example

Fresh air might be thought of as 'pure', but it's chemically impure. It's a mixture of nitrogen, oxygen, argon, carbon dioxide, water vapour and various other gases.

Lots of mixtures are really useful, but sometimes chemists need to obtain a pure sample of a substance.

Tip: There are lots of ways to extract a pure substance from a mixture. There's more about them on pages 102-105.

Testing for purity

A chemically pure substance will have a specific, sharp boiling or melting point. For example, pure ice melts at 0 °C, and pure water boils at 100 °C.

If a substance is a mixture then it will melt gradually over a range of temperatures. An impure substance will also melt over a range of temperatures. This is because impure substances are essentially mixtures of different elements or compounds.

This means you can test the purity of a sample by measuring its melting point, and comparing it with the melting point of the pure substance (which you can find from a data book). Here's how to do it:

- Measure the melting point of the sample using melting point apparatus (see Figure 1 on the next page).
- This apparatus allows you to heat up a small sample of a solid very slowly, so it is easy to see the exact temperature that the sample starts to melt at.
- If the melting point is the same as the expected melting point, then the substance is pure. If it's different, then it's a mixture.

Tip: A water bath and a thermometer can be used instead of melting point apparatus, but it is harder to control the temperature as exactly.

Example

**Adil's teacher gives him samples of four powdered solids, labelled A, B, C and D. He uses melting point apparatus to determine the melting point of each of the solids. Adil's results are shown in the table below.
Which of the four solids, A, B, C or D, was a mixture?**

Solid	A	B	C	D
Melting point (°C)	82	72-79	101	63

Adil's results show that solid B must be a mixture, because it melted over a range of temperatures (rather than melting at a specific temperature, as the other three solids did).

Figure 1: *Laboratory melting point apparatus.*

Practice Question — Fact Recall

Q1 Explain the difference between a pure substance and a mixture.

Practice Question — Application

Q1 A scientist has samples of three solids, labelled X, Y and Z. She grinds them to a powder, and uses melting point apparatus to measure their melting points. The results of her experiment are shown in the table below.

Solid	Melting point (°C)
X	115
Y	127-129
Z	65-73

a) Which of the solids, X, Y or Z, was pure? Explain your answer.

b) Suggest which of the solids was the most impure.
Give a reason for your answer.

4. Distillation

Distillation is used to separate mixtures that include a liquid. There are two kinds you need to know about — simple and fractional distillation.

Learning Objective:
- Be able to explain the experimental techniques for separation of mixtures by simple distillation and fractional distillation.

Specification Reference 2.7

Simple distillation

CORE PRACTICAL

Simple distillation is used to separate out a liquid from a mixture. It's used in industry to get pure water from sea water (see p.113). This is the method used in the lab:

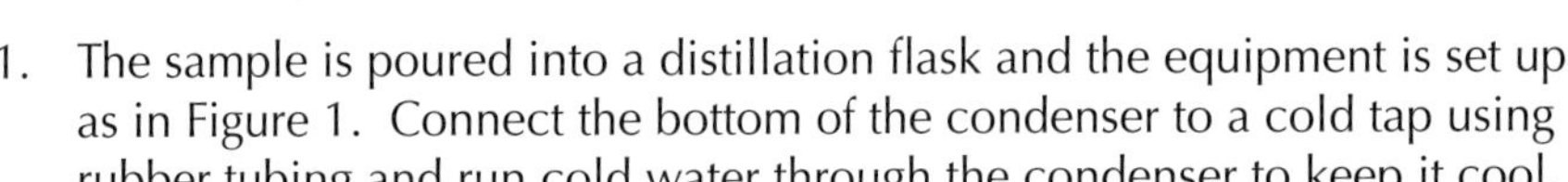

1. The sample is poured into a distillation flask and the equipment is set up as in Figure 1. Connect the bottom of the condenser to a cold tap using rubber tubing and run cold water through the condenser to keep it cool.
2. The distillation flask is gradually heated. The component of the mixture that has the lowest boiling point evaporates — in this case, it's water.
3. As the vapour rises it passes into the condenser, where it is cooled by the water, condenses (turns back into liquid) and is collected in a container below the condenser.
4. Components of the mixture with higher boiling points are left behind in the flask (like the salt).

Tip: If the liquid you're heating is flammable, use an electric heater or a water bath to heat it, rather than a Bunsen burner.

Tip: Make sure that the water goes in at the bottom of the condenser and out at the top so that the condenser fills fully.

Tip: You can use simple distillation to separate out the components of an ink (see page 111).

Tip: Remember to carry out a risk assessment before you do any experiment in the lab.

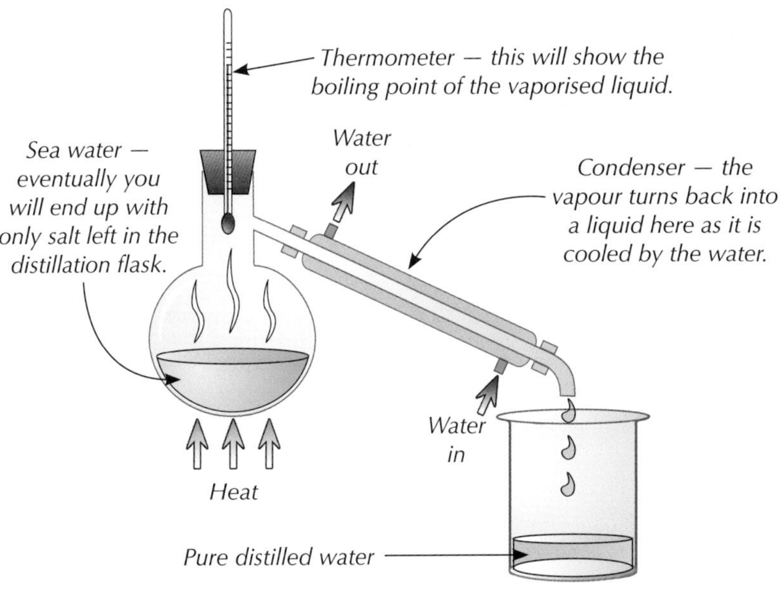

Figure 1: *The simple distillation of salt water.*

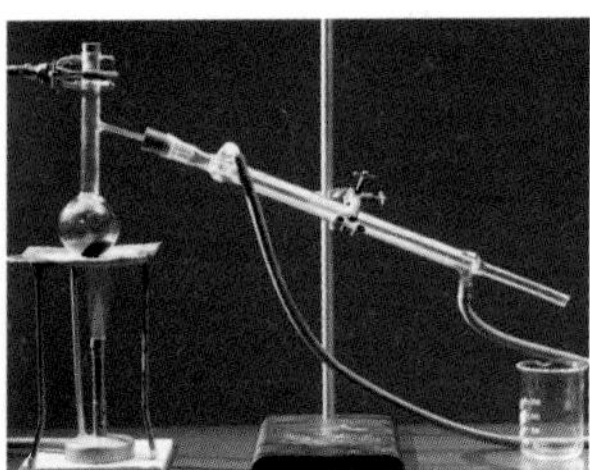

Figure 2: *Simple distillation apparatus being used to separate ink from water.*

Simple distillation can be used to separate substances with **boiling points** significantly apart from one another. But if the boiling points of the substances are close to each other simple distillation doesn't work. The temperature may rise above the boiling point of more than one of the substances, and they'll end up mixing again.

Fractional distillation

Fractional distillation can be used for separating a mixture of different liquids and is especially useful when the liquids have similar boiling points.

1. Figure 4 shows the set-up of equipment that you need. You place the mixture in a flask, attach a fractionating column and gradually heat it.
2. The different liquids will all have different boiling points — so they will evaporate at different temperatures.
3. The liquid with the lowest boiling point evaporates first. When the temperature on the thermometer matches the boiling point of this liquid, its vapour has reached the top of the column and passed into the condenser. It will then cool and condense and run out of the end. The pure liquid can then be collected.
4. Liquids with higher boiling points might also start to evaporate. But the column is cooler towards the top. So they will only get part of the way up before condensing and running back down towards the flask.
5. When the first liquid has been collected, you raise the temperature to the next lowest boiling point of the liquids in the mixture.

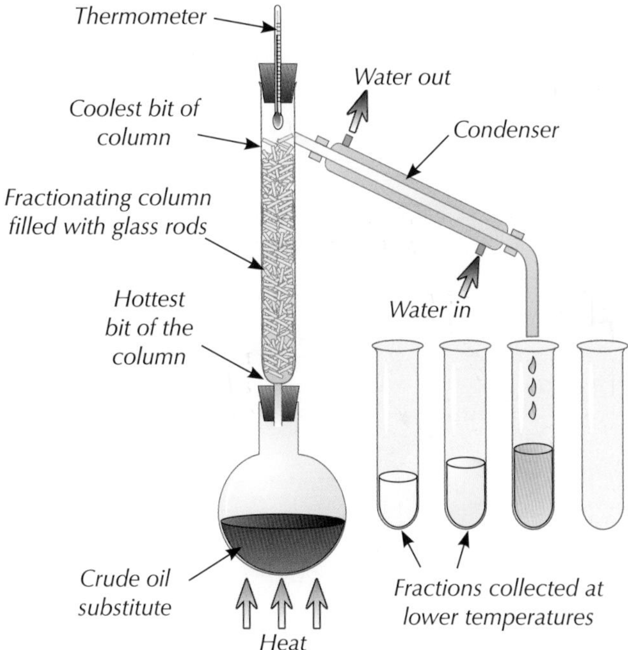

Figure 4: Fractional distillation of a crude oil substitute.

Tip: Although fractional distillation is a technique commonly used in industry to separate liquid mixtures, for example separating crude oil into different groups (see p.220-221), it is also used in the lab.

Figure 3: A fractionating column containing glass beads. The beads act as a surface for the vapour to condense on as it makes its way up the column.

Exam Tip
You need to be able to describe how to carry out simple distillation and fractional distillation and know when you would use each technique.

Practice Questions — Application

Q1 A student tries to separate a mixture of ethanol, boiling point 78 °C, and propanol, boiling point 97 °C, using simple distillation.

a) Suggest a reason why she was not successful.

b) Suggest another method of separation that would be successful.

Q2 A mixture contains methanol, ethanol and propanol. The boiling points of the components are 65 °C, 78 °C and 97 °C respectively. Describe a process that could be used to separate the mixture.

5. Filtration and Crystallisation

Learning Objective:

- Be able to explain the experimental techniques for separation of mixtures by filtration and crystallisation.

Specification Reference 2.7

Filtration and crystallisation are two more physical processes that are used to separate mixtures. They can be used to separate solids from liquids.

Separating an insoluble solid and a liquid

Filtration is often used if your desired product is an **insoluble** solid that needs to be separated from a liquid reaction mixture. It's also a useful technique for purification. For example, solid impurities in a reaction mixture can be removed using filtration. Here's how it's done:

1. Fold a piece of filter paper into a cone. You can do this by folding the paper in half and then in half again, and then gently separating one leaf of paper from the rest so that you've got a cone shape.
2. Place the filter paper point down into a filter funnel that's sitting in the neck of a container such as a conical flask — see Figure 2.
3. Pour the mixture containing the insoluble solid into the funnel lined by the filter paper. Make sure that none of the mixture goes over the top or down the side of the filter paper.
4. The liquid will pass through the filter paper but the solid won't — it will be left behind in the funnel.

Tip: An insoluble solid is one that can't be dissolved in the liquid.

Figure 1: *Filtering a copper sulfate ($CuSO_4$) solution to remove any undissolved copper sulfate crystals.*

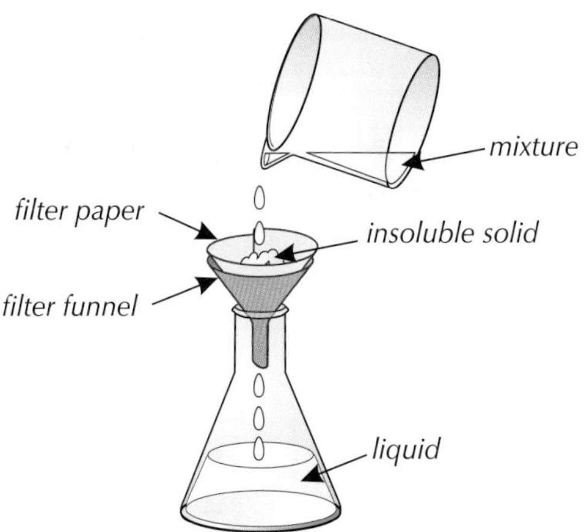

Figure 2: *Filtering out an insoluble solid from a mixture using filter paper and a filter funnel.*

Separating a soluble solid and a solution

If a solid can be dissolved it is said to be **soluble**. You can use **crystallisation** to separate a soluble product from a solution.

You can crystallise soluble solids using this method:

1. Place an evaporating dish on top of a tripod with a gauze mat. Place a Bunsen burner underneath the tripod (see Figure 3).
2. Pour the solution into the evaporating dish and gently heat it. Some of the water will evaporate and the solution will get more concentrated.
3. Once some of the water has evaporated, or when you see crystals start to form (the point of crystallisation), remove the dish from the heat and leave the solution to cool.
4. The dissolved compound should start to form crystals as it becomes insoluble in the cold, highly concentrated solution.
5. Filter the crystals out of the solution, and leave them in a warm place to dry. You could also use a drying oven or a desiccator.

Tip: Make sure you use tongs to move very hot evaporating dishes.

Tip: The longer the solution is left to cool following heating, the larger the crystals will be.

Tip: A desiccator contains chemicals which remove water from surroundings.

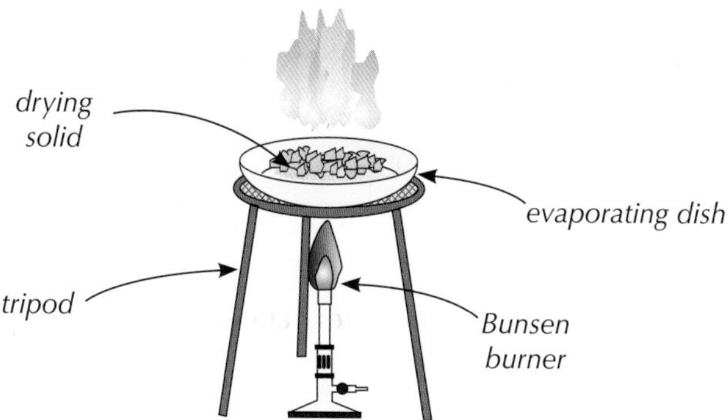

Figure 3: *Diagram of the apparatus required to carry out crystallisation.*

Figure 4: *Hydrated copper sulfate crystals can be obtained from an aqueous copper sulfate solution using crystallisation.*

Practice Questions — Fact Recall

Q1 Give one technique that can be used to separate an insoluble solid from a liquid.

Q2 What is the final stage in crystallisation?

Practice Questions — Application

Q1 Silver bromide is insoluble in water. A student needs to separate a mixture containing water and silver bromide. Describe a method to remove the silver bromide from water.

Q2 A student separated a mixture of lead bromide and sodium sulfate solution by filtration followed by crystallisation. Lead bromide is insoluble in water whereas sodium sulfate is soluble. Which component of the mixture was separated out at:

a) filtration?

b) crystallisation?

6. Choosing a Separation Method

Learning Objective:
- Be able to describe an appropriate experimental technique to separate a mixture, knowing the properties of the components of the mixture.

Specification Reference 2.8

The last few pages have covered a few different methods that you can use to separate mixtures. However, not all mixtures are the same — you've got to be able to choose a suitable separating method for a certain mixture.

Selecting an appropriate purification method

When choosing a technique to separate a mixture, the best technique to use will depend on the properties of the substances in the mixture.

Tip: Room temperature is often taken to be about 20 °C.

Example

A mixture is composed of two substances, X and Y. The table below shows some information about the properties of substances X and Y.

Substance	Melting point (°C)	Boiling point (°C)	State at room temperature
X	5	60	liquid
Y	745	1218	solid

Substance Y dissolves completely in substance X.
Suggest a purification method you could use to obtain:

a) A pure sample of substance X,

b) A pure sample of substance Y.

a) To get X on its own, you need to distil it from the solution. You can use simple distillation here — there's no need for fractional distillation as there's only one liquid in the solution. So, you could obtain a pure sample of substance X using simple distillation.

b) In theory, if you distilled the mixture until all of substance X had evaporated off, you'd end up with just substance Y left in the flask. But there might be traces of substance X still present — crystallisation is a better way of obtaining a pure sample of a solid from a solution. So, the most suitable method for obtaining a pure sample of substance Y would be crystallisation.

Exam Tip
You might have to pick one of the techniques covered in the last few pages to separate a mixture. Make sure you're comfortable with simple distillation (p.102), fractional distillation (p.103), filtration (p.104) and crystallisation (p.105).

Practice Question — Application

Q1 A student has a sample of magnesium carbonate and sodium chloride in water. Magnesium carbonate is insoluble in water, whilst sodium chloride is soluble. Suggest how the student could obtain a pure sample of sodium chloride from this mixture.

7. Paper Chromatography

Paper chromatography is often used in labs to separate a mixture.

How chromatography works

Chromatography is a method used to separate a mixture of soluble substances and identify them. There are many different types of chromatography — but they all have two 'phases':

- A **mobile phase**, where the molecules can move. The mobile phase is always a liquid or a gas.
- A **stationary phase**, where the molecules can't move. This can be a solid or a really thick liquid.

In chromatography, the mobile phase passes over the stationary phase. The components in the mixture separate out as the mobile phase moves over the stationary phase, which causes them to all end up in different places on the stationary phase. This happens because each of the chemicals in a mixture will spend different amounts of time dissolved in the mobile phase and stuck to the stationary phase. How fast a chemical moves over the stationary phase depends on how it 'distributes' itself between each of the two phases — the more time it spends in the mobile phase, the faster it will move.

Each component in a mixture produces a 'spot' on a chromatogram (see p.108).

How to carry out paper chromatography

CORE PRACTICAL

In paper chromatography, the stationary phase is a piece of filter paper, and the mobile phase is a liquid solvent (e.g. water or ethanol). It can be used to separate mixtures made up of liquids of different colours. An example of this is the use of paper chromatography to separate different dyes in an ink. Here's how you can do it:

1. Draw a line near the bottom of a sheet of filter paper. This is known as the baseline. (Use a pencil to do this — pencil marks are **insoluble** and won't move with the solvent.)
2. Spot the ink by placing a small amount on the line in a single place. Then put the sheet upright in a beaker of **solvent**, e.g. water. The solvent used depends on what's being tested. Some compounds dissolve well in water, but sometimes other solvents, like ethanol, are needed. Make sure the ink isn't touching the solvent initially — you don't want it to be washed away.
3. Place a watch glass on top of the beaker to stop the solvent evaporating.
4. The solvent will start to move up the paper. When the chemicals in the ink dissolve in the solvent, they will move up the paper too.
5. The different dyes in the ink will move up the paper at different rates, so the dyes will separate out and form spots in different places. If any of the dyes in the ink are insoluble (won't dissolve) in the solvent you've used, they'll stay on the baseline.

Learning Objectives:

- Be able to describe paper chromatography as the separation of mixtures of soluble substances by running a solvent (mobile phase) through the mixture on the paper (containing the stationary phase), which causes the substances to move at different rates over the paper.
- Be able to explain the experimental technique for separation of mixtures by paper chromatography.
- Be able to interpret a paper chromatogram to identify substances by calculation and use of R_f values, identify substances by comparisons with known substances and distinguish between pure and impure substances.

Specification References
2.7, 2.9, 2.10

Tip: Make sure to carry out a risk assessment before you try this practical.

Tip: 'Spot' or 'spotting' inks is just a technical term for placing a dot of the ink on the pencil line.

Tip: Make sure the level of solvent in the beaker is <u>below</u> the baseline before you place the sheet in the beaker. If there's too much solvent in the beaker, the separation won't work properly.

Tip: Sometimes, a solvent will start to evaporate off the paper before you have time to mark the solvent front with a pencil. To get around this, you could put a mark near the top of the paper before you place it in the beaker, and then take out the paper once the solvent has reached that mark.

6. The point the solvent has reached as it moves up the paper is known as the **solvent front**. When the solvent front has nearly reached the top of the paper, take the paper out of the beaker, draw a line with a pencil along the solvent front and leave to dry.

7. The end result is a pattern of spots called a **chromatogram**.

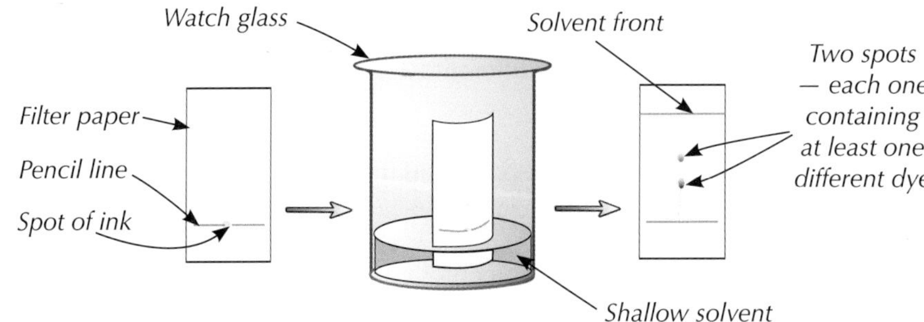

Figure 1: A diagram showing the stages of carrying out paper chromatography.

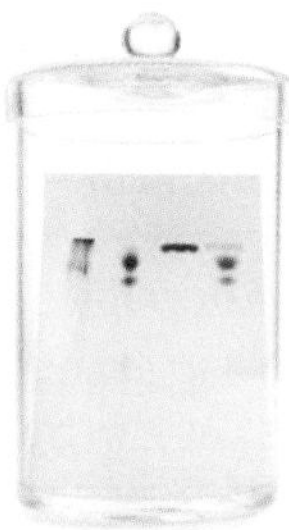

Figure 2: A finished chromatogram, showing the different dyes in 4 different samples of ink.

You can use chromatography to separate out more than one ink at a time. Figure 2 shows a chromatogram with four mixtures separated out. Follow the same steps as above, but instead of adding a spot of just one mixture to the pencil line, spot all the inks you want to separate in different places along the line. Make sure they're far enough apart that they won't run into each other.

Factors affecting the distance a compound moves

The amount of time the molecules spend in each phase (and therefore how far the molecules move up the paper) depends on:

1. How soluble they are in the solvent.
2. How attracted they are to the paper.

Molecules with a higher solubility in the solvent, and which are less attracted to the paper, will spend more time in the mobile phase — and they'll be carried further up the paper.

Tip: If any substances in a mixture are insoluble in one solvent, you could try re-running the experiment with the same mixture, but using a different solvent. You may find this separates out the components, allowing you to find their R_f values.

R_f values

The result of a chromatography experiment is called a chromatogram. Each substance on a chromatogram has an **R_f value**. This is the ratio between the distance travelled by the dissolved substance (the solute) and the distance travelled by the solvent (see Figure 3 on the next page). The further through the stationary phase a substance moves, the larger the R_f value. You can calculate R_f values using the formula:

$$R_f \text{ value} = \frac{\text{distance travelled by solute } (B)}{\text{distance travelled by solvent } (A)}$$

To find the distance travelled by the solute, measure from the baseline to the centre of the spot.

Tip: If you know that you have chemicals in your mixture that are colourless (e.g. amino acids), you might have to spray the chromatogram with a chemical called a locating agent to show where the spots are.

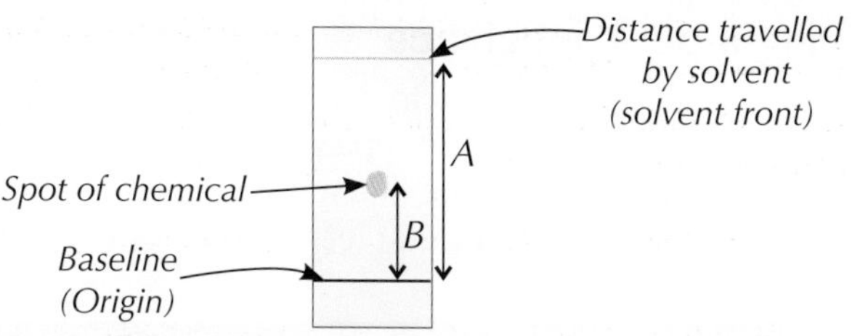

Figure 3: *A chromatogram for paper chromatography.*

Example

A finished chromatogram is shown below. The solvent travelled 7.0 cm up the paper and the substance travelled 2.8 cm.

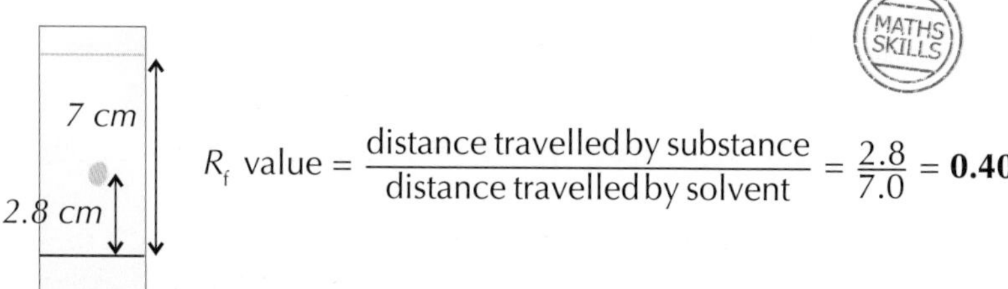

$$R_f \text{ value} = \frac{\text{distance travelled by substance}}{\text{distance travelled by solvent}} = \frac{2.8}{7.0} = \mathbf{0.40}$$

Tip: The chromatogram on the left only shows one spot, so it could be a mixture that hasn't separated in this solvent, or it could be a pure substance.

Interpreting paper chromatograms

Identifying a substance using a reference

Paper chromatography is often carried out to see if a certain substance is present in a mixture. To do this, you run a pure sample of that substance (a reference) alongside the unknown mixture. If the R_f values of the reference and one of the spots in the mixture match, the substance may be present.

Example

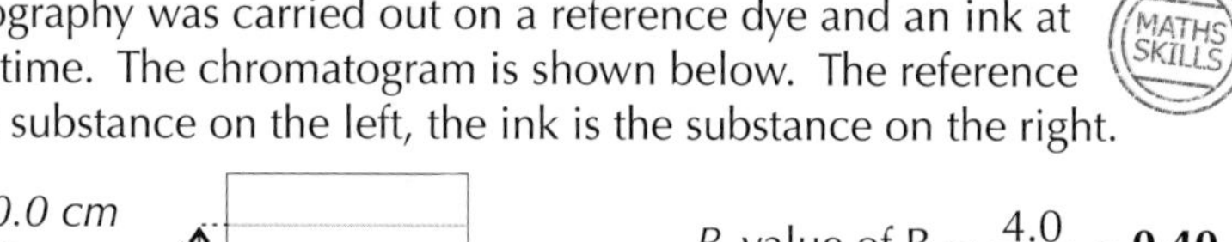

Chromatography was carried out on a reference dye and an ink at the same time. The chromatogram is shown below. The reference dye is the substance on the left, the ink is the substance on the right.

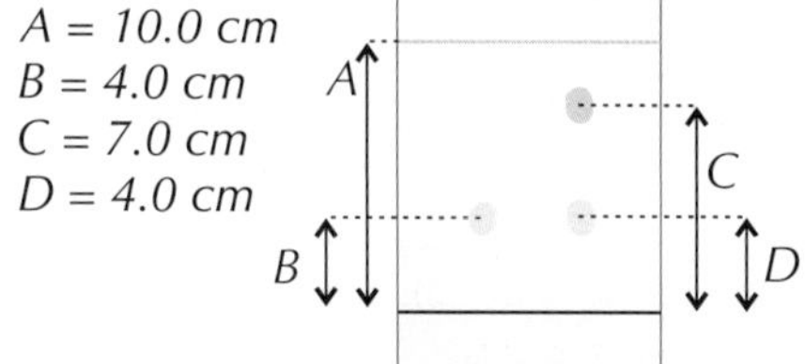

R_f value of B = $\frac{4.0}{10.0}$ = **0.40**

R_f value of C = $\frac{7.0}{10.0}$ = **0.70**

R_f value of D = $\frac{4.0}{10.0}$ = **0.40**

As the R_f values of B and D are the same, you can suggest that the reference dye may be in the ink. However, this isn't proof that B and D are the same substance, as other dyes may have the same R_f value in this solvent.

Tip: Chemists sometimes run samples of pure substances called standard reference materials (SRMs) next to a mixture to check the identities of its components. SRMs have controlled concentrations and purities.

If the R_f values match in one solvent, you can check to see if the chemicals are the same by repeating with a different solvent. If they match again, there's a greater chance that they're the same.

Identifying a pure substance

You can also use chromatography to determine whether a substance is pure or not. A pure substance won't be separated by chromatography — it'll move as one spot. An impure substance (i.e. a mixture) will separate out during chromatography, and will produce at least two spots.

Practice Questions — Fact Recall

Q1 In chromatography, what's the name of the phase which can't move?

Q2 During paper chromatography, why must you make sure the ink spot doesn't touch the solvent when you place the filter paper into the solvent?

Q3 Why do you place a lid on top of the container whilst carrying out paper chromatography?

Q4 What is the pattern of spots produced by paper chromatography known as?

Q5 Give the equation used to calculate R_f values.

Practice Questions — Application

Q1 On a chromatogram, a solvent travelled 12.3 cm and a substance travelled 6.9 cm. Calculate the R_f value of the substance.

Q2 A red spot and a blue spot are on a chromatogram. The R_f value of the red substance is 0.77, the blue substance has an R_f value of 0.52.

a) Which substance has travelled furthest up the chromatogram?

b) Which substance spent the most time in the mobile phase?

Q3 A student used paper chromatography to analyse a substance in 5 different solvents. In each solvent only one spot appeared. The R_f value of the spot was different in each solvent.

a) Make a prediction about the purity of this substance.

b) Suggest why the R_f value of the spots were different.

Q4 A student analysed a chromatogram of a mixture containing three substances. A red spot was 3.5 cm from the baseline, a purple spot was 4.7 cm from the baseline and a yellow spot had travelled 5.3 cm. The solvent had travelled 8.3 cm.

a) Calculate the R_f values of the red, purple and yellow substances.

b) The student thinks that the purple substance is methyl violet. Suggest how she could investigate whether she is correct.

Exam Tip

R_f values are <u>always</u> less than 1. So if you get an answer that's greater than 1 you need to go back and do the calculation again — you'll have made a mistake somewhere.

8. Analysing the Composition of Inks

Separating techniques are useful on their own, but they can be combined to investigate and separate mixtures.

Learning Objective:

- Be able to investigate the composition of inks using simple distillation and paper chromatography (Core Practical).

Specification Reference 2.11

Analysing a mixture using a combination of separation techniques

Sometimes mixtures are complicated enough that you need to use more than one technique to separate them. For example, a mixture of simple distillation and chromatography can be used to analyse the composition of an ink.

Analysing the solvent using simple distillation

Ink is a mixture of different dyes dissolved in a solvent. You could use a simple distillation to work out what solvent the ink contains. Simple distillation allows you to evaporate off the solvent and collect it (assuming that the solvent has the lowest boiling point of all the substances in the ink, and will evaporate first).

The thermometer in the distillation set-up will read the boiling point of the solvent when it's evaporating (and therefore when it's being collected). You can use the boiling point of the solvent to try to determine what it is by comparing it to the boiling points of common solvents. For example, if the solvent in a certain ink evaporated at 100 °C, it would be quite likely to be water.

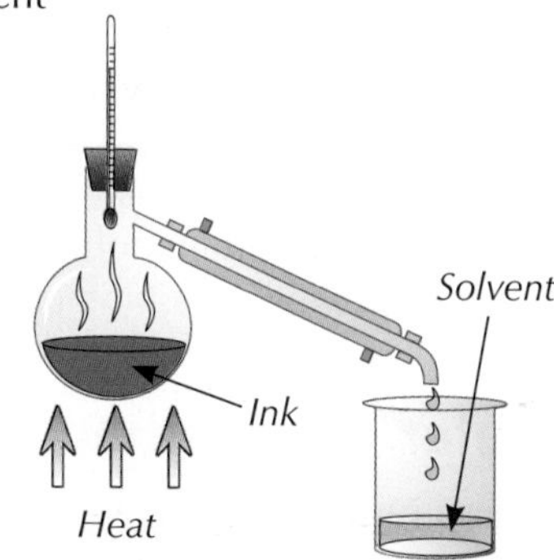

Figure 1: *The simple distillation of an ink.*

Tip: For full details on how to run distillation and chromatography experiments, look back at pages 102 and 107.

Tip: Be sure to carry out a full risk assessment before you try any of this practical work in class.

Analysing the dyes using paper chromatography

After evaporating off the solvent, you could then carry out paper chromatography on a sample of the ink — this will separate out the different dyes in the ink, so that you can see how many there are.

You can compare the R_f values of the different spots on the chromatogram produced with reference values (or run further chromatography experiments with pure substances) to work out what dyes are in the ink.

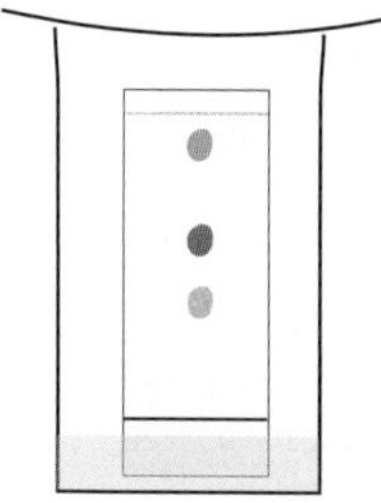

Figure 2: *Separation of the dyes in an ink on a chromatogram.*

Practice Question — Application

Q1 A student is investigating the composition of an ink using simple distillation and paper chromatography. Describe how the results of these experiments could be used to identify the solvent and dyes present in the ink.

9. Water Treatment

Water has to be treated before it can be made potable (safe to drink). How water is treated depends upon where you live...

Learning Objectives:

- Be able to describe how waste and ground water can be made potable, including the need for sedimentation, filtration and chlorination.
- Be able to describe how sea water can be made potable by using distillation.
- Be able to describe why water used in analysis must not contain any dissolved salts.

Specification Reference 2.12

Sources of water

In the UK, there are a number of sources of water which can be purified to provide us with **potable water** (water that is fit to drink). The main sources of water in the UK are:

- **Surface water**: from lakes, rivers and reservoirs. In much of England and Wales, these sources start to run dry during the summer months.
- **Ground water**: from aquifers (rocks that trap water underground). In parts of south-east England, where surface water is very limited, as much as 70% of the domestic water supply comes from ground water.
- **Waste water**: from water that's been contaminated by a human process, e.g. as a by-product from some industrial processes. Treating waste water is often better for the environment than simply disposing of it, as waste water can contain pollutants. How easy waste water is to treat depends on the levels of contaminants in it.

Water purification

Water from some sources is dirtier than from others, and so requires a lot more treatment to make it drinkable. Ground water from aquifers is normally quite clean, but waste water and surface water need far more treatment.

Tip: Water is purified in special facilities called water treatment plants.

The process of purification

No matter the source, all water has to go through a basic process of purification to make it potable. This process includes:

1. Filtration — a wire mesh screens out large twigs, etc., and then gravel and sand beds filter out any solid bits.
2. Sedimentation — iron sulfate or aluminium sulfate is added to the water, which makes fine particles clump together and settle at the bottom.
3. Chlorination — chlorine gas is bubbled through to kill harmful bacteria and other microbes.

Tip: Some soluble impurities that are dissolved in the water are not removed as they can't be filtered out — these include the minerals which cause water hardness.

Figure 1: *Sedimentation tanks at a water treatment plant.*

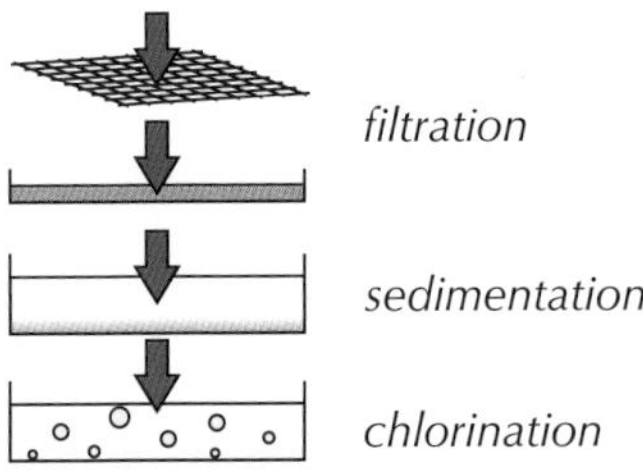

Figure 2: *A diagram showing the main steps of water treatment.*

Distilling sea water

In some dry countries, e.g. Kuwait, there's not enough surface water or ground water, so instead sea water must be distilled to provide potable water. The sea water is boiled to produce steam, which is then condensed — this separates the water from the dissolved salts.

Distillation requires a lot of energy, so it's really expensive, especially if it's used to produce large quantities of fresh water. Countries don't tend to use this if there are other sources of water available.

Tip: Have a look back at page 102 for more on how sea water can be distilled in the lab.

Deionised water

A lot of analytical chemistry involves carrying out experiments to work out what something is, or how a substance will react. For experiments that involve mixing or dissolving something in water, you should use something called deionised water.

Deionised water is water that has had the ions (such as calcium, iron and copper ions) that are present in normal tap water removed. These ions, although present in small amounts and harmless in tap water, can interfere with reactions. So using normal water could give your experiment a false result.

Practice Questions — Fact Recall

Q1 What is potable water?

Q2 Describe the source of ground water in the UK.

Q3 What is waste water?

Q4 Describe the sedimentation step of water purification.

Q5 What is meant by the term 'deionised water'?

Practice Question — Application

Q1 Describe the technique used to produce potable water from sea water.

Topic 2 Checklist — Make sure you know...

States of Matter

- [ ] That the three states of matter are solid, liquid and gas.
- [ ] That particles in solids don't have much energy and are held together in fixed positions by strong forces of attraction.
- [ ] That particles in liquids have more energy than those in solids, so can move past each other (but normally stick close together in a random arrangement).
- [ ] That the forces of attraction between particles in a liquid are weaker than those in a solid.
- [ ] That particles in gases have more energy than those in liquids.
- [ ] That the forces of attraction between particles in a gas are very weak, so the gas particles are free to move constantly in random motion.

Changes of State

- [ ] That changes of state are physical changes, so can be undone by heating or cooling a substance.
- [ ] The names used for the changes of state that occur between solids, liquids and gases.
- [ ] How the arrangement, movement and energy of particles in a substance change when that substance changes state.
- [ ] That chemical changes result in bonds breaking between atoms and atoms changing places, so they are difficult to reverse.
- [ ] How to predict which state of matter a substance is in, under given conditions.

Purity

- [ ] That in chemistry, a pure substance is completely made up of only one element or compound.
- [ ] That in chemistry, a mixture is a substance that contains more than one compound, or different elements that don't make up a single compound.
- [ ] That a pure substance melts at a specific temperature, whilst a mixture melts over a range of temperatures.

Distillation

- [ ] That simple distillation is used to separate a liquid from a mixture where the components have large differences in boiling points.
- [ ] That fractional distillation is used to separate a mixture of different liquids, and is useful when the liquids have similar boiling points.
- [ ] How to carry out simple and fractional distillation.

cont...

Filtration and Crystallisation

- [ ] That filtration is used to separate an insoluble solid from a liquid.
- [ ] That crystallisation is used to separate a soluble solid from a solution.
- [ ] How to carry out filtration and crystallisation.

Choosing a Separation Method

- [ ] That a suitable separation method depends on the properties of the substances in a mixture.
- [ ] How to select an appropriate method to separate a given mixture.

Paper Chromatography

- [ ] That chromatography can be used to separate and identify soluble substances from a mixture.
- [ ] That the stationary phase is a solid or a very thick liquid where the molecules can't move.
- [ ] That the mobile phase is a liquid or a gas that carries the molecules over the stationary phase.
- [ ] That the rate a substance moves over the paper depends on how long it spends in the mobile or stationary phase.
- [ ] How to carry out paper chromatography.
- [ ] That the R_f value is the ratio between the distance that a solute travels and the distance travelled by the solvent.
- [ ] How to calculate the R_f value of a spot on a chromatogram.
- [ ] That R_f values can be used to analyse the components of a mixture by comparison with the R_f values of known compounds.
- [ ] That a pure substance can't be separated out by chromatography so will only produce one spot.

Analysing the Composition of Inks

- [ ] How to use simple distillation and chromatography to investigate the composition of an ink (Core Practical).

Water Treatment

- [ ] That potable water has been treated to make it safe to drink.
- [ ] How ground water and waste water can be purified using a process of filtration, sedimentation and chlorination.
- [ ] How sea water can be purified through a process of distillation.
- [ ] That water used in analysis must be deionised, as the dissolved ions in normal water could affect the results of an experiment or procedure.

Exam-style Questions

1 A substance in two different states is represented in Figure 1 using the particle model.

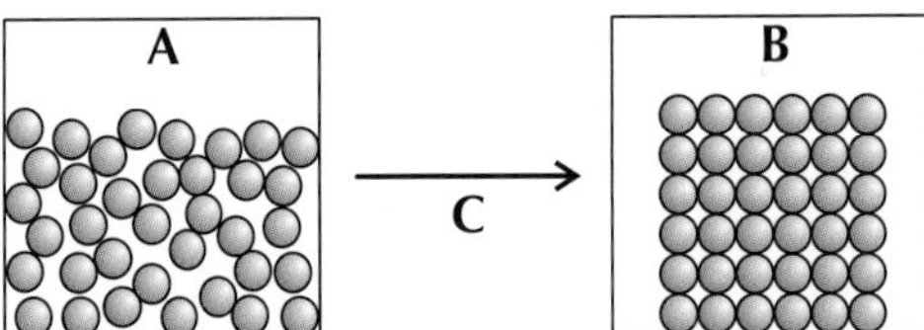

Figure 1

(a) Which states are represented in boxes **A** and **B** of Figure 1?

(2 marks)

(b) Name the change of state represented by arrow **C** in Figure 1 and describe the changes that occur within the substance during it.

(3 marks)

(c) A change of state is a physical change. Describe the difference between a physical change and a chemical change.

(2 marks)

(d) The substance has a melting point of -31 °C and a boiling point of 156 °C. Which state will the substance be in at -123 °C?

(1 mark)

2 A chemist carried out paper chromatography on a sample of a reaction mixture following completion of the reaction. The chromatogram is shown in Figure 2.

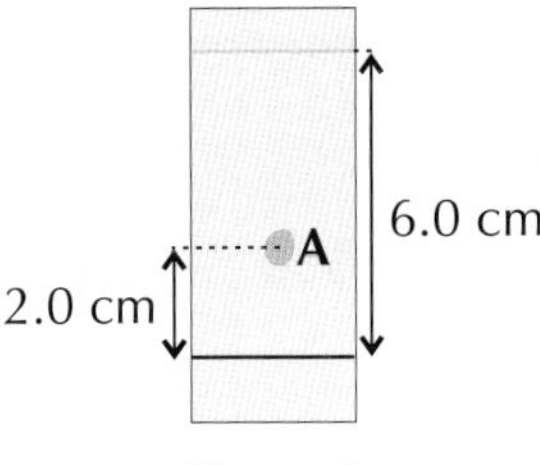

Figure 2

(a) Calculate the R_f value for the spot, A.

(1 mark)

(b) Give **one** factor that affects the distance a compound moves in chromatography.

(1 mark)

(c) Describe how a standard reference material could be used to identify the substance that corresponds to the spot, A.

(2 marks)

3 A student is using crystallisation to obtain hydrated copper sulfate crystals from a solution of copper sulfate. She gently heats copper sulfate solution in an evaporating dish using a Bunsen burner. After some of the water has evaporated, the student turns off the Bunsen burner and leaves the solution to cool before filtering it.

(a) Explain why the student leaves the solution to cool before filtration.

(1 mark)

(b) Give **one** example of a piece of equipment that the student could use to dry the copper sulfate crystals.

(1 mark)

4 A student wants to investigate the components that make up an ink.
Using the equipment in Figure 3, she carries out a simple distillation on the ink.

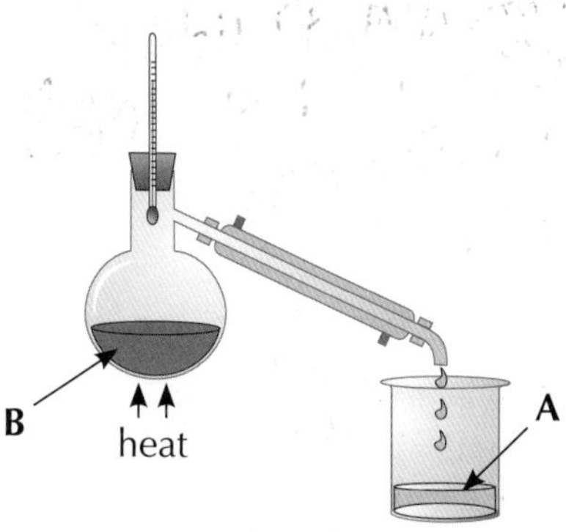

Figure 3

(a) Name the component of the ink labelled **A** in Figure 3.

(1 mark)

(b) Which liquid has a lower boiling point, **A** or **B**?
Give a reason for your answer.

(1 mark)

(c) Suggest a method that the student could use to separate and analyse the mixture **B**.

(1 mark)

5 This question is on potable water and water treatment.

(a) Fresh water is sourced from ground water or is in lakes and rivers.
Describe the steps required to produce potable water from fresh water.

(3 marks)

(b) In certain countries such as Singapore where fresh water is scarce, treated waste water can be recycled as potable water. Suggest one other possible method of producing water in countries without enough fresh water.

(1 mark)

Learning Objectives:
- Know that a neutral solution has a pH of 7, and that acidic solutions have lower pH values and alkaline solutions have higher pH values.
- Know that acids in solution are sources of hydrogen ions.
- Know that a base is any substance that reacts with an acid to form a salt and water only.
- Know that alkalis are soluble bases.
- Know that alkalis in solution are sources of hydroxide ions.
- H Know that the higher the concentration of hydrogen ions in an acidic solution, the lower the pH.
- H Know that the higher the concentration of hydroxide ions in an alkaline solution, the higher the pH.
- Be able to describe the effects of acids and alkalis on indicators (including litmus, methyl orange and phenolphthalein).

Specification References
3.1-3.4, 3.9, 3.10

1. Acids and Bases

Solutions can be classed as acidic, alkaline or neutral depending on their pH. How acidic or basic a solution is can tell you a lot about its chemistry.

The pH scale

pH is a measure of how acidic or alkaline a solution is. The **pH scale** goes from 0 to 14 (see Figure 1).

- Anything that forms a solution with a pH of less than 7 is an **acid**. The lower the pH, the more acidic the solution.
- Anything that forms a solution with a pH of greater than 7 is an **alkali**. The higher the pH, the more alkaline the substance is.
- **Neutral substances** are neither acidic nor alkaline and have a pH of exactly 7. Pure water is an example of a neutral substance.

Acids and bases in solution

When a substance is dissolved in water, the pH of the solution depends on the type of ions that are released by the substance. Acids release hydrogen ions (H^+) when they are in an aqueous solution. A **base** is a substance that reacts with an acid to produce a salt and water. An alkali is a base that is soluble in water. Alkalis form OH^- ions (otherwise known as hydroxide ions) in water.

Concentrations of ions Higher

The higher the concentration of hydrogen ions in a solution, the more acidic it is, so the lower its pH will be. So, as the concentration of hydrogen ions increases, the pH decreases. In alkaline solutions, the higher the concentration of OH^- ions, the higher the pH.

Measuring the pH of a solution

You can measure the pH of a solution using an **indicator**. An indicator is a dye that changes colour depending on whether it's above or below a certain pH.

Indicators are simple to use — add a few drops to the solution you're testing, then compare the colour the solution goes to a pH chart for that indicator. For example, **Universal indicator** gives the colours shown in Figure 1.

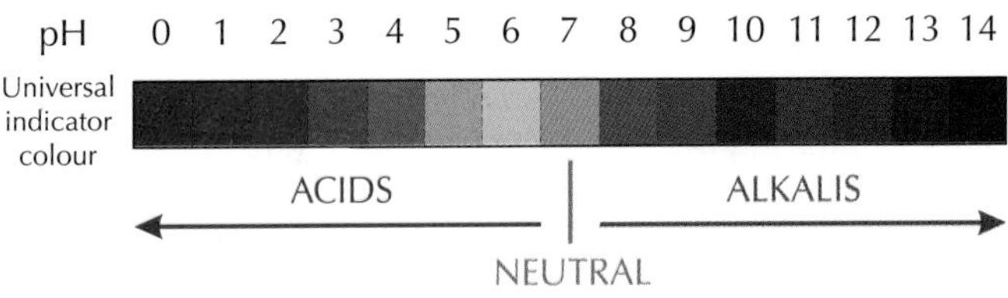

Figure 1: *The colour of Universal indicator at different pHs.*

Tip: You could also measure the pH of a solution using a pH probe (see p.245).

There are three indicators that you need to know the colour changes of — **litmus**, **methyl orange** and **phenolphthalein**. Figure 2 shows the colour that each indicator changes in certain solutions.

Indicator	Acidic Solutions	Neutral Solutions	Alkaline Solutions
litmus	red	purple	blue
methyl orange	red	yellow	yellow
phenolphthalein	colourless	colourless	pink

Figure 2: *The colour changes that occur when a few drops of litmus, methyl orange and phenolphthalein are added to acidic, neutral and alkaline solutions.*

Tip: You don't need to add a lot of indicator when testing solutions, three or four drops is more than enough.

Figure 3: *Phenolphthalein in acid (far left) and alkali (2nd from left). Methyl orange in acid (2nd from right) and alkali (far right).*

Practice Questions — Fact Recall

Q1 What is pH a measure of?

Q2 If a solution is neutral, what pH will it have?

Q3 What range of pHs show that a substance is an alkali?

Q4 What type of ions are released when an acid dissolves in water?

Q5 a) What type of ions are released when an alkali dissolves in water?

b) Describe the relationship between the concentration of these ions and the pH of a solution.

Practice Questions — Application

Q1 State whether the following solutions are acidic or alkaline.

a) A solution of hydrogen sulfide with a pH of 4.2.

b) A solution of calcium hydroxide with a pH of 12.4.

Q2 a) After adding litmus to a colourless solution, the colour changes to red. Suggest the pH of this solution.

b) Another solution has a pH of 9. Suggest what colour this solution will go if litmus is added to it.

Q3 The base lithium hydroxide reacts with hydrochloric acid. A salt is formed. What is the other product of this reaction?

Tip: Remember that acidic solutions have a pH less than 7 and alkaline solutions have a pH greater than 7.

Learning Objectives:

- Be able to describe a neutralisation reaction as a reaction between an acid and a base.
- Know that an acid-alkali neutralisation is a reaction in which hydrogen ions (H^+) from the acid react with hydroxide ions (OH^-) from the alkali to form water.
- Be able to describe and carry out an experiment to investigate the change in pH on adding powdered calcium hydroxide or calcium oxide to a fixed volume of dilute hydrochloric acid (Core Practical).

Specification References 3.6, 3.13, 3.14

Figure 1: Universal indicator turning green at the end of a neutralisation reaction.

Tip: You should always complete a risk assessment before you do an experiment in class.

WORKING SCIENTIFICALLY

Tip: You can do this experiment with calcium hydroxide too.

2. Neutralisation Reactions

Acids react with bases in neutralisation reactions. You need to know what happens in these reactions and how to investigate them...

What are neutralisation reactions?

An acid will react with a base to form a salt and water — this is called a **neutralisation** reaction. The general equation for a neutralisation reaction is shown below.

acid + base → salt + water

Neutralisation reactions between acids and bases can also be shown as an ionic equation (see p.26) in terms of H^+ and OH^- ions. During neutralisation reactions, hydrogen ions (H^+) from the acid react with hydroxide ions (OH^-) from the base to produce water. The equation for this reaction is:

$$H^+_{(aq)} + OH^-_{(aq)} \rightarrow H_2O_{(l)}$$

When an acid neutralises a base (or vice versa), the solution that's formed is neutral — it has a pH of 7. At pH 7, the concentration of hydrogen ions is equal to the concentration of hydroxide ions. An indicator can be used to show that a neutralisation reaction is over.

Example

Universal Indicator turns green at the end of a neutralisation reaction — see Figure 1. This shows that the solution has become neutral (and therefore that the reaction has finished).

Investigating neutralisation reactions

CORE PRACTICAL

You've got to know how to investigate how the pH of a solution of dilute hydrochloric acid changes on addition of calcium oxide. Calcium oxide is a base. It reacts with hydrochloric acid to give calcium chloride (a salt) and water. The equation for the reaction is:

$$2HCl + CaO \rightarrow CaCl_2 + H_2O$$

Here's how you'd carry out this experiment:

1. Measure out 150 cm^3 of dilute hydrochloric acid into a conical flask. Use a pipette or a measuring cylinder for this (see p.243-244).
2. Measure out 0.5 g of calcium oxide using a mass balance.
3. Carefully add the calcium oxide to the hydrochloric acid.
4. Wait for the base to completely react, then record the pH of the solution, using either a pH probe (see page 245) or Universal indicator paper. (You can use a glass rod to spot samples of the solution onto the paper).

5. Repeat steps 2 to 4 until all the acid has reacted. You'll know you've reached this point when unreacted calcium oxide starts to collect at the bottom of the flask.
6. You can then plot a graph to see how pH changes with the mass of base added (see Figure 3).

Figure 2: *Calcium oxide is a white solid.*

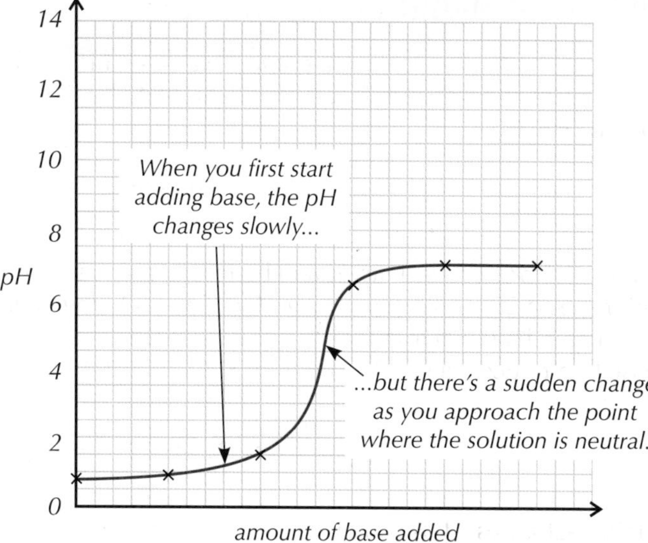

Figure 3: *Graph showing how pH changes during the neutralisation reaction of dilute hydrochloric acid with calcium oxide.*

Tip: In this reaction, the hydrochloric acid is neutralised by the calcium oxide.

Practice Questions — Fact Recall

Q1 State the products that are formed during a neutralisation reaction.

Q2 Write an equation to show the reaction of a hydrogen ion with a hydroxide ion. Include state symbols in your answer.

Practice Question — Application

Q1 A student is investigating the reaction between dilute hydrochloric acid and calcium hydroxide. She adds some calcium hydroxide to a beaker containing dilute hydrochloric acid. A reaction occurs. One of the products of the reaction is calcium chloride.

a) Write a word equation for the reaction that takes place.

b) The student records the pH of the solution, before adding more calcium hydroxide. She repeats these steps until the reaction finishes.

i) How could the student tell that the reaction has finished?

ii) Give one way that the student could measure the pH of the solution.

iii) Sketch a graph showing how you would expect the pH of the solution to change with the amount of base added.

Learning Objectives:

- H Be able to explain the terms weak and strong acids, with respect to the degree of dissociation into ions.
- H Be able to explain the terms dilute and concentrated, with respect to amount of substances in solution.
- H Know that as hydrogen ion concentration in a solution increases by a factor of 10, the pH of the solution decreases by 1.

Specification References
3.5, 3.7, 3.8

3. Strong and Weak Acids

Not all acids are created equal, some like to give up more of their H^+ ions in water than others — some are strong, some are weak.

Dissociation of acids

When acids are added to an aqueous solution they ionise (or dissociate) to produce H^+ ions and another type of ion (which is negatively charged).

Example — Higher

Hydrogen chloride dissolves in water to form hydrogen ions and chloride ions:

$$HCl_{(g)} \rightarrow H^+_{(aq)} + Cl^-_{(aq)}$$

Acid strength

The strength of an acid tells you about the proportion of acid particles that will dissociate to produce H^+ ions in solution.

Strong acids

Strong acids, such as sulfuric (H_2SO_4), hydrochloric (HCl) and nitric acid (HNO_3), ionise almost completely in water — most of the acid particles dissociate to release H^+ ions. Strong acids tend to have low pHs (pH 0-2).

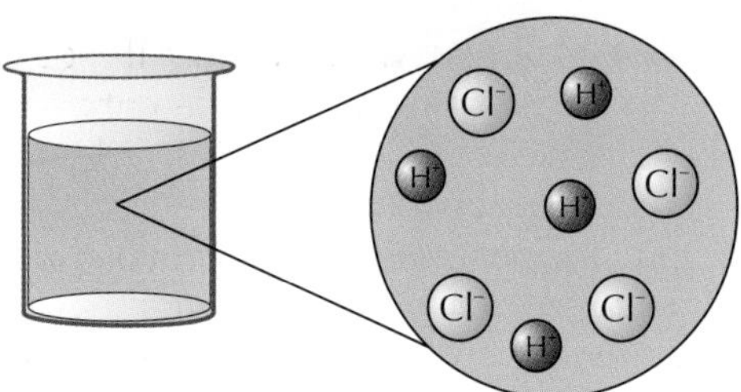

Figure 1: *Hydrochloric acid dissociates completely in water.*

Tip: H Acids don't produce hydrogen ions until they meet water. So, for example, hydrogen chloride gas isn't acidic.

Examples — Higher

Nitric acid ionises completely in water to form hydrogen ions and nitrate ions:

$$HNO_{3(l)} \rightarrow H^+_{(aq)} + NO_3^-{}_{(aq)}$$

Sulfuric acid also ionises completely but releases two hydrogen ions for every molecule of sulfuric acid:

$$H_2SO_{4(l)} \rightarrow 2H^+_{(aq)} + SO_4^{2-}{}_{(aq)}$$

Weak acids

Weak acids only partially ionise in water — if you put a sample of a weak acid in water, only some of the acid molecules will ionise and release H^+ ions. Carboxylic acids are weak acids (they don't ionise completely when dissolved in water) as are citric and carbonic acids. Weak acids tend to have pHs around 2-6.

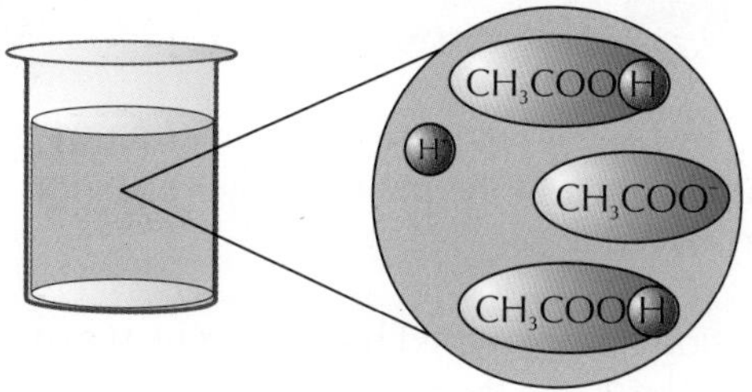

Figure 2: *Ethanoic acid dissociates partially in water.*

Ionisation of a weak acid is a reversible reaction, which sets up an equilibrium between the undissociated and dissociated acid. Since only a few of the acid particles release H^+ ions, the position of equilibrium lies well to the left.

Examples — Higher

Ethanoic acid does not fully ionise in water, creating an equilibrium:

$$CH_3COOH_{(aq)} \rightleftharpoons H^+_{(aq)} + CH_3COO^-_{(aq)}$$

Carbonic acid also only partially ionises in water:

$$H_2CO_{3(aq)} \rightleftharpoons 2H^+_{(aq)} + CO_3^{2-}{}_{(aq)}$$

Tip: In a reversible reaction, the products are able to react together to form the reactants again. The symbol '$\rightleftharpoons$' is used in place of a normal reaction arrow for reversible reactions to show that the reaction can go both ways. For more on this, have a look at page 169.

Tip: If the equilibrium is to the left there are more reactants than products.

Strong acids vs concentrated acids

Acid strength (i.e. if an acid is strong or weak) tells you what proportion of the acid molecules ionise in water. This is different to the **concentration** of an acid, which measures how much acid there is in a litre (1 dm^3) of water.

An acid with a large number of acid molecules compared to the volume of water is said to be concentrated. An acid with a small number of acid molecules compared to the volume of water is said to be dilute. Note that concentration describes the total number of dissolved acid molecules — not the number of acid molecules that produce hydrogen ions.

The more grams (or moles) of acid per dm^3, the more concentrated the acid is. So you can have a dilute strong acid, or a concentrated weak acid.

Tip: H Concentration is basically how watered down an acid is. If an acid is dilute, then it's been watered down a lot.

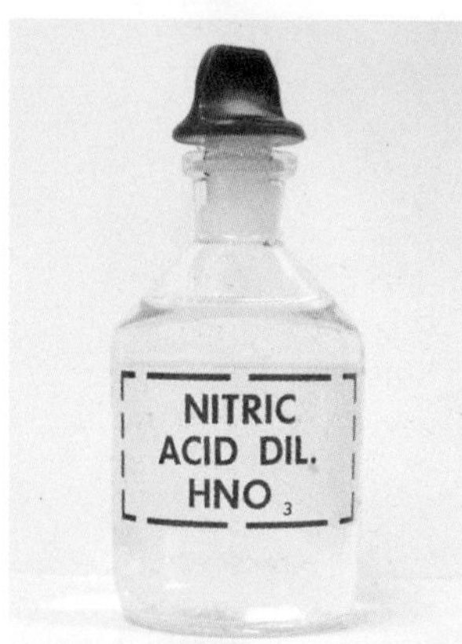

Figure 3: *A bottle of dilute nitric acid (a strong acid).*

Concentration and pH

The pH of an acid is dependent on the acid's concentration — increasing the concentration of H^+ ions leads to a decrease in the pH. If the concentration of H^+ ions increases by a factor of 10, the pH decreases by 1. So if the H^+ ion concentration increases by a factor of 100 (= 10 × 10), the pH decreases by 2 (= 1 + 1), and so on.

Decreasing the H^+ ion concentration has the opposite effect — a decrease by a factor of 10 in the H^+ concentration means an increase of 1 on the pH scale.

Tip: H Concentration is measured in g dm^{-3} or mol dm^{-3}.

Exam Tip H
You can check your answer by making sure that, if the pH has decreased, then the concentration of H^+ ions has increased.

Example 1 **Higher**

A solution with a hydrogen ion concentration of 0.001 mol dm^{-3} has a pH of 3. What would happen to the pH if the hydrogen ion concentration was increased to 0.01 mol dm^{-3}?

The H^+ concentration has increased by a factor of 10, so the pH would decrease by 1. So the new pH would be 3 – 1 = 2.

Tip: H Due to this relationship between concentration and pH, an acid with a pH of 2 is 100 times more concentrated than an acid with a pH of 4 (not 2 times more concentrated, as the numbers might suggest).

Example 2 **Higher**

A solution with a hydrogen ion concentration of 0.25 mol dm^{-3} has a pH of 0.6. What would happen to the pH if the hydrogen ion concentration was decreased to 0.00025 mol dm^{-3}?

The H^+ concentration has decreased by a factor of (10 × 10 × 10 =) 1000, so the pH would increase by 3. So the new pH would be 0.6 + 3 = 3.6.

Practice Questions — Fact Recall

Q1 Give the definition of a strong acid.

Q2 Give the definition of a weak acid.

Q3 Give the equation for the dissociation of ethanoic acid (CH_3COOH). Include state symbols in your answer.

Q4 Describe the difference between the strength and the concentration of an acid.

Practice Questions — Application

Q1 The pH of a strong acid is lower than the pH of a weak acid at the same concentration. Explain why.

Q2 A student added acid to an alkaline solution. The concentration of H^+ ions increased by a factor of 100. What effect would this have had on the pH of the solution?

Q3 A solution had a hydrogen ion concentration of 0.02 mol dm^{-3} and a pH of 1.7. The hydrogen ion concentration was decreased to 0.002 mol dm^{-3}. Calculate the pH of the new solution.

Q4 Following the addition of alkali to an acid solution the pH of the solution changed from 4 to 7. By how many times did the concentration of H^+ ions change?

Tip: H To answer Q4, work out the change in pH first, and then convert that to multiples of 10 to find the change in H^+ ion concentration.

4. Reactions of Acids

Acids can react with all sorts of things, most of the time through neutralisation reactions. Here are some you need to know...

Learning Objectives:

- Be able to explain the general reactions of aqueous solutions of acids with metals, metal oxides, metal hydroxides and metal carbonates to produce salts.
- Be able to describe the chemical tests for hydrogen and carbon dioxide (using limewater).

Specification References 3.11, 3.12

Reaction with metal oxides and metal hydroxides

All metal oxides and hydroxides are **bases**. Soluble metal hydroxides are alkalis because they dissolve in water to form OH^- ions. A base reacts with an acid to form a salt and water. So the general equation for the reaction of metal oxides or metal hydroxides with acids is:

acid + metal oxide or metal hydroxide → salt + water

Which salt is formed?

The name of the salt produced depends on the metal ion in the oxide or hydroxide and the acid that is used. The first part of the name of the salt is the metal ion in the oxide/hydroxide and the second part of the name comes from the acid that is used.

Example

Reacting hydrochloric acid with copper oxide will give you copper chloride:

hydrochloric acid + copper oxide → copper chloride + water

Reaction with hydrochloric acid gives chlorides, with sulfuric acid gives sulfates and with nitric acid gives nitrates.

Examples

hydrochloric acid + sodium hydroxide → sodium chloride + water

$HCl_{(aq)} + NaOH_{(aq)} \rightarrow NaCl_{(aq)} + H_2O_{(l)}$

sulfuric acid + zinc oxide → zinc sulfate + water

$H_2SO_{4(aq)} + ZnO_{(s)} \rightarrow ZnSO_{4(aq)} + H_2O_{(l)}$

sulfuric acid + calcium hydroxide → calcium sulfate + water

$H_2SO_{4(aq)} + Ca(OH)_{2(s)} \rightarrow CaSO_{4(aq)} + 2H_2O_{(l)}$

nitric acid + magnesium oxide → magnesium nitrate + water

$2HNO_{3(aq)} + MgO_{(s)} \rightarrow Mg(NO_3)_{2(aq)} + H_2O_{(l)}$

nitric acid + potassium hydroxide → potassium nitrate + water

$HNO_{3(aq)} + KOH_{(aq)} \rightarrow KNO_{3(aq)} + H_2O_{(l)}$

Tip: Bases are substances that can react with acids in neutralisation reactions — see page 120.

Tip: Salts are ionic compounds (see pages 54-55 for more on ionic compounds).

Tip: The reactions of acids with metal oxides and hydroxides are examples of neutralisation reactions.

Tip: To work out the formula of an ionic compound, you need to balance the charges of the positive and negative ions so the overall charge of a compound is neutral. For more on ionic formulas, see p.49-50.

Tip: Whether you use an oxide or a hydroxide isn't important — it's the metal in the compound that determines which salt you'll get.

Reaction with metals

Acids can react with metals to produce a metal salt and hydrogen gas. Some metals react violently with acid (the reaction of potassium with hydrochloric acid produces enough heat to ignite the hydrogen gas formed in the reaction). Other metals, such as magnesium and aluminium, react more gently with acid. The general equation for the reaction of a metal with an acid is:

acid + metal → metal salt + hydrogen

Tip: The reaction of nitric acid with metals can be more complicated. You get a nitrate salt, but instead of hydrogen gas, the other products are usually a mixture of water, NO and NO_2.

Examples

Aluminium and magnesium react with hydrochloric acid to form chloride salts:

magnesium	+	hydrochloric acid	→	magnesium chloride	+	hydrogen
Mg	+	2HCl	→	$MgCl_2$	+	H_2
aluminium	+	hydrochloric acid	→	aluminium chloride	+	hydrogen
2Al	+	6HCl	→	$2AlCl_3$	+	$3H_2$

Magnesium metal reacts with sulfuric acid to form a sulfate salt:

magnesium	+	sulfuric acid	→	magnesium sulfate	+	hydrogen
Mg	+	H_2SO_4	→	$MgSO_4$	+	H_2

Test for hydrogen

If you hold a lit splint at the open end of a test tube containing hydrogen, you'll get a "squeaky pop". (The noise comes from the hydrogen burning quickly with the oxygen in the air to form H_2O.)

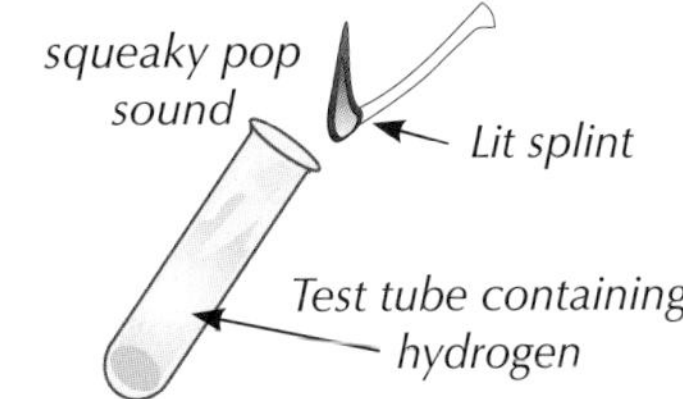

Figure 1: *Testing for hydrogen.*

Reaction with metal carbonates

Metal carbonates react with acids to make a salt, carbon dioxide and water. The general equation for the reaction of metal carbonates and acids is:

metal carbonate + acid → metal salt + carbon dioxide + water

The type of salt produced depends on the type of acid used and the metal in the carbonate.

Figure 2: *Reaction of calcium carbonate and hydrochloric acid forming calcium chloride, carbon dioxide and water.*

Examples

If calcium carbonate reacts with sulfuric acid, a sulfate is produced.

calcium carbonate + sulfuric acid → calcium sulfate + carbon dioxide + water

$$CaCO_3 + H_2SO_4 \rightarrow CaSO_4 + CO_2 + H_2O$$

If calcium carbonate reacts with hydrochloric acid, a chloride is produced.

calcium carbonate + hydrochloric acid → calcium chloride + carbon dioxide + water

$$CaCO_3 + 2HCl \rightarrow CaCl_2 + CO_2 + H_2O$$

When zinc carbonate reacts with nitric acid, zinc nitrate is formed.

zinc carbonate + nitric acid → zinc nitrate + carbon dioxide + water

$$ZnCO_3 + 2HNO_3 \rightarrow Zn(NO_3)_2 + CO_2 + H_2O$$

Exam Tip
You might be asked to write equations for the reactions of different carbonates with different acids, so make sure you can work them out. Remember, with sulfuric acid you always get a sulfate, with hydrochloric acid you always get a chloride and with nitric acid you always get a nitrate.

Test for carbon dioxide

If you make a solution of calcium hydroxide in water (called limewater) and bubble gas through it, the solution will turn cloudy if there's carbon dioxide in the gas. The cloudiness is caused by the formation of calcium carbonate.

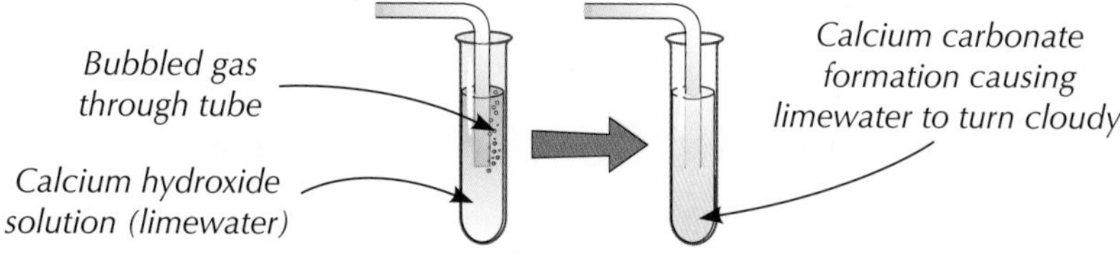

Figure 3: *Testing for carbon dioxide.*

Practice Question — Fact Recall

Q1 Describe the chemical test for:

a) hydrogen gas

b) carbon dioxide gas

Practice Questions — Application

Q1 Name the salt that is produced when:

a) magnesium carbonate reacts with hydrochloric acid.

b) potassium oxide reacts with nitric acid

c) sodium reacts with sulfuric acid

Q2 Name the gas that is formed when magnesium carbonate reacts with sulfuric acid.

5. Making Insoluble Salts

Not every salt will dissolve in water. The next couple of pages are about predicting if a salt will be soluble, and how to make an insoluble salt.

Learning Objectives:

- Know that all common sodium, potassium and ammonium salts are soluble in water.
- Know that all nitrates are soluble in water.
- Know that common chlorides are soluble in water, except those of silver and lead.
- Know that common sulfates are soluble in water, except those of lead, barium and calcium.
- Know that common carbonates and hydroxides are insoluble in water, except those of sodium, potassium and ammonium.
- Be able to predict, using solubility rules, whether or not a precipitate will be formed when named solutions are mixed together.
- Be able to name the precipitate formed during the reaction between named solutions.
- Be able to describe the method used to prepare a pure, dry sample of an insoluble salt.

Specification References
3.19-3.21

Solubility of different salts

How you make a salt depends on whether it's **soluble** or **insoluble**. You may need to work out if, when two solutions are mixed, a salt will form as a precipitate (i.e. it's an insoluble salt), or whether it will just form in solution (i.e. it's a soluble salt). Figure 1 is a handy guide to whether some common substances are soluble in water or not.

Substance	Soluble or Insoluble?
common salts of sodium, potassium and ammonium	soluble
nitrates	soluble
common chlorides	soluble (except silver chloride and lead chloride)
common sulfates	soluble (except lead, barium and calcium sulfate)
common carbonates and hydroxides	insoluble (except for sodium, potassium and ammonium ones)

Figure 1: *Table showing the solubility in water of some common salts.*

Making insoluble salts from soluble salts

To make a pure, dry sample of an insoluble salt, you can use a precipitation reaction. Precipitation occurs when an insoluble solid (known as a **precipitate**) forms in a solution. You just need to pick the right two soluble salts and react them together to get your insoluble salt.

Example

You can make lead chloride (an insoluble salt) by mixing together lead nitrate and sodium chloride (both soluble salts).

lead nitrate + sodium chloride → lead chloride + sodium nitrate

$$Pb(NO_3)_{2(aq)} + 2NaCl_{(aq)} \rightarrow PbCl_{2(s)} + 2NaNO_{3(aq)}$$

Here's how you would do it in the lab:

1. Add one spatula of lead nitrate to a test tube. Add some deionised water in order to dissolve it. Shake the test tube thoroughly to ensure that all the lead nitrate has dissolved.
2. Repeat step 1 in a separate test tube, except this time use one spatula of sodium chloride.
3. Tip the two solutions into a small beaker, and stir thoroughly to make sure the solutions are fully mixed. The lead chloride should precipitate out (see Figure 3 on the next page).

Tip: Deionised water has been purified so it doesn't contain any salts. This means that there are no other ions in solution that could interfere with the reaction.

4. Fold a piece of filter paper and place it into a filter funnel. Place the funnel into the top of a conical flask.

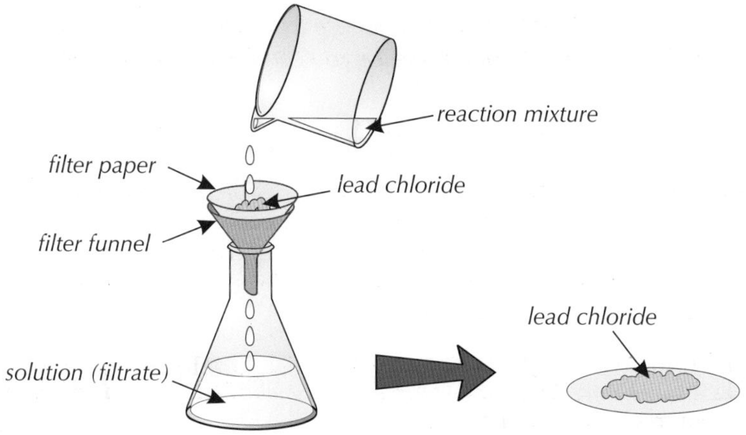

Figure 2: *Filtering out lead chloride from the reaction mixture using filter paper and a filter funnel.*

Figure 3: *Insoluble lead chloride precipitate forms in the reaction of lead nitrate with sodium chloride.*

Tip: The liquid that ends up in the conical flask after passing through the filter paper is known as the filtrate.

5. Pour the contents of the beaker into the middle of the filter paper. Make sure that the solution doesn't go above the top of the filter paper — otherwise some of the solid lead chloride could end up in the filtrate.
6. Swill out the beaker with more deionised water, and tip this into the filter paper. This will ensure all the precipitate is taken from the beaker.
7. Rinse the contents of the filter paper with deionised water to make sure that all the soluble sodium nitrate has been washed away.
8. Scrape the lead chloride onto fresh filter paper and leave it to dry in an oven or a desiccator.

Practice Questions — Fact Recall

Q1 State whether the following salts will be soluble or insoluble in water:

a) sodium hydroxide b) silver nitrate

c) barium chloride d) potassium iodide

Q2 What type of reaction is used to make insoluble salts?

Exam Tip
You need to remember whether the substances in Figure 1 on the previous page are soluble or not. Learning them could get you easy marks in the exam.

Practice Questions — Application

Q1 Sam wants to make the insoluble salt magnesium carbonate ($MgCO_3$). To do this he plans to mix magnesium sulfate ($MgSO_4$) with sodium sulfate (Na_2SO_4). Explain why this reaction won't produce magnesium carbonate.

Q2 A scientist is making the insoluble salt barium sulfate ($BaSO_4$) by reacting barium chloride ($BaCl_2$) with sodium sulfate (Na_2SO_4).

a) Write the word equation for this reaction.

b) Describe the experimental method used to make this salt.

Learning Objectives:

- Be able to describe an experiment to investigate the preparation of pure, dry hydrated copper sulfate crystals from copper oxide, including the use of a water bath (Core Practical).
- Be able to explain why excess insoluble reactant is used in the preparation of a soluble salt from an acid and an insoluble reactant.
- Be able to explain why excess insoluble reactant is removed at the end of the preparation of a soluble salt, and why the solution left at the end contains only the salt dissolved in water.
- Be able to explain why the acid and the soluble reactant are mixed in the correct proportions during the preparation of a soluble salt from a soluble reactant, and why the resulting solution contains only salt and water.
- Be able to explain why a titration must be used when soluble salts are prepared from an acid and a soluble reactant.
- Be able to describe how to carry out an acid-alkali titration, using a burette, a pipette and a suitable indicator, to prepare a pure, dry salt.

Specification References 3.15-3.18

6. Making Soluble Salts

There are a couple of methods you can use to make soluble salts. You can react an acid with an insoluble base, or you can use a titration.

Soluble salts from acids and insoluble reagents

Soluble salts (salts that dissolve in water) can be made by reacting an acid with a metal or an insoluble base (such as a metal oxide, metal hydroxide or metal carbonate). When making a soluble salt, the first thing you need to do is choose appropriate reagents to produce that particular salt. You should be able to work out which are the right reagents to choose from the name of the salt you want to produce.

Example

If you want to make copper chloride, you could mix hydrochloric acid and copper oxide:

$$2HCl_{(aq)} + CuO_{(s)} \rightarrow CuCl_{2\,(aq)} + H_2O_{(l)}$$

Making copper sulfate

You can make copper sulfate (a soluble salt) by adding copper oxide (an insoluble reagent) to warm sulfuric acid.

$$CuO_{(s)} + H_2SO_{4\,(aq)} \rightarrow CuSO_{4\,(aq)} + H_2O_{(l)}$$

The copper oxide is added in excess and separated out at the end of the reaction using filter paper. Many metal oxides and some metal carbonates are insoluble, so this is also the method you'd use if you're using any of those. Here's what you do:

1. Put the sulfuric acid in a beaker. Gently warm the dilute acid by placing the beaker in a water bath (see p.248 for more on water baths) — this speeds up the reaction between the acid and the insoluble base. Carry out this step in a fume cupboard to avoid releasing acid fumes into the room.

2. Add the copper oxide (the base) to the acid and stir — they will react with each other to form copper sulfate (a soluble salt) and water.

3. Keep adding the copper oxide until it is in excess. When it reaches excess, the oxide will start to sink to the bottom and won't react — this shows that all the acid has been neutralised and the reaction has finished. It's important that the base is in excess, as this ensures that you won't have any leftover acid in your product.

4. Then you need to filter out the excess copper oxide to separate it from the copper sulfate solution. This ensures that the copper sulfate salt isn't contaminated with copper oxide once it's dried. This stage is done using filter paper and a filter funnel (see Figure 1 on the next page).

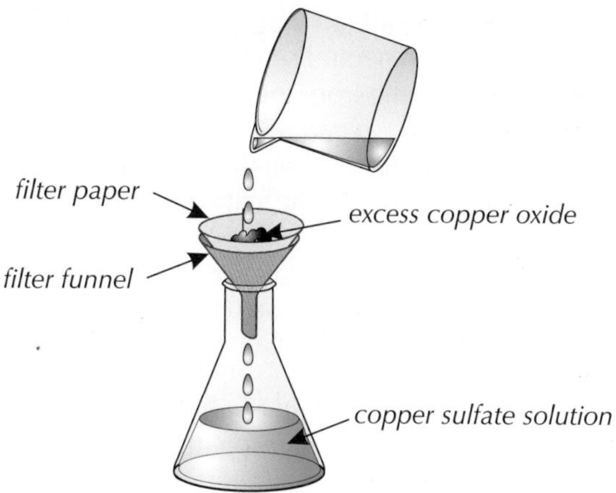

Figure 1: *Filtering out the excess copper oxide using filter paper and a filter funnel.*

Tip: Make sure you carry out a risk assessment before doing any practical and that you use the correct safety equipment. WORKING SCIENTIFICALLY

5. At the end of the filtration, you'll be left with a solution of copper sulfate salt dissolved in water. You can convert this into pure, solid crystals of copper sulfate using crystallisation. To do this you first need to heat the salt solution using a Bunsen burner and an evaporating dish (see p.105), in order to evaporate some of the water and make the solution more concentrated.

6. Then, stop heating it and leave the solution to cool. Blue crystals of hydrated copper sulfate should form, which can be filtered out of the solution and then dried.

Figure 2: *Hydrated copper sulfate forms blue crystals.*

Making a soluble salt using acid-alkali reactions

Soluble salts can be made by reacting an acid with an alkali. It is not always obvious when the reaction has finished, as there's no signal that all the acid has been neutralised. You also can't just add an excess of alkali to the acid, because the salt is soluble and would be contaminated with the excess alkali.

In order to overcome these problems you need to work out exactly the right amount of alkali to neutralise the acid. For this, you need to do a **titration** using an **indicator**. Here's what you do:

1. Measure out a set amount of acid into a conical flask using a pipette. Add a few drops of indicator, then place the flask on a white tile.

2. Fill a burette with alkali and record the volume.

3. Slowly add alkali to the acid, gently swirling the flask all the time, until you reach the end point — this is when the acid's been exactly neutralised and the indicator changes colour (see Figure 3).

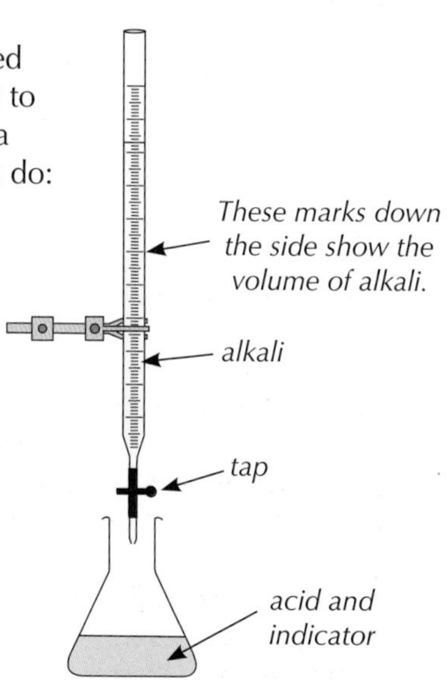

Figure 3: *A burette set up for a titration.*

Tip: A titration is an experiment that lets you see what volume of a reactant is needed to react completely with a certain volume of another reactant.

Tip: For a titration, you should use an indicator with a single, clear colour change (like phenolphthalein or methyl orange). Universal indicator is no good as its colour change is too gradual.

Tip: When you're taking a reading from a burette, make sure that your eyes are in line with the top of the liquid. It won't be as accurate if you try and read it from too high up.

4. Read the final volume of alkali left in the burette. Calculate the amount of alkali that was needed to neutralise the acid by subtracting the final volume of alkali in the burette from the initial volume.

5. Then, carry out the reaction using exactly the same volumes of alkali and acid but with no indicator, so the salt won't be contaminated with indicator.

6. The solution that remains when the reaction is complete contains only the salt and water. This is because all the alkali has reacted with all the acid.

7. Slowly evaporate off some of the water and then leave the solution to crystallise (see page 105 for more on crystallisation). Filter off the solid and dry it — you'll be left with a pure, dry salt.

Practice Questions — Application

Q1 A scientist is making the soluble salt zinc chloride ($ZnCl_2$) by reacting an excess of the insoluble base, zinc oxide (ZnO), with hydrochloric acid (HCl).

a) Write the word equation for this reaction.

b) Explain why zinc oxide is used in excess in this reaction.

c) i) Suggest how the scientist will separate the excess zinc oxide from the solution at the end of the reaction.

ii) Why does the excess zinc oxide need to be removed from the solution?

Q2 A student is carrying out a titration to find how much potassium hydroxide to add to nitric acid to make a pure salt.

a) Describe a method by which the student could carry out the titration.

b) Explain why the student needs to know the exact volume of potassium hydroxide that reacts with the nitric acid.

7. Electrolysis

Don't be put off by the fancy name, electrolysis is simply a process where substances are split using electricity.

What is electrolysis?

If you pass an electric current through an ionic substance that's molten or in solution, the ions in the liquid or solution will move towards the electrodes, where they can react, causing the ionic substance to decompose. This process of breaking down a substance using electricity is called **electrolysis**. For example, the electrolysis of molten aluminium oxide breaks aluminium oxide down into aluminium and oxygen.

Electrolytes

Electrolysis requires a liquid to conduct the electricity, called the **electrolyte**. Electrolytes contain free ions — they're usually a molten or dissolved ionic compound (see Figure 1). In either case, it's the free ions which conduct the electricity and allow the whole thing to work.

Sodium chloride solution (sodium chloride dissolved in water).

The ions are free to move throughout the substance, so can carry an electric charge.

Molten sodium chloride.

Figure 1: *Free ions in molten and dissolved sodium chloride.*

How electrolysis works

Electrolysis is based on an electrical circuit that includes an electrolyte and two **electrodes** — an electrode is a solid that conducts electricity and is submerged in the electrolyte. In electrolysis, the electrodes are placed into the electrolyte and ions move from one electrode to the other — this allows the conduction of electricity through the circuit. The positive ions (cations) in the electrolyte will move towards the negative electrode (the **cathode**) and gain electrons. The negative ions (anions) in the electrolyte will move towards the positive electrode (the **anode**) and lose electrons. As ions gain or lose electrons they become atoms or molecules and are discharged (released) from the electrolyte. These atoms or molecules are the products of electrolysis.

Electrolysis and redox Higher

Electrolysis always involves an oxidation reaction and a reduction reaction. Reduction is occurring at the negative electrode as the positive ions are gaining electrons. Oxidation occurs at the positive electrode as the negative ions are losing electrons.

Practice Questions — Fact Recall

Q1 Why are dissolved ionic substances able to conduct electricity?

Q2 What type of ions are attracted towards the negative electrode?

Learning Objectives:

- Be able to describe electrolysis as a process in which electrical energy, from a direct current supply, decomposes electrolytes.
- Know that electrolytes are ionic compounds in the molten state or dissolved in water.
- Be able to explain the movement of ions during electrolysis, in which positively charged cations migrate to the negatively charged cathode, and negatively charged anions migrate to the positively charged anode.
- H Be able to explain oxidation and reduction in terms of loss or gain of electrons.
- H Know that reduction occurs at the cathode and that oxidation occurs at the anode.
- Be able to predict the products of electrolysis of binary, ionic compounds in the molten state.
- Be able to explain the formation of the products in the electrolysis of molten lead bromide using inert electrodes.
- H Be able to write half equations for reactions occurring at the anode and cathode in electrolysis.

Specification References
3.22-3.29

Tip: H See page 153 for more on redox.

Tip: Electrodes should be made out of an inert material, such as graphite or platinum, so they don't react.

Electrolysis of molten ionic substances

Binary compounds are ionic compounds containing two elements which are ions — a positive metal ion and a negative non-metal ion. Solid ionic compounds cannot be electrolysed because the ions are in fixed positions and can't move. However, molten ionic compounds can be electrolysed because the ions can move freely and conduct electricity. Electrolysis of molten binary compounds gives the neutral metal and non-metal elements. During the electrolysis of these substances, the metal ions move to the cathode and gain electrons to become neutral, while the non-metal ions move to the anode and lose electrons to become neutral.

Tip: Lead bromide only contains two elements so can be described as a binary compound.

Tip: In the electrolysis of lead bromide, you'd see a brown vapour of bromine gas at the anode and a silver coloured liquid at the cathode as molten lead is formed.

Tip: H During the electrolysis of lead bromide, lead ions gain electrons. This is a reduction reaction, and the lead ions are said to be reduced. Bromide ions lose electrons. This is an oxidation reaction, and the bromide ions are said to be oxidised.

Example

Lead bromide ($PbBr_2$) is an ionic compound, so when it is molten, it will conduct electricity. Electrolysis of lead bromide breaks it down into lead (Pb) and bromine (Br_2). So, the electrolyte is lead bromide and the products of electrolysis are lead and bromine. Here's how it works...

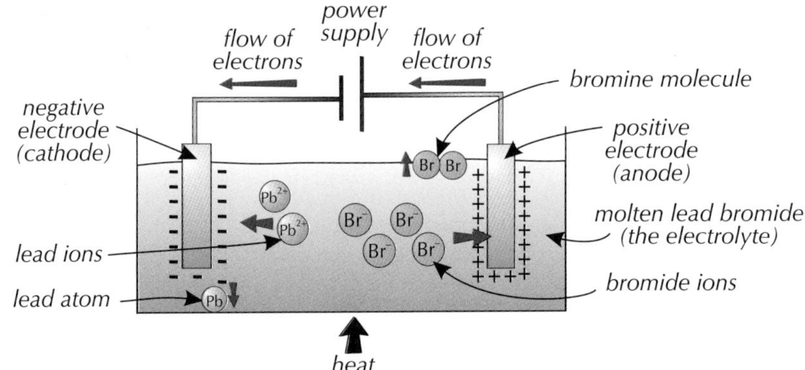

Figure 2: *The electrolysis of lead bromide.*

Molten lead bromide contains positively charged lead ions and negatively charged bromide ions.

- The positive ions are attracted towards the negative electrode. Here, each lead ion gains two electrons and becomes a lead atom.
- The negative ions are attracted towards the positive electrode. Here, bromide ions lose one electron each and form bromine molecules (Br_2).

Half equations Higher

Half equations show how electrons are transferred during the reactions at the electrodes. Here's how to write a half equation for the reaction that takes place at the negative electrode:

Step 1: Write the symbol for the positive ion in the electrolyte on the left-hand side of the equation.

Step 2: Write the symbol for the neutral atoms or molecules produced on the right-hand side of the equation.

Step 3: Balance the number of atoms in the equation.

Step 4: Balance the charges by adding or subtracting electrons (shown as e^-).

You can do the same to get the half equation for the reaction at the positive electrode, starting with the negative ion on the left-hand side of the equation.

Example **Higher**

These are the half equations for the electrolysis of lead bromide:

Negative electrode:

Step 1: Pb^{2+}

Step 2: $Pb^{2+} \rightarrow Pb$

Step 3: There's one lead ion on the left and one lead atom on the right, so the number of atoms is balanced.

Step 4: A charge of 2+ on the left hand side needs to be balanced out by two electrons, so that the overall charge of both sides is the same (0). So the half equation for the reaction at the negative electrode is:

$Pb^{2+} + 2e^- \rightarrow Pb$

Positive electrode:

Step 1: Br^-

Step 2: $Br^- \rightarrow Br_2$

Step 3: There are two bromine atoms on the right so there need to be two bromide ions on the left to balance the equation.

$2Br^- \rightarrow Br_2$

Step 4: A charge of 2– on the left hand side needs to be balanced out by two electrons on the right hand side, so that the overall charge on both sides is equal (2–). So the half equation for the reaction at the negative electrode is:

$2Br^- \rightarrow Br_2 + 2e^-$

Or, you could subtract two electrons from the left-hand side to give both sides a charge of zero. This would give you this half equation:

$2Br^- - 2e^- \rightarrow Br_2$

The charges in this half equation are still balanced because $(-2) - (-2) = 0$

Tip: H For the half equation to show the reaction at the positive electrode, you can balance the charges by adding or subtracting electrons. For the half equation for the negative electrode you can only add electrons.

Tip: H These equations are called half equations because each one only shows half of the overall reaction that takes place.

Exam Tip H
You can check your half equations are correct by making sure that the charges balance and the atoms balance. If they don't, you've gone wrong somewhere.

Practice Questions — Application

Q1 Molten zinc chloride can undergo electrolysis. The ions in the electrolyte are Zn^{2+} and Cl^-. The electrodes are made of graphite.

a) Give the name of the electrolyte.

b) Which electrode do the Cl^- ions move towards?

c) Describe what happens to the Cl^- ions at this electrode.

d) Are the zinc ions oxidised or reduced during electrolysis?

Q2 Complete the half equations below to show the reactions that happen during the electrolysis of two different solutions:

a) $Br^- \rightarrow Br_2$ and $H^+ \rightarrow H_2$

b) $Cu^{2+} \rightarrow Cu$ and $O^{2-} \rightarrow O_2$

8. Predicting Products of Electrolysis

Learning Objectives:

- Be able to explain the formation of the products in the electrolysis, using inert electrodes, of copper chloride, sodium chloride and sodium sulfate solutions.
- Be able to explain the formation of the products in the electrolysis, using inert electrodes, of water acidified with sulfuric acid.

Specification Reference 3.25

When you electrolyse substances dissolved in water, you need to think about the ions in the water when working out what the products will be.

Electrolysis of aqueous solutions

Sometimes there are more than two types of free ions in the electrolyte. For example, if a salt is dissolved in water there will be some H^+ and OH^- ions as well as the ions from the salt in the solution. In this situation, the products of electrolysis depend on how reactive the elements involved are.

At the negative electrode (the cathode), if metal ions and H^+ ions are present, the metal ions will stay in solution if the metal is more reactive than hydrogen (e.g. sodium). This is because the more reactive an element, the more likely it is to stay as ions. So, hydrogen will be produced unless the metal is less reactive than it. If the metal is less reactive than hydrogen (e.g. copper), then a solid layer of pure metal will be produced instead.

At the positive electrode (the anode), if OH^- and halide ions (Cl^-, Br^-, I^-) are present then molecules of chlorine, bromine or iodine will be formed. If no halide is present, then the OH^- ions are discharged and oxygen and water will be formed.

Tip: There's more about the reactivity of metals on pages 148-151.

Tip: H^+ and OH^- ions form in water when a water molecule dissociates in a reversible reaction:
$H_2O_{(l)} \rightleftharpoons H^+_{(aq)} + OH^-_{(aq)}$
(You can read more about reversible reactions on p.169.)

Example 1

A solution of copper chloride ($CuCl_2$) contains four different ions: Cu^{2+}, Cl^-, H^+ and OH^-.

Copper metal is less reactive than hydrogen. So at the cathode, copper metal is produced and coats the electrode.

$Cu^{2+} + 2e^- \rightarrow Cu$

As Cl^- (halide) ions are present, molecules of chlorine are produced at the anode. The chlorine can be seen as bubbles.

$2Cl^- \rightarrow Cl_2 + 2e^-$

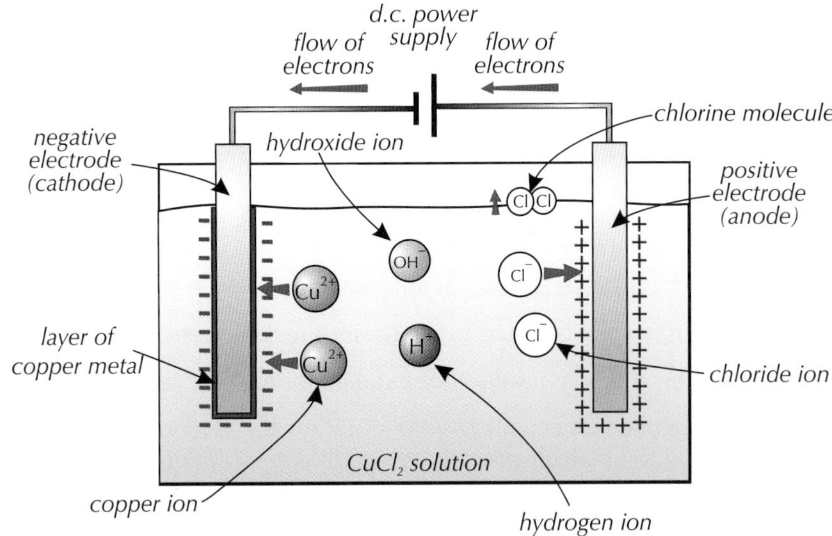

Figure 2: *The electrolysis of an aqueous solution of copper chloride.*

Figure 1: *Electrolysis of an aqueous solution of NaCl.*

Exam Tip H
If you are taking the higher tier paper, you need to know how to write half equations for the electrolysis of aqueous solutions.

Example 2

A solution of sodium chloride (NaCl) contains four different ions: Na^+, Cl^-, OH^- and H^+.

Sodium metal is more reactive than hydrogen. So, at the cathode, hydrogen gas is produced: $2H^+ + 2e^- \rightarrow H_2$.

Chloride ions are present in the solution. So, at the anode, chlorine gas is produced: $2Cl^- \rightarrow Cl_2 + 2e^-$.

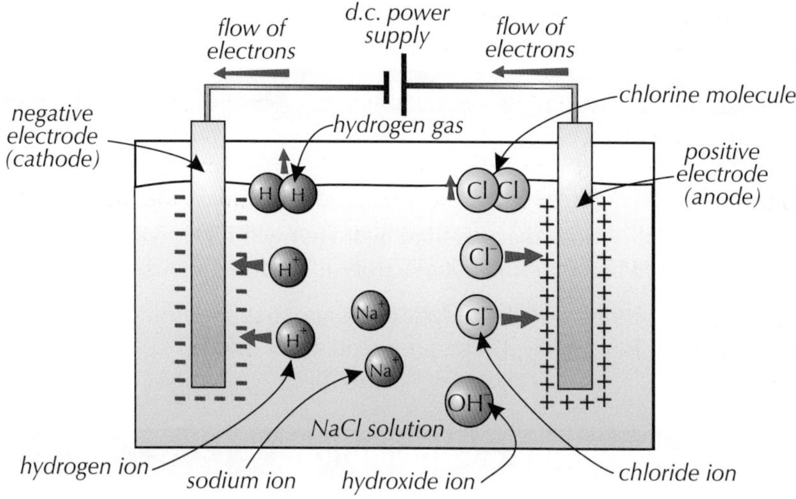

Figure 3: *Electrolysis of an aqueous solution of sodium chloride.*

Example 3

A solution of sodium sulfate (Na_2SO_4) contains four different ions: Na^+, SO_4^{2-}, H^+ and OH^-.

Sodium metal is more reactive than hydrogen. So at the cathode, hydrogen gas is produced: $2H^+ + 2e^- \rightarrow H_2$.

There aren't any halide ions present so at the anode oxygen and water are produced. The oxygen can be seen as bubbles: $4OH^- \rightarrow O_2 + 2H_2O + 4e^-$.

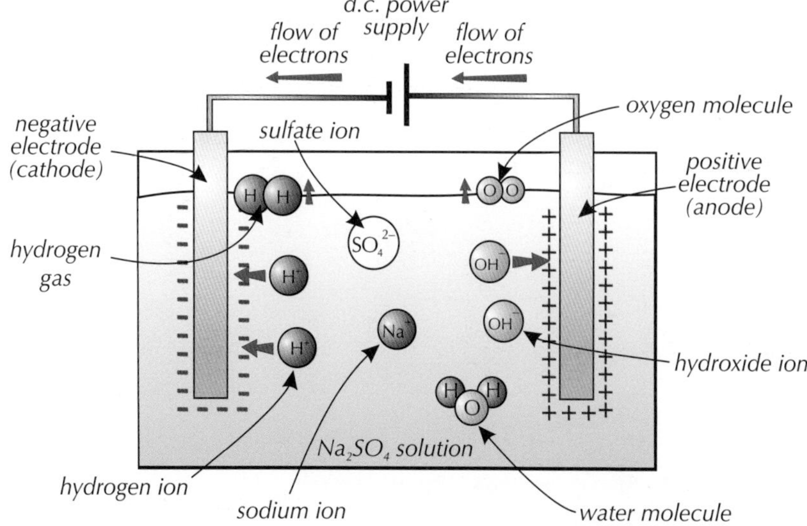

Figure 4: *The electrolysis of an aqueous solution of sodium sulfate.*

Tip: If you're drawing the apparatus for an electrolysis experiment, remember to include a d.c. power supply, wires and labels for the anode and the cathode. The anode is the electrode on the same side as the longer line of the d.c. power supply symbol.

Example 4

A solution of dilute sulfuric acid (H_2SO_4) contains three different ions: SO_4^{2-}, OH^- and H^+.

As there is no metal present, hydrogen gas is produced at the cathode: $2H^+ + 2e^- \rightarrow H_2$.

There are no halide ions present in solution. So, at the anode, oxygen and water are produced: $4OH^- \rightarrow O_2 + 2H_2O + 4e^-$.

Tip: Inert electrodes are unreactive, so they don't affect the products formed from electrolysis.

Practice Questions — Fact Recall

Q1 What determines the products of electrolysis of an aqueous solution using inert electrodes?

Q2 If a metal is more reactive than hydrogen will it be produced at the cathode when carrying out electrolysis on an aqueous solution?

Q3 When carrying out electrolysis of an aqueous solution containing bromide ions, what will be produced at the anode?

Tip: You can find out if a metal is more or less reactive than hydrogen by using the reactivity series — there's one on page 148.

Practice Questions — Application

Q1 When aqueous sodium chloride solution is electrolysed, hydrogen is produced at the cathode. Explain why sodium is not produced.

Q2 A solution of dilute sulfuric acid (H_2SO_4) is electrolysed using inert electrodes.

a) State the ions present in the solution.

b) Give the products formed at each electrode.

Q3 Electrolysis is carried out on an aqueous solution of sodium sulfate. Suggest the products of the reaction. Give reasons for your answer.

Q4 A student suggests that the electrolysis of an aqueous solution of copper chloride will produce copper and chlorine gas. Is the student correct? Explain your answer.

Q5 The electrolysis of an aqueous solution of sodium carbonate produces oxygen and hydrogen gas. Give half equations for the reactions at the anode and cathode.

9. Electrolysis of Copper Sulfate

These pages are about investigating the electrolysis of copper sulfate solution — you'll even get to do the experiment in class. First, how to set it up...

Using an electrochemical cell

CORE PRACTICAL

Here's how you set up the electrolysis of an aqueous solution:

- Get two inert electrodes (e.g. platinum or carbon). Clean the surfaces of the electrodes using a piece of emery paper (or sandpaper).
- From this point on, be careful not to touch the surfaces of the metals with your hands — you could transfer grease back onto the electrodes.
- Place both electrodes into a beaker filled with electrolyte and place them so they are inside inverted test tubes containing the aqueous solution.
- Connect the electrodes to a power supply using crocodile clips and wires. When you turn the power supply on, a current will flow through the cell.

As the reaction progresses, gases may form and collect inside the test tubes.

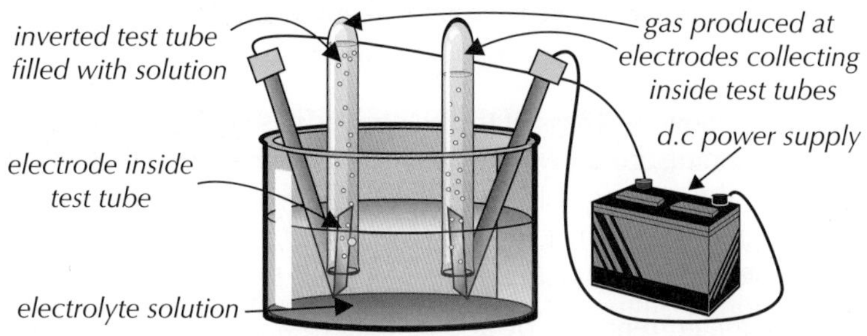

Figure 1: *Diagram of the experimental set-up for an electrolysis experiment.*

Electrolysis of copper sulfate using inert electrodes

A solution of copper sulfate ($CuSO_4$) contains four different ions: Cu^{2+}, SO_4^{2-}, H^+ and OH^-. When you electrolyse a solution of $CuSO_4$ with inert electrodes:

- Copper metal is less reactive than hydrogen. So at the cathode, copper metal is produced and coats the electrode: $Cu^{2+} + 2e^- \rightarrow Cu$.
- There aren't any halide ions present so at the anode oxygen and water are produced. The oxygen can be seen as bubbles: $4OH^- \rightarrow O_2 + 2H_2O + 4e^-$.

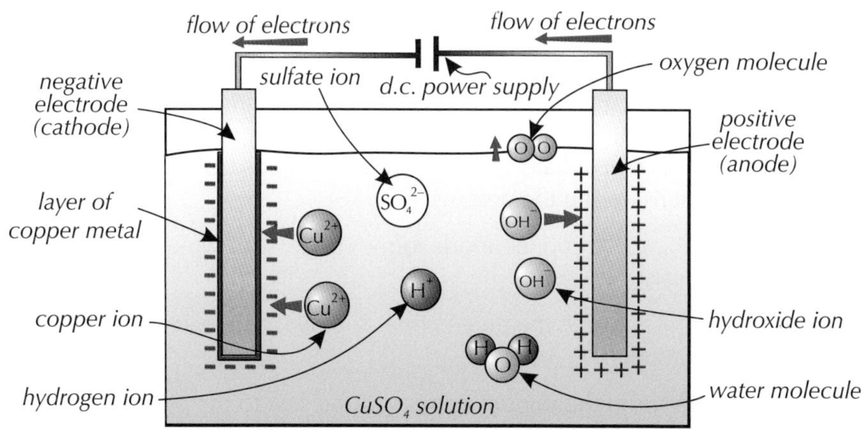

Figure 2: *The electrolysis of an aqueous solution of copper sulfate.*

Learning Objectives:

- Be able to describe and carry out an experiment to investigate the electrolysis of copper sulfate solution with inert electrodes and copper electrodes (Core Practical).
- Be able to explain the formation of the products in the electrolysis of copper sulfate solution, with copper electrodes, and how this electrolysis can be used to purify copper.

Specification References 3.30, 3.31

Tip: An electrochemical cell is a circuit, made up of the anode, cathode, electrolyte, a power source and the wires that connect the two electrodes.

Tip: You only need to use test tubes if you want to collect and test any gases that are produced during electrolysis.

Tip: Make sure you do a risk assessment before doing any electrolysis in class.

Tip: The voltage of the cell decreases as the electrolysis continues and the reactants get used up.

Tip: You could put an ammeter or bulb in series with your circuit to check you've set it up correctly.

Electrolysis of copper sulfate using non-inert electrodes

If you set up an electrochemical cell in the same way as the one on the previous page, but using copper electrodes in a solution of copper sulfate instead of inert electrodes, the result is different.

As the reaction continues, the mass of the anode will decrease and the mass of the cathode will increase. This is because copper is transferred from the anode to the cathode. The reaction is quite slow, so the cell should be left for around 30 minutes in order to achieve a measurable change in mass.

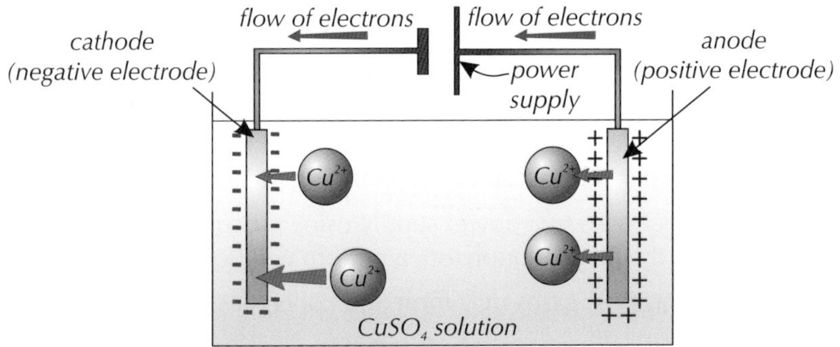

Figure 3: *Electrolysis of copper sulfate with copper electrodes.*

Tip: H The half equations for this experiment are: $Cu_{(s)} \rightarrow Cu^{2+}_{(aq)} + 2e^-$ at the anode and $Cu^{2+}_{(aq)} + 2e^- \rightarrow Cu_{(s)}$ at the cathode.

You can measure how the mass of the electrodes has changed during the experiment by finding the difference between the masses of the electrodes before and after the experiment. You should make sure the electrodes are dry before weighing them, as any copper sulfate solution on the electrodes may mean they appear to have a higher mass than they really do.

Tip: The reactions at the anode and cathode mean that the concentration of Cu^{2+} ions in solution is constant — they're produced and removed at the same rate.

If you increase the current (e.g. by adding batteries) you will increase the rate of electrolysis. This means there will be a bigger difference between the mass of the two electrodes after the same amount of time.
The electrical supply acts by:

- removing electrons from copper atoms at the anode (making Cu^{2+} ions).
- donating electrons at the cathode to nearby Cu^{2+} ions (making copper atoms).

Figure 4: *Copper plates being stacked at a refinery. The cathode plates are coated with pure copper.*

Purification of copper using electrolysis

Copper can be extracted from its ore by reduction with carbon (see p.155), but copper made in this way is impure. Electrolysis can be used to purify the copper using an electrochemical cell with copper electrodes.

When copper is purified using electrolysis, the anode starts off as a big lump of impure copper and the cathode starts off as a thin piece of pure copper. The electrolyte is copper sulfate solution (which contains Cu^{2+} ions).
Here's what happens during the process:

1. Copper in the impure copper anode forms copper ions which dissolve into the electrolyte.
2. The copper ions move to the pure copper cathode, and react to form a layer of pure copper.
3. Any impurities from the impure copper anode sink to the bottom of the cell, forming a sludge.

Electrolysis of a molten ionic substance

A different method is needed to electrolyse an ionic substance if it's not in solution. Here's how you'd do it:

1. Put your solid ionic substance (this becomes your electrolyte) in a crucible.
2. Heat the crucible with a Bunsen burner until the solid melts. You should do this in a fume cupboard to avoid releasing any toxic fumes into the room.
3. Once the solid is melted, put two clean, inert electrodes into the electrolyte.
4. Then, connect the electrodes to a power supply using wires and clips.

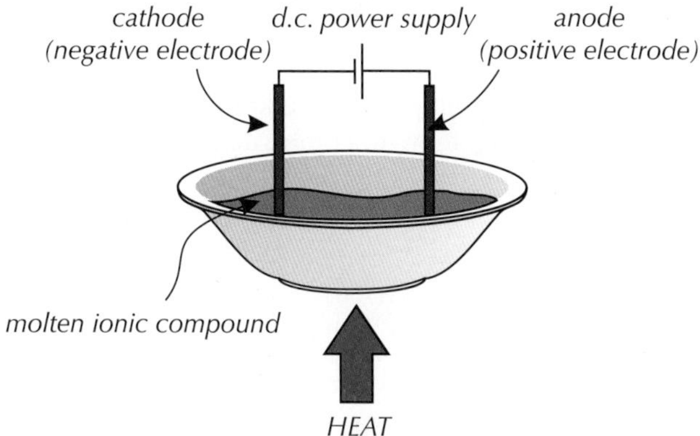

Figure 5: *Electrolysis of a molten ionic compound.*

Tip: Have a look back at page 134 for a recap on the electrolysis of molten lead bromide.

Tip: Molten is the term used to describe a solid substance that has melted.

Tip: When you turn the power supply on, a current should flow through the circuit.

Practice Question — Fact Recall

Q1 Describe the electrodes used for the purification of copper by electrolysis.

Practice Questions — Application

Q1 Explain what occurs at the cathode and anode when copper sulfate solution is electrolysed using inert electrodes.

Q2 Copper sulfate can be electrolysed using non-inert electrodes.

a) Explain why the mass of the anode decreases and the mass of the cathode increases during this process.

b) Describe how you would carry out this electrolysis.

Topic 3 Checklist — Make sure you know...

Acids and Bases

- ☐ That solutions with a pH of less than 7 are acidic, solutions with a pH of more than 7 are alkaline and solutions with a pH of exactly 7 are neutral.
- ☐ That acids release H^+ ions in solution.
- ☐ That a base is a substance that reacts with an acid to form only a salt and water.

cont...

- ☐ That an alkali is a base that is soluble in water.
- ☐ That alkalis release OH^- ions in solution.
- ☐ H That the higher the concentration of hydrogen ions in a solution, the lower the pH, and the higher the concentration of hydroxide ions in a solution, the higher the pH.
- ☐ The colours of the indicators litmus, methyl orange and phenolphthalein at different pHs.

Neutralisation Reactions

- ☐ That in a neutralisation reaction, water is produced when hydrogen ions (from an acid) react with hydroxide ions (from a base).
- ☐ How to carry out an experiment to measure the change in pH when a known mass of calcium oxide or calcium hydroxide is added to a fixed volume of dilute hydrochloric acid (Core Practical).

Strong and Weak Acids

- ☐ H That acids that ionise completely are strong acids and acids that partially ionise are weak acids.
- ☐ H That the concentration of an acid measures how much acid there is in a litre of water.
- ☐ H That a concentrated acid has a large number of acid molecules compared to the volume of water and a dilute acid has a small number of acid molecules compared to the volume of water.
- ☐ H That the pH of a solution changes by 1 if the H^+ ion concentration changes by a factor of 10.

Reactions of Acids

- ☐ That the reaction of an acid with a metal hydroxide or a metal oxide forms a salt and water.
- ☐ That an acid will react with a metal to produce a metal salt and hydrogen.
- ☐ That placing a lit splint in to a test tube containing hydrogen will produce a 'squeaky pop' sound.
- ☐ That carbon dioxide, a salt and water are formed from the reaction of a metal carbonate and an acid.
- ☐ That carbon dioxide will turn a solution of limewater cloudy if it is bubbled through it.

Making Insoluble Salts

- ☐ That common salts of sodium, potassium and ammonium will dissolve (are soluble) in water.
- ☐ That all nitrate salts will dissolve in water.
- ☐ That common chloride salts, except those of silver and lead, will dissolve in water.
- ☐ That common sulfate salts, except those of barium, lead and calcium, will dissolve in water.
- ☐ That common carbonates and hydroxides, except those of sodium, potassium and ammonium, will not dissolve (are insoluble) in water.
- ☐ How to use knowledge about the solubility of different salts to predict whether a precipitate will form when two solutions are mixed together, and be able to name the precipitate formed.
- ☐ How to prepare a pure, dry sample of an insoluble salt.

cont...

Making Soluble Salts

- [ ] How to prepare crystals of pure dry, hydrated copper sulfate from copper oxide.
- [ ] That excess insoluble reactant is used in the preparation of a soluble salt in order to ensure that all the acid in the solution has reacted to produce a salt.
- [ ] That excess insoluble reactant is removed at the end of the preparation of a soluble salt to make sure that the salt produced is pure, so the remaining solution contains only the salt and water.
- [ ] Why a reaction of an acid and soluble reactant, mixed in the correct proportions using a titration, will give a salt and water only.
- [ ] How to prepare a pure, dry salt using an acid-alkali titration.

Electrolysis

- [ ] That a dissolved or molten ionic compound will break down if a current is passed through it.
- [ ] That electrolytes are molten or dissolved ionic compounds.
- [ ] That during electrolysis, the positive ions (cations) in the electrolyte move towards the negative electrode (cathode) and the negative ions (anions) move towards the positive electrode (anode).
- [ ] H That, in electrolysis, positive ions are reduced (gain electrons) and negative ions are oxidised (lose electrons) at the electrodes.
- [ ] That when an ionic compound containing two elements is melted and electrolysed, the metal forms at the negative electrode and the non-metal forms at the positive electrode.
- [ ] That electrolysed molten lead bromide forms lead (at the cathode) and bromine gas (at the anode).
- [ ] H How to write half equations for the reactions that occur at the electrodes.

Predicting Products of Electrolysis

- [ ] That the products of the electrolysis of an aqueous solution using inert electrodes are determined by the reactivity of the elements.
- [ ] That water can break down into H^+ and OH^- ions and these ions can be discharged in electrolysis.
- [ ] That if the metal ion dissolved in the aqueous solution forms an elemental metal that is more reactive than hydrogen, then hydrogen will be formed at the cathode.
- [ ] That if the solution contains halide ions, then the halogen will be formed at the anode, but, if no halides are present, then oxygen and water will be produced.
- [ ] The products formed during the electrolysis of copper chloride, sodium chloride, sodium sulfate and dilute sulfuric acid solutions.

Electrolysis of Copper Sulfate

- [ ] How to carry out the electrolysis of copper sulfate solution, using inert and copper electrodes.
- [ ] How to explain the formation of the products of the electrolysis of copper sulfate solution.
- [ ] How the electrolysis of copper sulfate solution can be used to purify copper.

Exam-style Questions

1 There are a number of different ways to make soluble salts.
One way of making soluble salts involves reacting acids with metal oxides.

(a) Copy and complete the general equation for this reaction shown below:

acid + metal oxide → ________ + ________

(2 marks)

(b) What type of reaction is the reaction between a metal oxide and an acid?

(1 mark)

2 A student carried out a titration to make a soluble salt from nitric acid and sodium hydroxide solution. This is the equipment that she used:

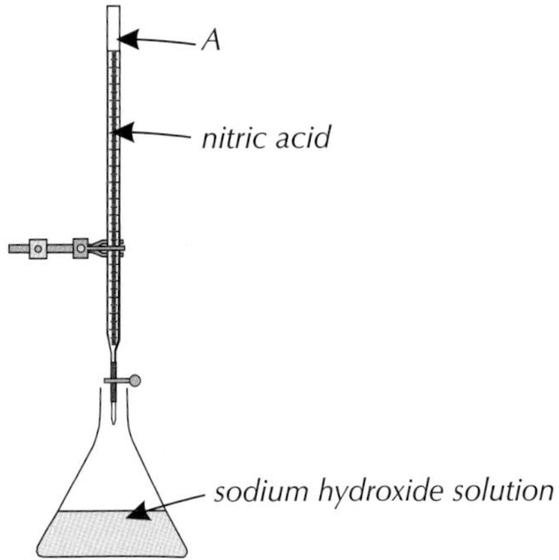

(a) Name the piece of equipment labelled A in the diagram.

(1 mark)

(b) The student adds an indicator to the sodium hydroxide solution before starting the titration. Explain why.

(2 marks)

(c) The student has the option of using either Universal indicator or phenolphthalein as the indicator. Which indicator should the student use? Give a reason for your answer.

(2 marks)

(d) The student repeats the experiment without indicator in order to make the salt. Explain why the student does not add indicator to the sodium hydroxide solution during the repeat of the experiment.

(1 mark)

(e) Describe how the student could obtain the salt from the salt-containing solution at the end of the reaction.

(3 marks)

3 Acids can have different strengths.

(a) Ethanoic acid is a weak acid. Describe how ethanoic acid ionises in solution.

(1 mark)

(b) A 1 mol dm^{-3} solution of hydrochloric acid has a pH of 0 and a 1 mol dm^{-3} solution of citric acid has a pH of 3. State which acid is stronger.

(1 mark)

(c) Sulfuric acid is a stronger acid than ethanoic acid. State which of the acids would react more vigorously with magnesium, and give a word equation for the reaction.

(2 marks)

4 The insoluble salt lead sulfate ($PbSO_4$) can be made in the precipitation reaction of magnesium sulfate ($MgSO_4$) and lead nitrate ($Pb(NO_3)_2$).

(a) Write a balanced symbol equation, including state symbols, for this reaction.

(2 marks)

(b) Suggest another suitable salt that could be reacted with lead nitrate in order to form lead sulfate.

(1 mark)

(c) Predict the insoluble salt formed when silver nitrate is mixed with sodium chloride.

(1 mark)

5 Copper chloride is an ionic compound. When dissolved in water it forms copper chloride solution. Copper chloride solution can undergo electrolysis.

(a) Give the name of the electrolyte used in this electrolysis.

(1 mark)

(b) The ions present in the electrolyte are Cu^{2+}, Cl^-, H^+ and OH^-.
What compound do the H^+ and OH^- ions come from?

(1 mark)

(c) Copper ions move towards the negative electrode.
Describe what happens to the copper ions at the negative electrode.

(2 marks)

(d) Complete the half equation for the reaction that occurs at the positive electrode.

$$\ldots\ldots Cl^- \rightarrow Cl_2 + \ldots\ldots e^-$$

(1 mark)

(e) Give the half equation for the reaction that occurs at the negative electrode.

(2 marks)

Learning Objective:
- Explain oxidation as the gain of oxygen and reduction as the loss of oxygen.

Specification Reference 4.5

Tip: H Reduction and oxidation can also be defined in terms of electrons (see page 153).

1. Oxidation and Reduction

The next couple of pages are about oxidation and reduction. Oxidation is when you add oxygen to a substance, and reduction is when you remove oxygen.

The gain and loss of oxygen

Oxidation can be defined as the gain of oxygen by an element or compound.

Examples

Magnesium is oxidised to make magnesium oxide.

$$2Mg + O_2 \rightarrow 2MgO$$

magnesium + oxygen → magnesium oxide

Copper is oxidised to make copper oxide.

$$2Cu + O_2 \rightarrow 2CuO$$

copper + oxygen → copper oxide

Reduction can be defined as the loss of oxygen from a compound.

Examples

Lead oxide is reduced to make lead.

$$2PbO + C \rightarrow 2Pb + CO_2$$

lead oxide + carbon → lead + carbon dioxide

Zinc oxide is reduced to make zinc.

$$2ZnO + C \rightarrow 2Zn + CO_2$$

zinc oxide + carbon → zinc + carbon dioxide

Reduction and oxidation happen simultaneously. Oxygen is removed from one compound and added to something else.

Example

Both reduction and oxidation occur when iron oxide reacts with carbon monoxide.

$$Fe_2O_3 + 3CO \rightarrow 2Fe + 3CO_2$$

iron oxide + carbon monoxide → iron + carbon dioxide

- Iron oxide is reduced to iron (as oxygen is removed).
- Carbon monoxide is oxidised to carbon dioxide (as oxygen is added).

Combustion reactions involve oxidation and reduction. They're always exothermic.

Example

The reaction of methane with oxygen is a combustion reaction.

$$CH_4 + 2O_2 \rightarrow CO_2 + 2H_2O$$

methane + oxygen → carbon dioxide + water

- Both the carbon and hydrogen are oxidised — they gain oxygen.
- The oxygen molecules are reduced as the oxygen atoms get split up by the reaction.

Tip: Combustion reactions are reactions where something burns in oxygen.

Tip: Exothermic reactions give out energy. Have a look at page 210 for more about this.

Practice Questions — Fact Recall

Q1 Define oxidation in terms of the loss or gain of oxygen.

Q2 Define reduction in terms of the loss or gain of oxygen.

Practice Questions — Application

Q1 A sample of copper (II) oxide, CuO, is reacted with hydrogen gas. Copper metal and water are produced.

a) Write a balanced symbol equation for this reaction.

b) In terms of the loss or gain of oxygen, state whether the copper oxide has been oxidised or reduced during the reaction. Explain your answer.

Q2 State the element(s) being reduced in the following reactions:

a) $CuO + 2HCl \rightarrow CuCl_2 + H_2O$

b) $MnO_2 + 4HCl \rightarrow MnCl_2 + 2H_2O + Cl_2$

Q3 State the element(s) being oxidised in the following reactions:

a) $MnO_2 + 4HCl \rightarrow MnCl_2 + 2H_2O + Cl_2$

b) $C_6H_{12}O_6 + 6O_2 \rightarrow 6CO_2 + 6H_2O$

Tip: Writing balanced equations comes up all the time. Have a look back at pages 23-24 if you need a reminder of how to do it.

Figure 1: *Glucose ($C_6H_{12}O_6$) burning in oxygen.*

2. Reactivity of Metals

The reactivity series tells you how reactive a metal is relative to another. It's all to do with how easily a metal is oxidised.

Learning Objectives:

- Explain the reactivity series of metals (potassium, sodium, calcium, magnesium, aluminium, (carbon), zinc, iron, (hydrogen), copper, silver, gold) in terms of the reactivity of the metals with water and dilute acids and that these reactions show the relative tendency of metal atoms to form cations.
- Explain how a metal's relative resistance to oxidation is related to its position in the reactivity series.
- Deduce the relative reactivity of some metals, by their reactions with water, acids and salt solutions.

Specification References
4.1, 4.3, 4.9

The reactivity series

The **reactivity series** is a list of metals that are arranged in order of how reactive they are. The reactivity of a metal is derived from how easily it forms cations (positive ions). The metals at the top of the reactivity series are the most reactive — they easily lose their electrons to form cations. Reactive metals also gain oxygen (are oxidised) more easily.

The metals at the bottom of the reactivity series are less reactive — they don't give up their electrons to form cations as easily. They're more resistant to oxidation than the metals higher up the reactivity series.

As well as the metals, carbon is often included in reactivity series — a metal's position in the reactivity series compared to carbon dictates how it's extracted from its ore (see page 155). Hydrogen can be included in the reactivity series too — this shows the reactivity of metals with dilute acids (see next page).

Tip: If a metal is below hydrogen in the reactivity series, it's less reactive than hydrogen and won't react with dilute acids.

Figure 1 shows an example of a reactivity series.

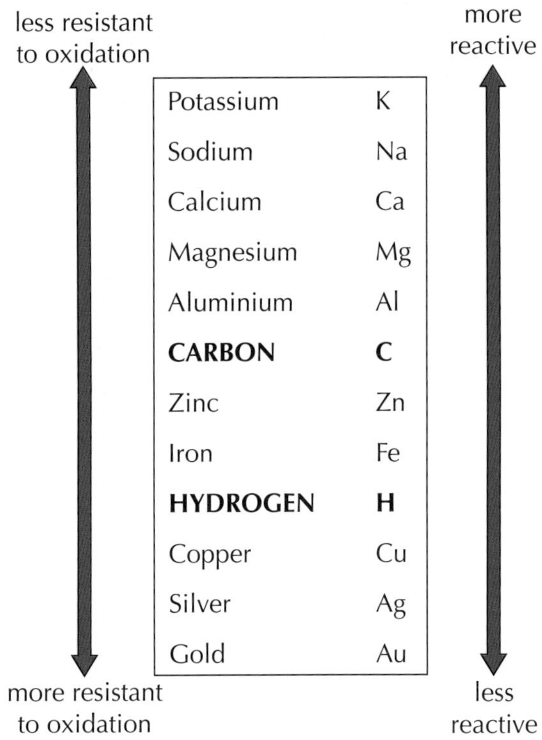

Figure 1: *A reactivity series.*

Finding an order of reactivity from experiments

If you compare the relative reactivity of different metals with either an acid or water and put them in order from most reactive to the least reactive, the order you get is a reactivity series. The higher a metal is in the reactivity series, the more easily it loses its outer electrons to form a positive ion and so the more easily it reacts with the water or acid.

You can also investigate the reactivity of metals by measuring the temperature change of the reaction with an acid or water over a set time period. If you use the same mass and surface area of metal each time, then the more reactive the metal, the greater the temperature change should be.

Reactions of metals with acids

The reaction of a metal and acid produces a salt and hydrogen, as shown in the equation below.

acid + metal → salt + hydrogen

Tip: This reaction can be used to make soluble salts using the technique shown on pages 130-131.

You can see how reactive different metals are by monitoring the rate of hydrogen production when they react with an acid. The more reactive the metal, the faster the reaction will go. The speed of the reaction is indicated by the rate at which bubbles of hydrogen are given off — a speedy reaction is shown by bubbles being produced rapidly.

Tip: The reactions of some Group 1 metals and acids are very dangerous and should not be attempted in a classroom.

The production of hydrogen can be detected using the burning splint test. This involves putting a lit splint at the mouth of the tube containing the metal and the acid. If hydrogen is there, you'll hear a 'squeaky pop'. The more reactive the metal, the more hydrogen is produced in a certain amount of time and the louder the 'squeaky pop'. You could measure the production of hydrogen more precisely by attaching a gas syringe to the test tube at the beginning of the reaction, and measuring the volume of gas given off at regular time intervals.

Tip: There's more about testing for hydrogen on page 126.

Very reactive metals like potassium, sodium, lithium and calcium react explosively with dilute acids, but less reactive metals such as magnesium, zinc and iron react less violently. Copper won't react with cold, dilute acids.

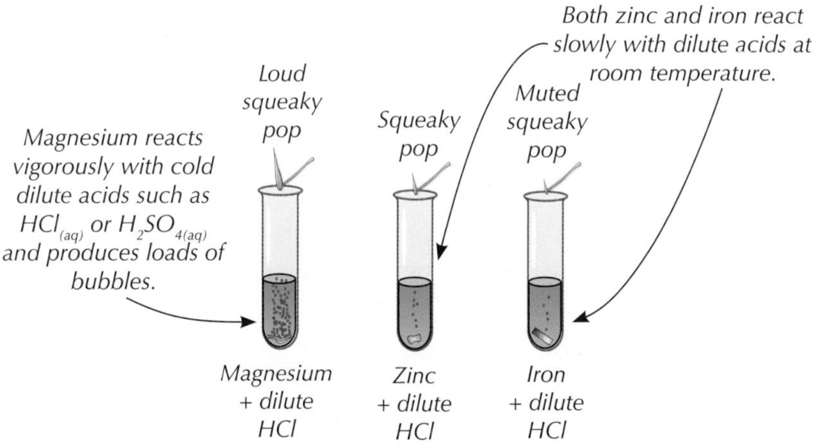

Magnesium reacts vigorously with cold dilute acids such as $HCl_{(aq)}$ or $H_2SO_{4(aq)}$ and produces loads of bubbles.

Loud squeaky pop

Squeaky pop

Muted squeaky pop

Both zinc and iron react slowly with dilute acids at room temperature.

Magnesium + dilute HCl

Zinc + dilute HCl

Iron + dilute HCl

***Figure 2:** The reactivity of different metals in the presence of hydrochloric acid.*

Tip: To be able to compare the reactivities of metals in the reactions between metals and acid, you need to keep the volume and concentration of acid, the mass and surface area of the metal and the starting temperature of the reactions the same.

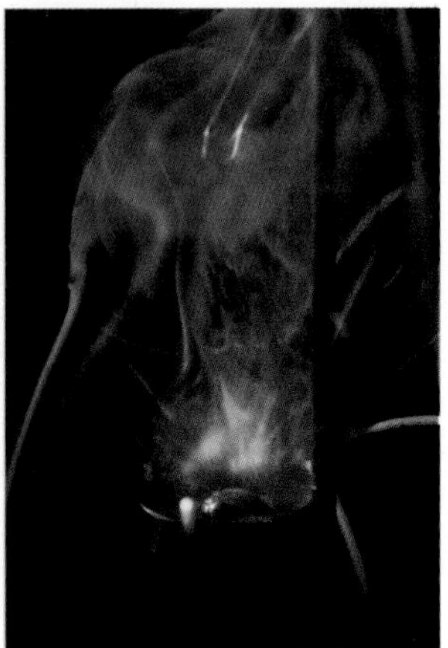

Figure 3: Potassium reacts explosively with water.

Tip: You can see more on the reactions of Group 1 metals with water on page 178.

Tip: The reaction of metals with acids and water is exothermic (they give out energy in the form of heat).

Reactions of metals with water

Some metals form positive ions when they react with water, so the reaction can be used to compare their reactivity. The reaction at room temperature produces a metal hydroxide and hydrogen gas as shown in the general equation below.

metal + water → metal hydroxide + hydrogen

Reactive metals such as the Group 1 metals potassium, sodium and lithium as well as the Group 2 metal calcium, will all react vigorously with water.

Metals that aren't very reactive, such as magnesium, zinc and iron won't react much with cold water. They will however react with steam. You could show this in the lab using the apparatus in Figure 4.

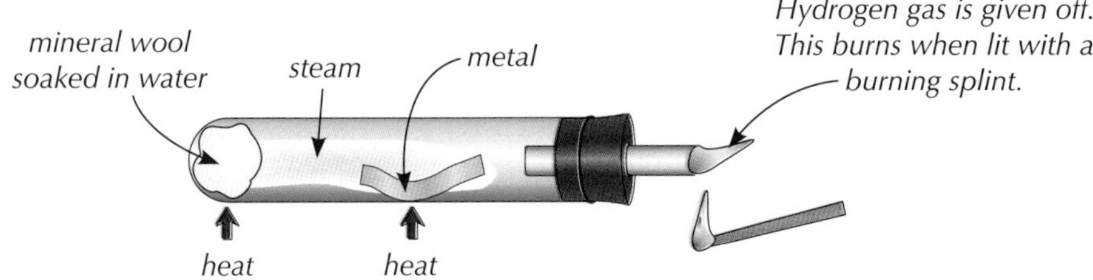

Figure 4: Apparatus used to react metals with steam in the laboratory.

Copper, silver and gold are very unreactive. They won't react with either steam or water.

Reactions of metals with salt solutions

Tip: H These are displacement reactions. Have a look at page 153 for more.

As well as using water and acids to determine the reactivity of metals, you can use salt solutions (solutions containing a dissolved metal compound). The advantage of this is it allows you to directly compare the reactivity of one metal with another.

If you put a reactive metal into a solution of a less reactive metal salt, the reactive metal will replace the less reactive metal in the salt.

Example

If you put an iron nail in a solution of copper sulfate, the more reactive iron will "kick out" the less reactive copper from the salt.

$Fe + CuSO_4 \rightarrow FeSO_4 + Cu$

iron + copper sulfate → iron sulfate + copper

If you put a less reactive metal into a solution of a more reactive metal salt, nothing will happen.

Example

If you put a small piece of silver metal into a solution of copper sulfate, nothing will happen. The more reactive metal (copper) is already in the salt.

Tip: You can use the reactivity series to work out whether a reaction will happen or not. Remember, metals lower down the reactivity series are less reactive. They won't displace metals that are higher in the reactivity series than them.

You can use reactions between metals and salt solutions to work out where in the reactivity series a metal should go.

Example

A student adds some metals to salt solutions and records whether any reactions happen. She records her results in the table below.

Substance	copper nitrate	magnesium chloride	zinc sulfate
copper	no reaction	no reaction	no reaction
magnesium	magnesium nitrate and copper formed	no reaction	magnesium sulfate and zinc formed
zinc	zinc nitrate and copper formed	no reaction	no reaction

- Magnesium displaces both copper and zinc, so it's more reactive than both.
- Copper is displaced by both magnesium and zinc, so it's less reactive than both.
- Zinc can displace copper, but not magnesium, so it must go between them.
- The order of reactivity, from most to least, is: magnesium, zinc, copper.

Tip: The more reactive the metal is compared to the metal ion in the salt, the more vigorous the reaction will be.

Tip: Have a look back at the reactivity series on page 148 — these observations agree with the order of the metals in the reactivity series.

Practice Questions — Fact Recall

Q1 What does a reactivity series show?

Q2 Is an element at the top of the reactivity series more or less reactive than the elements below it?

Q3 Which is more reactive: calcium or zinc?

Q4 Which of these metals is the hardest to oxidise: sodium, iron or silver?

Q5 Write a word equation for the general reaction of a metal with acid.

Q6 Why does iron displace copper in a solution of copper sulfate?

Tip: Have a look back at Figure 1 on page 148 for help answering Q3, Q4 and Q6.

Figure 5: *The reaction of iron and hydrochloric acid.*

Tip: You could use the reactivity series on page 148 to help you answer Q2 and Q4.

Practice Questions — Application

Q1 Give the balanced symbol equation for the reaction of iron and hydrochloric acid. The salt produced is iron chloride ($FeCl_2$).

Q2 A student wants to compare the reactivity of aluminium and iron by reacting them with hydrochloric acid. She decides to add samples of each metal to test tubes containing hydrochloric acid, and measure the volume of gas produced by each reaction at regular intervals using a gas syringe.

a) Name the gas that will be produced by the reactions.

b) State two things that the student should keep the same to ensure that the investigation is a fair test.

c) Which reaction would you expect to produce a larger volume of gas in the same amount of time? Explain your answer.

Q3 Three metals, A, B and C were placed into a test tube containing water. Metal A reacted vigorously and produced a gas which gave a loud, squeaky, popping noise on testing with a lit splint. Metal B did not react on addition of water but produced some bubbles of gas upon heating. Metal C produced a lower rate of bubbles than A and gave a quiet, squeaky pop when tested with a lit splint.
Give the order of reactivity of the metals A, B and C, going from least to most reactive.

Q4 A student added zinc to a solution of iron(II) sulfate.
A reaction occurred forming a precipitate.

a) Give the word equation for this reaction.

b) In a second experiment, copper was used instead of zinc.
Explain why no reaction occurred.

3. Displacement Reactions and Redox Higher

Oxidation and reduction aren't just the gain or loss of oxygen. Confusingly, they can also mean the loss or gain of electrons by a chemical species.

Learning Objectives:

- H Explain oxidation and reduction in terms of loss or gain of electrons.
- H Explain displacement reactions as redox reactions, in terms of gain or loss of electrons.

Specification References
3.28, 4.2

What is a redox reaction?

Redox reactions occur when electrons are transferred between substances.

- Oxidation is a loss of electrons.
- Reduction is a gain of electrons.

Both oxidation and reduction happen at the same time, hence the term redox. Oxidation and reduction can also be defined in terms of loss or gain of oxygen (p.146) but on this page they're referring to the transfer of electrons.

Tip: H A useful mnemonic to help remember what oxidation and reduction are is OIL RIG: Oxidation Is Loss, Reduction Is Gain (of electrons).

Displacement reactions and redox

Displacement reactions are a type of redox reaction. In displacement reactions, a more reactive element reacts to take the place of a less reactive element in a compound (see page 148 for more on the reactivity of metals).

In displacement reactions involving metals and salts, a more reactive metal will displace a less reactive metal in a salt solution. The more reactive metal loses electrons and the less reactive metal gains electrons. So, during a displacement reaction, the more reactive metal is oxidised and the less reactive metal is reduced.

Tip: H You met oxidation and reduction in terms of electrons back on page 133. But it's important here in understanding how displacement reactions work.

Example **Higher**

If you place zinc in a solution of copper sulfate ($CuSO_4$), the more reactive zinc will displace the less reactive copper from the solution. You end up with zinc sulfate solution and copper metal.

zinc	+	copper sulfate	→	zinc sulfate	+	copper
$Zn_{(s)}$	+	$CuSO_{4(aq)}$	→	$ZnSO_{4(aq)}$	+	$Cu_{(s)}$

- Zinc loses 2 electrons to become a 2+ ion — it's oxidised.
  $Zn \rightarrow Zn^{2+} + 2e^-$
- The copper ion gains 2 electrons to become a copper atom — it's reduced.
  $Cu^{2+} + 2e^- \rightarrow Cu$

Figure 1: Displacement reaction of zinc and copper sulfate. The blue colour of the copper sulfate solution fades as copper metal is precipitated out of solution.

Tip: H Equations that show electrons being lost or gained are called half equations. There's more about them on pages 134-135.

Exam Tip H
If you're sitting the higher papers, you'll need to know both definitions of oxidation and reduction.

Practice Questions — Fact Recall

Q1 Define oxidation in terms of the transfer of electrons.

Q2 Define reduction in terms of the transfer of electrons.

Q3 Describe what happens during a displacement reaction between a reactive metal and a solution containing the salt of a less reactive metal.

Practice Questions — Application

Q1 A student adds a sample of zinc to an aqueous solution of iron sulfate. A displacement reaction occurs.

$$Zn_{(s)} + Fe_2(SO_4)_{3\,(aq)} \rightarrow \text{Products}$$

a) Complete the reaction above by giving the formulas, including state symbols, of the products of this reaction, and balancing the equation.

b) State whether the zinc is being oxidised or reduced during the reaction.

c) Which metal is more reactive, zinc or iron?

Q2 Magnesium reacts with hydrochloric acid to form magnesium chloride and hydrogen.

$$Mg + 2HCl \rightarrow MgCl_2 + H_2$$

Explain why the above reaction is considered a redox reaction.

Figure 2: Magnesium reacting with hydrochloric acid.

4. Extracting Metals from their Ores

Most metals are not found in the ground in pure form, they have to be extracted from their ores somehow. Here are some of the ways it's done...

Metals and their ores

Some unreactive metals, such as gold and platinum, are present in the Earth's crust as uncombined elements, rather than as a compound. These metals can be mined straight out of the ground, but they usually need to be refined before they can be used.

The rest of the metals we get by extracting them from metal ores, which are mined from the ground. A metal ore is a rock which contains enough metal to make it profitable to extract the metal from it. In many cases the ore is an oxide of the metal.

Example

The main aluminium ore is called bauxite — it's aluminium oxide (Al_2O_3).

Extraction of metals by reduction with carbon

A metal below carbon in the reactivity series can be extracted from its ore by reducing it in a reaction with carbon. In this reaction, the ore is reduced as oxygen is removed from it and carbon gains oxygen so is oxidised.

Only metals below carbon in the reactivity series can be extracted by reduction using carbon. This is because carbon can only take the oxygen away from metals which are less reactive than carbon itself.

Metals higher than carbon in the reactivity series, or that react in different ways with carbon, have to be extracted using electrolysis, which is expensive (see pages 157-158).

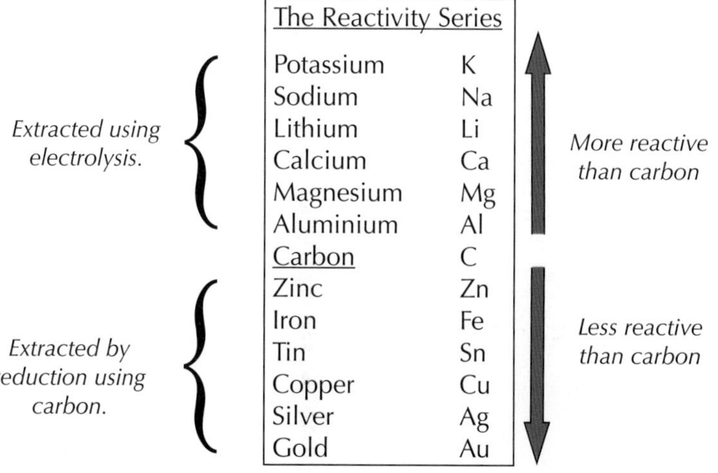

Figure 1: *The reactivity series of metals showing which are extracted using reduction with carbon and which are extracted via electrolysis.*

Learning Objectives:

- Recall that unreactive metals are found in the Earth's crust as uncombined elements.
- Recall that most metals are extracted from ores found in the Earth's crust.
- Recall that the extraction of metals involves reduction of ores.
- Explain why the method used to extract a metal from its ore is related to its position in the reactivity series and the cost of the extraction process, illustrated by heating with carbon (including iron).

Specification References
4.4, 4.6, 4.7

Tip: H Oxidation and reduction can also be defined in terms of the loss and gain of electrons (see page 153).

Tip: During a reduction reaction, oxygen is removed from the ore and the ore is said to be <u>reduced</u>.

Exam Tip
Make sure you can explain why different metals are extracted from their ores in different ways, as well as how they are extracted.

Tip: When you reduce metal oxides with carbon, most of the time you actually get a mixture of carbon dioxide (CO_2) and carbon monoxide (CO).

Tip: Iron oxide can also be reduced by carbon monoxide in a blast furnace. The equation for this reaction is on page 146.

Figure 2: *A blast furnace.*

Tip: Have a look at the reactivity series on the previous page to help you with these questions. You could also look back to page 148 for more about reactivity series.

Example

Iron(III) oxide (the ore of iron) is reduced in a blast furnace to make iron. Iron is less reactive than carbon so when iron oxide and carbon react the oxygen is removed from the iron ore, leaving iron metal.

$2Fe_2O_3$	+	$3C$	→	$4Fe$	+	$3CO_2$
iron(III) oxide	+	carbon	→	iron	+	carbon dioxide

Practice Questions — Fact Recall

Q1 Name a metal which is found in the earth as the metal itself.

Q2 What is a metal ore?

Q3 True or false? Sodium can be extracted from its ore by reduction with carbon.

Practice Questions — Application

Q1 Name the cheapest process that could be used to extract each of these metals from their metal oxides.

a) Iron

b) Calcium

c) Zinc

d) Potassium

Q2 Lithium is commonly extracted from lithium chloride using electrolysis. Explain why reducing lithium chloride with carbon doesn't work.

5. Electrolysis of Metal Ores

Now, the electrolysis of metal ores to get pure metals. The basics of electrolysis are the same as on pages 133-141, but there are a few twists to learn...

Learning Objective:

- Explain why the method used to extract a metal from its ore is related to its position in the reactivity series and the cost of the extraction process, illustrated by electrolysis (including aluminium).

Specification Reference 4.7

Extracting metals using electrolysis

If a metal is too reactive to be reduced with carbon (see page 155), then electrolysis can be used to extract it. The metal ore is melted, then an electric current is passed through it. The metal is discharged at the cathode and the non-metal at the anode.

Example

The main ore of aluminium is bauxite, which can be mined and purified to give aluminium oxide, Al_2O_3. Aluminium is then extracted by electrolysis.

Aluminium oxide (Al_2O_3) has a very high melting point of over 2000 °C — so melting it would be very expensive. Instead, the aluminium oxide is dissolved in molten cryolite (a less common ore of aluminium). This brings the melting point down to about 900 °C, which saves energy, making the process cheaper and easier.

The electrolysis of aluminium oxide is shown in Figure 1.

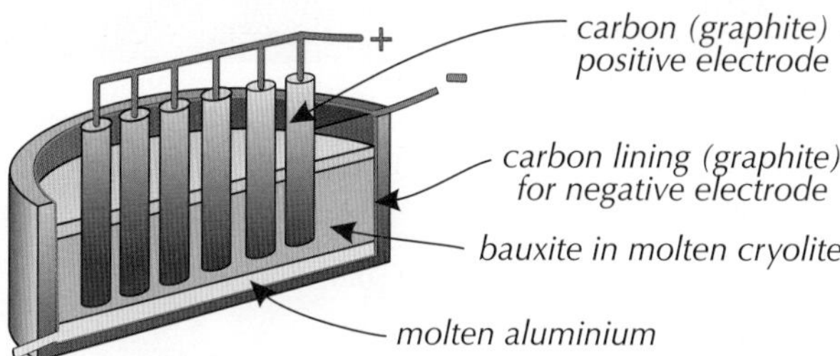

Figure 1: *The electrolysis of aluminium oxide.*

The electrodes are made of carbon (graphite), a good conductor of electricity. The positive Al^{3+} ions are attracted to the negative electrode where they each pick up three electrons and turn into neutral aluminium atoms. These sink to the bottom of the electrolysis tank. The negative O^{2-} ions are attracted to the positive electrode where they each lose two electrons. The neutral oxygen atoms combine to form O_2 molecules.

Some of the oxygen produced reacts with the carbon in the electrode to produce carbon dioxide. This means that the positive electrodes gradually get 'eaten away' and have to be replaced every now and again.

The overall equation for the reaction is: $2Al_2O_3 \rightarrow 4Al + 3O_2$

Tip: In electrolysis, the ore has to be molten (i.e. a liquid), so that the ions are free to move.

Figure 2: *Electrolysis cells at an aluminium factory.*

Half equations Higher

You can write half equations to show the transfer of electrons at each electrode.

Example Higher

The half equations for the reactions taking place at the electrodes when aluminium oxide is electrolysed are:

Negative electrode: $Al^{3+} + 3e^- \rightarrow Al$
Positive electrode: $2O^{2-} \rightarrow O_2 + 4e^-$

Exam Tip H
Make sure you're happy with how to work out the half equations for the reaction during electrolysis. (Have a look at page 134 for the steps.)

Tip: Electrolysis uses a lot of energy. If this energy is produced using fossil fuels, it can be damaging to the environment (see pages 233-235).

Tip: Other factors, e.g. abundance, affect how much a metal costs.

Disadvantages of extracting metals by electrolysis

In order to run electrolysis to extract metals from their ores, you need large amounts of electricity. Electricity is expensive, making electrolysis a pretty pricey process. There are also costs associated with melting or dissolving the metal ore so it can conduct electricity.

In comparison, extracting metals using reduction with carbon is much cheaper. Carbon is cheap, and also acts as a fuel to provide the heat needed for the reduction reaction to happen. This means that, in general, metals lower down the reactivity series (less reactive metals) are cheaper to extract than those higher up the reactivity series (more reactive metals).

Practice Questions — Fact Recall

Q1 Describe what happens at the negative electrode during electrolysis of a metal ore.

Q2 Write the half equation to show the reaction at the positive electrode during the electrolysis of aluminium oxide.

Practice Question — Application

Q1 A manufacturer is studying the materials that can be used for components in a car. It decides the components could be made of either zinc or aluminium.

a) i) Name two processes that the manufacturer could use to extract zinc from its ore.

ii) What process would the manufacturer need to use to extract aluminium from its ore?

b) To make the component, the manufacturer wants to use the metal that is the cheapest to extract from its ore. Using your answers to a), suggest which metal the manufacturer should use.
Explain your answer.

Tip: If you need to, have a quick look back at page 155 to see how to work out the method needed to extract a metal from its ore.

6. Alternative Methods of Extracting Metals

Conventional methods of extracting metals are not sustainable, and metal-rich ores are limited. So, we need to think of other ways to get the metal we need.

Learning Objective:
- H Evaluate alternative biological methods of metal extraction (bacterial and phytoextraction).

Specification Reference 4.8

Extracting metals and sustainability

The supply of some metal-rich ores is running low. For example, the supply of copper-rich ores is limited and the demand for copper is growing — this could lead to shortages in the future. To help with this, scientists are developing new ways of extracting these metals from low-grade ores (ores that only contain small amounts of the metal) or from the waste that is produced when metal is extracted. Using traditional methods to extract metals from these low-grade ores is expensive. Examples of new methods to extract metals from low-grade ores are **bioleaching** and **phytoextraction**.

Bioleaching

Bioleaching is a bacterial method of extracting metals. It uses bacteria which convert metal compounds in the ore into soluble metal compounds, separating out the metal from the ore in the process. The leachate (the solution produced by the process) contains metal ions, which can be extracted, for example by electrolysis or displacement with a more reactive metal.

Tip: H There's more information about electrolysis on page 133.

Example — Higher

Scrap iron is often used to displace copper from these solutions as it's cheap and reduces the amount of scrap iron going to landfill.

Tip: H You can read more about displacement reactions on page 153.

Phytoextraction

Phytoextraction involves growing plants in soil that contains metal compounds. The plants can't use or get rid of the metals so the metal compounds gradually build up in the leaves. The plants can be harvested, dried and burned in a furnace. The ash contains metal compounds from which the metal can be extracted by electrolysis or displacement reactions.

Tip: H The ash produced by phytoextraction contains a higher concentration of metal ions than the soil the plants were grown in, so it can be extracted in reasonable quantities.

Bioleaching and phytoextraction — pros and cons

Traditional methods of mining are pretty damaging to the environment. These new methods of extraction are cheap and have a much smaller environmental impact. For example, they require less energy which is good for the environment because energy use often contributes to climate change and other environmental problems. The low-grade ores used don't need to be mined in the same ways as high-grade ores, which protects habitats as large amounts of earth don't need to be dug up, shifted and disposed of in order to obtain the ores.

Tip: H As well as using more environmentally friendly processes to extract metals, we can recycle metals to prevent us having to extract more raw materials (see page 161).

The disadvantage of these new extraction methods is that they're slow. For example, in phytoextraction, it takes a long time for plants to grow and take up the metal.

Practice Questions — Fact Recall

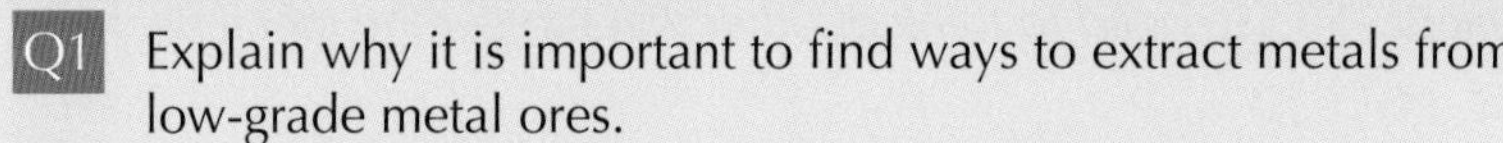

Q1 Explain why it is important to find ways to extract metals from low-grade metal ores.

Figure 1: *Bioleaching of copper sulfide ores at a copper mine.*

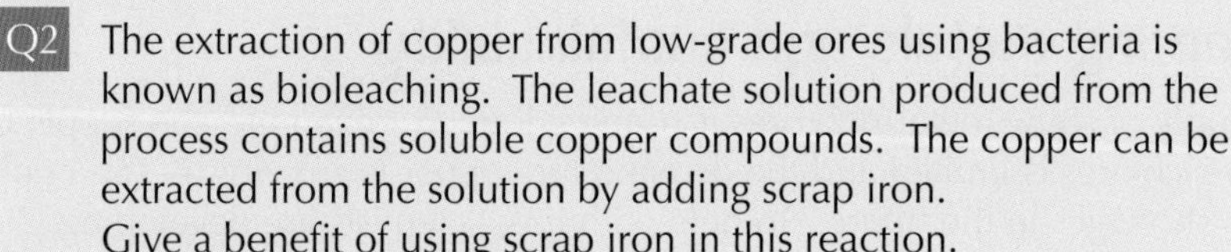

Q2 The extraction of copper from low-grade ores using bacteria is known as bioleaching. The leachate solution produced from the process contains soluble copper compounds. The copper can be extracted from the solution by adding scrap iron.
Give a benefit of using scrap iron in this reaction.

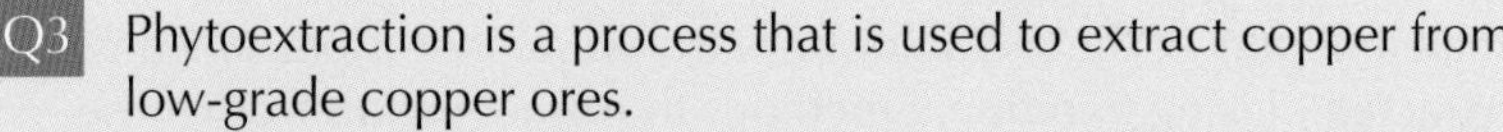

Q3 Phytoextraction is a process that is used to extract copper from low-grade copper ores.

a) Describe how phytoextraction is used to extract copper from low-grade copper ores.

b) State one advantage and one disadvantage of using phytoextraction as a way of extracting copper.

7. Recycling

As many of the materials we use are from non-renewable resources, finding ways to reduce our consumption of them is important to improve sustainability.

Learning Objective:

- Evaluate the advantages of recycling metals, including economic implications and how recycling can preserve both the environment and the supply of valuable raw materials.

Specification Reference 4.10

What is recycling?

Recycling involves using waste materials to make new products. For example, yoghurt pots can be melted down and the plastic used to make other products.

Advantages of recycling

Conserving energy and resources

Extracting raw materials can take large amounts of energy, lots of which comes from burning fossil fuels. Fossil fuels are running out (they're a non-renewable resource) so it's important to conserve them. Not only this, but burning them contributes to acid rain and climate change (see pages 226 and 235). Recycling materials saves energy as this process often only uses a small fraction of the energy needed to extract and refine the material from scratch.

Tip: Non-renewable resources are resources that are being used up faster than they are being made. (They can also be known as finite resources.)

As there's a finite amount of many raw materials, e.g. metals, on Earth, recycling conserves these resources too. Metals, like fossil fuels, are non-renewable. It's particularly important to recycle materials that are rare.

Tip: Recycling of most materials results in a reduction of waste, fewer finite resources being used and a lower environmental impact due to lower energy consumption.

Environmental benefits

Extracting metals also impacts on the environment. Mines are damaging to the environment and destroy habitats — not to mention the fact that they're a bit of an eyesore. Recycling more metals means that we don't need so many mines.

Recycling materials also cuts down on the amount of rubbish that gets sent to landfill. Landfill takes up space and pollutes the surroundings.

Economic benefits

As you saw above, extracting materials often requires more energy than just recycling them, and energy doesn't come cheap. So recycling saves money. It is particularly beneficial to the economy to recycle metals that are expensive to extract or buy.

Tip: Economic benefits have a positive impact on a country's financial state.

Recycling is also a massive industry and creates lots of jobs. The materials to be recycled have to be transported to recycling centres, where they then need to be processed. They are then reprocessed into new products which can be sold. Jobs are created at every stage of this process — far more than are created by simply disposing of waste by dumping it into landfill.

Example

If you didn't recycle aluminium, you'd have to mine more aluminium ore — 4 tonnes for every 1 tonne of aluminium you need. But mining makes a mess of the landscape (and these mines are often in rainforests). The ore then needs to be transported, and the aluminium extracted (which uses loads of electricity). And don't forget the cost of sending your used aluminium to landfill.

So it's a complex calculation, but for every 1 kg of aluminium cans you recycle, you save:

- 95% or so of the energy needed to mine and extract 'fresh' aluminium,
- 4 kg of aluminium ore,
- a lot of waste.

Figure 1: *Used aluminium that's been compressed into cubes for recycling.*

Practice Questions — Fact Recall

Q1 Give two environmental benefits of recycling materials.

Q2 Give one economic benefit associated with recycling.

Practice Question — Application

Q1 Information about the energy saved by recycling certain metals, and their abundance in the Earth's crust, is shown in the table below.

Metal	Energy saved by recycling compared to extraction (%)	Abundance in Earth's crust (%)
Aluminium	95	8.1
Iron	65	5.6
Zinc	60	0.007

a) Which metal saves the highest proportion of energy when it's recycled, compared to when it's extracted from its ore?

b) Give one reason why it might be more important to recycle zinc than aluminium.

Exam Tip
In the exam, you could be given a table containing data that you need to use to answer a question. Best get the practice in now.

8. Life Cycle Assessments

Life cycle assessments are becoming increasingly popular with manufacturers as a way to measure the effects on the environment of a new product.

Learning Objectives:

- Describe that a life time assessment for a product involves consideration of the effect on the environment of obtaining the raw materials, manufacturing the product, using the product and disposing of the product when it is no longer useful.
- Evaluate data from a life cycle assessment of a product.

Specification References
4.11, 4.12

Stages in a life cycle assessment

Life cycle assessments (LCAs) assess the environmental impact of the entire lifetime of a product. The stages of the lifetime of a product can be seen as:

- Getting the raw materials
- Manufacturing and packaging
- Using the product
- Product disposal

At each stage certain factors need to be considered, including the amount of energy that is needed, how much water and other resources are used, the amount of pollution produced, how much waste is formed and how this waste is disposed of.

Tip: Life cycle assessments can also be called life time assessments.

Getting the raw materials

Extracting raw materials needed for a product can damage the local environment, e.g. mining metals. Extraction can also result in pollution due to the amount of energy needed.

The transportation of raw materials to where they are used in manufacturing can result in greenhouse gas emissions from the combustion of fossil fuels.

Raw materials often need to be processed to extract the desired materials and this often needs large amounts of energy. E.g. extracting metals from ores or fractional distillation of crude oil. There are often large amounts of waste associated with these processes which need to be disposed of.

Raw materials for chemical manufacture often come from crude oil. Crude oil is a non-renewable resource, and supplies are decreasing.

Exam Tip
In the exam you may be asked to evaluate the use of different materials for a particular product, using an LCA.

Manufacturing and packaging

Manufacturing products and their packaging can use a lot of energy and other resources. It can also cause a lot of pollution, e.g. harmful fumes such as carbon monoxide or hydrogen chloride.

The chemical reactions used to make compounds from their raw materials can produce waste products. Some waste can be recycled and turned into other useful chemicals, reducing the amount that ends up polluting the environment.

Most chemical manufacture needs water. Businesses have to make sure they don't put polluted water back into the environment at the end of the process.

Tip: The environmental impact of transporting the materials and the product needs to be considered at each stage of an LCA.

Tip: LCAs are a method scientists use to assess how a new product or process might affect the environment.

WORKING SCIENTIFICALLY

Using the product

The use of a product can damage the environment.

Examples

Paint gives off toxic fumes.
Burning fuels releases greenhouse gases and other harmful substances.
Fertilisers can leach into streams and rivers causing damage to ecosystems.

How long a product is used for or how many uses it gets is a factor considered by LCAs — products that need lots of energy to produce, but are used for ages, may mean less waste and raw materials are needed in the long run.

Product disposal

Energy is used to transport waste to landfill, which causes pollutants to be released into the atmosphere. The waste kept in landfill takes up space and can pollute land and water, e.g. if paint peels off a product and gets into rivers. If the material is biodegradable, the space taken up by landfill may only be temporary. However, non-biodegradable materials, such as many plastics, may take up to a thousand years to degrade.

Another way to dispose of products is incineration. This is when waste is burnt at very high temperatures. This cuts down on waste going to landfill and can be used to generate electricity but can cause air pollution.

If all or part of the product can be recycled or reused, it will reduce the amount of waste going to landfill.

Tip: Products that can be made using recycled materials will need fewer raw materials to be manufactured, which improves their life cycle assessment.

Evaluating life cycle assessments

Life cycle assessments can be used to evaluate different products and allow decisions to be made on which product has the least environmental impact.

Example

A company is carrying out a life cycle assessment to work out which car, A, B or C, it should make. Using the data in the table, explain which car the company should produce to minimise the environmental impact.

Car	A	B	C
CO_2 emissions (tonnes)	17	21	34
Waste solid produced (kg)	10 720	5900	15 010
Water used (m^3)	8.2	6.0	17
Expected life span of product (years)	11	17	12

- Car A produces the least CO_2 but produces the second highest amount of waste solids and uses the second highest amount of water. It also has the shortest life span.
- Car B produces more CO_2 than car A, but produces by far the least waste solid, uses the least water and also has the longest life span. On balance, this looks a better choice than car A.
- Car C produces the most CO_2, the most waste solid, uses the most water, and has almost as short a life span as car A. This looks like the worst choice. So, on balance, car B looks like the one that will have the least environmental impact.

Exam Tip
You may be asked to interpret LCAs based on data only or those that include judgements based on opinion.

Practice Questions — Fact Recall

Q1 What is the purpose of a life cycle assessment?

Q2 State the four stages that are assessed in a life cycle assessment.

Practice Question — Application

Q1 A furniture firm carried out a life cycle assessment to decide whether to make tables out of wood or plastic.

	Wooden Table	Plastic Table
Raw Materials	Timber	Crude oil
Manufacturing and Packaging	Wood is cut and treated using low energy processes.	Fractional distillation, cracking and then polymerisation. Manufacture process uses a high amount of energy.

a) Using the information in the table above, explain which table has a smaller environmental impact.

b) Suggest one other variable that the furniture firm should consider when creating their life cycle assessment.

Topic 4a Checklist — Make sure you know...

Oxidation and Reduction

- [ ] That oxidation can be defined as the gain of oxygen and reduction as the loss of oxygen.

Reactivity of Metals

- [ ] That the reactivity series places metals and some non-metals in order of their ability to form positive ions, and so their reactivity.
- [ ] That the more reactive a metal is, the more easily it forms positive ions.
- [ ] How the resistance of a metal to oxidation is related to its position in a reactivity series.
- [ ] How to work out the order of reactivity of metals, based on their reactions with acids, water and metal salt solutions.
- [ ] That the reaction of metals with dilute acids produces salts and hydrogen.
- [ ] That the reaction of certain metals and water forms metal hydroxides and hydrogen.
- [ ] That a more reactive metal will displace a less reactive one in a compound.

cont...

Displacement Reactions and Redox

- [ ] **H** That oxidation can be defined as the loss of electrons and reduction as the gain of electrons.
- [ ] **H** That redox reactions describe when oxidation and reduction happen simultaneously.
- [ ] **H** That displacement reactions are examples of redox reactions.
- [ ] **H** How to identify which species are being oxidised and reduced in displacement reactions.

Extracting Metals from their Ores

- [ ] That unreactive metals are present as uncombined elements in the Earth's crust.
- [ ] That most metals are found as ores in the Earth's crust, which are often an oxide of the metal.
- [ ] That a metal less reactive than carbon (e.g. iron) can be extracted from its ore by reduction with carbon.
- [ ] That electrolysis is used to extract metals that are more reactive than carbon.
- [ ] That extracting metals from their ores using carbon is much cheaper than using electrolysis.

Electrolysis of Metal Ores

- [ ] That electrolysis is used to extract metals, such as aluminium, from their ores if they're too reactive to be extracted by reduction with carbon.
- [ ] That aluminium oxide is dissolved in molten cryolite before electrolysis takes place, as this reduces the temperature at which it can be melted, and so reduces the cost.
- [ ] That during the electrolysis of aluminium oxide, aluminium is formed at the negative electrode and oxygen is formed at the positive electrode.
- [ ] That the oxygen produced reacts with the carbon in the electrode to form carbon dioxide.

Alternative Methods of Extracting Metals

- [ ] **H** That supplies of some metal-rich ores are limited and traditional extraction techniques are damaging to the environment.
- [ ] **H** That new methods of extracting metals from low-grade ores and waste from traditional extraction include bioleaching and phytoextraction, and the pros and cons associated with these methods.

Recycling

- [ ] What recycling means, and the advantages of recycling metals.

Life Cycle Assessments

- [ ] What life cycle assessments are and what stages of a product's life they consider.
- [ ] How to interpret the environmental impact of a product using a life cycle assessment.

Exam-style Questions

1 A student is investigating the reactivity of three metals, **X**, **Y** and **Z**. She reacts a sample of each metal with cold hydrochloric acid in turn, and watches what happens.

(a) The student's results are shown in Figure 1 below.

Figure 1

Metal	X	Y	Z
Observation	Bubbles of gas slowly form on the surface of the metal.	No reaction occurs.	There is fizzing and lots of small bubbles of gas are produced.

Which of the following correctly shows the order of reactivity of the metals, starting with the most reactive?

A Z, Y, X

B X, Y, Z

C Y, X, Z

D X, Z, Y

(1 mark)

(b) Describe a technique that could be used to measure the amount of gas produced by the reaction.

(2 marks)

2 Figure 2 shows a reactivity series.

Figure 2

Sodium	Na
Magnesium	Mg
Aluminium	Al
Carbon	C
Zinc	Zn
Iron	Fe
Silver	Ag

(a) Name an element in Figure 2 that could be extracted from its ore by both reduction with carbon and by electrolysis.

(1 mark)

(b) Name an element in Figure 2 that can only be extracted from its ore by electrolysis.

(1 mark)

(c) Magnesium (Mg) is placed in an aqueous solution of zinc sulfate ($ZnSO_4$) and a reaction occurs.

(i) Give the word equation for the reaction.

(2 marks)

(ii) State which species has been oxidised and which species has been reduced.

(1 mark)

(iii) The reaction was attempted again with silver instead of magnesium. Would you expect a reaction to occur? Explain your answer.

(2 marks)

(iv) Magnesium also reacts with dilute sulfuric acid (H_2SO_4). Describe in terms of oxidation and reduction what happens in the reaction.

(2 marks)

3 A manufacturer is constructing a life cycle assessment for three types of shopping bag. The data is shown in Figure 3.

Figure 3

Bag	Material consumption (kg)	Waste (g)	Energy use (MJ)	Greenhouse emissions (CO_2 eqv.)
A	4.30	14.5	218	8.55
B	7.89	29.7	55	5.78
C	2.05	9.2	103	2.81

(a)* Use the data in Figure 3 to compare the environmental impacts of the bags.

(6 marks)

(b) Explain how the way a product is disposed of affects its impact on the environment.

(2 marks)

4 Copper can be extracted from copper oxide, CuO, by heating with carbon.

(a) Write a balanced equation to show the reaction of copper oxide with carbon.

(2 marks)

(b) Copper extracted using a reaction with carbon usually has to be purified using electrolysis. How might this impact on the cost of extracting copper for use? Explain your answer.

(2 marks)

(c) Copper can be extracted from low-grade ores using a process called bioleaching.

(i) Describe the process of bioleaching.

(3 marks)

(ii) State **one** disadvantage of using bioleaching to extract copper, compared to using traditional methods.

(1 mark)

1. Reversible Reactions

If a reaction is reversible this means it can run in both directions. Sounds a bit complicated, but don't worry — all will be revealed in the next few pages.

Learning Objectives:

- Recall that some chemical reactions are reversible.
- Understand the use of the symbol $\rightleftharpoons$ in chemical equations.
- Describe the formation of ammonia as a reversible reaction between nitrogen (extracted from air) and hydrogen (obtained from natural gas) and that it can reach a dynamic equilibrium.
- Recall the conditions for the Haber process (450 °C, 200 atmospheres and an iron catalyst).
- Explain what is meant by dynamic equilibrium.
- Know that the direction of some reversible reactions can be altered by changing the reaction conditions.

Specification References 4.13-4.16

What is a reversible reaction?

A **reversible reaction** is one where the products of the reaction can themselves react to produce the original reactants. Reversible reactions can be represented like this:

$$A + B \rightleftharpoons C + D$$

The double arrow means that the reaction can go in either direction.

Example

The **Haber process** is an industrial reaction that is an example of a reversible reaction. During the Haber process, nitrogen and hydrogen react to produce ammonia.

$$N_2 + 3H_2 \rightleftharpoons 2NH_3$$

- The nitrogen (N_2) is obtained easily from the air, which is about 78% nitrogen.
- The hydrogen (H_2) can be extracted from hydrocarbons from sources such as natural gas and crude oil.
- The reaction is carried out at 450 °C, with a pressure of 200 atmospheres and an iron catalyst.

Exam Tip
You could be asked about the reaction, starting materials and the conditions of the Haber process in the exam, so make sure you memorise them.

Dynamic Equilibrium

If a reversible reaction takes place in a closed system then a state of **dynamic equilibrium** will always be reached. Dynamic equilibrium is when the amounts of reactants and products reach a balance — their concentrations stop changing. A 'closed system' just means that none of the reactants or products can escape and nothing else can get in.

As the reactants react in a reversible reaction, their concentrations fall — so the forward reaction will slow down. But as more and more products are made and their concentrations rise, the backward reaction will speed up. After a while the forward reaction will be going at exactly the same rate as the backward one — the system has reached dynamic equilibrium. Both reactions are still happening, but the overall effect is nil because the forward and reverse reactions cancel each other out.

Tip: The plural of equilibrium is equilibria.

When a reaction's at equilibrium it doesn't mean the amounts of reactants and products are equal:

- If the equilibrium lies to the right, the concentration of products is greater than that of the reactants.
- If the equilibrium lies to the left, the concentration of reactants is greater than that of the products.
- The exact position of equilibrium depends on the conditions, as well as the reaction itself.

Tip: 'Dynamic equilibrium' is often just referred to as 'equilibrium'.

Tip: H There's more about changing the position of equilibrium on pages 172-173.

Changes in the position of equilibrium

Three things can change the position of equilibrium (which changes the amounts of products and reactants present at equilibrium).
These are:

- temperature,
- pressure (when some or all of the products or reactants are gases),
- and the concentrations of reactants or products.

Example

Ammonium chloride can thermally decompose to form ammonia and hydrogen chloride. This reaction can also run in reverse — ammonia and hydrogen chloride can react with each other to form ammonium chloride.

$$\text{ammonium chloride} \rightleftharpoons \text{ammonia} + \text{hydrogen chloride}$$

- Heating the reaction means that the position of equilibrium moves to the right and more of the products are produced (more ammonia and hydrogen chloride).
- Cooling the reaction means that the position of equilibrium moves to the left and more of the reactants are produced (more ammonium chloride).

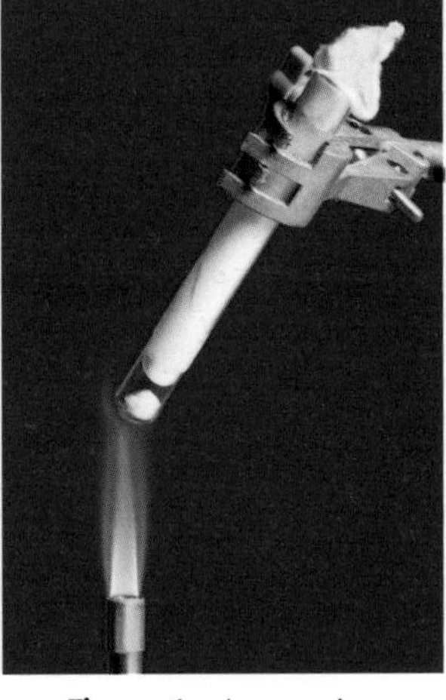

Figure 1: *Ammonium chloride thermally decomposes to form ammonia and hydrogen chloride. These gases can react together to reform the solid ammonium chloride.*

Practice Questions — Fact Recall

Q1 What is a reversible reaction?

Q2 A reversible reaction involves the reactants A and B and the products C and D. Write an equation to represent this reaction.

Q3 At what temperature and pressure is the Haber process carried out?

Q4 Compare the rates of the forward and reverse reactions when dynamic equilibrium is reached.

Q5 State three things that can affect the position of equilibrium for a reversible reaction.

Practice Questions — Application

Q1 Hydrogen gas ($H_{2(g)}$) reacts with nitrogen gas ($N_{2(g)}$) during the Haber process to form ammonia ($NH_{3(g)}$).
Write a balanced symbol equation for this reversible reaction.

Q2 A student adds bismuth chloride to water. It dissolves and reacts with water to form a white precipitate of bismuth oxychloride and a colourless solution of hydrochloric acid. The equation for the reaction is shown below.

$$BiCl_{3(aq)} + H_2O_{(l)} \rightleftharpoons BiOCl_{(s)} + 2HCl_{(aq)}$$

a) After a period of time, the reaction reaches dynamic equilibrium. Describe what 'dynamic equilibrium' means.

b) Explain why altering the pressure of this reaction would not effect the position of equilibrium.

Q3 A student carries out the thermal decomposition of calcium carbonate to form calcium oxide and carbon dioxide.
The equation for the reaction is shown below.

$$CaCO_{3(s)} \rightleftharpoons CaO_{(s)} + CO_{2(g)}$$

The student did not carry out the reaction in a closed system.
Explain why the reaction will not reach equilibrium.

Exam Tip
Remember, if you come across a reaction you're not familiar with in an exam, you can tell whether it's reversible by the arrow symbol. Double arrows ($\rightleftharpoons$) mean it's reversible.

Figure 2: *When it's heated, calcium carbonate thermally decomposes to form calcium oxide and carbon dioxide.*

2. Le Chatelier's Principle Higher

Henri Le Chatelier (1850-1936) developed a principle to explain how yield is affected when you change conditions for reversible reactions. Clever chap.

Learning Objective:

- H Be able to predict how the position of a dynamic equilibrium is affected by changes in temperature, pressure and concentration.

Specification Reference 4.17

What is Le Chatelier's principle?

Le Chatelier's principle is the idea that if you change the conditions of a reversible reaction at equilibrium, the system will try to counteract the change. This means the effect of any changes to a system can be predicted. So by altering the temperature, pressure or concentration of the reactants, you can alter the **yield** of the reaction — making sure that you end up with more of the product you want (and less of the reactants).

Tip: The yield is the amount of product you get from a reaction.

Temperature

All reversible reactions are **exothermic** in one direction and **endothermic** in the other.

- If you raise the temperature, the equilibrium will move in the endothermic direction. So the yield of the endothermic reaction will increase and the yield of the exothermic reaction will decrease.
- If you reduce the temperature, the equilibrium will move in the exothermic direction. So the yield of the exothermic reaction will increase and the yield of the endothermic reaction will decrease.

Tip: Turn to page 210 for more about exothermic and endothermic reactions.

Example — Higher

The reaction below is used to make sulfur trioxide (SO_3). It's exothermic in the forward direction and endothermic in the reverse direction.

Exothermic →

$$2SO_{2(g)} + O_{2(g)} \rightleftharpoons 2SO_{3(g)}$$

← Endothermic

- If you increase the temperature, the endothermic reverse reaction will be favoured and absorb the extra energy. This would result in a higher yield of SO_2 and O_2.
- If you decrease the temperature, the exothermic forward reaction will be favoured and release more energy. This would result in a higher yield of SO_3 — the product that you want.

Tip: H In descriptions of Le Chatelier's principle you might see different phrases like 'equilibrium shifts to the right', 'forward reaction is favoured' and 'yield of the forward reaction is increased' — they all mean the same thing.

Pressure

Changing the pressure affects reactions where the reactants and products are gases. Many of these reactions have a greater volume on one side (either of products or reactants). Greater volume means there are more gas molecules on that side of the equation and less volume means there are fewer gas molecules.

- Raising the pressure favours the reaction which produces less volume (the fewest number of gas molecules).
- Lowering the pressure favours the reaction which produces more volume (the greatest number of gas molecules).

Tip: Remember — changing the pressure only affects the equilibrium position of reactions where some of the reactants or products are gases.

Example — Higher

The reaction below is used to make hydrogen gas. It has two gas molecules on the left and four on the right.

$$CH_{4(g)} + H_2O_{(g)} \rightleftharpoons CO_{(g)} + 3H_{2(g)}$$

- If you increase the pressure, the reverse reaction will be favoured because the left side has fewer gas molecules than the right. This would result in a higher yield of CH_4 and H_2O.
- If you decrease the pressure, the forward reaction will be favoured because the right side has more gas molecules than the left. This would result in a higher yield of CO and H_2 — the products that you want.

Tip: Remember — all of these reactions happen in closed systems. Have a look back at page 169 for a reminder about what that means.

Concentration

If you change the concentration of either the reactants or the products, the system will no longer be at equilibrium. So the system will respond to bring itself back to equilibrium again.

- If you increase the concentration of a reactant, the system tries to decrease it by making more products.
- If you decrease the concentration of a product, the system tries to increase it again by reducing the amount of reactants.

Tip: H The general idea here is that when you make any change to the conditions, the reaction will try to counteract it. In other words, it will do whatever it can to get the temperature, pressure or concentration back to what it was before you started meddling with it.

Example — Higher

Nitrogen and hydrogen can react together in a reversible reaction to form ammonia through the Haber process.

$$N_{2(g)} + 3H_{2(g)} \rightleftharpoons 2NH_{3(g)}$$

- If the concentration of N_2 or H_2 is increased, the forward reaction will be favoured so more NH_3 is produced.
- If NH_3 is removed, lowering the concentration, again, the forward reaction will be favoured so more NH_3 is produced.

Predicting Changes in Equilibria

You can apply the rules from this page and the last to any reversible reaction to work out how changing the conditions will affect the equilibrium position. This has useful applications in industry — you can increase the yield of a desired product by changing the conditions to shift the equilibrium position to the right (towards the products).

WORKING SCIENTIFICALLY

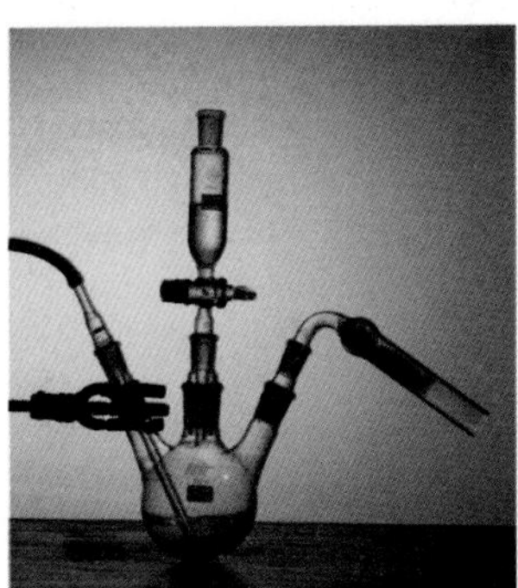

Figure 1: The laboratory apparatus used for the production of phosphorus pentachloride from phosphorus trichloride and chlorine gas.

Example **Higher**

The compound phosphorus pentachloride (PCl_5) can be made using this reaction:

$$PCl_{3(g)} + Cl_{2(g)} \rightleftharpoons PCl_{5(g)}$$

Explain what would happen to the equilibrium position and to the yield of PCl_5 if you increased the pressure that the reaction was being performed at.

- According to Le Chatelier's Principle, if you increase the pressure, the position of equilibrium will move towards the side with fewer moles of gas to reduce the pressure. In this reaction there are 2 moles of gas in the reactants and 1 in the products.
- So, the position of equilibrium will move to the right, since that is the side with fewer moles of gas. This shifts the equilibrium towards the products, so the yield of PCl_5 will increase.

Practice Questions — Fact Recall

Q1 What is the name of the principle which states that if you change the conditions of a reversible reaction at equilibrium, the system will try to counteract the change?

Q2 If you decrease the temperature of a reversible reaction, is the endothermic or exothermic reaction favoured?

Q3 In a reversible reaction involving gases, what effect does increasing the pressure have on the position of equilibrium?

Q4 What happens to the position of equilibrium if you decrease the concentration of the products in a reversible reaction?

Tip: H You might come across double arrow symbols with words above and below them. For example:

$$\underset{\text{cool}}{\overset{\text{heat}}{\rightleftharpoons}} \quad \underset{\text{exothermic}}{\overset{\text{endothermic}}{\rightleftharpoons}}$$

The words 'heat' and 'cool' indicate how the conditions need to change for the reaction to run in the direction indicated — e.g. heat causes the reaction to run to the right.
The words 'endothermic' and 'exothermic' indicate what type of reaction is taking place in each direction (endo or exothermic).

Practice Questions — Application

Q1 Ammonium chloride decomposes when heated to 338 °C to form ammonia and hydrogen chloride. On cooling the reaction can be reversed. The equation for the reaction is shown below.

$$NH_4Cl_{(s)} \underset{\text{exothermic}}{\overset{\text{endothermic}}{\rightleftharpoons}} NH_{3(g)} + HCl_{(g)}$$

a) i) What would happen to the position of equilibrium if the temperature was lowered to 250 °C?

ii) Which compound(s) will have a higher yield as a result?

b) How could the pressure be altered to favour the production of NH_3?

Q2 Sulfur dioxide reacts with oxygen to produce sulfur trioxide.

$$2SO_{2(g)} + O_{2(g)} \rightleftharpoons 2SO_{3(g)}$$

What effect will decreasing the pressure have on the yield of SO_3? Explain your answer.

Topic 4b Checklist — Make sure you know...

Reversible Reactions

- ☐ That the products of reversible reactions can react to re-form the original reactants.
- ☐ That equations showing reversible reactions are written with a double arrow ($\rightleftharpoons$).
- ☐ That the Haber process is an example of a reversible reaction and can reach dynamic equilibrium.
- ☐ That the Haber process is a reaction between nitrogen, which can be extracted from the air, and hydrogen, which can be extracted from natural gas.
- ☐ That the Haber process is carried out at 450 °C, with a pressure of 200 atmospheres and in the presence of an iron catalyst.
- ☐ That at dynamic equilibrium the forward and reverse reactions are occurring at exactly the same rate.
- ☐ That the conditions a reversible reaction takes place in can affect the overall direction of the reaction and the relative amounts of reactants and products.

Le Chatelier's Principle

- ☐ H That Le Chatelier's principle states that if you change the conditions of a reversible reaction the system will react to counteract that change by shifting the position of equilibrium.
- ☐ H That increasing the temperature of a reversible reaction will move the position of equilibrium in the endothermic direction, and decreasing the temperature will move it in the exothermic direction.
- ☐ H That increasing the pressure of a reversible reaction will move the position of equilibrium in the direction that has fewer gas molecules, and decreasing the pressure will move it in the direction that has more gas molecules.
- ☐ H That increasing the concentration of a reactant or decreasing the concentration of a product in a reversible reaction will move the position of equilibrium in the forwards direction.

Exam-style Questions

1 The Haber process is an industrial process that is important in the manufacture of fertilisers. The reaction that occurs during the Haber process is shown below.

$$N_{2(g)} + 3H_{2(g)} \underset{\text{endothermic}}{\overset{\text{exothermic}}{\rightleftharpoons}} 2NH_{3(g)}$$

(a) State a source of hydrogen for use in the Haber process.

(1 mark)

(b) State what type of catalyst is used in the Haber process.

(1 mark)

(c) Suggest **one** way that the yield of ammonia could be increased during the Haber process.

(1 mark)

2 A reusable hand warmer contains a solution of sodium acetate trihydrate. When the hand warmer is activated, the sodium acetate trihydrate crystallises and energy is released. The word equation for this reaction is shown below.

$$\text{sodium acetate trihydrate solution} \rightleftharpoons \text{solid sodium acetate trihydrate}$$

(a) Using the information above, explain why hand warmers that contain sodium acetate trihydrate are reusable.

(1 mark)

(b) The hand warmer can be reset after use by heating it.
Suggest why heating the hand warmer makes it ready to be used again.

(2 marks)

3 Ethanol is produced using a reversible reaction between ethene and steam, as shown in the equation below.

$$C_2H_{4(g)} + H_2O_{(g)} \underset{\text{endothermic}}{\overset{\text{exothermic}}{\rightleftharpoons}} C_2H_5OH_{(g)}$$

This reaction is carried out at 300 °C and 60-70 atmospheres in a closed system.

(a) The temperature that the reaction is carried out at is increased.
What effect would this have on the yield of ethanol? Explain your answer.

(2 marks)

(b) The pressure that the reaction is carried out at is increased.
What effect would this have on the yield of ethanol? Explain your answer.

(2 marks)

1. Group 1 — The Alkali Metals

The elements in Group 1 are commonly known as the alkali metals. The next few pages are all about these metals and their properties.

Learning Objectives:

- Be able to explain why some elements can be classified as alkali metals (Group 1), based on their position in the periodic table.
- Know that alkali metals are soft and have relatively low melting points.
- Be able to explain the pattern of reactivity of alkali metals in terms of electronic configurations.
- Be able to describe the reactions of lithium, sodium and potassium with water.
- Be able to describe the pattern in reactivity of lithium, sodium and potassium with water, and be able to use the pattern to predict the reactivity of other alkali metals.

Specification References
6.1-6.5

Properties of the alkali metals

The **alkali metals** are the elements in Group 1 of the periodic table — they are lithium, sodium, potassium, rubidium, caesium and francium (see Figure 1).

They're all silvery solids that have to be stored in oil and handled with forceps (they can cause chemical burns on the skin).

The alkali metals all have one electron in their outer shell. This gives them similar chemical properties. They're all very reactive and they react in similar ways.

The alkali metals all have similar physical properties too. For example, all the alkali metals have low melting and boiling points (compared with other metals). They are also very soft — they can all be cut with a knife.

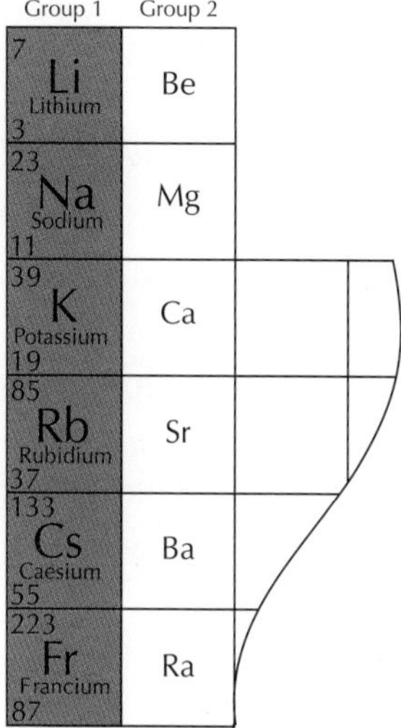

Figure 1: *Group 1 of the periodic table.*

Reactivity of the alkali metals

Group 1 metals readily lose their single outer electron to form a 1+ ion with a stable electronic structure (see Figure 2).

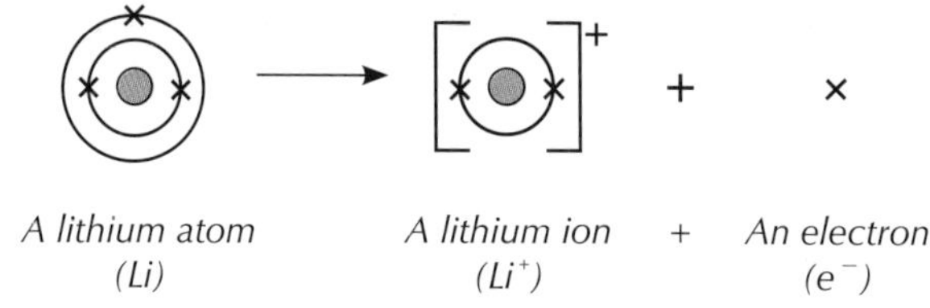

A lithium atom (Li) + *A lithium ion (Li^+)* + *An electron (e^-)*

Figure 2: *An atom of the alkali metal lithium (Li) loses an electron to form a lithium ion (Li^+).*

The more readily a metal loses its outer electrons, the more reactive it is. This is why the Group 1 metals are so reactive. As you go down Group 1, the reactivity of the alkali metals increases. The outer electron is more easily lost because it's further from the nucleus (the **atomic radius** is larger), so it's less strongly attracted to the nucleus and less energy is needed to remove it.

The alkali metals only form ionic compounds. As their single outer electron is so easily lost, they don't form covalent bonds.

Exam Tip
In the exams, you might be asked to predict how a Group 1 element will react based on its position in the group.

Reaction with water

The alkali metals react with cold water to form a metal hydroxide and hydrogen gas. The general equation for this reaction is:

alkali metal + water → metal hydroxide + hydrogen

Exam Tip
Make sure you can write balanced symbol equations for the reactions of the alkali metals with water. It's the same equation each time — all you need to change is the metal reactant and the metal in the hydroxide product.

Examples

- Sodium reacts with water to form sodium hydroxide and hydrogen:

$$2Na_{(s)} + 2H_2O_{(l)} \rightarrow 2NaOH_{(aq)} + H_{2(g)}$$

- Potassium reacts with water to form potassium hydroxide and hydrogen:

$$2K_{(s)} + 2H_2O_{(l)} \rightarrow 2KOH_{(aq)} + H_{2(g)}$$

Metal hydroxide solutions

The hydroxides that are formed when the alkali metals react with water will dissolve in water to give alkaline solutions. This is where the name 'alkali metals' comes from. The reaction of sodium with water is illustrated in Figure 3. The reaction is similar for the other alkali metals but becoming more vigorous as you go down the group.

Tip: You can test for the production of hydrogen in these reactions using a burning splint. A lighted splint will indicate hydrogen by producing the notorious "squeaky pop" as the H_2 ignites. See page 126 for more about this.

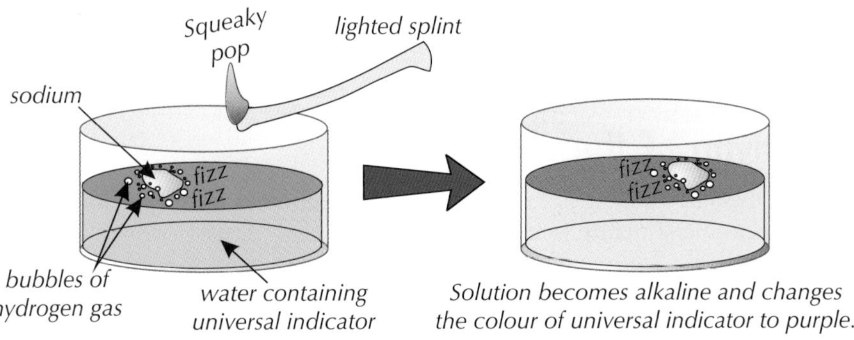

Figure 3: *The reaction of sodium with water.*

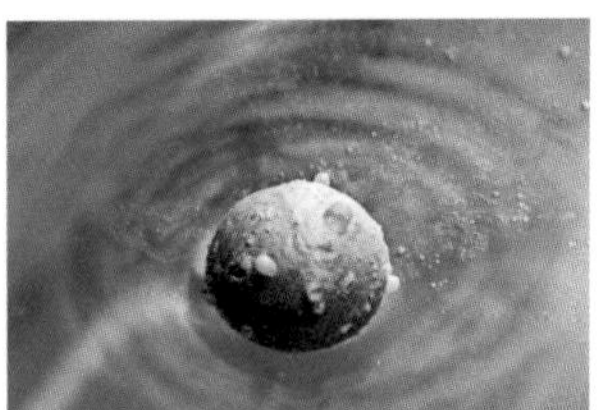

Figure 4: *Sodium reacting with water.*

The reactivity of Group 1 metals with water (and dilute acid) increases down the group because the outer electron is lost more easily in the reaction (see previous page). This results in the reaction becoming more violent:

- Lithium will move around the surface of the liquid, fizzing furiously.
- Sodium and potassium do the same, but also melt in the heat of the reaction. Potassium gets hot enough to ignite the hydrogen gas being produced.

Because you know the reactivity trend in Group 1 (the elements get more reactive as you go down the group), you can make predictions about the reactions of elements further down the group.

Example

Rubidium and caesium are near the bottom of Group 1. You may predict that the reactions of these two elements will be more violent than the reaction of potassium with water. And sure enough, rubidium and caesium react violently with water and tend to explode when they get wet.

Practice Questions — Fact Recall

Q1 Which group in the periodic table are the alkali metals?

Q2 Compared to other metals, do the alkali metals have low melting points or high melting points?

Q3 State the trend in reactivity as you go down Group 1.

Q4 Explain the trend in reactivity seen in Group 1.

Q5 a) Write down the general word equation for the reaction of an alkali metal with water.

b) Will the solution formed when a Group 1 metal reacts with water be acidic, neutral or alkaline?

Q6 State what you would observe in the reaction between:

a) lithium and water,

b) potassium and water.

Practice Questions — Application

Q1 Which is more reactive:

a) sodium or potassium?

b) lithium or rubidium?

Q2 The melting points of Group 1 metals decrease as you go down the group. State which has the higher melting point:

a) lithium or potassium?

b) caesium or potassium?

Q3 Is potassium hydroxide a covalent compound or an ionic compound?

Q4 Write a balanced symbol equation, including state symbols, for the reaction of rubidium with water.

Tip: You might need to have a peek back at the order of the elements in Group 1 at the top of page 177 to help you answer these questions.

2. Group 7 — The Halogens

The halogens are found in Group 7 of the periodic table. The next few pages will cover all you need to know about their properties and reactivities.

Learning Objectives:
- Be able to explain why some elements can be classified as halogens (Group 7), based on their position in the periodic table.
- Be able to recall the colours and physical states of chlorine, bromine and iodine at room temperature.
- Be able to describe the pattern in the physical properties of chlorine, bromine and iodine, and use this pattern to predict the physical properties of other halogens.
- Be able to describe the chemical test for chlorine.
- Be able to explain the relative reactivity of the halogens in terms of electronic configurations.
- Be able to describe the reactions of chlorine, bromine and iodine with metals to form metal halides, and use this pattern to predict the reactions of other halogens.
- Know that chlorine, bromine and iodine form hydrogen halides which dissolve in water to form acidic solutions, and be able to use this pattern to predict the reactions of other halogens.

Specification References
6.1, 6.6-6.10, 6.13

Properties of the halogens

Group 7 is made up of fluorine, chlorine, bromine, iodine and astatine (see Figure 1). These elements are known as the **halogens**. They all have 7 electrons in their outer shell, so they all have similar chemical properties.

The halogens exist as diatomic molecules (e.g. Cl_2, Br_2, I_2). Sharing one pair of electrons in a covalent bond (see p.56) gives both atoms a full outer shell.

The halogens also have similar physical properties. As you go down Group 7, melting points and boiling points of the halogens increase. This means that at room temperature:

- Chlorine (Cl_2) is a fairly reactive, poisonous, green gas.
- Bromine (Br_2) is a poisonous, red-brown liquid, which gives off an orange vapour at room temperature.
- Iodine (I_2) is a poisonous, dark grey crystalline solid which gives off a purple vapour when heated.

Group 6	Group 7	Group 0
		He
O	19 F Fluorine 9	Ne
S	35.5 Cl Chlorine 17	Ar
Se	80 Br Bromine 35	Kr
Te	127 I Iodine 53	Xe
Po	210 At Astatine 85	Rn

Figure 1: *Group 7 of the periodic table.*

Predicting the physical properties of the halogens

You can use the trends in physical properties from chlorine to iodine to predict the properties of halogens further down the group.

Examples

- Melting point increases down the group, and the colours of the halogens get darker (see Figure 4 on the next page).
- So, you could predict that astatine (which comes below iodine) would be a dark-coloured solid at room temperature. Scientists believe that this is the case, but because pure astatine is very unstable it is very difficult to produce enough of it to properly determine its properties.

Test for chlorine

Chlorine (Cl_2) bleaches damp **litmus paper**, turning it from blue to white (it may turn red for a moment first though — that's because a solution of chlorine is acidic.)

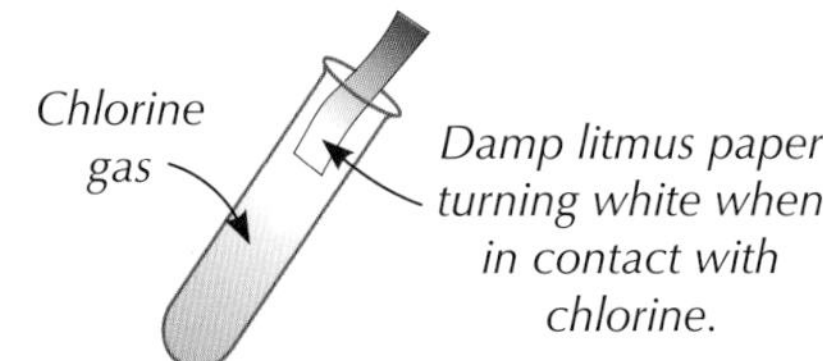

Figure 2: *Testing for chlorine gas.*

Tip: There's more on predicting properties using the periodic table on page 187.

Reactivity and electronic structure in Group 7

As you go down Group 7, the reactivity of the halogens decreases. A halogen atom only needs to gain one electron to form a 1– ion (known as a **halide ion**) with a stable electronic structure (see Figure 3).

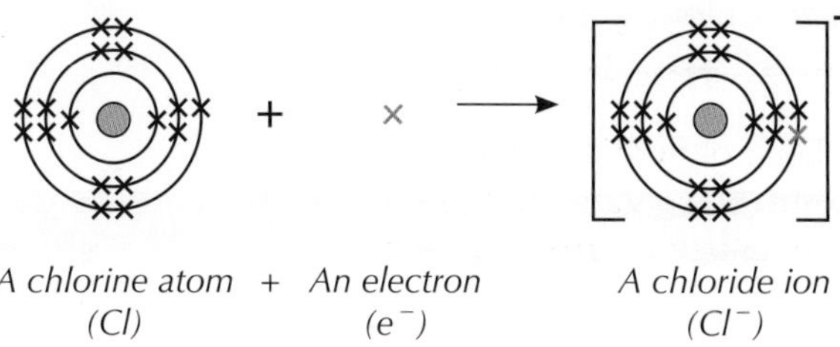

Figure 3: *An atom of the halogen chlorine (Cl) gains an electron to form a chloride ion (Cl^-).*

Figure 4: *Some of the elements in Group 7 — chlorine, bromine and iodine.*

The easier it is for a halogen atom to attract an electron, the more reactive the halogen will be. As you go down Group 7, the atomic radius gets larger, and the halogens become less reactive. This is because it gets harder to attract the extra electron to fill the outer shell when it's further away from the nucleus.

Since all halogens have the same number of electrons in their outer shells, they all have similar reactions. So you can use the reactions of chlorine, bromine and iodine to predict how fluorine and astatine will react.

Reaction with metals

The halogens will react vigorously with some metals to form salts called '**metal halides**'. Halogens higher up in Group 7 are more reactive because they can attract the outer electron of the metal more easily (see above).

Examples

- Chlorine reacts with sodium to form sodium chloride:

$$Cl_2 + 2Na \rightarrow 2NaCl$$

- Bromine reacts with potassium to form potassium bromide:

$$Br_2 + 2K \rightarrow 2KBr$$

Tip: Metals lose electrons and form positive ions when they react. When halogens react with metals, the metal halides that are formed are ionic compounds (see p.54).

Tip: To know what type of compound is formed by a halogen, just replace '-ine' with '-ide'. E.g. chlor<u>ine</u> forms chlor<u>ide</u> compounds.

Reaction with hydrogen

Halogens can also react with hydrogen to form **hydrogen halides**.

Examples

- Chlorine reacts with hydrogen to form hydrogen chloride:

$$Cl_2 + H_2 \rightarrow 2HCl$$

- Iodine reacts with hydrogen to form hydrogen iodide:

$$I_2 + H_2 \rightarrow 2HI$$

Hydrogen halides are soluble, and they can dissolve in water to form acidic solutions.

Example

Hydrogen chloride is a gas. It dissolves in water to form an aqueous solution of hydrochloric acid.

Practice Questions — Fact Recall

Q1 State the trend in melting points as you go down Group 7.

Q2 Describe the appearance of bromine at room temperature.

Q3 Describe the chemical test for chlorine gas.

Q4 Where are the most reactive halogens found — at the top of Group 7 or at the bottom of Group 7?

Q5 What is the charge on a halide ion?

Q6 Describe and explain the trend in reactivity going down Group 7.

Practice Questions — Application

Q1 Which is more reactive:

a) chlorine or iodine? b) bromine or fluorine?

Q2 Which has the higher melting point:

a) fluorine or iodine? b) chlorine or bromine?

Q3 Write a balanced symbol equation for the reaction that would occur between:

a) iodine and potassium

b) chlorine and lithium

Q4 Suggest a name for the acid that forms when hydrogen bromide dissolves in water.

3. Halogen Displacement Reactions

The reaction of a halogen with an aqueous solution of a halide salt is a type of displacement reaction. Read on to find out more...

Learning Objectives:

- Be able to describe the relative reactivity of chlorine, bromine and iodine, as shown by their displacement reactions with halide ions in aqueous solution.
- H Be able to explain why the halogen displacement reactions are redox reactions, in terms of gain and loss of electrons.
- H Be able to identify which species are oxidised and reduced in displacement reactions.
- Be able to use the pattern in the relative reactivity of chlorine, bromine and iodine to predict the reactions of astatine.

Specification References
6.11, 6.12

Displacement reactions

A more reactive halogen can displace (kick out) a less reactive halogen from an aqueous solution of its salt.

Examples

- Chlorine is more reactive than bromine, so chlorine will displace bromine from an aqueous solution of its salt (a bromide). For example:

  chlorine + potassium bromide → bromine + potassium chloride

  $$Cl_{2(g)} + 2KBr_{(aq)} \rightarrow Br_{2(aq)} + 2KCl_{(aq)}$$

- Chlorine is more reactive than iodine, so chlorine will displace iodine from an aqueous solution of its salt (an iodide). For example:

  chlorine + sodium iodide → iodine + sodium chloride

  $$Cl_{2(g)} + 2NaI_{(aq)} \rightarrow I_{2(aq)} + 2NaCl_{(aq)}$$

- Bromine is more reactive than iodine, so bromine will displace iodine from an aqueous solution of its salt (an iodide). For example:

  bromine + lithium iodide → iodine + lithium bromide

  $$Br_{2(g)} + 2LiI_{(aq)} \rightarrow I_{2(aq)} + 2LiBr_{(aq)}$$

A less reactive halogen will not displace a more reactive halogen from the aqueous solution of the more reactive halogen's salt.

Example

If you mixed bromine with sodium chloride, nothing would happen — there wouldn't be any reaction. This is because chlorine is more reactive than bromine, so the bromine cannot displace the chlorine from the chloride salt.

Redox reactions Higher

Like all displacement reactions (see p.153), the halogen displacement reactions are redox reactions. In redox reactions, both **reduction** and **oxidation** occur. The halogens gain electrons (reduction) whilst the halide ions lose electrons (oxidation).

Tip: H In a halogen displacement reaction, the more reactive halogen always gets reduced, whilst the less reactive halogen always gets oxidised.

Example Higher

Chlorine is more reactive than bromine (it's higher up Group 7). If you add chlorine water (an aqueous solution of Cl_2) to potassium bromide solution, the chlorine will displace the bromine from the salt solution.

Tip: H All equations for halogen displacement reactions follow this pattern.

Tip: H You can see the loss and gain of electrons by looking at the ionic equation. The bromide ions on the left-hand side are negatively charged, and lose electrons during the reaction to become neutral. The chlorine atoms on the left-hand side gain electrons when they form the negative chloride ions.

Tip: Remember to carry out a risk assessment before starting any practical work.

- The chlorine is reduced to chloride ions, so the salt solution becomes potassium chloride:

  chlorine + potassium bromide → bromine + potassium chloride

  $Cl_2 + 2KBr \rightarrow Br_2 + 2KCl$

- An ionic equation shows that the bromide ions are oxidised to bromine:

  chlorine + bromide ions → bromine + chloride ions

  $Cl_2 + 2Br^- \rightarrow Br_2 + 2Cl^-$

Demonstrating reactivity trends

You can use displacement reactions to show the reactivity trend of halogens.

1. Measure out a small amount of a halide salt solution in a test tube.
2. Add a few drops of a halogen solution to it and shake the tube gently.
3. If you see a colour change, then a reaction has happened — the halogen has displaced the halide ions from the salt. If no reaction happens, there won't be a colour change — the halogen is less reactive than the halide and so can't displace it.
4. Repeat the process using different combinations of halide salt and halogen.

Figure 1: Chlorine water being added to potassium bromide. The chlorine displaces the bromide ions and bromine (orange) is formed.

Example

The table below shows what should happen when you mix different combinations of chlorine, bromine and iodine water with solutions of the salts potassium chloride, potassium bromide and potassium iodide. All the starting solutions of the halide salts are initially colourless.

Start with:	Potassium chloride solution — $KCl_{(aq)}$	Potassium bromide solution — $KBr_{(aq)}$	Potassium iodide solution — $KI_{(aq)}$
Add chlorine water, $Cl_{2\,(aq)}$ — pale yellow to colourless	no reaction	orange solution (Br_2) formed	brown solution (I_2) formed
Add bromine water, $Br_{2\,(aq)}$ — orange	no reaction	no reaction	brown solution (I_2) formed
Add iodine water, $I_{2\,(aq)}$ — brown	no reaction	no reaction	no reaction

- Chlorine displaces both bromine and iodine from salt solutions.
- Bromine can't displace chlorine, but it does displace iodine.
- Iodine can't displace chlorine or bromine.

This shows the reactivity trend — the halogens get less reactive as you go down the group. You can use this trend to predict how astatine might react. Since astatine is the least reactive halogen, you'd predict it wouldn't displace any other halogens from their salt solutions.

Practice Questions — Fact Recall

Q1 What is a halogen displacement reaction?

Q2 Name the type of halide ion formed by:

a) chlorine

b) bromine

Q3 a) What would happen if you added a less reactive halogen to solution of a more reactive halide salt?

b) Give an explanation for the answer you gave in part a).

Q4 Describe how you could carry out a halogen displacement reaction. How could you tell whether the reaction is successful?

Practice Questions — Application

Q1 Would a displacement reaction occur between the following reactants?

a) Chlorine and sodium bromide solution.

b) Bromine and magnesium chloride solution.

c) Iodine and lithium chloride solution.

d) Chlorine and calcium iodide.

Q2 Write a balanced symbol equation, including state symbols, for the reaction that would occur between:

a) Chlorine (Cl_2) and potassium iodide (KI).

b) Bromine (Br_2) and sodium iodide (NaI).

Q3 Which halogen is oxidised and which halogen is reduced in the following reactions?

a) The reaction between chlorine (Cl_2) and potassium bromide (KBr).

b) The reaction between bromine (Br_2) and lithium iodide (LiI).

4. Group 0 — The Noble Gases

Learning Objectives:

- Be able to explain why some elements can be classified as noble gases (Group 0), based on their position in the periodic table.
- Be able to explain why the noble gases are chemically inert, compared with the other elements, in terms of their electronic configurations.
- Be able to explain how the uses of noble gases depend on their inertness, low density and non-flammability.
- Be able to describe the pattern in the physical properties of some noble gases and use this pattern to predict the physical properties of other noble gases.

Specification References
6.1, 6.14-6.16

Group 0 elements aren't very reactive at all. This is because they have a stable arrangement of electrons in their outer shell.

Properties of the Group 0 elements

Group 0 elements are called the **noble gases** and include the elements helium, neon and argon (plus a few others).

They all have a full outer shell of electrons. For most of the noble gases, this means there are eight outer electrons. Helium, however, only has electrons in the first shell, which only needs two electrons to be filled. As their outer shell is energetically stable they don't need to give up or gain electrons to become more stable. This means they are more or less **inert** — they don't react with much at all. As they are inert they're non-flammable (they won't set on fire).

At room temperature they all exist as colourless monatomic gases — single atoms not bonded to anything else.

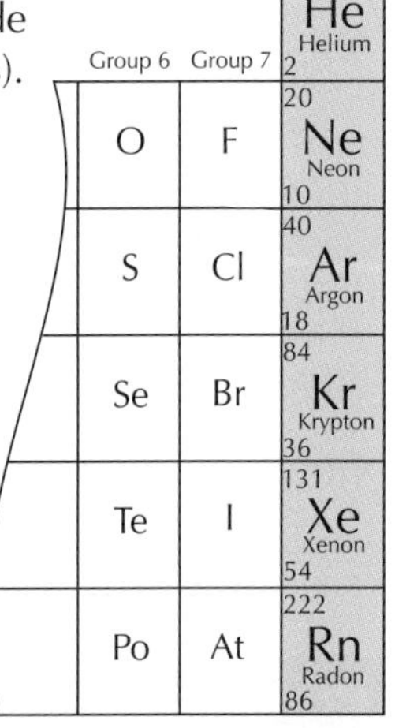

Figure 1: *Group 0 of the periodic table.*

Uses of the noble gases

Noble gases have a unique set of properties, which makes them suitable for a variety of everyday uses.

Inertness

The noble gases are very unreactive, so are often used to provide an inert atmosphere.

Examples

- Argon provides an inert atmosphere in filament lamps (light bulbs). It's non-flammable, so it stops the very hot filament from burning away.
- Flash photography uses the same principle — argon, krypton and xenon stop the flash filament from burning up in the high temperature flashes.
- Argon and helium can also be used to protect metals that are being welded. The inert atmosphere stops the hot metal reacting with oxygen.

Tip: The properties of the noble gases make them pretty hard to observe — it took a long time for them to be discovered.

Density

Group 0 gases have low densities. Helium and neon are less dense than air.

Example

Helium is used in airships and party balloons. Since helium has a lower density than air, it makes balloons float. It is also non-flammable which makes it safer to use than hydrogen gas (which used to be used for the same purpose but is dangerously flammable).

Figure 2: *Helium can be used to make airships, like this one, float.*

Predicting properties of elements in Group 0

As you go down Group 0, the density of the noble gases increases. The melting and boiling points of the noble gases also increase as you go down the group. As with other groups, trends in physical properties within Group 0 mean that you can use information about some elements to predict the properties of other elements in the group. Here are some examples:

Example 1

The densities of helium and argon are 0.2 kg m^{-3} and 1.8 kg m^{-3} respectively. Neon comes between helium and argon in the group, so you can predict that its density will be roughly halfway between their densities:

$(0.2 + 1.8) \div 2 = 2.0 \div 2 = 1.0$

MATHS SKILLS

Neon should have a density of about 1.0 kg m^{-3}.

Exam Tip
There are other methods you could use for these types of question, but don't worry — you'd get marks for any sensible answer.

Example 2

The boiling points of neon, argon and krypton are –246 °C, –186 °C and –153 °C respectively. Using this information, you can calculate the average gap between boiling points and therefore estimate the boiling point of xenon.

Gap between neon and argon: (–186) – (–246) = 60 °C
Gap between argon and krypton: (–153) – (–186) = 33 °C
Average gap: (60 + 33) ÷ 2 = 46.5 °C

You know that boiling points increase as you go down Group 0. So, xenon will have a higher boiling point than neon, argon and krypton. You can predict xenon's boiling point by adding 46.5 to the boiling point of krypton.

Estimated boiling point of xenon: (–153) + 46.5 = –106.5 °C

Exam Tip
You could also use these methods to predict the properties of other elements from the trends within their group, e.g. Group 1 and Group 7 elements.

Practice Questions — Fact Recall

Q1 What are the elements in Group 0 of the periodic table commonly known as?

Q2 Give one example of a use of noble gases.

Practice Questions — Application

Q1 Argon is an inert gas.

a) How many electrons does argon have in its outer shell?

b) Explain how the electron arrangement of argon affects its reactivity.

Q2 The boiling points of the noble gases increase down Group 0. The boiling points of xenon and argon are –108 °C and –186 °C respectively. Use this data to predict the boiling point of helium.

Topic 6 Checklist — Make sure you know...

Group 1 — The Alkali Metals

- [ ] That the Group 1 elements, known as the alkali metals, all have one electron in their outer shell.
- [ ] That the elements in Group 1 are soft and have relatively low melting points.
- [ ] That reactivity increases down Group 1 because the outer electron is lost more easily.
- [ ] That the alkali metals react with water to form hydrogen and metal hydroxides. These hydroxides form alkaline solutions when dissolved in water.
- [ ] What happens when lithium, sodium and potassium react with water.
- [ ] That the reaction of alkali metals with water gets more vigorous as you go down the group, and how to predict the reactivity of other alkali metals from the reactions of lithium, sodium and potassium.

Group 7 — The Halogens

- [ ] That the elements in Group 7, known as the halogens, all have seven electrons in their outer shell.
- [ ] That chlorine is a green gas, bromine is a red-brown liquid and iodine is a dark grey solid at room temperature.
- [ ] The trends in the physical properties of chlorine, bromine and iodine and how to use these trends to predict the physical properties of other halogens.
- [ ] That damp litmus paper turns from blue to white in the presence of chlorine.
- [ ] That reactivity decreases down Group 7, as it becomes harder to attract the extra electron needed to form a full outer shell.
- [ ] That chlorine, bromine and iodine react with metals to form metal halides and with hydrogen to form hydrogen halides (which dissolve in water to form acidic solutions).
- [ ] How to predict the reactivity of other halogens from trends in the reactions of chlorine, bromine and iodine.

Halogen Displacement Reactions

- [ ] That a less reactive halogen will be displaced from an aqueous solution of its salt when reacted with a more reactive halogen.
- [ ] H That displacement reactions are redox reactions, and how to work out which halogens are oxidised or reduced in a given reaction.
- [ ] How to use the trend in displacement reactions of chlorine, bromine and iodine to predict the reactions of astatine.

Group 0 — The Noble Gases

- [ ] That Group 0 elements, known as noble gases, are unreactive as they have a full outer shell of electrons.
- [ ] That noble gases have a wide range of uses due to their inertness, low density and non-flammability.
- [ ] The trends in the physical properties of the noble gases and how to predict the properties of noble gases from these trends.

Exam-style Questions

1 The elements in Group 1 of the periodic table are commonly known as the alkali metals. The alkali metals show trends in their reactivities and their physical properties.

(a) The alkali metals react vigorously with water. When sodium is added to water, the metal fizzes and bubbles of gas can be seen. What gas is produced when sodium reacts with water?

(1 mark)

(b) If Universal indicator was added to the solution at the end of the reaction between sodium and water, the solution would turn purple, showing that it was alkaline. Explain why the solution is alkaline.

(2 marks)

(c) **Figure 1** shows the melting points and boiling points of some Group 1 metals.

Figure 1

Group 1 Metal	Boiling Point (°C)	Melting Point (°C)
Sodium	883	98
Potassium		63
Rubidium	688	
Caesium	671	28

Use the information in **Figure 1** to predict the boiling point of potassium and the melting point of rubidium.

(2 marks)

(d)* Describe and explain the relative reactivities of sodium, potassium and rubidium.

(6 marks)

2 Magnesium generally reacts to form ionic compounds containing magnesium ions with a 2+ charge. For example, magnesium chloride can be formed by reacting magnesium with chlorine.

(a) What group of the periodic table is chlorine in?

(1 mark)

(b) Explain why the reaction of magnesium and bromine is similar to the reaction of magnesium and chlorine.

(1 mark)

(c) Describe a reaction that could be used to make magnesium chloride from magnesium bromide.

(2 marks)

(d) Magnesium does not react with argon. Explain why not.

(2 marks)

Learning Objective:

- Be able to suggest practical methods for determining the rate of a given reaction.

Specification Reference 7.2

1. Measuring Rates of Reaction

Chemical reactions don't all happen at the same rate — some are fast and some are slow. You need to know how to measure rates of reaction...

Calculating rates of reaction

The **rate** of a reaction is how quickly a reaction happens. You can find the rate of a reaction either by measuring how quickly the reactants are used up or how quickly the products are formed (although it's usually a lot easier to measure the products forming). Once you've taken these measurements, you can work out the mean reaction rate using this formula:

Tip: The mean rate of a reaction tells you what the average rate was as a certain amount of product was formed.

$$\text{Mean rate of reaction} = \frac{\text{Quantity of reactant used or product formed}}{\text{Time}}$$

Example

In a reaction, 14.4 cm³ of oxygen gas was produced in the first 8 seconds. Calculate the mean rate of this reaction.

MATHS SKILLS

$$\text{Mean rate} = \frac{\text{Quantity of product formed}}{\text{Time}} = \frac{14.4}{8} = \mathbf{1.8\ cm^3/s}$$

Units of rate

The units of rate will depend on the units you used to measure the amount of product or reactant. The general form of the units will be 'units of amount of substance'/'units of time' or 'units of concentration of substance'/'units of time'.

Tip: The units of time could be different. For example, if you'd measured the time in minutes, the units would be, e.g. g/min rather than g/s.

For example, when the product or reactant is a gas you usually measure the amount in cm^3. If it's a solid, then you use grams (g). If you're measuring concentration, then you might use g/dm^3. Time is often measured in seconds (s). This means that the units for rate may be in cm^3/s, g/s or $g/dm^3/s$. These units can also be written as $cm^3\ s^{-1}$, $g\ s^{-1}$ or $g\ dm^{-3}\ s^{-1}$.

Measuring the formation of product

There are a few different ways that you can measure the formation of products during a reaction, and so calculate the rate.

Precipitation

Tip: A precipitate is a solid that is formed in a solution during a chemical reaction (see page 128 for more).

You can record the visual change in a reaction if the initial solution is transparent and the product is a **precipitate** which clouds the solution (so it becomes opaque). You can observe a mark through the solution and measure how long it takes for the mark to disappear (see Figure 1). The quicker the mark disappears, the quicker the reaction.

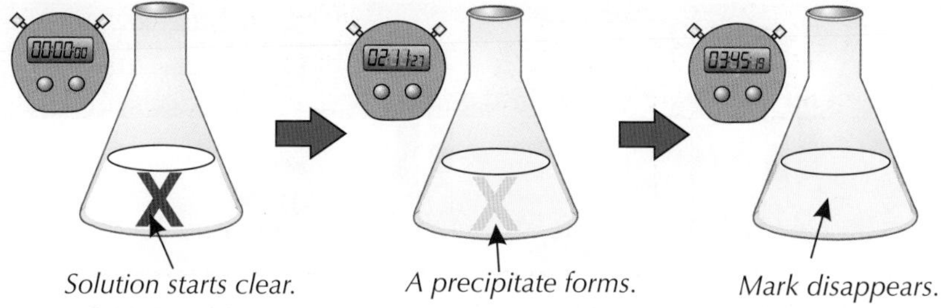

Figure 1: *Measuring the rate of a precipitation reaction.*

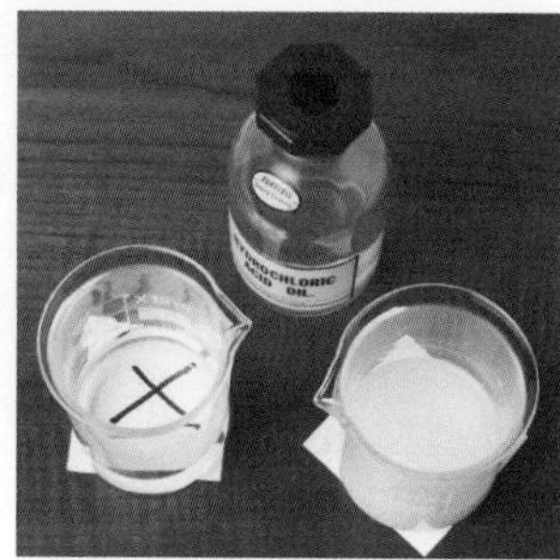

Figure 2: *A reaction that produces a precipitate. When enough precipitate has formed, the cross disappears.*

If the reactants are coloured and the products are colourless (or vice versa), you can time how long it takes for the solution to lose (or gain) colour.

This method is simple and easy to do but it only works for reactions where there's a visual change in the solution as the reaction occurs. The results are very subjective — different people might not agree over the exact point when the mark 'disappears' or the solution changes colour. Also, if you use this method, you can't plot a rate of reaction graph from the results.

Tip: Choosing the right method and equipment to make sure an investigation is accurate and reliable is an important part of Working Scientifically.

Change in mass

You can measure the speed of a reaction that produces a gas using a mass balance. You just place the reaction vessel on the balance. Then add your reactants to a conical flask and put a piece of cotton wool in the neck. As the gas is released the mass disappearing is easily measured — see Figure 3. The quicker the reading on the balance drops, the faster the reaction.

You know the reaction has finished when the reading on the mass balance stops changing. If you take measurements at regular intervals, you can plot a graph of the mass against time which can be used to find the rate at a particular point (see page 195 for more).

Figure 3: *Measuring the rate of a reaction using a change in mass.*

Tip: Some gases don't weigh very much so the change in mass can be quite small. The trick is to use a mass balance with a high resolution, so that very small changes in mass can be detected. See page 12 of the Working Scientifically section for more on resolution.

This is the most accurate of the three methods described here because the mass balance is very accurate. But it has the disadvantage of releasing the gas straight into the room — so if the gas is harmful, you need to take appropriate safety precautions (such as carrying out the reaction in a fume cupboard).

Volume of gas given off

You can also measure the rate of a reaction that produces a gas by using a gas syringe to measure the volume of gas given off — see Figures 4 and 5. The more gas given off during a given time interval, the faster the reaction. You can tell the reaction has finished when no more gas is produced. You can take measurements at regular intervals and plot a graph of volume of gas given off against time in order to find the rate of the reaction at a particular point.

Tip: Rate isn't constant during a reaction — it slows down. Drawing a graph can let you calculate the rate of reaction at a particular point in time during the reaction.

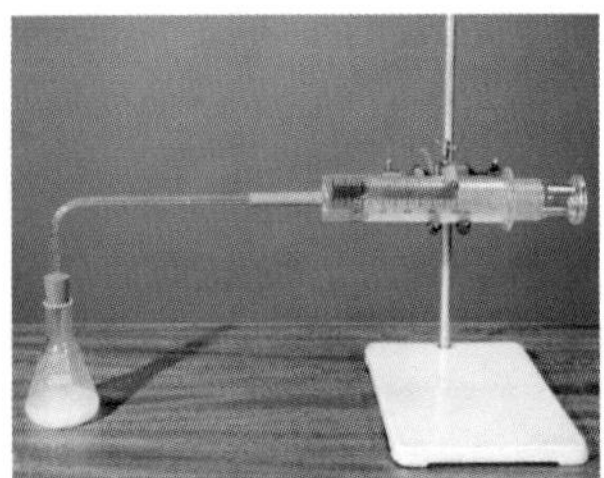

Figure 4: The volume of gas produced in a reaction being measured.

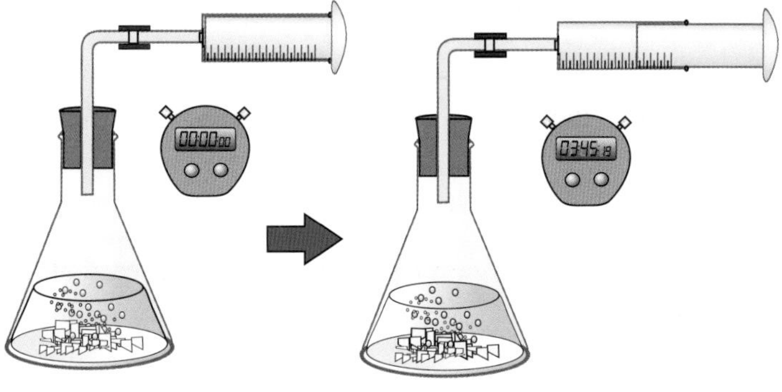

Figure 5: Measuring the rate of a reaction using the volume of gas produced.

Gas syringes usually give volumes to the nearest cm^3, so they're quite sensitive. Also, the gas isn't released into the room, which is useful if the gas produced is poisonous. You have to be careful that you're using the right size gas syringe for your experiments though — if the reaction is too vigorous, you can easily blow the plunger out of the end of the syringe.

Practice Questions — Fact Recall

Q1 What is the formula for calculating the mean rate of a reaction?

Q2 Describe how you could measure the rate of a reaction between two transparent solutions where one of the products was a precipitate.

Q3 A student is measuring the rate of a reaction using a gas syringe.

a) Discuss the advantages and disadvantages of this technique.

b) Suggest another method that the student could use to measure the rate of this reaction.

Tip: Remember — the tiny letters in brackets that you find in some equations are called state symbols. They tell you what state each chemical is in:

- (s) means solid,
- (l) means liquid,
- (g) means gas,
- (aq) means dissolved in water.

For more about state symbols, see page 25.

Practice Questions — Application

Q1 The equation below shows the reaction between sulfuric acid and sodium hydrogen carbonate:

$$H_2SO_{4(aq)} + 2NaHCO_{3(s)} \rightarrow Na_2SO_{4(aq)} + 2H_2O_{(l)} + 2CO_{2(g)}$$

Suggest a method for measuring the rate of this reaction.

Q2 The equation below shows the reaction of sodium hydroxide with magnesium chloride:

$$2NaOH_{(aq)} + MgCl_{2(aq)} \rightarrow 2NaCl_{(aq)} + Mg(OH)_{2(s)}$$

Suggest a method for measuring the rate of this reaction. (If you need a clue, have a look at Figure 6.)

Q3 A reaction produced 4.3 cm^3 of carbon dioxide gas in the first 5.0 seconds. Calculate the rate of this reaction in cm^3/s.

Q4 Some lithium metal was added to water and the change in mass was measured on a mass balance. In the first 8.0 seconds, the mass of the reaction decreased from 34.31 g to 32.63 g. Calculate the rate of this reaction in g/s.

Figure 6: The reaction of sodium hydroxide with magnesium chloride.

2. Rate of Reaction Graphs

Once you've measured the rate of a reaction, you can plot the data on a graph.

Learning Objective:
- Be able to interpret graphs of mass, volume or concentration of reactant or product against time.

Specification Reference
7.5

Graphs showing the rate of a reaction

If you plot the amount of product formed or the amount of reactant left in a reaction against time, you'll get a graph similar to one of the ones in Figure 1.

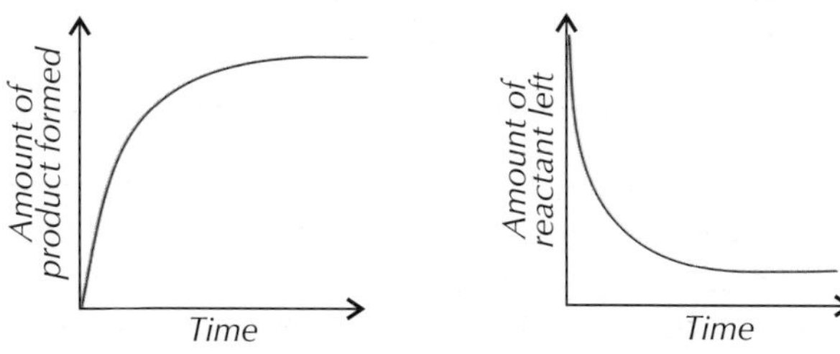

Figure 1: *Typical graphs of the amount of product formed and reactant left against time.*

On a graph showing the amount of product or reactant against time, the rate of the reaction is shown by the gradient (steepness) of the line. The steeper the line, the faster the rate (as it shows that products are being formed, or reactants used up, more quickly).

Graphs of product formed or reactant left against time aren't straight lines — they're curves that start steep, get shallower and then level off. This is because reactions start quickly, then slow down and eventually stop. The reaction has finished at the point at which the line on the graph goes flat.

Tip: Have a look at pages 16-17 for tips on how to draw graphs from a table of data.

Exam Tip
Always look really carefully at any graphs you're asked to interpret — don't assume you know what they show. Make sure you read the labels for each axis and the units that the data is in.

Comparing rates of reaction

The rate of a reaction is affected by the reaction conditions, e.g. the temperature at which the reaction takes place. You can compare the rate of a reaction performed under different conditions (e.g. at different temperatures) by plotting a series of lines on one graph. All of the lines will be curves, but the exact shape of each curve will depend on the rate of reaction and the amount of reactants that you started with.

- The fastest reaction will be the line with the steepest slope at the beginning. Also, the faster a reaction goes, the sooner it finishes, which means that the line will become flat earlier.
- Reactions that start off with the same amount of reactants will give lines that finish at the same level on the graph.

Tip: There's more on factors affecting the rates of reactions on pages 202-203.

Example

A student added some magnesium metal to an excess of hydrochloric acid that had been heated to 30 °C. He recorded the amount of gas formed at regular intervals.

The student repeated the experiment with the acid heated to 40 °C and then to 50 °C. Finally he tried heating the acid to 50 °C and adding double the mass of magnesium. The graph on the next page shows all of his results.

Tip: There are more examples of rate of reaction graphs coming up on the next few pages.

Exam Tip
You need to be able to interpret graphs like this in your exam so make sure you understand why the shapes of these curves are different.

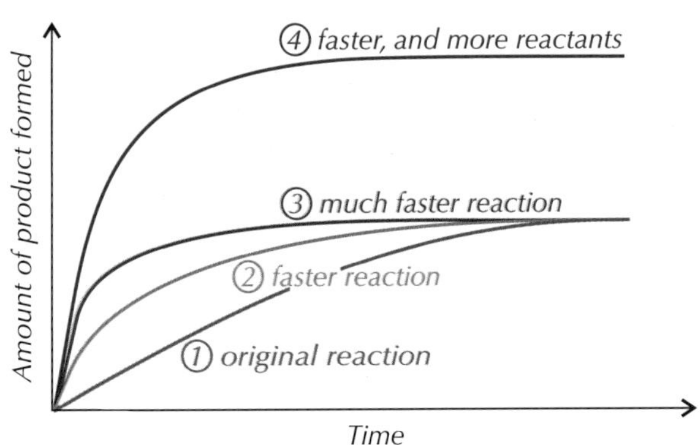

- Line 1 shows the original (fairly slow) reaction at 30 °C. The graph isn't very steep at the start and it takes a long time to level off.
- Lines 2 and 3 show the same reaction taking place at 40 °C and 50 °C. The initial rate of the reaction gets faster as the temperature increases, so the slope of the graphs gets steeper too.
- Lines 1, 2 and 3 all end up at the same level because they produce the same amount of product (though they take different times to get there).
- Line 4 shows the reaction taking place at 50 °C with double the mass of magnesium. It goes faster than the original reaction. It also finishes at a higher level because more reactants were added to begin with.

Finding the gradient of a straight line

The gradient of a straight line is given by the equation:

$$\text{gradient} = \frac{\text{change in } y}{\text{change in } x}$$

You can use this formula to work out the gradient (and therefore rate) of a section of a graph that's a straight line.

Example

Calculate the rate of the reaction between 0 and 20 seconds.

- The section of the graph between 0 and 20 seconds is a straight line.
- So, you can draw a line straight down from the higher point (20 seconds) and straight across from the lower one (0 seconds) to make a triangle.

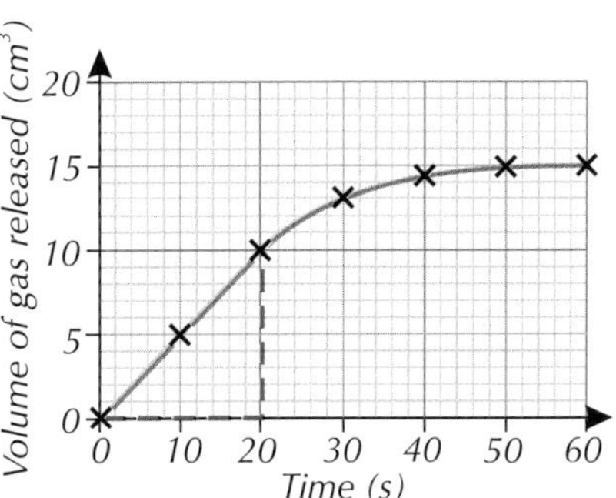

- The height of your triangle = change in y = 10 – 0 = 10
  The base of your triangle = change in x = 20 – 0 = 20

- Use the formula to work out the gradient, and therefore the rate:
  Gradient = change in y ÷ change in x = 10 ÷ 20 = 0.5 cm^3/s

Tip: The units of the rate are just: units of y-axis ÷ units of x-axis.

Mean rates from graphs

To find the mean rate for the whole reaction from a graph of the amount of a substance against time, you just work out the overall change in the y-value (the amount of substance) and then divide this by the total time taken for the reaction. You can also use the graph to find the mean rate of reaction between any two points in time, even when the graph is a curve:

Example

MATHS SKILLS

The graph shows the concentration of the reactant, measured at regular intervals. Find the mean rate of reaction between 10 s and 30 s.

Mean rate = change in y ÷ change in x
= (10 g/dm³ – 2 g/dm³) ÷ 20 s
= **0.4 g/dm³/s**

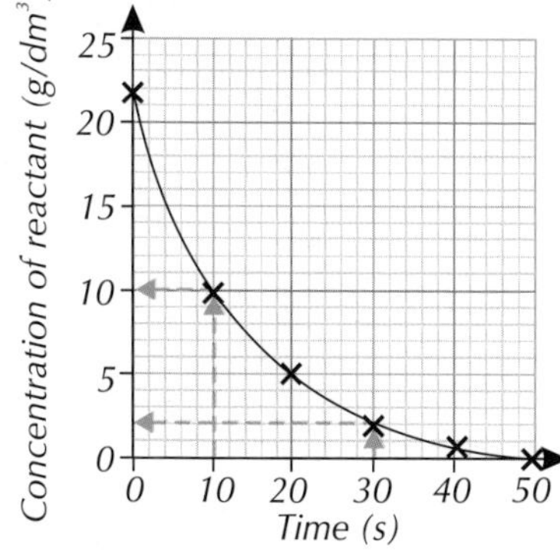

Exam Tip
If you're asked to find the mean rate of reaction for the whole reaction, remember that the reaction finishes as soon as the line on the graph goes flat.

Tip: g/dm³/s means the same as g dm⁻³ s⁻¹.

Tangents and rates

The rate at a particular point in a reaction can be found by drawing a **tangent** to the curve. A tangent is a straight line that touches the curve at a particular point without crossing it.

Example

Here's how to draw a tangent at 90 s on the graph below.

MATHS SKILLS

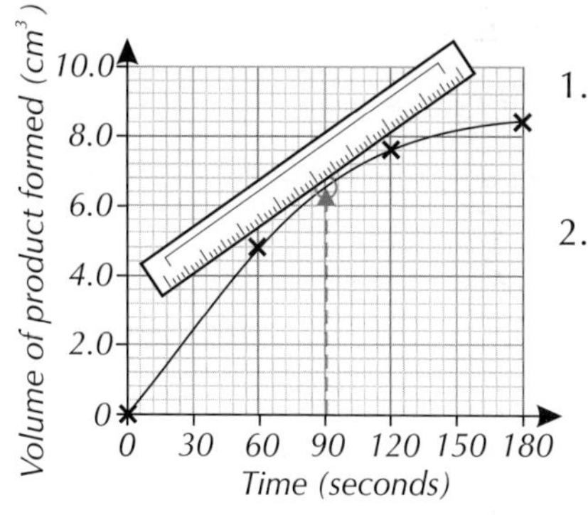

1. To draw the tangent at 90 s, place a ruler at the point on the curve at 90 s so that it's just touching the curve.
2. Adjust the ruler until the space between the ruler and the curve is equal on both sides of the point.
3. Draw a line along the ruler to make the tangent.

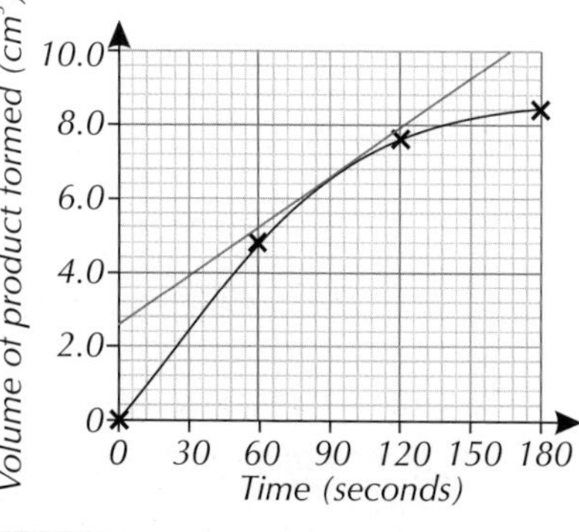

Exam Tip
Always use a ruler and a sharp pencil to draw tangents.

By drawing tangents at various points along the curve of a reaction, you can see how the rate changes over time. The steeper the slope of the tangent, the faster the rate.

Calculating rates from tangents Higher

Once you've drawn a tangent, you can also calculate its gradient. The value you calculate will be equal to the rate of reaction at that particular point in time.

Tip: H The rate is the same as the value of the gradient, not the sign. So if the gradient's negative, just change the sign to positive to give the rate.

Example — Higher

MATHS SKILLS

Find the rate at 40 seconds for the reaction shown in the following graph:

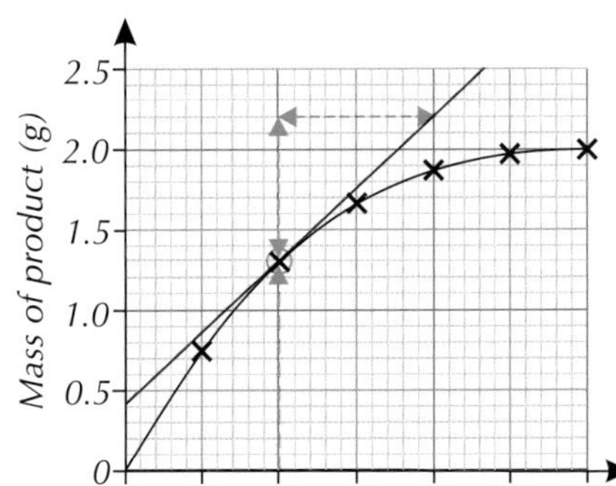

1. Draw a tangent to the curve at the point where you want to know the rate — here it's 40 s.
2. Pick two points on the line that are easy to read. Use them to calculate the gradient of the tangent in order to find the rate:

gradient = change in y ÷ change in x
= (2.2 – 1.3) ÷ (80 – 40)
= 0.90 ÷ 40 = 0.023

So, the rate of reaction at 40 s was **0.023 g/s.**

Tip: Remember, g/s can also be written as g s^{-1}.

Practice Questions — Application

Q1 A reaction took 200 s to finish and produced 24 cm^3 of gas.

a) Which of the graphs below shows the volume of gas produced against time over the course of this reaction?

A

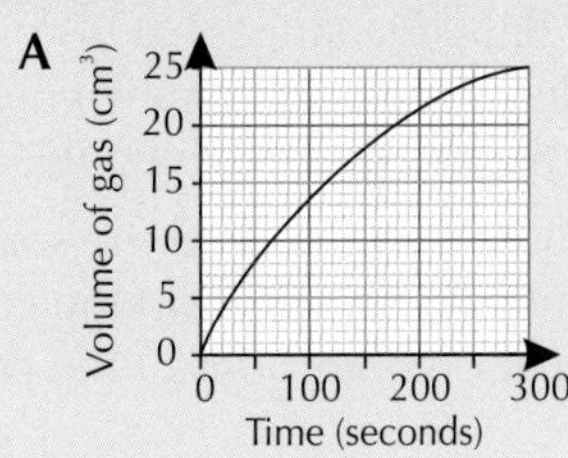

B

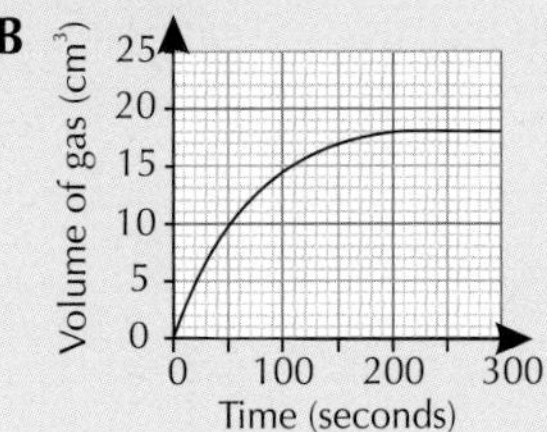

C

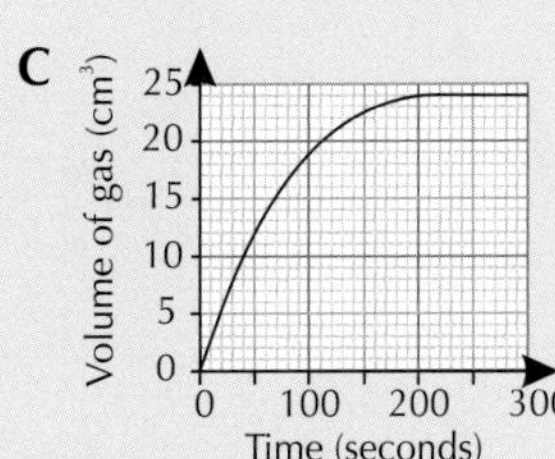

D

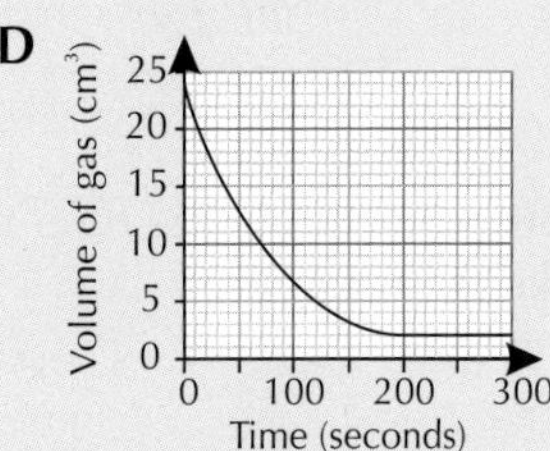

b) Under different conditions the reaction took 150 s to finish and produced 24 cm^3 of gas. At the beginning of this reaction, would you predict the gradient of a graph of the amount of gas produced against time to be steeper or shallower than the original reaction?

Q2 The graph below shows the same reaction performed at three different temperatures. All other conditions were kept the same.

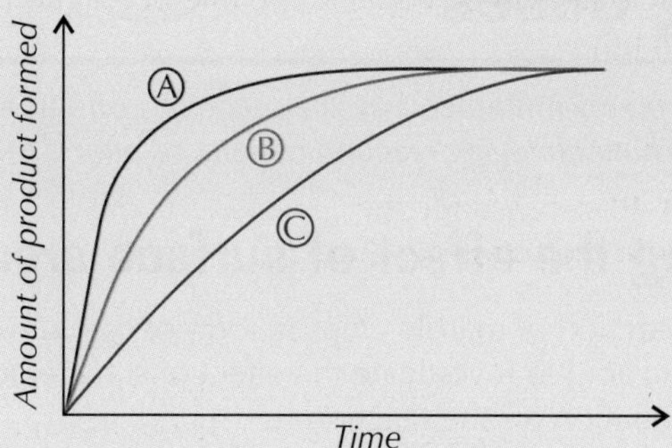

Temperature increases the rate of a reaction.
Which of these reactions (A, B or C) was performed at the highest temperature? Explain your answer.

Q3 The graph below shows the amount of product formed over time in a reaction.

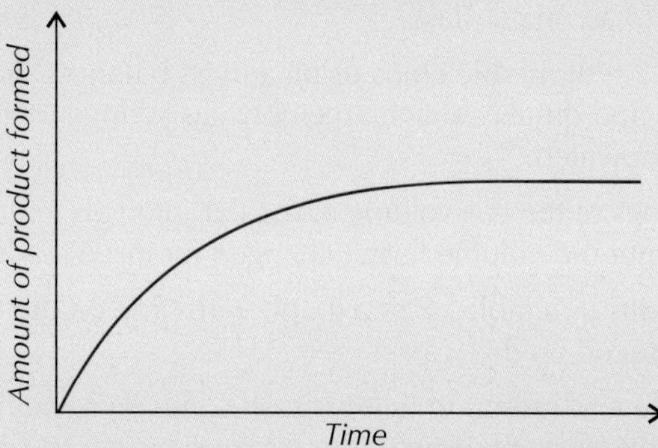

Copy this graph and sketch on the curve that would be produced if the reaction was performed with double the amount of reactant.

Q4 The graph below shows the change in concentration of a reactant against time during a reaction. After 60 seconds, the reaction is complete.

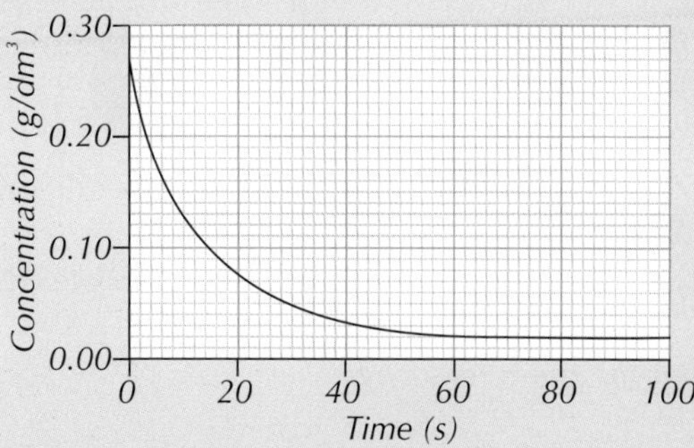

a) Find the mean rate of the entire reaction.

b) Find the rate of the reaction at 20 seconds.

Tip: See page 202 for more on how and why temperature affects the rate of reaction.

Exam Tip
If you need to draw on a graph make sure you use a pencil rather than a pen. If you use pen you won't be able to rub it out if you make a mistake. Also, if you obscure something on the graph that you later need to read you'll be in trouble.

3. Rate Experiments Involving Gases

Learning Objective:

- Be able to investigate the effects of changing the conditions of a reaction on its rate, and do so by measuring the production of a gas — as shown by the reaction between hydrochloric acid and marble chips (Core Practical).

Specification Reference 7.1

The rate of a reaction is influenced by the reaction conditions. You need to be able to investigate how changing reaction conditions affects the rate of a reaction.

Investigating the effect of surface area on rate

You can use the reaction of marble chips (a form of calcium carbonate) with dilute hydrochloric acid to investigate the effect of surface area on the rate of a reaction. The equation for the reaction is:

$$2HCl_{(aq)} + CaCO_{3\,(s)} \rightarrow CaCl_{2\,(aq)} + H_2O_{(l)} + CO_{2\,(g)}$$

This reaction gives off carbon dioxide gas, so you can follow the rate of the reaction by measuring the volume of gas produced using a gas syringe. Here's what you do:

- Use a measuring cylinder to measure 100 cm^3 of dilute hydrochloric acid and add it to a conical flask.
- Weigh out 2 g of marble chips using a mass balance. Add the chips to the acid and quickly attach an empty gas syringe to the flask. Start the stopwatch.
- Take readings of the gas volume at regular intervals (e.g. every 30 seconds) until the volume hasn't changed for three readings in a row.
- Put the results in a table. Plot a graph with time on the *x*-axis and volume of gas produced on the *y*-axis.
- Use a pestle and mortar to lightly crush some more marble chips, and repeat the experiment using these. Make sure you use exactly the same volume and concentration of acid, and exactly the same mass of marble chips. This will ensure your experiment is a fair test — see page 10.
- Repeat the experiment again with the same mass of powdered chalk.

Tip: Make sure you complete a risk assessment before you do this experiment.

Tip: Marble and chalk are both made of the same thing — calcium carbonate ($CaCO_3$).

Tip: It's important your system is air tight so no gas escapes.

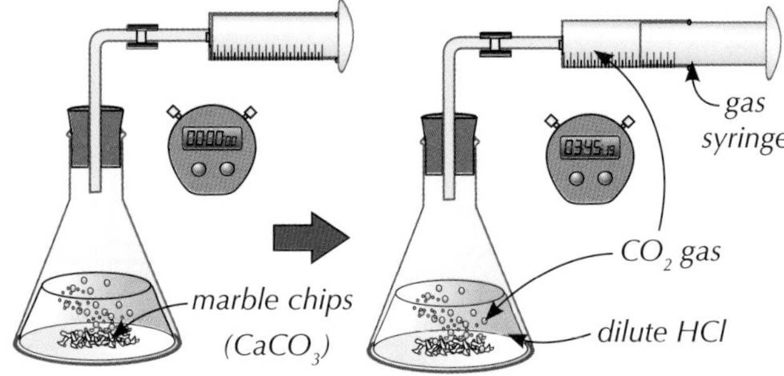

Figure 1: *Investigating the rate of reaction between hydrochloric acid and marble chips.*

Figure 2: *The reaction of hydrochloric acid with calcium carbonate powder (left) and marble chips (right).*

The results

Changing the size of the marble chips changes the surface area of the solid reactant. Smaller particles have a bigger surface area to volume ratio than larger particles — so as you go from large chips to crushed chips to powdered chalk, the surface area to volume ratio of the calcium carbonate increases.

Figure 3 on the next page is an example of the type of thing you would expect to see if you carried out the experiment and plotted your results.

Lines 1 to 3 in Figure 3 show that the finer the particles are (and therefore the greater the surface area of the solid reactant), the sooner the reaction finishes and so the faster the reaction.

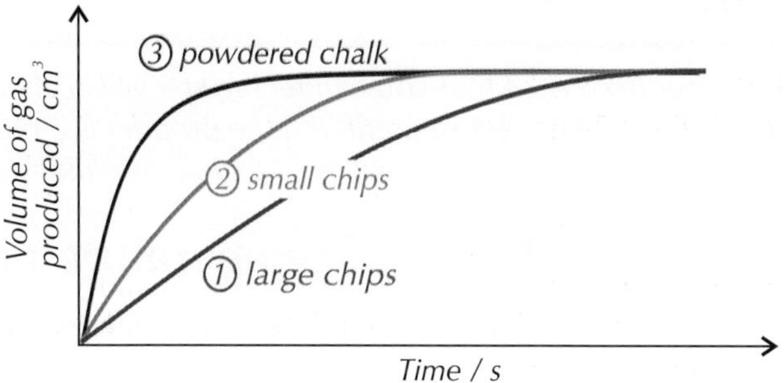

Figure 3: *Graph to show rates of reaction between dilute hydrochloric acid and varying sizes of calcium carbonate.*

Tip: You could also measure the rate of this reaction by measuring the loss of mass as the gas is produced (see page 191).

Investigating the effect of concentration on rate

The reaction between marble chips and hydrochloric acid is also good for measuring how changing the reactant concentration affects reaction rate.

You can measure the effect of concentration on rate by following the same method described on the previous page. However, this time you repeat the experiment with exactly the same mass and surface area of marble chips and exactly the same volume of acid, but using different concentrations of acid. Figure 4 shows the results you might expect to get. Lines 1 to 3 in Figure 4 show that a higher concentration gives a faster reaction, with the reaction finishing sooner.

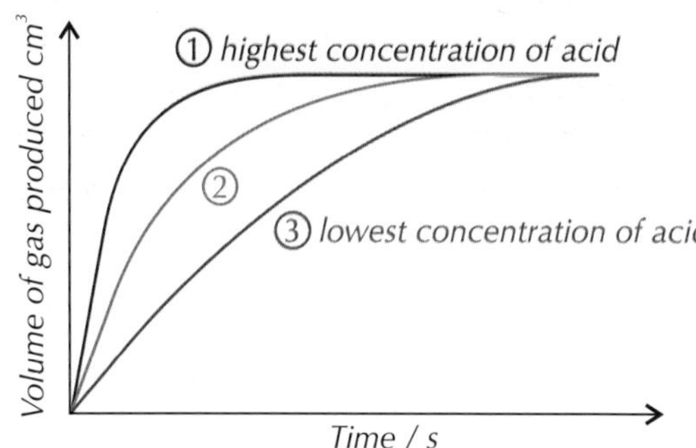

Figure 4: *Graph to show rates of reaction between calcium carbonate and varying concentrations of hydrochloric acid.*

Tip: The effects of surface area and concentration on the rate of a reaction can be explained by collision theory. See pages 202-204 for more.

Practice Question — Fact Recall

Q1 Describe how you would carry out an experiment to investigate the effect of concentration on the rate of the reaction between marble chips and hydrochloric acid.

4. Rate Experiments Involving Precipitation

Learning Objective:

- Be able to investigate the effects of changing the conditions of a reaction on its rate, and do so by observing a colour change — as shown by the reaction between sodium thiosulfate and hydrochloric acid (Core Practical).

Specification Reference
7.1

Tip: Always carry out a risk assessment before you do an experiment in class. This reaction releases sulfur dioxide, which is a toxic gas, so the experiment should be carried out in a well-ventilated place, e.g. a fume cupboard.

Tip: Remember, a precipitate is a solid formed in a solution during a chemical reaction.

Tip: Check the temperature of your solutions using a thermometer.

Tip: As well as the depth, the concentration and volume of the solutions must be kept the same in each repeat.

You might remember from *p.74* *that you can record the visual change in a reaction if the initial solution is transparent and the product is a precipitate. This is one way of investigating how changing reaction conditions affects rate.*

Investigating the effects of temperature on rate

You can see how temperature affects reaction rate by looking at the reaction between sodium thiosulfate and hydrochloric acid. Sodium thiosulfate and hydrochloric acid are both colourless solutions. They react together to form a yellow precipitate of sulfur, so the reaction mixture will become more turbid (cloudy) as the reaction continues:

$$2HCl_{(aq)} + Na_2S_2O_{3(aq)} \rightarrow 2NaCl_{(aq)} + SO_{2(g)} + S_{(s)} + H_2O_{(l)}$$

This experiment involves looking through the reaction solution at a black cross and timing how long it takes to disappear (see Figure 1).

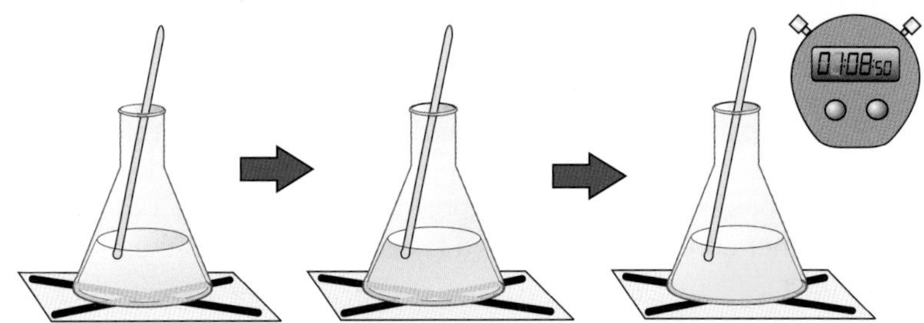

Figure 1: *Investigating the rate of the reaction between sodium thiosulfate and hydrochloric acid.*

- Start by measuring out 50 cm^3 of dilute sodium thiosulfate solution and 10 cm^3 of dilute hydrochloric acid. Use a water bath to gently heat both solutions to the same desired temperature before you mix them.
- Mix the solutions in a conical flask. Place the flask on a piece of paper with a black cross drawn on it and start the stopwatch.
- Now watch the black cross through the cloudy, yellow sulfur and time how long it takes to disappear. Record your results in a table.
- Repeat the reaction a few more times, but each time heat the solutions of hydrochloric acid and sodium thiosulfate to a different temperature — e.g. you could carry out the reaction at 20 °C, 30 °C, 40 °C and 50 °C. Repeat the reaction three times at each temperature and calculate the mean time taken for the cross to disappear. This will make your results more precise.
- The depth of the solutions must be kept the same, so make sure you use the same reaction flask each time you repeat the experiment. Also, different people might think the cross has disappeared at slightly different times, so the same person should observe the cross each time, to make it a fair test.

The results

You can plot the time taken for the mark to disappear against the temperature of the reacting solutions (see Figure 2).

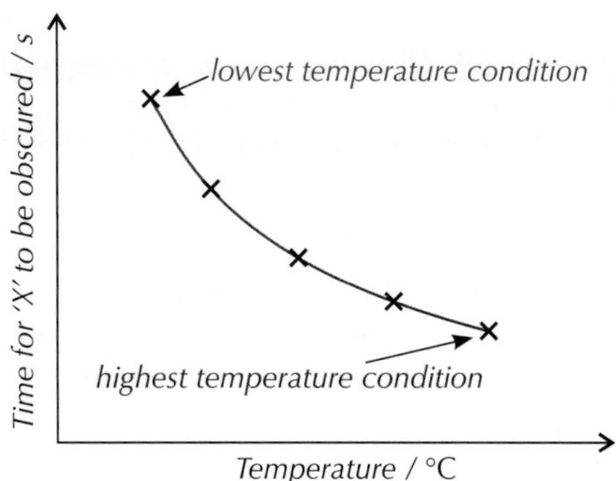

Figure 2: *Graph to show how changing the temperature of a reaction mixture affects the time taken for a mark to be obscured.*

If you look at Figure 2, you can see that the reactions that happened at lower temperatures took longer to obscure the mark, whereas the reactions happening at higher temperatures finished sooner. So increasing the temperature increases the rate of the reaction.

Tip: The effect of temperature on the rate of a reaction can be explained using collision theory — see next page.

Tip: Figure 2 isn't a rate of reaction graph — it doesn't show amount of product formed/reactant used against time.

Practice Question — Fact Recall

Q1 Describe one way that you could measure how the temperature affects the rate of the reaction between sodium thiosulfate and hydrochloric acid.

Practice Question — Application

Q1 Two scientists investigate how long it takes for a colour change to happen in a reaction that takes place in solution at different temperatures. They repeat their experiment at each temperature a number of times.

a) State what the independent and dependent variables are in this experiment.

b) Name two other variables that should be controlled in this experiment.

c) What is the purpose of repeating the experiment at each temperature?

d) Why is it important that only one of the scientists decides when the colour change is complete for every repeat?

Learning Objectives:

- Be able to explain how reactions occur when particles collide and that rates of reaction are increased when the frequency and/or energy of collisions is increased.
- Be able to explain, in terms of frequency and/or energy of collisions between particles, the effect of changes in temperature, concentration, pressure (of reactions involving gases) and surface area to volume ratio of a solid on rates of reaction.

Specification References
7.3, 7.4

5. Collision Theory

Collision theory can be used to explain why some reactions go faster than others.

Factors that affect the rate of a reaction

There are four main factors that affect how quickly a reaction goes:

1. Temperature — the higher the temperature, the faster the reaction.
2. Concentration (or pressure for gases) — the more concentrated the reactants (or the higher the pressure), the faster the reaction goes.
3. Surface area (which depends on the size of solid pieces) — the larger the surface area (the smaller the pieces), the faster the reaction goes.

Collision theory

Reaction rates are explained by **collision theory**. Collision theory just says that the rate of a reaction depends on two things:

1. The collision frequency of reacting particles (how often they collide). The more collisions there are in a certain amount of time, the faster the reaction is.
2. The energy transferred during a collision. Particles have to collide with enough energy for the collision to be successful.

Changing either of these factors will change the rate of reaction, meaning there are two ways to increase the rate of a reaction. One way is to increase the frequency of collisions, so that the probability of a **successful collision** (a collision that results in a reaction) increases. The other way is to increase the energy of the collisions, so that more of the collisions are successful.

1. Increasing the frequency of collisions

The effects of temperature, concentration (or pressure) and surface area on the rate of reaction can be explained in terms of how often the reacting particles collide.

Tip: Being able to use a theoretical model, such as collision theory, to explain an experimental observation is an important part of Working Scientifically.

Temperature

When the temperature is increased the particles all move quicker. If they're moving quicker, they're going to collide more often and more collisions means a faster rate of reaction — see Figure 1.

Cold

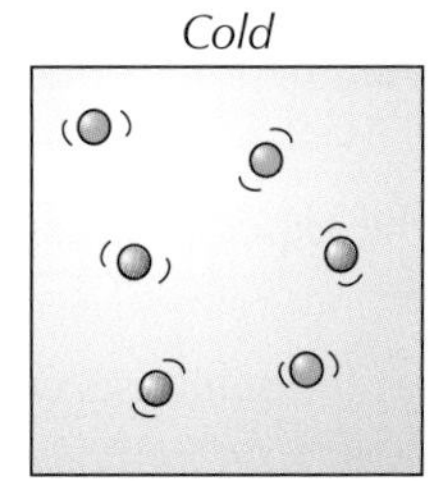

Particles move slowly.
Not many collisions.

Hot

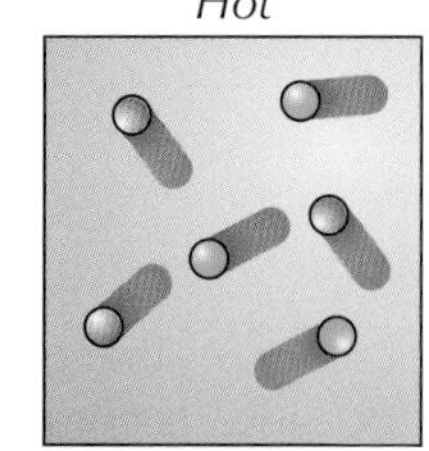

Particles move quickly.
Lots of collisions.

Figure 1: *A diagram showing why increasing the temperature increases the rate of a reaction.*

Tip: Increasing the temperature also increases the energy of the collisions — more on this on the next page.

Concentration (or pressure)

If a solution is made more concentrated it means there are more particles of reactant knocking about between the other molecules, which makes collisions between the important particles more likely.

Similarly, in a gas, increasing the pressure means the particles are more squashed up together, so there will be more frequent collisions (see Figure 2). More frequent collisions means a faster rate of reaction.

Low concentration (or low pressure)

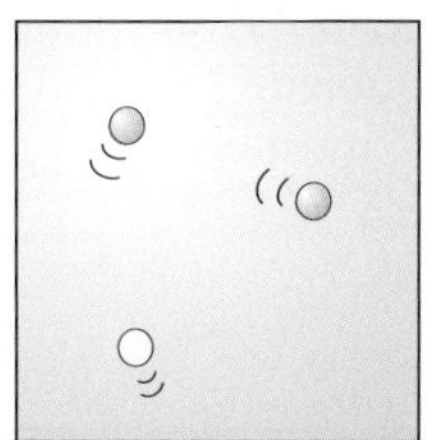

The particles are far apart — they don't collide often.

High concentration (or high pressure)

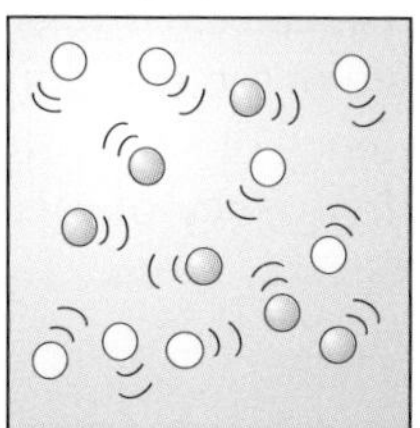

The particles are close together — they collide often.

Figure 2: *A diagram showing why increasing the concentration (or pressure) increases the rate of a reaction.*

Tip: This makes sense if you think about it — you're much more likely to bump into someone when you're in a crowd of people than when there aren't many people around.

Tip: The rate of a reaction slows down as the reaction progresses (see p.193) because the concentration of the reactants decreases.

Surface area

If one of the reactants is a solid then breaking it up into smaller pieces will increase its **surface area to volume ratio**. This means that, for the same volume of solid, the particles around it in the solution will have more area to work on, so there'll be more frequent collisions and the rate of reaction will be faster — see Figure 3.

Small surface area

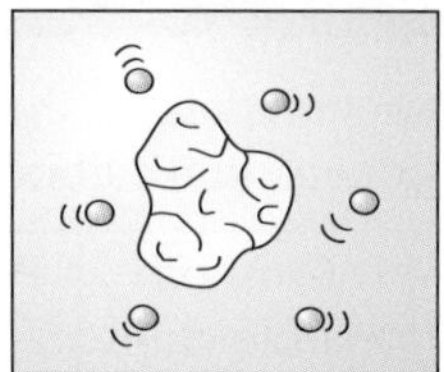

Less area for collisions. Collisions are less frequent.

Large surface area

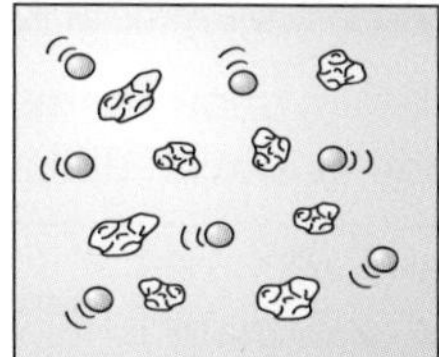

More area for collisions. Collisions are more frequent.

Figure 3: *A diagram showing why increasing the surface area increases the rate of a reaction.*

Tip: You get the fastest rates of reactions with powders because powders have a very large surface area.

Figure 4: *Powdered calcium carbonate (top) has a larger surface area than a piece of calcium carbonate (above).*

2. Increasing the energy of collisions

The effect of temperature on reaction rate can also be explained in terms of how much energy the particles have when they collide. A higher temperature doesn't only increase the frequency of collisions — it also increases the energy of the collisions, because it makes all the particles move faster.

Reactions only happen if the particles collide with enough energy. The minimum amount of energy that particles must have in order to react is called the **activation energy**. At a higher temperature there will be more particles colliding with enough energy to make the reaction happen.

Tip: For a collision to be successful, the energy of the particles must be greater than or equal to the activation energy. If the particles don't have enough energy, they will just bounce off each other without reacting.

Rate and proportionality

The rate of a reaction is directly proportional to the frequency of successful collisions. This means that, if the frequency of successful collisions doubles, the rate will also double. If the frequency of successful collisions triples, the rate triples, and so on.

Example

Magnesium and hydrochloric acid react to form magnesium chloride and hydrogen gas. When the temperature at which the reaction is carried out is increased from 15 °C to 25 °C, the mean rate of the reaction is found to have doubled.
So the frequency of successful collisions at 25 °C must be double the frequency of successful collisions at 15 °C.

Practice Questions — Fact Recall

Q1 What must happen for a reaction to occur between two particles?

Q2 Give two reasons why increasing the temperature increases the rate of a reaction.

Q3 Explain why increasing the concentration of the reactants increases the rate of a reaction.

Q4 Describe what is meant by the term 'activation energy'.

Practice Question — Application

Q1 The table below shows some rate of reaction data for the reactions of hydrochloric acid with different forms of calcium carbonate:

Form of calcium carbonate	Marble chips	Crushed marble chips	Powdered chalk
Initial rate of reaction (cm^3/min)	0.6	1.2	5.6

a) Describe and explain the trend in these results.

b) The rate of reaction for the crushed marble chips is double the rate for the marble chips. State how the frequency of the collisions between particles has changed between these two reactions.

6. Catalysts

Catalysts are very important for commercial reasons. They increase reaction rate and reduce energy costs in industrial reactions.

Catalysts

Many reactions can be speeded up by adding a catalyst.

> A catalyst is a substance which can speed up a reaction, without being chemically changed or used up in the reaction, and without changing the reaction products.

As they're not changed or used up in reactions, catalysts don't appear in the chemical equation for the reaction. Sometimes they're written in over the arrow, but they'll never be shown in the reactants or products. You're also left with the same mass of catalyst at the end of the reaction as you had at the beginning.

And since catalysts don't change the products of a reaction, if a catalyst isn't used, the same reaction will still take place — just much more slowly.

Different catalysts are needed for different reactions, but they all work by decreasing the activation energy (see page 203) needed for the reaction to occur. They do this by providing an alternative reaction pathway with a lower activation energy. As a result, more of the particles have at least the minimum amount of energy needed for a reaction to occur when the particles collide. The reaction profile in Figure 1 shows that the activation energy for the catalysed reaction is much lower than for the uncatalysed reaction.

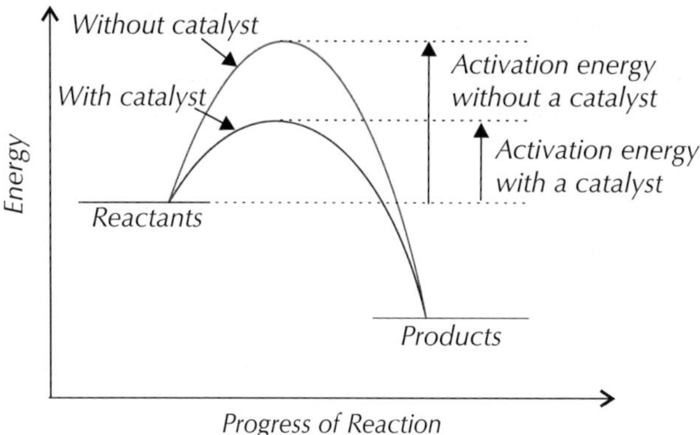

Figure 1: *The reaction profiles of the same reaction with and without a catalyst.*

Example

The reaction of ethene (C_2H_4) with hydrogen (H_2) is catalysed by nickel:

$$C_2H_4 + H_2 \xrightarrow{Ni} C_2H_6$$

The nickel catalyst provides a solid surface for the ethene and hydrogen to react on. This lowers the activation energy needed for the reaction to occur. The nickel is not used up during the reaction, so it is not part of the reaction equation.

Learning Objectives:

- Be able to describe a catalyst as a substance that speeds up the rate of a reaction without altering the products of the reaction, and is unchanged chemically and in mass at the end of the reaction.
- Be able to explain how the addition of a catalyst increases the rate of a reaction in terms of activation energy.
- Know that enzymes are biological catalysts and that enzymes are used in the production of alcoholic drinks.

Specification References 7.6-7.8

Tip: Because catalysts aren't used up in the reaction, you only need a tiny bit to catalyse large amounts of reactants.

Tip: Reaction profiles show the energy levels of the reactants and products in a reaction. There's more about reaction profiles on pages 211-212.

Tip: Think of the nickel as being like a host at a party, introducing two people who otherwise wouldn't have met.

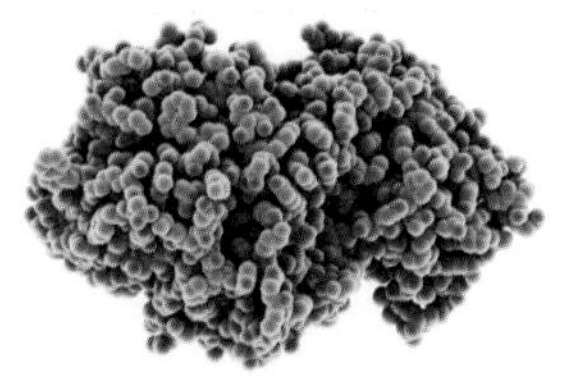

Figure 2: A molecular model showing an enzyme found in saliva that catalyses the breakdown of starch.

Enzymes

Enzymes are biological catalysts. This means that they catalyse (speed up) the chemical reactions inside living organisms. Like other catalysts, they work by lowering the activation energy of a reaction. An enzyme will generally only catalyse a certain reaction for a specific molecule.

For example, some enzymes help to break down specific molecules in food, whilst there are others which catalyse processes in the formation of proteins. Other reactions catalysed by enzymes include respiration and photosynthesis. Enzyme-controlled reactions are also often used in industry.

Example

Enzymes from yeast cells are used in the fermentation process which is used to make alcoholic drinks. They catalyse the reaction that converts sugars (such as glucose) into ethanol and carbon dioxide.

Practice Questions — Fact Recall

Q1 What is the definition of a catalyst?

Q2 What is an enzyme?

Q3 Give one example of an industrial process that uses enzymes.

Topic 7a Checklist — Make sure you know...

Measuring Rates of Reaction

- [ ] That the rate of a reaction that produces a precipitate can be measured by observing a mark through the solution and timing how long it takes for the mark to disappear.
- [ ] That the rate of a reaction that involves a colour change can be measured by timing how long it takes for the colour change to occur.
- [ ] That the rate of a reaction that produces a gas can be measured by monitoring the mass of the reaction over time (using a balance) or by measuring the volume of gas formed (using a gas syringe).

Rate of Reaction Graphs

- [ ] That if you plot a graph showing the amount of product formed (or reactant used) against time, the steepness of the curve shows the rate of the reaction — the steeper the curve, the faster the rate.
- [ ] That these types of graphs are usually curves because the reaction starts quickly, then slows down and eventually stops as the reactants get used up.
- [ ] How to use these graphs to find the rate of reaction between two points in time.
- [ ] H How to calculate the reaction rate at a particular point in time by drawing and using a tangent.

cont...

Rate Experiments Involving Gases

- [ ] How to investigate how changing the surface area or concentration of a reactant affects the rate of the reaction between calcium carbonate and hydrochloric acid (Core Practical).

Rate Experiments Involving Precipitation

- [ ] How to investigate how changing the temperature affects the rate of the reaction between sodium thiosulfate and hydrochloric acid (Core Practical).

Collision Theory

- [ ] That increasing the temperature, the concentration (or pressure), or the surface area of reactants will increase the rate of reaction, because they increase the frequency of collisions between particles.
- [ ] That in order for a reaction to take place, the reacting particles must collide with sufficient energy.
- [ ] That increasing the temperature also increases the rate because it increases the energy of collisions.
- [ ] That the minimum amount of energy required for a reaction to occur is called the activation energy.

Catalysts

- [ ] That a catalyst increases the rate of a reaction without being chemically changed or used up, and without changing the reaction products.
- [ ] That catalysts work by providing a different reaction pathway that has a lower activation energy.
- [ ] That catalysts in biological systems are known as enzymes.
- [ ] That enzymes are used to catalyse the fermentation process that is used to make alcoholic drinks.

Exam-style Questions

1 A student is investigating the rate of the reaction between dilute hydrochloric acid and calcium carbonate. The equation for this reaction is shown below:

$$2HCl_{(aq)} + CaCO_{3(s)} \rightarrow CaCl_{2(aq)} + CO_{2(g)} + H_2O_{(l)}$$

The student measured the volume of carbon dioxide produced by this reaction and recorded the volume every 2 minutes for 20 minutes.

(a) Suggest another technique that the student could have used to measure the rate of this reaction.

(1 mark)

The student's results are shown on this graph.

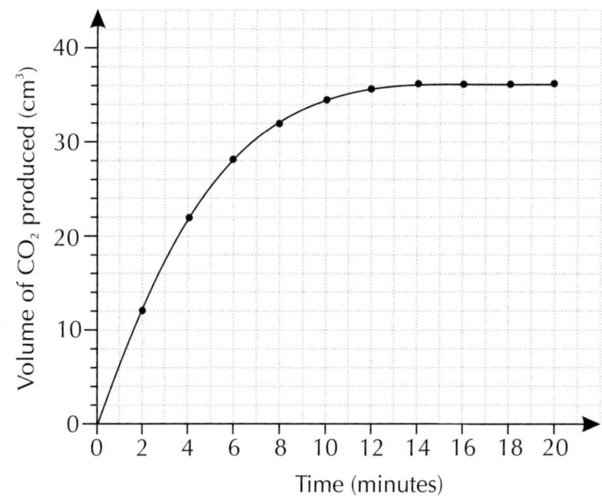

(b) Use the graph to estimate how long it took for all of the reactants to be used up in this reaction.

(1 mark)

(c) Calculate the mean rate of reaction during the first 2 minutes of this reaction. Give your answer in cm^3/min.

(2 marks)

(d) Explain why the rate of reaction slows down as the volume of CO_2 produced increases.

(2 marks)

(e) The student repeated his experiment using a higher concentration of hydrochloric acid. All other conditions were kept the same.

Sketch out a copy of the graph above and sketch a second curve on the same axes to show the results he might expect.

(2 marks)

2 A student mixes ethanol, ethanoic acid and hydrochloric acid together in a beaker. The following reaction takes place:

ethanol + ethanoic acid → ethyl ethanoate + water

The student carries out the experiment again, but this time leaves out the hydrochloric acid. The same reaction takes place, but it happens at a much slower rate.

(a) State two pieces of evidence that suggest that hydrochloric acid is a catalyst for the reaction.

(2 marks)

(b) Explain how catalysts work.

(2 marks)

(c) Other than adding hydrochloric acid, suggest one thing the student could do to increase the rate of the reaction.

(1 mark)

3 A student is investigating how the rate changes over the course of the following reaction:

$$2HCl_{(aq)} + Mg_{(s)} \rightarrow MgCl_{2(aq)} + H_{2(g)}$$

She does this by measuring the volume of hydrogen gas produced at regular intervals. Her results are shown in the table below.

Time (s)	0	20	40	60	80	100	120	140	160	180
Volume of gas produced (cm^3)	0.0	13.0	18.0	20.5	22.0	23.0	23.5	24.0	24.0	24.0

(a) State a piece of equipment the student could have used to accurately measure the volume of gas produced.

(1 mark)

(b) Plot a graph of the student's results. Draw a line of best fit.

(3 marks)

(c) State the units of the rate that would be given using these results.

(1 mark)

(d) Calculate the rate of reaction at 20 seconds.

(3 marks)

(e) After 40 s, the rate of reaction was half the rate it had been at 20 s.
State how the frequency of successful collisions changed between 20 s and 40 s.

(1 mark)

1. Endothermic and Exothermic Reactions

Learning Objectives:
- Be able to describe an exothermic change or reaction as one in which heat energy is given out.
- Be able to describe an endothermic change or reaction as one in which heat energy is taken in.
- Be able to draw and label reaction profiles for endothermic and exothermic reactions, identifying activation energy.
- Be able to explain the term activation energy.

Specification References
7.10, 7.11, 7.15, 7.16

During reactions, energy is transferred between the reaction mixture and the surroundings. Some reactions give out heat, while others take heat in.

Energy transfer

Chemicals store a certain amount of energy — and different chemicals store different amounts. If the products of a reaction store more energy than the original reactants, then they must have taken in some energy from the surroundings. But if they store less, then they must have transferred some of their energy to the surroundings during the reaction. The energy is normally transferred in the form of heat, so the temperature of a reaction mixture will almost always increase or decrease during a reaction.

Tip: The 'surroundings' could be the water that the reactants are dissolved in, or the air that gases are reacting in.

Exothermic reactions

An **exothermic reaction** is one which gives out heat energy to the surroundings. This is shown by a rise in temperature in the surroundings. The best example of an exothermic reaction is burning fuels (**combustion**). This gives out a lot of energy — it's very exothermic. **Neutralisation reactions** (between an acid and an alkali) are also exothermic as are many **oxidation** reactions.

Examples

- The reaction of potassium hydroxide with hydrochloric acid is a neutralisation reaction. This reaction releases energy — it's exothermic.
- When sodium is added to water, it's oxidised, releases energy and moves about on the surface of the water. The fact that energy is released shows that this is an exothermic reaction.

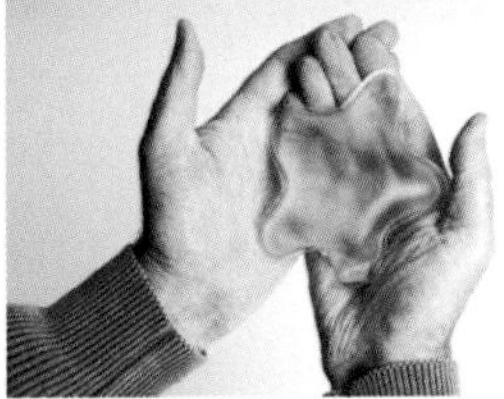

Figure 1: A chemical hand warmer. It uses an exothermic reaction.

Endothermic reactions

An **endothermic reaction** is one which takes in heat energy from the surroundings. This is shown by a fall in the temperature of the surroundings. Endothermic reactions are much less common than exothermic reactions, but the reaction between citric acid and sodium hydrogencarbonate is a good example, as are thermal decomposition reactions.

Tip: Physical processes can also take in or release energy. E.g. freezing is an exothermic process, melting is endothermic.

Example

The thermal decomposition of calcium carbonate is endothermic. Heat must be supplied to make calcium carbonate decompose into calcium oxide and carbon dioxide. The equation for this reaction is:

$$CaCO_3 \rightarrow CaO + CO_2$$

Reaction profiles

A **reaction profile** is a graph that shows how the energy in a reaction changes as the reaction progresses. The graph starts at the energy level of the reactants and finishes at the energy level of the products. These two points are usually joined by a smooth curve — see Figure 2.

There are three useful pieces of information you can find from a reaction profile:

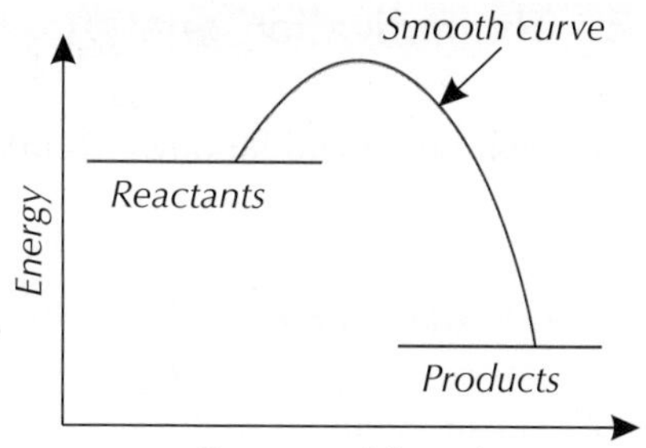

Figure 2: *A reaction profile showing how the energy in a reaction changes over time.*

Tip: Reaction profiles can also be called energy level diagrams.

1. The overall energy change

The overall energy change of a reaction is the difference between the energy of the reactants and the energy of the products. You can find the overall energy change of a reaction from a reaction profile by looking at the difference in height between the reactants and the products — see Figure 3.

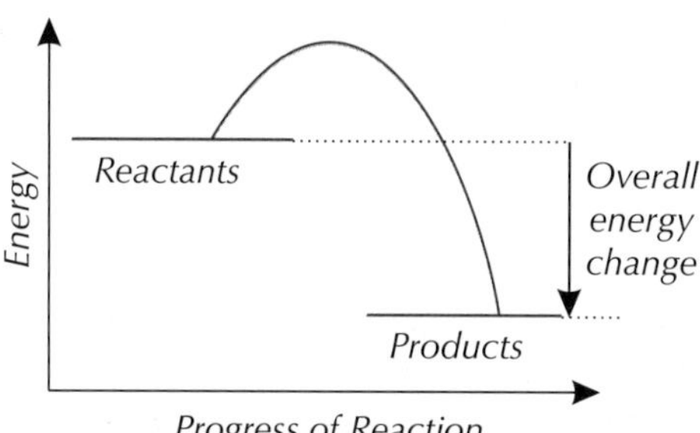

Figure 3: *Finding the overall energy change from a reaction profile.*

Tip: H You can also find the overall energy change of a reaction using bond energies — see page 216 for more.

2. Whether the reaction is exothermic or endothermic

Reaction profiles show the relative energies of the reactants and the products, so you can use them to work out whether a reaction is exothermic or endothermic.

In an exothermic reaction, the reactants have more energy than the products, because energy is released during the reaction. This means the reaction profile will start high and finish lower than where it started.

In an endothermic reaction, the products have more energy than the reactants, because energy is taken in during the reaction. This means the reaction profile will start low and finish higher than where it started — see Figure 4.

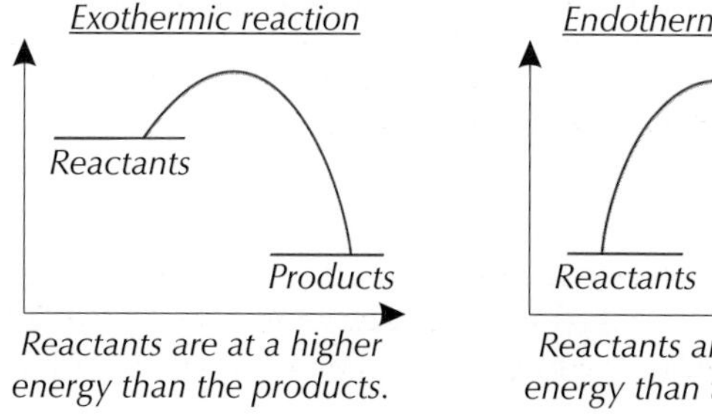

Figure 4: *The reaction profiles of an exothermic reaction and an endothermic reaction.*

Tip: Don't forget — an exothermic reaction transfers energy to the surroundings and an endothermic reaction takes in energy from the surroundings.

Tip: The activation energy is normally supplied through heating the reaction mixture.

Tip: Overcoming the activation energy is a bit like having to climb up one side of a hill before you can ski down the other side.

Tip: Adding a catalyst to the reaction mixture changes the shape of the reaction profile by decreasing the activation energy — see page 205 for more.

Exam Tip
You need to be able to draw reaction profiles, so make sure you know how they're set up and how the axes are labelled.

3. The activation energy

Reaction profiles don't normally go straight from the reactants to the products — the graph will curve upwards before it starts to go down again. This is because some energy usually has to be put in to break the bonds in the reactants and get the reaction started.

The **activation energy** (E_a) is the minimum amount of energy the reactant particles need when they collide with each other in order to react. The greater the activation energy, the more energy that is needed to start the reaction. If the energy input is less than the activation energy there won't be enough energy to start the reaction, so nothing will happen.

You can find the activation energy of a reaction from its reaction profile by looking at the difference between where the curve starts (the reactants) and the highest point on the curve — see Figure 5.

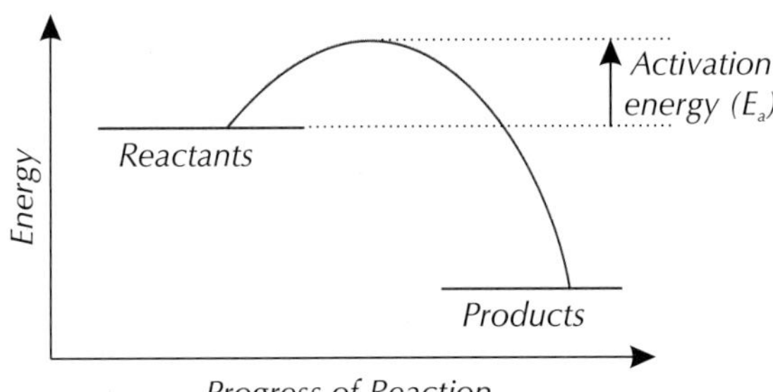

Figure 5: *Finding the activation energy from a reaction profile.*

Practice Questions — Fact Recall

Q1 What is an exothermic reaction?

Q2 When an endothermic reaction takes place, the temperature around the reaction decreases. Explain why.

Q3 Sketch a reaction profile for an exothermic reaction and add the following labels to it.

a) The energy of the reactants.

b) The energy of the products.

c) The activation energy.

d) The overall energy change.

Practice Question — Application

Q1 Which of the following reactions has the highest activation energy?

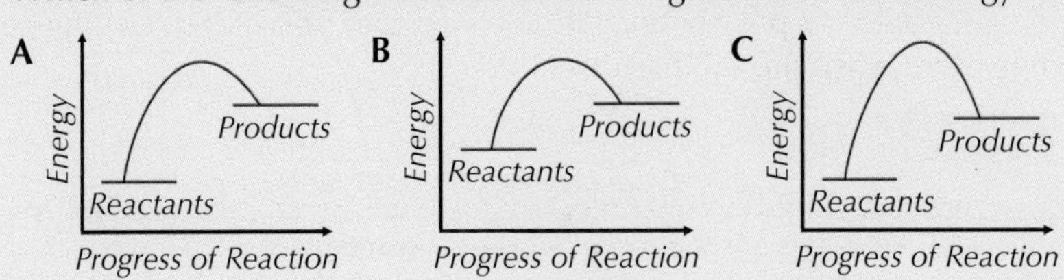

2. Measuring Temperature Changes

By measuring the temperature change, you can work out how much energy is transferred during an exothermic or endothermic reaction.

How to measure a temperature change

The amount of energy transferred during a reaction is proportional to the temperature change of that reaction. So you can use the temperature change as a measure of the heat energy transferred.

You can follow the change in temperature of a reaction mixture as a reaction takes place. Here's how:

1. Put a polystyrene cup into a beaker of cotton wool (the cotton wool gives insulation to help limit energy transfer to or from the reaction mixture).
2. Add a known volume of your first reagent to the cup.
3. Measure the initial temperature of the solution.
4. Add a measured mass/volume of your second reagent and use the thermometer to stir the mixture.
5. Put a lid on the cup to reduce any energy lost by evaporation.
6. Record the maximum or minimum temperature (depending on whether it's increasing or decreasing) that the mixture reaches during the reaction.
7. Calculate the temperature change.

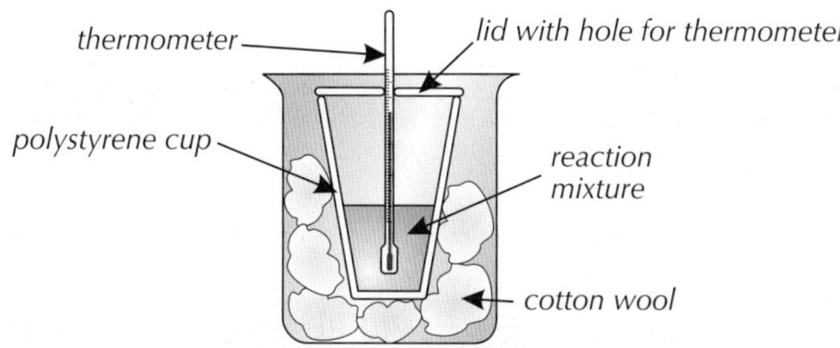

Figure 1: *Apparatus for measuring the energy change of a reaction in solution.*

Temperature changes of common reactions

You can measure the temperature change for different types of reaction. Whether there's an increase or decrease in temperature depends on which reagents take part in the reaction.

Dissolving salts in water

You can measure the temperature change when dissolving salts in water by adding the salt to a polystyrene cup of water and measuring the change in temperature when the salt has dissolved.

Examples

- Dissolving ammonium chloride decreases the temperature of the reaction mixture — it's endothermic.
- Dissolving calcium chloride causes the temperature of the solution to rise — it's exothermic.

Learning Objectives:

- Know that, when reactions take place in solution, temperature changes can be measured to reflect the heat energy changes.
- Know that a change in heat energy occurs when salts dissolve in water.
- Know that changes in heat energy occur during neutralisation, displacement and precipitation reactions.

Specification Reference 7.9

Tip: If your reaction is between two solutions, make sure they're the same temperature before you mix them together.

Tip: You can also use this method to see the effect that different variables have on the amount of energy transferred e.g. the mass or concentration of the reactants.

Figure 2: *A reaction taking place in a polystyrene cup with no insulation and no lid — it will lose lots of energy to the surroundings.*

Neutralisation reactions

In a neutralisation reaction (see page 120), an acid and a base react to form a salt and water.

Tip: Most neutralisation reactions occur without having to supply any extra heat to the system. This is because the activation energy is so low that the reaction is easily achieved at room temperature.

Examples

- Most neutralisation reactions are exothermic:
  e.g. $HCl + NaOH \rightarrow NaCl + H_2O$
- However, the neutralisation reaction between ethanoic acid and sodium carbonate is endothermic.

Displacement reactions

In a displacement reaction (see page 183), a more reactive element displaces a less reactive element in a compound. These types of reactions are accompanied by a release of energy — they're exothermic.

Example

- Zinc powder and copper sulfate react in a displacement reaction forming zinc sulfate and copper.

Precipitation reactions

Precipitates are insoluble solids which can sometimes form when two solutions are mixed together. All precipitation reactions are exothermic.

Tip: For more on precipitation reactions, see page 128.

Example

- The reaction between lead(II) nitrate solution and potassium iodide forming a lead iodide precipitate would result in an increase in the temperature of the surroundings.

Practice Question — Fact Recall

Q1 Give one type of reaction that results in a change in heat energy.

Practice Question — Application

Q1 A student wants to measure the temperature change when a solution of potassium hydroxide reacts with sulfuric acid.

a) Describe a method the student could use to measure the temperature change of this reaction.

b) The reaction between potassium hydroxide and sulfuric acid is exothermic. Describe the temperature change the student will observe.

3. Bond Energies

Chemical reactions are all about breaking old bonds and making new ones. You need to put in energy to break bonds, but making bonds releases energy. That's why there's a change in energy when a chemical reaction happens.

Learning Objectives:

- Know that the breaking of bonds is endothermic and the making of bonds is exothermic.
- Know that the overall heat energy change for a reaction is exothermic if more heat energy is released in forming bonds in the products than is required in breaking bonds in the reactants.
- Know that the overall heat energy change for a reaction is endothermic if less heat energy is released in forming bonds in the products than is required in breaking the bonds in the reactants.
- H Be able to calculate the energy change in a reaction given the energies of bonds in kJ mol^{-1}.

Specification References
7.12-7.14

Units of energy

Energy is usually measured in **joules** (J). Large energy values are often given in kilojoules (kJ) — there are 1000 joules in a kilojoule.

When measuring energy transfer in reactions, the amount of energy released or absorbed will depend on how much reactant is used. As a result, energy transfer is usually measured in kilojoules per mole of reactant (kJ mol^{-1}), so that comparisons can be made between different reactions.

Energy and bonding

Energy is transferred in chemical reactions because old bonds are broken and new bonds are formed.

- Energy must be supplied to break existing bonds — so bond breaking is an **endothermic** process (see Figure 1).
- Energy is released when new bonds are formed — so bond formation is an **exothermic** process (see Figure 1).

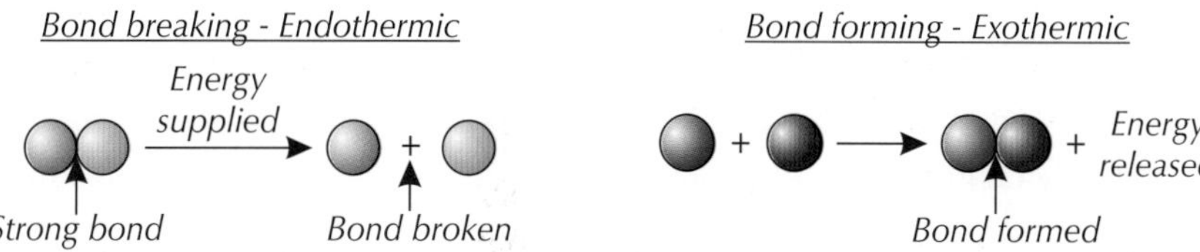

Figure 1: *Energy changes during bond breaking and bond forming.*

Bond energy and overall energy change

Whether a reaction is exothermic or endothermic depends on what bond breaking and bond making is going on. It all comes down to whether the amount of energy absorbed when the bonds in the reactants are broken is more or less than the amount of energy released when the bonds in the products are made.

In an exothermic reaction, the energy released in bond formation is greater than the energy used in breaking old bonds. The leftover energy is released into the surroundings and the temperature rises.

In an endothermic reaction, the energy required to break old bonds is greater than the energy released when new bonds are formed. The extra energy needed is absorbed from the surroundings and the temperature falls.

Figure 2: *Combustion reactions are very exothermic — they give off lots of energy.*

Bond energy calculations Higher

Not all bonds are the same strength — it requires more energy to break some bonds than others. Every chemical bond has a particular **bond energy** associated with it.

Examples Higher

- A carbon-carbon (C–C) bond has a bond energy of 348 kJ mol^{-1}. This means that it takes 348 kJ of energy to break one mole of C–C bonds. It also means that 348 kJ of energy is released when one mole of C–C bonds is formed.
- A carbon-hydrogen (C–H) bond has a bond energy of 413 kJ mol^{-1}. It takes 413 kJ of energy to break one mole of C–H bonds and 413 kJ of energy is released when one mole of C–H bonds are made.

Tip: H There are 1000 J in a kJ, so 348 kJ is the same as 348 000 J.

You can use these bond energies to calculate the overall energy change for a reaction. Here's what you have to do:

- Draw out the displayed formulas of the molecules in the reaction so you can see all the bonds that are being broken and made.
- Work out the amount of energy used in bond breaking by adding up the bond energies of all the bonds in all the reactants.
- Work out the amount of energy given out from bond making by adding up the bond energies of all the bonds in all the products.
- Then, use this formula to work out the overall energy change:

Energy change = Energy of bond breaking – Energy of bond making

Exam Tip H
Bond energies vary slightly depending on what compound the bond is in. But don't worry about this — you'll be given any bond energies that you need in the exam.

Example 1 Higher

Calculate the overall energy change for this reaction: $H_2 + Cl_2 \rightarrow 2HCl$

The bond energies you need are:
H–H: 436 kJ mol^{-1}; Cl–Cl: 242 kJ mol^{-1}; H–Cl: 431 kJ mol^{-1}.

MATHS SKILLS

If you draw out the displayed formulas of the molecules in this reaction, it looks like this:

$$\text{H—H} \quad + \quad \text{Cl—Cl} \rightarrow \begin{matrix}\text{H—Cl}\\ \text{H—Cl}\end{matrix}$$

As you can see, one mole of H–H bonds and one mole of Cl–Cl bonds are being broken and two moles of H–Cl bonds are being formed.

The amount of energy used in bond breaking is 436 + 242 = 678 kJ mol^{-1}

The amount of energy released in bond making is 2 × 431 = 862 kJ mol^{-1}

So the overall energy change of the reaction is 678 – 862 = –184 kJ mol^{-1}

Tip: H You don't have to draw out the displayed formulas if you don't want to, but it makes it much easier to see all the bonds if you do.

Example 2 Higher

Calculate the overall energy change for: $CH_4 + 2O_2 \rightarrow CO_2 + 2H_2O$

The bond energies you need are: C–H: 413 kJ mol⁻¹, O=O: 498 kJ mol⁻¹, C=O: 805 kJ mol⁻¹, O–H: 464 kJ mol⁻¹

Drawing out the displayed formulae of the molecules in this reaction gives you this:

MATHS SKILLS

```
   H
   |
H—C—H  +  O=O  →  O=C=O  +  H—O—H
   |      O=O                H—O—H
   H
```

Four moles of C–H bonds and two moles of O=O bonds are being broken. Two moles of C=O bonds and four moles of O–H bonds are being formed.

The amount of energy used in bond breaking is
$(4 \times 413) + (2 \times 498) = 2648$ kJ mol^{-1}

The amount of energy released in bond making is
$(2 \times 805) + (4 \times 464) = 3466$ kJ mol^{-1}

So the overall energy change of the reaction is $2648 - 3466 = -818$ kJ mol^{-1}

Exam Tip H
You might be asked to find the energy of one of the bonds using the total energy change and the bond energies of all the other bonds. To do this, rearrange the equation for overall energy change to make the unknown bond energy the subject. You can then substitute in all the other known values on the right hand side of the equation.

The overall energy change for a reaction can be positive or negative. If the energy change is negative, it shows that more energy was released in bond making than was used in bond breaking — so the reaction is exothermic. If the energy change is positive, it shows that more energy was used in bond breaking than was released in bond making — so the reaction is endothermic.

Exam Tip H
You can use the sign of the energy change to check your answer. If you know a reaction is exothermic and you end up with a positive energy change, you must have gone wrong somewhere.

Practice Questions — Fact Recall

Q1 Are the following processes exothermic or endothermic?

a) Breaking chemical bonds. b) Making chemical bonds.

Q2 Explain why energy is released to the surroundings during an exothermic reaction.

Practice Questions — Application

Q1 Use the information in the table to calculate the overall energy change for the reaction, $2H_2 + O_2 \rightarrow 2H_2O$.

Bond	H–H	O=O	O–H
Bond energy (kJ mol⁻¹)	436	498	464

Q2 Methanol burns in air to form carbon dioxide and water:

```
     H
     |
2 H—C—O—H + 3O=O → 2O=C=O + 4H—O—H
     |
     H
```

Calculate the overall energy change for this reaction.
Bond energies: C–H = 413 kJ mol⁻¹, C–O = 358 kJ mol⁻¹, O–H = 464 kJ mol⁻¹, O=O = 498 kJ mol⁻¹, C=O = 805 kJ mol⁻¹.

Figure 3: *Methanol burning in air.*

Topic 7b Checklist — Make sure you know...

Endothermic and Exothermic Reactions

- [ ] That during a chemical reaction, energy is either transferred from the reaction to the surroundings, or from the surroundings to the reaction.
- [ ] That exothermic reactions are reactions which transfer heat energy to the surroundings, resulting in an increase in temperature.
- [ ] That an endothermic reaction is a reaction which takes heat energy in from the surroundings, resulting in a decrease in temperature.
- [ ] That a reaction profile starts at the energy level of the reactants, ends at the energy level of the products and shows how the energy in a reaction changes as the reaction progresses with a smooth curve.
- [ ] That on a reaction profile, the overall energy change of the reaction is the difference in height from where the graph starts to where it finishes.
- [ ] That a reaction profile will start high and finish lower if the reaction is exothermic, and will start low and finish higher if the reaction is endothermic.
- [ ] That the activation energy is the minimum amount of energy the reactant particles need when they collide with each other in order to react.
- [ ] That on a reaction profile, the activation energy is the difference in height from where the graph starts to the highest point on the curve.

Measuring Temperature Changes

- [ ] How you can find the energy change of a reaction in solution by mixing the reactants in a well-insulated polystyrene cup and measuring the change in temperature of the reaction.
- [ ] That a change in heat energy occurs when a salt is dissolved in water, and that the energy change can be endothermic or exothermic.
- [ ] That a change in heat energy occurs during neutralisation reactions, and that most neutralisation reactions are exothermic.
- [ ] That a change in heat energy occurs during displacement reactions, and that all displacement reactions are exothermic.
- [ ] That a change in heat energy occurs during precipitation reactions, and that all precipitation reactions are exothermic.

Bond Energies

- [ ] That energy is released when bonds are made (bond making is exothermic) and energy must be absorbed to break bonds (bond breaking is endothermic).
- [ ] That in an exothermic reaction, more energy is released forming the bonds in the products than is absorbed breaking the bonds in the reactants — so energy is given out to the surroundings.
- [ ] That in an endothermic reaction, more energy is absorbed breaking the bonds in the reactants than is released forming the bonds in the products — so energy is absorbed from the surroundings.
- [ ] H How to calculate the overall energy change for a reaction from given bond energies.

Exam-style Questions

1 When magnesium reacts with sulfuric acid to form magnesium sulfate and hydrogen gas, energy is released.

(a) Draw a reaction profile to show how energy changes during the reaction.

(3 marks)

A student investigates how the concentration of the acid affects the amount of heat given out by the reaction. She carries out the reaction in a polystyrene cup and measures the initial and maximum temperatures of the reaction mixture.
She repeats the experiment with different concentrations of acid, but keeping everything else the same.

(b) Suggest why the student uses a polystyrene cup, rather than a glass beaker.

(1 mark)

(c) Why does she keep all the factors other than the concentration of the acid the same in each experiment?

(1 mark)

2 The Haber process is used to manufacture ammonia from nitrogen and hydrogen in the following reaction:

$$N_{2(g)} + 3H_{2(g)} \rightleftharpoons 2NH_{3(g)}$$

Here is the reaction profile for this reaction:

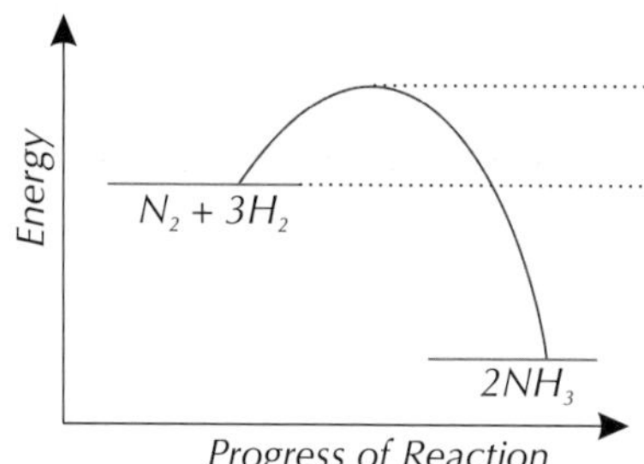

(a) Use the reaction profile to explain whether the formation of ammonia is endothermic or exothermic.

(2 marks)

(b) The bond energies of the bonds that are broken and made during this reaction are:
H–H = 436 kJ mol^{-1}, N≡N = 945 kJ mol^{-1}, N–H = 391 kJ mol^{-1}.
Calculate the overall energy change for this reaction.

(3 marks)

(c) Draw and label an arrow on a sketch of the reaction profile to show the overall energy change for this reaction.

(1 mark)

1. Fractional Distillation of Crude Oil

Learning Objectives:
- Be able to describe crude oil as a complex mixture of hydrocarbons, containing molecules in which carbon atoms are in chains or rings.
- Know that crude oil is a finite resource and an important source of useful substances, such as fuels and feedstock for the petrochemical industry.
- Be able to describe and explain the separation of crude oil into simpler, more useful mixtures by the process of fractional distillation.
- Know that petrol, kerosene and diesel oil are non-renewable fossil fuels obtained from crude oil, and methane is a non-renewable fossil fuel found in natural gas.
- Know the names and uses of the following fractions of crude oil: gases, petrol, kerosene, diesel oil, fuel oil and bitumen.

Specification References
8.2-8.4, 8.15

Crude oil is a fossil fuel that is formed deep underground. Many useful products can be made from crude oil using a technique called fractional distillation.

What is crude oil?

Crude oil is a complex **mixture** of many different **hydrocarbons** — compounds which contain only hydrogen and carbon (see page 223). It's formed at high temperatures and pressures from the remains of animals and plants that died millions of years ago. Because it takes so long for crude oil to form it's said to be a **finite resource** — once it's used up we can't replace it.

Crude oil is our main source of hydrocarbons and is used as a raw material (sometimes called a **feedstock**) to create lots of useful substances for the petrochemical industry. Most of the hydrocarbons in crude oil are alkanes (hydrocarbons with the general formula C_nH_{2n+2}). The carbon atoms in these molecules are arranged in chains or rings.

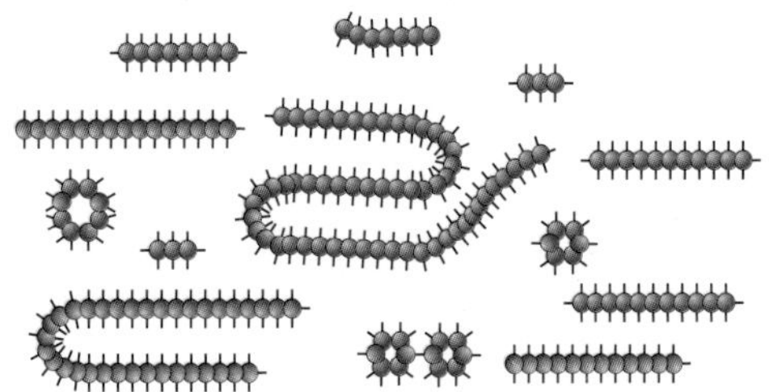

Figure 1: *The carbon atoms in the hydrocarbons that make up crude oil can be arranged in chains or rings.*

Fractional distillation

Crude oil can be split into separate groups of hydrocarbons (known as **fractions**) using a technique called **fractional distillation**. Fractions are simpler, more useful mixtures than crude oil. They contain groups of hydrocarbons of similar lengths (i.e. they have similar numbers of carbon and hydrogen atoms).

In fractional distillation, the crude oil is pumped into a piece of equipment known as a fractionating column. This fractionating column has a temperature gradient running through it — it's hottest at the bottom and coldest at the top.

The crude oil is heated so that most of it evaporates (turns into a gas). It's then piped in at the bottom of the column, where the liquid part (bitumen) is drained off. The gas rises up the column and gradually cools. Different compounds in the mixture have different boiling points, so they condense (turn back into a liquid) at different temperatures. This means they condense at different levels in the fractionating column.

Hydrocarbons that have a similar number of carbon atoms have similar boiling points, so they condense at similar levels in the column.

Examples

- Hydrocarbons with lots of carbon atoms have high boiling points, so they condense near the bottom of the column.
- Hydrocarbons with a small number of carbon atoms have low boiling points, so they condense near the top of the column.

Tip: The temperature at which a compound condenses is the same as its boiling point. E.g. if a compound had a boiling point of 120 °C, it would condense at 120 °C.

The various fractions are constantly tapped off from the column at the different levels where they condense. Each fraction contains a mixture of hydrocarbons with similar boiling points.

The process of fractional distillation is illustrated in Figure 3.

Figure 2: *A fractionating column.*

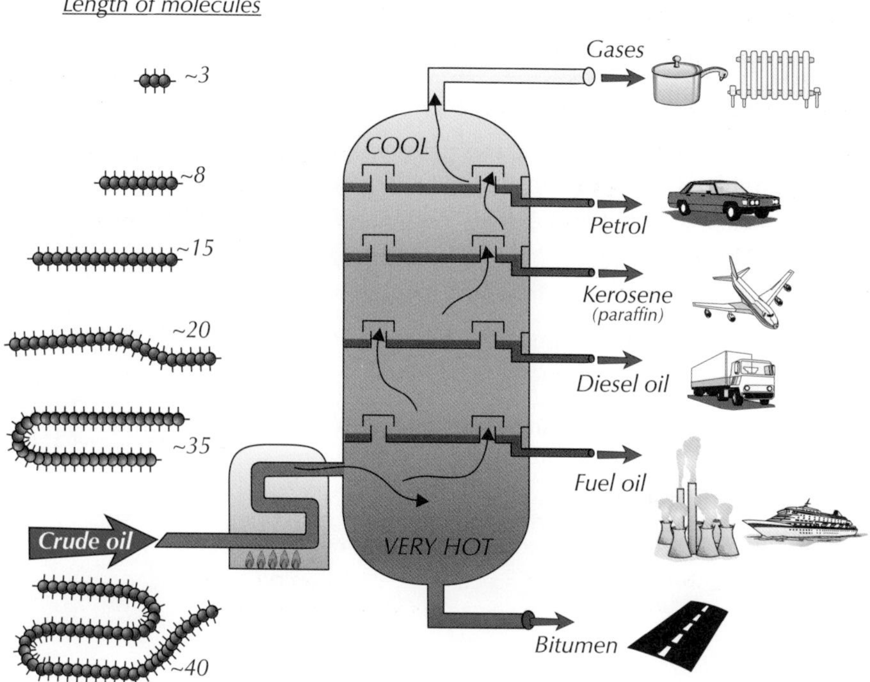

Figure 3: *The process of fractional distillation.*

Exam Tip
Don't worry — you don't need to know the lengths of specific fractions. Just make sure you understand the general principles of fractional distillation for the exam.

Uses of crude oil fractions

The fractions from fractional distillation are suitable for different uses:

- **Bitumen** is used to surface roads and the roofs of buildings.
- **Fuel oil** is used as a fuel for large ships and in some power stations.
- **Diesel oil** is used as a fuel in some cars and larger vehicles, such as trains.
- **Kerosene** can be used as a fuel in aircraft.
- **Petrol** is used as a fuel in cars.
- The **gases** that leave at the top of fractionating column are used in domestic heating appliances (such as central heating boilers) and cooking.

Most of the fractions from crude oil, e.g. petrol, kerosene and diesel, are examples of non-renewable fossil fuels.

Tip: Methane, the main component of natural gas, is another example of a non-renewable fossil fuel. Natural gas is a mixture of gases which forms underground in a similar way to crude oil.

Exam Tip
You need to learn the names and main uses of the fractions of crude oil for the exam.

Tip: Finite resources can also be called non-renewable resources.

Practice Questions — Fact Recall

Q1 What is a finite resource?

Q2 Give a use for the following crude oil fractions:

a) petrol

b) fuel oil

Practice Questions — Application

Tip: Don't forget — the fractionating column is hottest at the bottom and coolest at the top.

Q1 This table contains data on some of the fractions of crude oil that are separated out during fractional distillation.

Fraction	Petrol	Naphtha	Kerosene	Diesel
Approx. boiling temp. range (°C)	30 – 80	80 – 190	190 – 250	250 – 350

a) Which of the fractions in the table will be removed closest to the bottom of the fractionating column?

b) Hexane has a boiling point of 68 °C. At what temperature will hexane condense? In which fraction will it be found?

Q2 This table shows the number of carbon atoms in some of the hydrocarbons found in crude oil.

Hydrocarbon	Butane	Decane	Icosane	Tetracontane
Number of carbon atoms	4	10	20	40

Which of the hydrocarbons in the table will condense at the highest temperature?

2. Hydrocarbons

Crude oil fractions contain hydrocarbons. The physical properties of a crude oil fraction depend on how big the hydrocarbons in that fraction are.

What is a hydrocarbon?

A **hydrocarbon** is any molecule that is formed from carbon and hydrogen atoms only. So $C_{10}H_{22}$ (decane, an alkane) is a hydrocarbon, but $CH_3COOC_3H_7$ (an ester) is not — it contains oxygen.

Homologous series

Hydrocarbons which share similar chemical properties can be grouped together in **homologous series**. A homologous series is a family of molecules which have the same general formula and share similar chemical properties. The molecular formulae of neighbouring compounds in a homologous series differ by a CH_2 unit.

The physical properties of compounds in a homologous series vary between the different molecules. For example, there is a gradual increase in boiling point as the molecules get bigger (see Figure 1). Alkanes and alkenes (hydrocarbons with at least one double bond between carbon atoms) are two different homologous series of hydrocarbons. The hydrocarbons in fractions of crude oil are mostly alkanes.

Alkane	Molecular Formula	Boiling point (°C)	Fraction in crude oil
Methane	CH_4	–161	Gases
Ethane	C_2H_6	–89	Gases
Dodecane	$C_{12}H_{26}$	216	Kerosene
Icosane	$C_{20}H_{42}$	343	Diesel Oil
Tetracontane	$C_{40}H_{82}$	524	Fuel Oil

Figure 1: *Information about some of the members of the alkane homologous series.*

Properties of hydrocarbons

The size of a hydrocarbon determines which fraction of crude oil it will separate into (see page 221). Each fraction contains hydrocarbons (mostly alkanes) with similar numbers of carbon atoms, so all of the molecules in a fraction will have similar properties and behave in similar ways.

The physical properties are determined by the **intermolecular forces** that hold the chains together. The strength of these intermolecular forces is determined by the size of the hydrocarbon.

Learning Objectives:

- Know that a hydrocarbon is a compound that contains carbon and hydrogen only.
- Be able to explain a homologous series as a series of compounds which have the same general formula, differ by CH_2 in molecular formulae from neighbouring compounds, show a gradual variation in physical properties and have similar chemical properties.
- Know that hydrocarbons in crude oil are mostly members of the alkane homologous series.
- Be able to explain how hydrocarbons in different crude oil fractions differ from each other in the number of carbon and hydrogen atoms their molecules contain, boiling points, ease of ignition and viscosity.
- Be able to describe the complete combustion of hydrocarbon fuels as a reaction in which carbon dioxide and water are produced and energy is given out.

Specification References 8.1, 8.5-8.7

Tip: Intermolecular forces of attraction occur between molecules.

Boiling points

The intermolecular forces of attraction break a lot more easily in small molecules than they do in bigger molecules. This is because the forces are much stronger between big molecules than they are between small molecules.

Tip: Because they have higher boiling points, larger hydrocarbons tend to be liquids at room temperature, whilst smaller ones are normally gases.

A large molecule contains many points along its length where it can be attracted to another molecule. So, even if it can overcome these forces at a few points along its length, it's still got lots of other places where the force is still strong enough to hold it in place (see Figure 2).

Because of this, it takes a lot more energy to break the intermolecular forces between large molecules than between small molecules. That's why large molecules have higher boiling points than small molecules do.

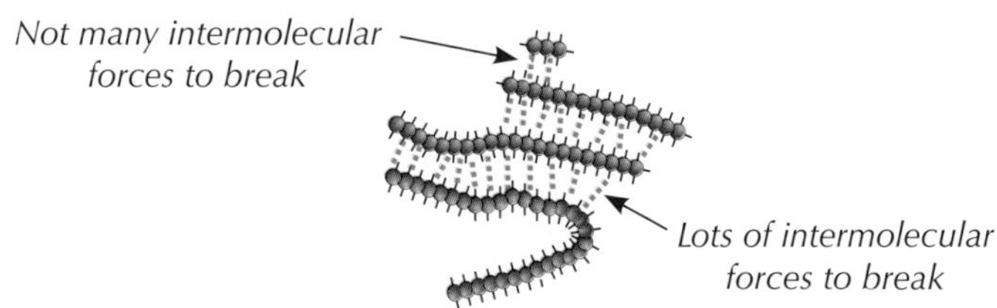

Figure 2: *Diagram showing the difference in intermolecular forces between small molecules and large molecules.*

Ease of ignition

Tip: When a substance ignites, it sets on fire.

Shorter hydrocarbons are easier to ignite than larger hydrocarbons because they have lower boiling points, so tend to be gases at room temperature. The gas molecules mix with oxygen in the air to produce a gas mixture which bursts into flames if it comes into contact with a spark. Longer hydrocarbons are usually liquids at room temperature. They have higher boiling points and are much harder to ignite.

Viscosity

Tip: A viscous substance, such as thick treacle, does not flow very easily.

Viscosity measures how easily a substance flows. The stronger the intermolecular forces are between hydrocarbon molecules, the harder it is for the liquid to flow. Fractions containing longer hydrocarbons have a higher viscosity and are very thick. Fractions made up of shorter hydrocarbons have a low viscosity and are much runnier.

Figure 3: *Bottled butane gas burning.*

Complete combustion of hydrocarbons

If you burn hydrocarbons, the carbon and hydrogen react with oxygen from the air to form carbon dioxide and water. Energy is also released (as the reaction is exothermic, see p.210). This makes hydrocarbons great fuels. When there's plenty of oxygen, the only products are carbon dioxide and water — this is called complete **combustion**. This is the equation for the complete combustion of a hydrocarbon:

hydrocarbon + oxygen → carbon dioxide + water

E.g. $C_3H_8 + 5O_2 \rightarrow 3CO_2 + 4H_2O$

Practice Questions — Fact Recall

Q1 What is a hydrocarbon?

Q2 Write down the general word equation for the complete combustion of a hydrocarbon in oxygen.

Tip: Incomplete combustion can occur when a hydrocarbon burns in a limited supply of oxygen (see p.226).

Practice Question — Application

Q1 The table below shows the boiling points of four hydrocarbons from the alkane homologous series.

Alkane	Molecular formula	Boiling point (°C)
Methane	CH_4	–161
Ethane	C_2H_6	–89
Butane	C_4H_{10}	–0.5
Decane	$C_{10}H_{22}$	174

a) Which alkane in the table has the strongest intermolecular forces of attraction between its molecules?

b) Explain why the boiling point of butane is higher than that of ethane. In your answer, refer to the strength of the intermolecular forces between molecules.

c) Which alkane would you expect to be the most viscous?

Learning Objectives:

- Be able to explain why the incomplete combustion of hydrocarbons can produce carbon and carbon monoxide.
- Be able to explain how carbon monoxide behaves as a toxic gas.
- Be able to describe the problems caused by incomplete combustion producing carbon monoxide and soot in appliances that use carbon compounds as fuels.
- Be able to explain how impurities in some hydrocarbon fuels results in the production of sulfur dioxide.
- Be able to explain some problems associated with acid rain caused when sulfur dioxide dissolves in rain water.
- Be able to explain why, when fuels are burned in engines, oxygen and nitrogen can react together at high temperatures to produce oxides of nitrogen, which are pollutants.
- Be able to evaluate the advantages and disadvantages of using hydrogen, rather than petrol, as a fuel in cars.

Specification References
8.8-8.14

3. Pollutants

Modern life depends on fossil fuels, but when they are burned they can lead to some pretty harmful chemicals being released into the air...

Incomplete combustion

In plenty of oxygen, hydrocarbons combust completely to produce only water and carbon dioxide (see p.224). However, when you burn them when there is insufficient oxygen in the air, they undergo **incomplete combustion**. This can happen in some appliances, e.g. boilers that use carbon compounds as fuels.

The products of incomplete combustion contain less oxygen than the products of complete combustion. Carbon dioxide and water are still produced, but carbon (in the form of soot) and the toxic gas carbon monoxide (CO) can also be produced.

Example

Here's an example of an equation for incomplete combustion:

$C_4H_8 + 5O_2 \rightarrow 2CO + 2CO_2 + 4H_2O$

However, depending on the amount of oxygen the reaction could also be:

$C_4H_8 + 3O_2 \rightarrow 2C + 2CO + 4H_2O$

Carbon monoxide

The carbon monoxide produced during incomplete combustion can combine with red blood cells and stop your blood from doing its proper job of carrying oxygen around the body. It does this by binding to the haemoglobin in your red blood cells that normally carries oxygen — so less oxygen is able to be transported round your body. A lack of oxygen in the blood supply to the brain can lead to fainting, a coma or even death. A household appliance producing carbon monoxide is a serious health hazard.

Soot

During incomplete combustion, tiny particles of carbon can be released into the atmosphere. When they fall back to the ground, they deposit themselves as the black dust we call soot. Soot makes buildings look dirty, reduces air quality and can cause or worsen respiratory problems. Appliances that produce soot are inefficient as well as dangerous.

Sulfur dioxide and acid rain

When fossil fuels are burned, they release mostly carbon dioxide gas (a major cause of global warming — see page 234). They also release other harmful gases — in particular sulfur dioxide and various nitrogen oxides. The sulfur dioxide (SO_2) comes from sulfur impurities present in fossil fuels.

When sulfur dioxide mixes with the water in the clouds, it reacts with water to form dilute sulfuric acid. This then falls as **acid rain** (see Figure 1 on the next page).

Figure 1: *The formation of acid rain.*

Figure 2: *Trees that have been killed by acid rain.*

Figure 3: *A statue that has been damaged by acid rain.*

Acid rain causes lakes to become acidic and many plants and animals die as a result. Acid rain also kills trees (see Figure 2), damages limestone buildings and ruins some stone statues (see Figure 3). It can also make metals corrode. Links between acid rain and human health problems have also been suggested.

Nitrogen oxides

When fuels are burned in the internal combustion engines of cars, they release a lot of energy in the form of heat. At the high temperatures reached inside combustion engines, the nitrogen and oxygen in the air can react to form nitrogen oxides.

Nitrogen oxides are harmful pollutants — they can contribute to acid rain and, at ground level, can cause photochemical smog. Photochemical smog is a type of air pollution that can cause breathing difficulties, headaches and tiredness. It often forms in large cities, where there is a lot of traffic.

Hydrogen as a fuel

Hydrogen can be used to power vehicles, as an alternative to petrol. It's also often used as a fuel in fuel cells.

Tip: A fuel cell is a device that converts the chemical energy of a fuel directly into electricity.

Advantages

Hydrogen is a very clean fuel. In a hydrogen fuel cell, hydrogen combines with oxygen to produce energy, and the only waste product is water. No harmful pollutants like carbon dioxide, toxic carbon monoxide or soot are produced (unlike in standard combustion engines).

Hydrogen is obtained from water which is a renewable resource, so it's not going to run out (unlike fossil fuels). Hydrogen can even be obtained from the water produced by the cell when it's used in fuel cells.

Tip: Hydrogen can be produced in the electrolysis of water (see pages 136-138).

Disadvantages

A special, expensive engine is required in order to use hydrogen as a fuel. Hydrogen gas also needs to be manufactured, which is expensive and often uses energy from another source — this energy often comes from burning fossil fuels, which produces pollutants.

Hydrogen is a highly flammable gas, so is hard to store safely. It is not widely available, which can make it more expensive to purchase than regular fuels.

Practice Questions — Fact Recall

Q1 Explain when incomplete combustion occurs.

Q2 Give one health problem associated with the production of carbon monoxide during incomplete combustion.

Q3 a) Name a gas that can cause acid rain.

b) Give two ways in which acid rain can damage the environment.

Q4 Under what condition will nitrogen oxides form when a hydrocarbon fuel is burned?

Exam Tip
You can tell from what's in a fuel what pollutants could be produced when it's burned. If it only contains carbon and hydrogen, carbon dioxide, carbon particles, carbon monoxide and oxides of nitrogen could be made. If it also contains sulfur, you could get sulfur dioxide as well.

Practice Questions — Application

Q1 A car manufacturer is developing a range of cars that are powered by hydrogen fuel cells. Describe one advantage and one disadvantage that these cars might have compared to cars powered by fossil fuels.

Q2 The composition of two fuels is shown below:

Fuel A: 80% carbon, 12% hydrogen, 8% sulfur

Fuel B: 72% carbon, 10% hydrogen, 18% sulfur

Which fuel would be the better choice to use in a car in order to reduce the chance of acid rain? Give a reason for your answer.

4. Cracking Crude Oil

Some fractions of crude oil are more useful than others — for example, short-chain hydrocarbons are often more useful than long-chain hydrocarbons. Cracking is used to break down long-chain hydrocarbons into shorter ones.

Learning Objectives:

- Be able to explain how cracking involves the breaking down of larger, saturated hydrocarbon molecules (alkanes) into smaller, more useful ones, some of which are unsaturated (alkenes).
- Be able to explain why cracking is necessary.

Specification References
8.16, 8.17

What is cracking?

Short-chain hydrocarbons are flammable so make good fuels and are in high demand. Long-chain hydrocarbons form thick gloopy liquids which aren't all that useful, so a lot of the longer saturated hydrocarbons (alkanes) produced from fractional distillation are turned into smaller, more useful ones by a process called **cracking**. Cracking produces both alkenes (which are unsaturated) and alkanes (which are saturated).

Some of the products of cracking are useful as fuels, like petrol for cars and kerosene for jet fuel. Cracking also produces alkene molecules such as ethene, which are needed for making polymers (mostly plastics). The process of cracking is illustrated in Figure 1.

Tip: The terms 'saturated' and 'unsaturated' are to do with the bonding in alkanes and alkenes.

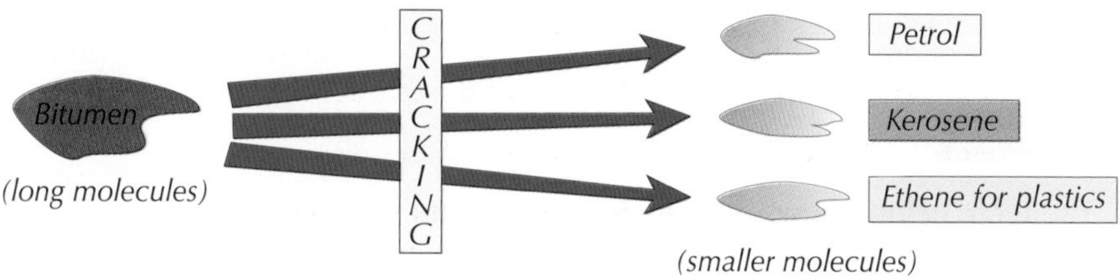

Figure 1: *Cracking. In this example, bitumen (a fraction containing long-chain hydrocarbons) is broken down into shorter-chain hydrocarbons found in petrol, kerosene and ethene.*

How cracking works

Cracking is a **thermal decomposition** reaction — breaking molecules down into at least two new ones by heating them. In cracking, vaporised hydrocarbons are passed over a powdered **catalyst**. A lot of energy is needed to break the strong covalent bonds in the long chain hydrocarbons, so cracking is carried out at temperatures of 400 °C – 700 °C. A pressure of 70 atm and an aluminium oxide catalyst are also used. The long-chain molecules split apart or 'crack' on the surface of the specks of catalyst.

Tip: A vaporised substance is one that has been turned into a gas.

Exam Tip
You don't need to remember the conditions used for cracking.

<u>Long-chain hydrocarbon molecule</u>

Decane ($C_{10}H_{22}$)
There's usually too much of this in crude oil.

CRACKING →

<u>Shorter alkane molecule</u>

Octane (C_8H_{18}) is useful for petrol.

\+

<u>Alkene</u>

Ethene (C_2H_4) is useful for making plastics.

Figure 2: *The cracking of decane into an alkane (octane) and an alkene (ethene).*

Figure 3: *Cracking machinery at an oil refinery.*

Tip: A catalyst speeds up a reaction (see page 205 for more).

The apparatus shown in Figure 4 can be used to crack alkanes in the lab. During this reaction, the alkane is heated until it is vaporised. It then breaks down when it comes into contact with the catalyst, producing a mixture of short-chain alkanes and alkenes.

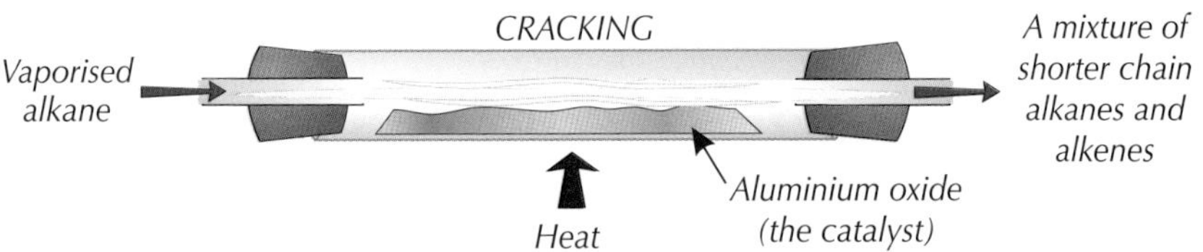

Figure 4: *The cracking of an alkane using an aluminium oxide catalyst.*

Interpreting data on cracking

The examiner might give you a table like the one below to show supply and demand for different crude oil fractions. A fraction will be suitable for cracking if it contains long-chain hydrocarbons and its demand is less than the percentage of crude oil that it makes up.

Example

The table below shows the supply and demand for various fractions of crude oil. Which fraction is most likely to be cracked to provide more petrol and diesel oil?

Fraction	Approximate % in crude oil	Approximate % demand
Gases	2	4
Petrol	16	27
Kerosene	13	8
Diesel Oil	19	23
Fuel Oil and Bitumen	50	38

You could use the kerosene fraction to provide more petrol and the fuel oil and bitumen fraction to supply extra diesel oil. Or you could crack the fuel oil and bitumen to provide both more petrol and more diesel oil. This might be the best option, as there's a lot more fuel oil and bitumen than kerosene.

Exam Tip
Make sure the fractions that you suggest cracking have longer chain hydrocarbons than the fractions you need more of.

Practice Questions — Fact Recall

Q1 What is cracking?

Q2 Name two types of hydrocarbon produced by cracking.

Q3 Why is cracking a necessary process in the petrochemical industry?

5. Evolution of the Atmosphere

The Earth's atmosphere is really important — without it, life as we know it wouldn't have evolved. But the atmosphere hasn't always been the way it is today. This is the story of how the atmosphere was formed...

Formation of the early atmosphere and oceans

The Earth's surface was originally molten for many millions of years. It was so hot that any atmosphere just dispersed into space. Eventually things cooled down a bit and a thin crust formed, but volcanoes kept erupting.

There was intense volcanic activity for the first billion years after the Earth was formed, and the volcanoes gave out lots of gas. Scientists think that these gases went on to form the early atmosphere and the oceans. There are lots of different theories, but the most popular theory suggests that the early atmosphere was probably mostly carbon dioxide (CO_2), with little or no oxygen (O_2). This is quite like the atmospheres of Mars and Venus today. Volcanic activity probably also released nitrogen, which built up in the atmosphere over time, as well as water vapour, and small amounts of methane (CH_4) and ammonia (NH_3).

As the Earth cooled, the water vapour in the atmosphere condensed, forming the oceans.

Decreasing the amount of carbon dioxide

Although the early atmosphere was mostly carbon dioxide, it didn't stay that way for long. Most of the carbon dioxide was gradually removed from the atmosphere. This happened in a number of ways.

Absorption by the oceans

The oceans are a natural store of carbon dioxide. When the oceans formed, a lot of the carbon dioxide from the atmosphere dissolved into them. This dissolved carbon dioxide then went through a series of reactions to form carbonate precipitates that formed sediments on the seabed. When marine animals evolved, their shells and skeletons contained carbonates from the oceans. When they died, they formed sedimentary rocks such as limestone, locking the carbon dioxide away.

Absorption by plants and algae

Green plants and algae evolved over most of the Earth. Algae evolved first — about 2.7 billion years ago. Then over the next billion years or so, primitive green plants also evolved. They absorbed some of the carbon dioxide in the atmosphere and used it for a process called photosynthesis (see next page).

Learning Objectives:

- Know that the gases produced by volcanic activity formed the Earth's early atmosphere.
- Be able to describe that the Earth's early atmosphere was thought to contain little or no oxygen, a large amount of carbon dioxide, water vapour and small amounts of other gases, and be able to interpret evidence relating to this.
- Be able to explain how condensation of water vapour formed oceans.
- Be able to explain how the amount of carbon dioxide in the atmosphere was decreased when carbon dioxide dissolved as the oceans formed.
- Be able to explain how the growth of primitive plants used carbon dioxide and released oxygen by photosynthesis and consequently the amount of oxygen in the atmosphere gradually increased.
- Be able to describe the chemical test for oxygen.

Specification References 8.18-8.23

Tip: Algae are organisms that can use photosynthesis to produce their food.

Increasing the amount of oxygen

As well as absorbing the carbon dioxide in the atmosphere, green plants and algae produced oxygen by photosynthesis — this is when plants use light to convert carbon dioxide and water into sugars:

$$\text{carbon dioxide} + \text{water} \xrightarrow{\text{light}} \text{glucose} + \text{oxygen}$$

$$6CO_2 + 6H_2O \xrightarrow{\text{light}} C_6H_{12}O_6 + 6O_2$$

Tip: Thanks to the plants, the amount of O_2 in the air gradually built up, and much of the CO_2 eventually got locked up as the plants died and formed sedimentary rocks and fossil fuels.

As the oxygen level built up in the atmosphere over time, organisms that couldn't tolerate it were killed off. The increase in oxygen allowed more complex life (like animals), that needed more oxygen, to evolve. The oxygen also created the ozone layer (O_3), which blocked harmful rays from the Sun and enabled even more complex organisms to evolve.

Tip: The nitrogen gas (N_2) found in the atmosphere today was created when ammonia reacted with oxygen. It was also released by denitrifying bacteria. N_2 isn't very reactive, so it built up in the atmosphere because it was being made but not broken down.

Eventually, as the levels of O_2 increased and CO_2 decreased, the atmosphere reached a composition similar to what it is today, with virtually no CO_2 left.

Test for oxygen

You can test for the presence of oxygen in the lab. To test for oxygen, put a glowing splint inside a test tube containing the gas. If oxygen is present it will relight the glowing splint — see Figure 1.

Tip: Remember to always carry out a risk assessment before doing any practical work.

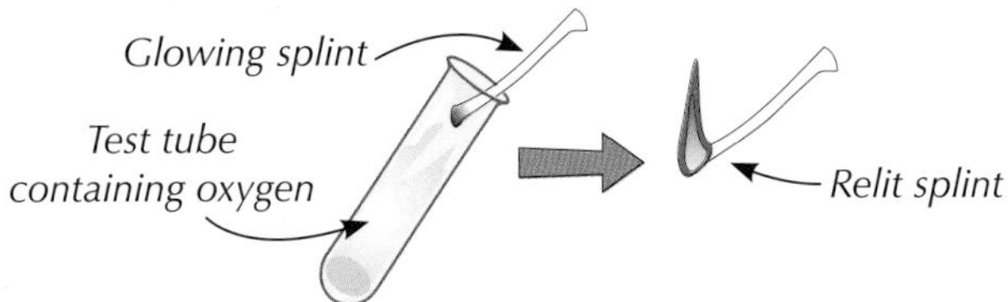

Figure 1: *Testing for oxygen.*

Practice Questions — Fact Recall

Q1 Describe the likely composition of the Earth's early atmosphere.

Q2 Describe why the formation of the oceans led to a decrease in the concentration of carbon dioxide in the atmosphere.

Practice Question — Application

Q1 A scientist is investigating how the composition of gases in the atmosphere may have changed over the last 4.5 billion years.

a) He suggests that, between 4.5 and 4 billion years ago, the concentration of water vapour in the atmosphere decreased rapidly. Explain this change.

b) The scientist finds that, as the level of carbon dioxide in the atmosphere decreased, the level of another gas increased. Suggest the identity of this gas, giving a reason for your answer.

6. Greenhouse Gases & Climate Change

Some of the gases in the atmosphere help to keep the Earth warm, which is great. But if their concentrations get too high, they can cause the climate to change.

What are greenhouse gases?

Greenhouse gases, such as carbon dioxide, methane and water vapour, are present in small amounts in the Earth's atmosphere. They act like an insulating layer, keeping the Earth warm. Here's how it works...

All particles absorb certain frequencies of radiation. The sun emits short wavelength electromagnetic radiation which passes through the Earth's atmosphere, as it isn't absorbed by greenhouse gases. The short wavelength radiation reaches the Earth's surface, is absorbed, and then re-emitted as long wavelength, infrared (IR) radiation. This radiation is absorbed by greenhouse gases in the atmosphere. The greenhouse gases then re-radiate it in all directions — including back towards Earth. The IR radiation is thermal radiation, so it warms the surface of the Earth. This is the **greenhouse effect**.

Figure 1: *The greenhouse effect.*

Human activity and greenhouse gases

WORKING SCIENTIFICALLY

It's thought that human activities have caused a rise in greenhouse gas concentrations in the atmosphere. For example, the level of carbon dioxide is increasing (as shown in Figure 2).

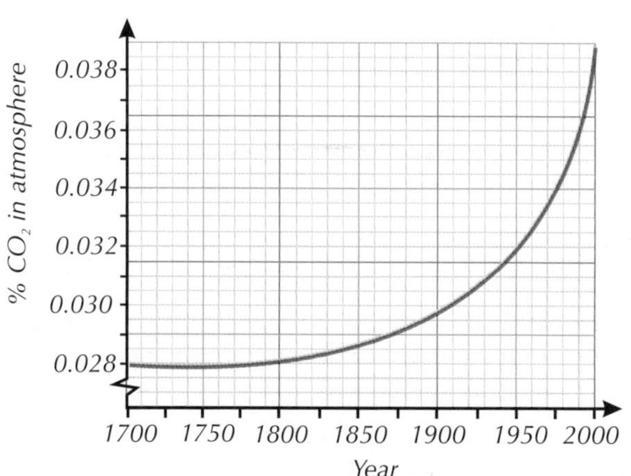

Figure 2: *A graph to show how the CO_2 level in the atmosphere has risen over the last 300 years.*

Learning Objectives:

- Be able to describe how various gases in the atmosphere, including carbon dioxide, methane and water vapour, absorb heat radiated from the Earth, subsequently releasing energy which keeps the Earth warm and that this is known as the greenhouse effect.
- Be able to evaluate the evidence for human activity causing climate change, considering:
  - the correlation between the change in atmospheric carbon dioxide concentration, the consumption of fossil fuels and temperature change;
  - the uncertainties caused by the location where these measurements are taken and historical accuracy.
- Be able to describe the potential effects on the climate of increased levels of carbon dioxide and methane generated by human activity, including burning fossil fuels and livestock farming, and that these effects may be mitigated (considering scale, risk and environmental implications).

Specification References
8.24-8.26

Tip: The greenhouse effect is very important — it's what keeps the Earth warm enough to support life.

Increased levels of greenhouse gases in the atmosphere enhance the greenhouse effect as more IR radiation is absorbed and radiated back towards Earth, which causes the Earth to get warmer — this is **global warming**.

The level of carbon dioxide in the atmosphere has increased because we are adding more CO_2 to the atmosphere and less is being removed from it (see below). We are also adding to the amount of other greenhouse gases in the atmosphere, such as methane.

Increasing energy consumption

Over the last 150 years or so, the world's human population has shot up and we've become more industrialised. Both of these factors mean that we've increased our energy consumption and are burning more and more fossil fuels.

Examples

- An increasing global population means that more energy is needed for lighting, heating, cooking, transport and so on.
- People's lifestyles are changing too. This means that the average energy demand per person is also increasing (since people have more electrical gadgets and more people have cars or travel on planes, etc.).

Tip: As the consumption of fossil fuels increases, so does the concentration of CO_2 in the atmosphere.

Burning more fossil fuels means that carbon, that was 'locked up' in the fuels, has been released into the atmosphere in the form of CO_2.

Deforestation

Figure 3: *Forests being cut down (deforestation) contributes to the increased level of carbon dioxide in the atmosphere.*

More people also means more land is needed to build houses and grow food. We've been chopping down forests (known as **deforestation**) to create this extra space. This is a problem as plants absorb carbon dioxide by photosynthesis. So fewer plants means less carbon dioxide is being removed from the atmosphere.

Methane and farming

The greenhouse gas methane is also causing problems. Like carbon dioxide, the concentration of methane has also risen a lot in recent years due to increased human activity. For example, in livestock farming, cows produce large amounts of methane. Paddy fields, in which rice is grown, produce a fair bit too. So the larger the population gets, the more we need to farm to produce food, and the more methane is produced.

Tip: CO_2 is also produced by volcanoes erupting.

Though it's currently only present in tiny amounts in our atmosphere, the increasing concentration of methane is an issue as it's a highly effective greenhouse gas.

Carbon dioxide and global warming

Historically, temperature change at the Earth's surface is correlated to the level of carbon dioxide in the atmosphere (see Figure 4). Recently, the average temperature at the Earth's surface has been increasing as the level of carbon dioxide has increased.

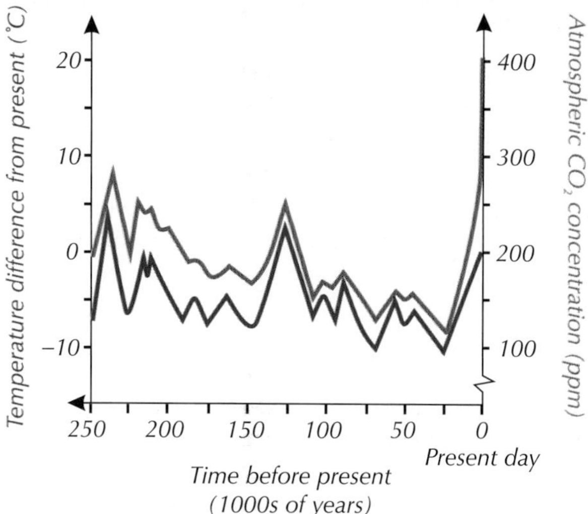

Figure 4: *A graph to show the correlation between atmospheric carbon dioxide level and temperature.*

Tip: Just because two variables are correlated, doesn't mean that one causes the other. However, in the case of temperature and CO_2 concentration, the correlation can be backed up with a plausible and scientific explanation. WORKING SCIENTIFICALLY

Even though the Earth's temperature varies naturally, most scientists agree that the extra greenhouse gases from human activity (mainly through burning fossil fuels) are causing an increase in temperature. This temperature increase is known as global warming and is a type of **climate change**. Global warming could even lead to further climate change — which may have lots of effects with negative consequences.

Tip: Don't get confused. Global warming and climate change aren't the same thing — global warming is a type of climate change.

Examples

- An increase in global temperature could lead to polar ice caps and glaciers melting, causing a rise in sea levels, increased flooding in coastal areas and coastal erosion.
- Changes in rainfall patterns (the amount, timing and distribution) may cause some regions to get too much or too little water. This, along with changes in temperature, may affect the ability of certain regions to produce food.
- The frequency and severity of storms may also increase.
- Changes in temperature and the amount of water available in a habitat may affect wild species, leading to differences in their distribution.

The vast majority of the scientific community agree that global warming is anthropogenic (caused by humans). But some scientists believe that the current rises in global temperature are just natural fluctuations and that we don't have enough data to prove that global warming is caused by increasing CO_2 emissions or human activity.

Tip: One of the best ways scientists have of predicting how the climate might change is by using computer modelling. WORKING SCIENTIFICALLY

Challenges in obtaining climate change data

The current average global temperature and carbon dioxide level can be worked out pretty accurately, as they're based on measurements taken all over the world. Historical data is less accurate — less data was taken over fewer locations and the methods used to collect the data were less accurate. If you go back far enough, there are no records of the global temperature and carbon dioxide level at all.

Tip: The width of a tree ring shows how much a tree has grown over a year. Tree rings can be used to make predictions about what the climate (e.g. rainfall, temperature) was like in the past.

But there are ways to estimate past data. For example, you can analyse fossils, tree rings or gas bubbles trapped in ice sheets to estimate past levels of atmospheric carbon dioxide. The problem with using these kinds of measurements is that they're much less precise than current measurements made using instrumental sampling. Another issue with measuring carbon dioxide level is the location of sampling. Different areas may have varying carbon dioxide levels and may be unrepresentative of the global level.

Mitigating the effects of climate change

In order to slow down or mitigate (lessen) climate change, we need to cut down on the amount of greenhouse gases we're releasing into the atmosphere. To reduce carbon dioxide emissions, we can try to limit our use of fossil fuels. This could be doing things on a personal level, like walking or cycling instead of driving or turning your central heating down.

On a larger scale, the UK government has formed plans to encourage the public and industry to become more energy efficient, to create financial incentives to reduce CO_2 emissions, to use more renewable energy and to increase research into new energy sources.

Figure 5: *The Thames Barrier is a flood defence that can be raised and lowered when required.*

Technology could also be used to reduce some of the effects of climate change. For example, flood defences can be used which could keep homes safe from flooding. However, the long-term effects of climate change are hard to predict and new technology may have knock-on environmental implications.

Practice Questions — Fact Recall

Q1 Explain how greenhouse gases help to keep the Earth warm.

Q2 State one way that human activity is leading to an increase in methane in the atmosphere.

Q3 Explain why there are uncertainties in measuring the current carbon dioxide level.

Q4 a) What is global warming?

b) Global warming may lead to further climate change. Suggest one consequence of climate change.

Q5 Suggest one way that the effects of climate change can be mitigated.

Topic 8 Checklist — Make sure you know...

Fractional Distillation of Crude Oil

- [ ] That crude oil is a complex mixture of different hydrocarbons which have their carbon atoms arranged in chains or rings.
- [ ] That crude oil is a finite (non-renewable) resource.
- [ ] That crude oil is a source of fuels and is a feedstock for the petrochemical industry.
- [ ] How fractional distillation is used to separate crude oil into simpler, more useful mixtures.
- [ ] That fractions of crude oil include gases, petrol, kerosene, diesel oil, fuel oil and bitumen.
- [ ] The uses of the different fractions of crude oil.
- [ ] That methane is a non-renewable fossil fuel found in natural gas.
- [ ] That petrol, kerosene and diesel oil are non-renewable fossil fuels.

Hydrocarbons

- [ ] That a hydrocarbon is a compound that contains only hydrogen and carbon.
- [ ] That a homologous series is a group of compounds which share similar chemical properties and have the same general formula.
- [ ] That neighbouring compounds in a homologous series differ by a CH_2 unit in their molecular formulae.
- [ ] That the physical properties (e.g. boiling points) of compounds in a homologous series gradually change as the sizes of the molecules increase.
- [ ] That the majority of hydrocarbons found in crude oil are alkanes.
- [ ] That fractions of crude oil contain hydrocarbons of similar sizes.
- [ ] Why hydrocarbons with longer carbon chains tend to have higher boiling points, be harder to ignite and be more viscous.
- [ ] That complete combustion occurs when a hydrocarbon is burned in plenty of oxygen.
- [ ] That the products of complete combustion are carbon dioxide and water.
- [ ] That energy is released when a hydrocarbon undergoes complete combustion.

Pollutants

- [ ] That incomplete combustion occurs when a hydrocarbon is burned in an insufficient amount of oxygen, and that carbon (in the form of soot) and carbon monoxide are produced.
- [ ] That carbon monoxide is a toxic gas that binds to the haemoglobin in red blood cells and prevents them from carrying oxygen around the body.
- [ ] That tiny particles of carbon, called soot, are produced during incomplete combustion and that they make buildings look dirty, reduce air quality and can lead to respiratory problems.
- [ ] That incomplete combustion can occur in appliances that use fossil fuels.
- [ ] That sulfur dioxide is produced when fossil fuels containing sulfur impurities are burned.
- [ ] That acid rain forms when sulfur dioxide dissolves in rain water.

cont...

- [ ] The problems associated with acid rain.
- [ ] That the high temperatures created in the internal combustion engines of cars can lead to the formation of nitrogen oxides from nitrogen and oxygen.
- [ ] That nitrogen oxides are pollutants that can cause photochemical smog.
- [ ] The advantages and disadvantages of using hydrogen as a fuel in cars, as opposed to petrol.

Cracking Crude Oil

- [ ] That cracking is used to break down large, saturated hydrocarbon molecules found in crude oil into smaller, more useful ones at high temperatures and pressures.
- [ ] That the products of cracking can be saturated (alkanes) or unsaturated (alkenes).
- [ ] That cracking is important as it allows the petrochemical industry to match the supply of chemicals and fuels with their demand.

Evolution of the Atmosphere

- [ ] That the gases that made up Earth's early atmosphere came from volcanic eruptions.
- [ ] That the Earth's early atmosphere contained barely any oxygen, a lot of carbon dioxide, water vapour and small amounts of various other gases such as methane and ammonia.
- [ ] That the oceans were formed when water vapour in the air condensed.
- [ ] That the level of carbon dioxide in the atmosphere decreased as carbon dioxide began to dissolve in the oceans, and plants started to photosynthesise.
- [ ] How the evolution of photosynthetic plants led to an increase in the level of oxygen in the atmosphere.
- [ ] That oxygen gas relights a glowing splint.

Greenhouse Gases & Climate Change

- [ ] That greenhouse gases absorb heat from the Earth and re-emit it back towards the Earth, warming it, and that this is known as the greenhouse effect.
- [ ] That carbon dioxide, methane and water vapour are greenhouse gases.
- [ ] How human activity, such as the increased use of fossil fuels and livestock farming, has increased the levels of greenhouse gases in the Earth's atmosphere.
- [ ] That in recent times there has been a sharp increase in the level of carbon dioxide in the Earth's atmosphere, which is strongly correlated with an increase in the temperature of the Earth and increased burning of fossil fuels, strongly indicating that human activity is causing climate change.
- [ ] Why climate change data taken in the past (historical data) is not as accurate as present-day data.
- [ ] That there are uncertainties in measuring global carbon dioxide level due to the location of sampling.
- [ ] The impact that increased levels of greenhouse gases, caused by human activity, could have on the Earth's climate.
- [ ] How the effects of climate change can be mitigated.

Exam-style Questions

1 Many modern cars use petrol as their fuel source.
Petrol is produced from crude oil by a process known as fractional distillation.

(a) Explain why fractional distillation is used to produce petrol and other fractions from crude oil.

(1 mark)

(b) Petrol is removed from near the top of the fractionating column.
What does this tell you about the hydrocarbons that make up petrol?

(1 mark)

(c) Petrol often contains heptane (C_7H_{16}).
Write a word equation for the complete combustion of heptane.

(2 marks)

2 Alkanes are a homologous series of saturated hydrocarbons.

(a) State the formula of the unit that the molecular formulae of neighbouring hydrocarbons in the alkane homologous series differ by.

(1 mark)

This table contains information about some common alkanes.

Alkane	Formula	Number of carbon atoms in chain
Propane	C_3H_8	3
Heptane	C_7H_{16}	7
Decane	$C_{10}H_{22}$	10

(b) Which of the alkanes in the table is likely to be the hardest to ignite?
Explain your answer.

(2 marks)

(c) Which of the alkanes in the table would be the most likely to leave a fractionating column close to the top? Explain your answer.

(3 marks)

Hydrocarbons are often used as a fuel in the internal combustion engines of cars.

(d) (i) Nitrogen oxides are pollutants.
Describe how nitrogen oxides are formed in the engines of cars.

(2 marks)

(ii) Give **one** example of a type of pollution that nitrogen oxides can cause.

(1 mark)

3 Crude oil is an important source of useful chemicals.

(a) Certain fractions of crude oil can be turned into more useful products by breaking them up into smaller molecules at high temperatures and pressures. Name this process.

(1 mark)

(b) Diesel oil is a fraction of crude oil that is in high demand. Give **one** use of diesel oil.

(1 mark)

4 The composition of the Earth's atmosphere has changed a lot over the last 4.5 billion years.

(a) Where did the gases that formed the Earth's early atmosphere come from?

(1 mark)

Scientists think that the most abundant gas in the atmosphere 4.5 billion years ago was carbon dioxide. Now, there is very little carbon dioxide in our atmosphere.

(b) Give **two** reasons why the concentration of carbon dioxide in the atmosphere decreased to the level that it is at today.

(2 marks)

(c) The burning of fossil fuels is now causing the concentration of carbon dioxide in the atmosphere to rise again. Give **one** environmental impact that an increased level of carbon dioxide in the atmosphere may cause.

(1 mark)

5 A cattle farm is investigating how it could reduce the amount of greenhouse gases and pollutants that it produces.

(a) The biggest contributor to the total greenhouse gas emissions from the farm is methane gas. Suggest why this is.

(1 mark)

(b) (i) The farm has a generator that runs off a hydrocarbon fuel. The farmer notices that a layer of soot has formed around the generator. Explain how this soot may have formed.

(1 mark)

(ii) Give two ways in which soot can affect health and the environment if it gets into the atmosphere.

(2 marks)

(iii) The reaction that causes soot to form can also result in the production of a harmful gas. State what this gas is and explain why it can be harmful to health.

(2 marks)

(c) The farm is considering replacing the current generator with one powered by a hydrogen fuel cell. Describe how using a hydrogen-powered generator could reduce the levels of pollutants and greenhouse gases that the farm produces.

(2 marks)

1. Drawing Equipment

As part of the chemistry topics in GCSE Combined Science, you'll have to do at least five practicals, called Core Practicals. You'll also need to know how to use various pieces of apparatus and carry out different scientific techniques. And not only do you need to carry out the practicals and techniques, you could also be asked about them in the exams. Luckily, all the Core Practicals are covered in this book, and the next few pages cover some of the other techniques that you'll need to know about.

Tip: The Core Practicals in this book are marked with a big stamp like this...

Scientific drawings

When you're writing out a method for your experiment, it's always a good idea to draw a labelled diagram showing how your apparatus will be set up. The easiest way to do this is to use a scientific drawing, where each piece of apparatus is drawn as if you're looking at its cross-section. Some basic pieces of equipment that you're likely to need to draw are shown in Figures 1 and 2.

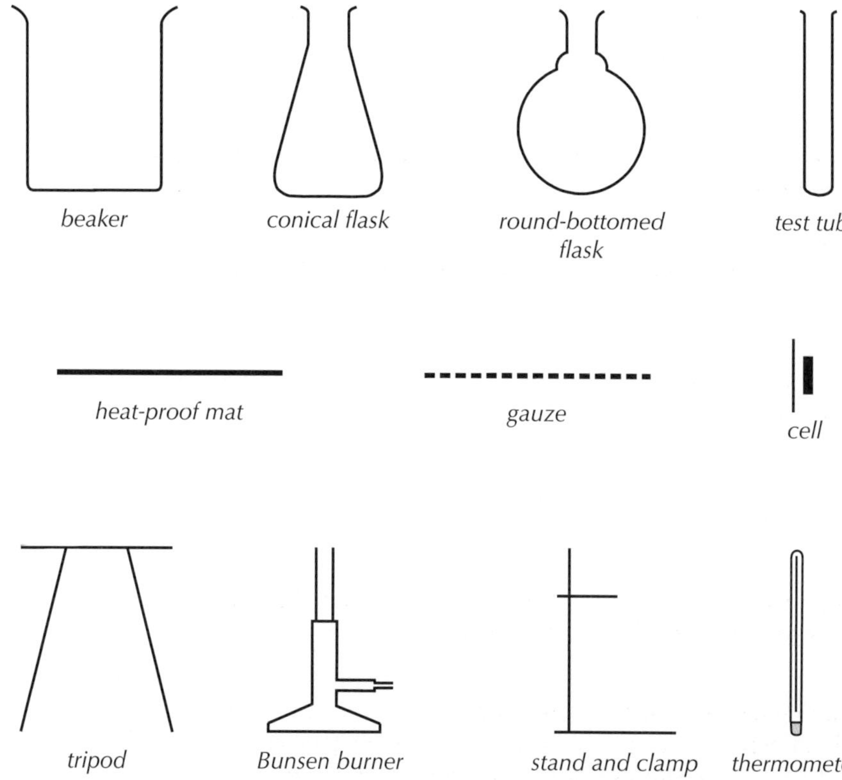

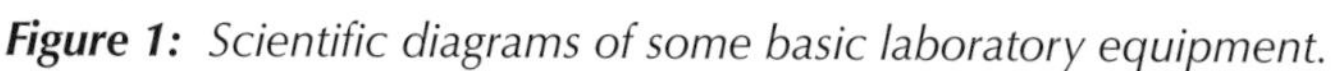

Figure 1: *Scientific diagrams of some basic laboratory equipment.*

Tip: In the scientific drawing of a cell, the longer line is the positive side, and the shorter line is negative.

Tip: There's more information on using pipettes, burettes and measuring cylinders on pages 243-244.

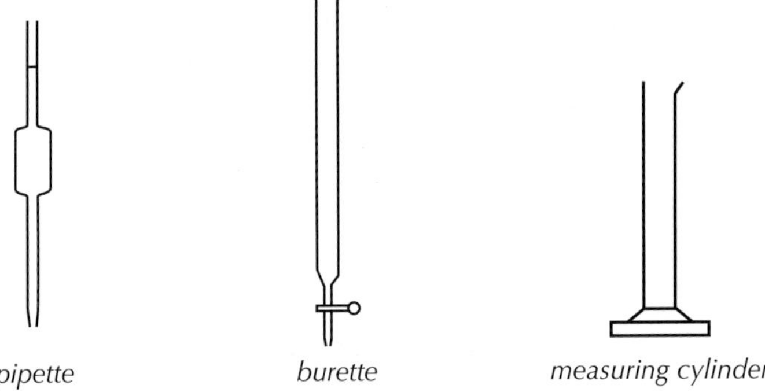

***Figure 2:** Scientific diagrams of some more basic laboratory equipment.*

Exam Tip
Always make sure the set-up is drawn correctly in your diagrams. This might mean making sure your diagram shows a closed system if you're collecting a gas, making sure any thermometers are positioned at the right point for where you're measuring the temperatures, or making sure that any equipment with a water flow shows it going in the right direction.

None of the pieces of glassware (such as the conical flask) shown in Figure 1 have been drawn with tops. If you see this, it means that the equipment is open to the air, so things can get in and out. For experiments where the equipment needs to be sealed, make sure that you draw a bung in the top of the flask.

Example

To measure the volume of gas given off in a reaction, the equipment needs to be sealed so no gas can escape, as shown in Figure 3.

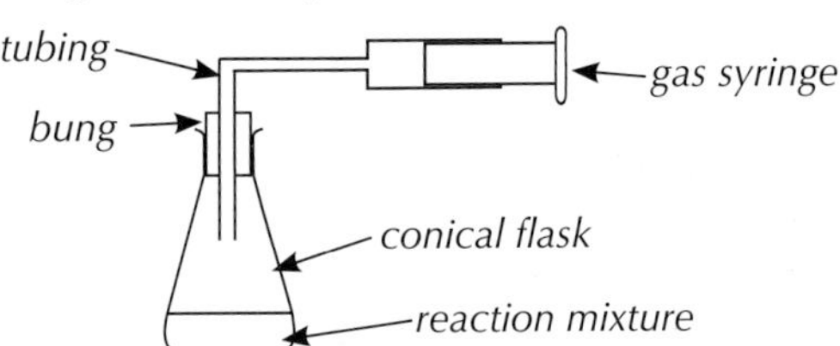

***Figure 3:** Equipment for measuring the volume of gas produced by a reaction.*

2. Measuring Substances

The results of an experiment won't be any good if you don't know how to measure and record things properly. Some of this may seem obvious, but measuring things carefully is key to getting good results.

Measuring the mass of solids

You weigh solids using a balance. To do this you should put the container you are weighing your substance into on the balance, and make sure the balance is set to exactly zero. Then, start weighing out your substance. Once you've measured a quantity of a substance you need to be careful you don't lose any. In particular, think about how to minimise losses if you're transferring the solid from the measuring equipment into another container. For example, if you're dissolving the solid in a solvent to make a solution, you could wash any remaining solid into the new container using the solvent.

Tip: If you don't set your mass balance to exactly zero, your results will have 'zero errors' (see page 13).

Another way you could measure the mass of solid is to set the balance to zero before you put your weighing container on it. Then reweigh the weighing container after you've transferred the solid. Use the difference in mass to work out exactly how much solid you added to your experiment.

Measuring the volumes of liquids

There are a few methods you might use to measure the volume of a liquid. Whichever method you use, always read the volume from the bottom of the meniscus (the curved upper surface of the liquid) when it's at eye level (see Figure 1).

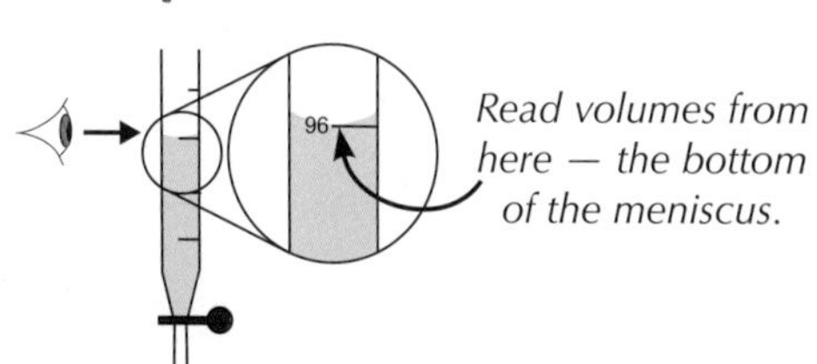

Figure 1: *The technique for correctly measuring the volume of a liquid.*

Measuring cylinders

Measuring cylinders are the most common way to measure out a liquid. They come in all different sizes. Make sure you choose one that's the right size for the measurement you want to make. It's no good using a huge 1000 cm^3 cylinder to measure out 2 cm^3 of a liquid — the graduations will be too big, and you'll end up with massive errors. It'd be much better to use one that measures up to 10 cm^3.

Figure 2: *A student using a burette.*

Burettes

Burettes measure from top to bottom (so when they are full, the scale reads zero). They have a tap at the bottom which you can use to release the liquid into another container (you can even release it drop by drop). To use a burette, take an initial reading, and once you've released as much liquid as you want, take a final reading. The difference between the readings tells you how much liquid you used.

Tip: Burettes and pipettes are both used in titration experiments — see pages 131-132 for more about titrations.

Pipettes

Pipettes are long, narrow tubes that are used to suck up an accurate volume of liquid and transfer it to another container. They are often calibrated to allow for the fact that the last drop of liquid stays in the pipette when the liquid is ejected. This reduces transfer errors.

To use a pipette, you'll need to attach a pipette filler to the top. This could be a plastic tube with a wheel that you turn to draw liquid into the pipette. To release the liquid, either turn the wheel in the opposite direction, or press the quick release lever on the side. Alternatively, it could be a rubber ball with three valves. To use it, press the top valve and squeeze air out of the rubber ball. Then press the valve just below the rubber ball to suck liquid into the pipette. To release liquid, press the valve on the side-arm.

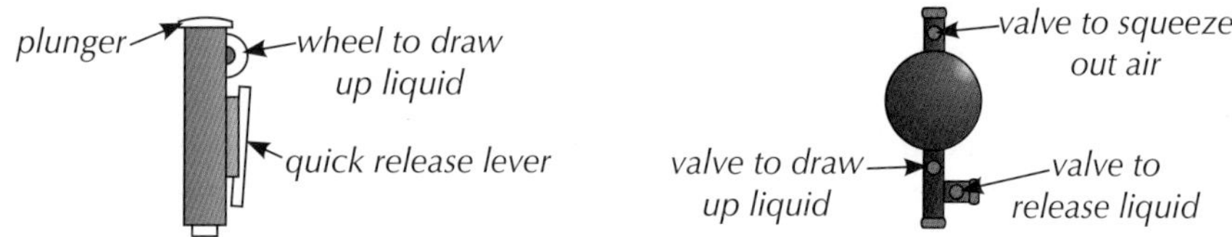

Figure 3: *Different pipette fillers.*

Figure 4: *A dropping pipette being used to add Universal indicator to an acid.*

Dropping pipettes

If you only want a couple of drops of liquid and don't need it to be accurately measured, you can use a dropping pipette to transfer it. For example, you'd use a dropping pipette to add indicator to a liquid or solution (see p.118-119).

Measuring the volumes of gases

There are times when you might want to collect the gas produced by a reaction. When you're measuring a gas, your equipment has to be sealed or gas will escape and your results won't be accurate. You should take all your measurements at the same temperature and pressure, as both these factors affect the volume of a gas. Here are a couple of methods you could use:

Gas syringes

The most accurate way to measure the volume of a gas is with a gas syringe. You should use a gas syringe that's the right size. Before you use the syringe, you should make sure it's completely sealed and that the plunger moves smoothly.

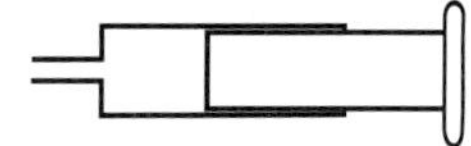

Figure 5: *A scientific diagram of a gas syringe.*

Tip: Gas syringes can be used to follow the rate of a reaction (see pages 191-192).

Collecting gases over water

You can collect gases by displacing water from a measuring cylinder. To do this, you should first fill a measuring cylinder with water, and carefully place it upside down in a container of water. Record the initial level of the water in the measuring cylinder. Then position a delivery tube coming from the reaction vessel so that it's inside the measuring cylinder, pointing upwards. Any gas that's produced will pass through the delivery tube and into the measuring cylinder. As the gas enters the measuring cylinder, the water is pushed out. Record the level of water in the measuring cylinder. You can calculate the volume of gas produced by subtracting the final volume of liquid in the measuring cylinder from the initial volume.

This method is less accurate than using a gas syringe to measure the volume of gas produced. This is because some gases can dissolve in water, so less gas ends up in the measuring cylinder than is actually produced.

If just want to collect a sample to test (and don't need to measure a volume), you can collect it over water as above using a test tube. Once the test tube is full of gas, you can stopper it and store the gas for later.

Figure 6: *Collecting the gas produced in a reaction by displacing water from a test tube.*

Measuring temperature

You can use a thermometer to measure the temperature of a substance. Always wait for the temperature to stabilise before taking an initial reading and if you're using a thermometer with a scale, read off your measurement at eye level to make sure it's accurate. Think about where you need to take your measurement from — if you're measuring the temperature of a liquid, the bulb of the thermometer should be submerged in the liquid. If you're measuring the temperature of a gas as it evaporates from a liquid during distillation, then the bulb of your thermometer should be at the outlet of the distillation apparatus (see Figure 7). This is so you know the temperature being measured is the same as the temperature of the substance that is being distilled.

Tip: Measuring temperature accurately is important for investigating how different factors affect the temperature change of a reaction (see p.213).

***Figure 7:** Distillation apparatus. The bulb of the thermometer is level with the outlet to the condenser.*

Measuring time

You should use a stopwatch to time experiments. These measure to the nearest 0.1 s so are pretty sensitive. Make sure you start and stop the stopwatch at exactly the right time. For example, if you're investigating the rate of an experiment, you should start timing the moment you mix the reagents and start the reaction. If you're measuring the time taken for a precipitate to form, you should stop timing the moment the reaction goes cloudy.

Tip: There's more about distillation on pages 102-103.

Measuring pH

You need to be able to decide the best method for measuring pH, depending on what your experiment is. There are two methods you might come across.

Indicators

Indicators are dyes that change colour depending on the pH. You use them by adding a couple of drops of the indicator to the solution you're interested in. They're useful for titration reactions, when you want to find the point at which a solution is neutralised.

Tip: There's loads more on pH on page 118.

Universal indicator is a mixture of indicators that changes colour gradually as pH changes. It doesn't show a sudden colour change. It's useful for estimating the pH of a solution based on its colour.

Indicators can be soaked into paper and strips of this paper can be used for testing pH. If you use a dropping pipette to spot a small amount of a solution onto some indicator paper, it will change colour depending on the pH of the solution. Indicator paper is useful when you don't want to change the colour of all of the substance. You can also hold a piece of damp indicator paper in a gas sample to test the pH of the solution it forms.

Examples

- Litmus paper is red in acidic conditions and blue in basic conditions.
- Universal indicator paper can be used to estimate pH based on its colour. It's blue or purple in alkaline conditions, green in neutral conditions and yellow, orange or red in acidic conditions.

Exam Tip
In the exam, you may have to read a method or look at a diagram of equipment and work out whether an experiment would be valid. Experiments can only be valid if everything's been measured correctly, so make sure you know these measuring techniques.

pH probes

A pH meter is an electronic gadget that can be used to give a precise and accurate value for the pH of a solution. They're made up of a probe attached to a digital display. You put the probe in the solution you're measuring and read the pH off the display.

3. Handling and Mixing Substances

So now you know how to measure things carefully. But that's not the end, I'm afraid. In order to carry out an experiment safely, you also need to know how to handle and mix substances properly. And that's what this page is on.

Tip: Being able to plan and carry out experiments safely is a key part of Working Scientifically.

Handling chemicals

There are lots of hazards in chemistry experiments, so before you start any experiment, you should read any safety precautions to do with your method or the chemicals you're using.

The substances used in chemical reactions are often hazardous. For example, they might catch fire easily (they're flammable), or they might irritate or burn your skin if you come into contact with them. Whenever you're doing an experiment, you should wear a lab coat, safety goggles and gloves. Always be careful that the chemicals you're using aren't flammable before you go lighting any Bunsen burners, and make sure you're working in an area that's well ventilated.

If you're doing an experiment that might produce nasty gases (such as chlorine), you should carry out the experiment in a fume hood so that the gas can't escape out into the room you're working in.

Tip: There's more about safety in experiments on pages 28-29.

Never directly touch any chemicals (even if you're wearing gloves). Use a spatula to transfer solids between containers. Carefully pour liquids between different containers, using a funnel to avoid spillages, and make sure you transfer things below eye level. For example, if you're filling a burette, you should adjust the height of the burette so that the opening is below your eyes, rather than reaching up to fill it. This reduces the risk of splashing chemicals into your eyes.

***Figure 1:** Dissolving copper sulfate in water to make a solution.*

Mixing chemicals

Be careful when you're mixing chemicals, as a reaction might occur.

Examples

- If you're diluting a liquid, add the concentrated substance to the water (not the other way around) or the mixture could get very hot.
- To dissolve a solid, you should always add the solid to the liquid. Then, to mix the substances properly, you should either use a glass stirrer, or put a bung in the top of the container and carefully invert it a few times. If you're using the second method, make sure the substances don't react to form a gas, or the pressure will build up in the container and the bung could fly off the top.
- If you're carrying out a reaction that involves a catalyst, you should mix the reactants first and then add the catalyst.

4. Heating substances

If you need to heat a substance, you can't always just hold it over a Bunsen burner until it's the right temperature. The way you heat something depends on how flammable it is and how accurate its final temperature needs to be.

Bunsen burners

Bunsen burners are good for heating things quickly. You can easily adjust how strongly they're heating. But you need to be careful not to use them if you're heating flammable compounds as the flame means the substance would be at risk of catching fire.

To use a Bunsen burner, you should first connect it to a gas tap, and check that the hole is closed. Place it on a heatproof mat. Next, light a splint and hold it over the Bunsen burner. Now, turn on the gas. The Bunsen burner should light with a yellow flame. The more open the hole is, the more strongly the Bunsen burner will heat your substance. Open the hole to the amount you want. As you open the hole more, the flame should turn more blue.
Heat things just above the blue cone, as this is the hottest part of the flame.

Tip: Some things take a long time to cool down, and you can't necessarily tell by looking whether they're hot or cold. So, after heating equipment, you should always handle it with tongs so you don't get burnt.

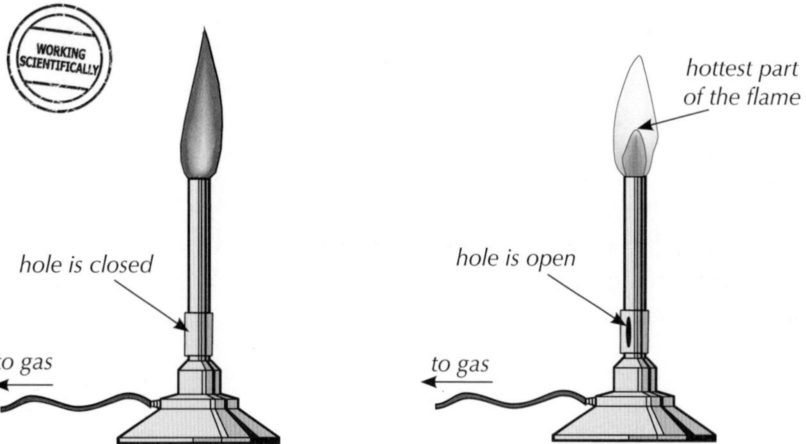

Figure 1: *A Bunsen burner with the hole closed (left) and the hole open (right).*

If your Bunsen burner is alight but not heating anything, make sure you close the hole so that the flame becomes yellow and clearly visible. If you're heating something so that the container (e.g. a test tube) is in the flame, you should hold the vessel at the top, furthest away from the substance (and so the flame) using a pair of tongs. If you're heating something over the flame (e.g. an evaporating dish), you should put a tripod and gauze over the Bunsen burner before you light it, and place the vessel on this.

Tip: Many organic substances, such as alkanes, are very flammable, so you shouldn't heat them with a Bunsen burner.

Example

You could use a Bunsen burner to heat the mixture you wanted to separate during a simple distillation. As the mixture warms up, a substance will evaporate when the temperature of the mixture reaches the boiling point of that particular substance. You could then re-condense and collect the substance in a beaker (see page 102 for more).

Electric heaters

Figure 2: An electric heater.

WORKING SCIENTIFICALLY

Electric heaters are often made up of a dish of metal that can be heated to a particular temperature. The reaction vessel goes on top of the hot plate (see Figure 2). The mixture is only heated from below, so you'll usually have to stir the reaction mixture to make sure it's heated evenly.

Electric heaters don't have a flame, so can be used to safely heat flammable substances. It's also easy to control how strongly they heat. And unlike water baths (see below), they can heat things to above 100 °C.

Example

If you wanted to distil a flammable mixture, you couldn't use a Bunsen burner. An electric heater could be used instead.

Water baths

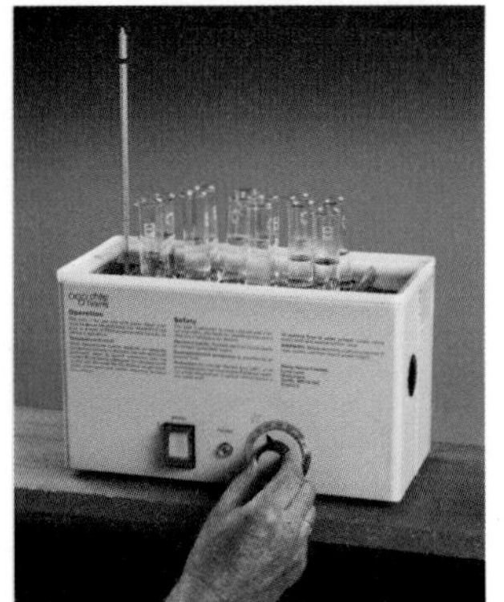

Figure 3: A water bath.

WORKING SCIENTIFICALLY

A water bath is a container filled with water that can be heated to a particular temperature. To use one, start by setting the temperature on the water bath, and allow the water to heat up. Place the container with the substance you want to heat in the water bath using a pair of tongs. The level of the water outside the container should be just above the level of the substance inside the vessel. The substance will then heat up until it reaches the same temperature as the water.

As the substance in the container is surrounded by water, the heating is very even. Water boils at 100 °C though, so you can't use a water bath to heat something to a higher temperature than this — the water won't get hot enough.

Example

You could use a water bath to get two liquids or solutions to the same temperature before mixing them. This could be used in an experiment to find the temperature change over the course of a reaction (see page 213).

Maths skills for GCSE Combined Science

Maths is an important part of GCSE Combined Science, so you need to be confident using your maths skills by the time you sit your exams. There are loads of examples using maths skills throughout this book but, to be extra useful, here's a section entirely about maths. How delightful.

Exam Tip
Around 20% of the marks in the exams will depend on your maths skills. That's a lot of marks so it's definitely worth making sure you're up to speed.

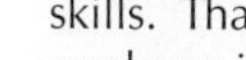

1. Calculations

Calculations are the cornerstone of maths in science. So being able to carry them out carefully is pretty important.

Making estimates

Estimates are useful when it's difficult to be accurate. For example, when you're using something that's hard to measure, or can't be measured directly. Estimates are also useful for checking whether an answer to a calculation is sensible.

Tip: All the examples in this book that include the kind of maths you could get in your exam are clearly marked. You can spot them by the little stamp that says...

Example

During a chromatography experiment, a mixture separates into two spots. Spot A travels 2.4 cm up the filter paper, and spot B travels 1.1 cm. The solvent front travels 5.0 cm. From this data, you can calculate the R_f of spot A is 0.48 and the R_f of spot B is 0.22.

You can check your answer is sensible by doing a quick estimate. The distance travelled by spot A is just over double the distance travelled by spot B. So the R_f of A should be just over double the R_f of B. It is, so there's a good chance that the calculations have been done correctly.

Exam Tip
If you've done a calculation in your head, make sure you check it using a calculator. (Unless you're really, really confident that you've got it right.)

Fractions and decimals

Values that aren't whole numbers can either be written as fractions or as decimals. Decimal numbers are equivalent to a fraction. Here are some common equivalents that could be useful to know.

Examples

$0.5 = \frac{1}{2}$ $0.33... = \frac{1}{3}$ $0.25 = \frac{1}{4}$ $0.1 = \frac{1}{10}$

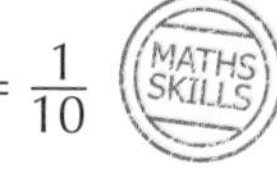

You can do calculations with numbers that contain fractions or decimals.

Example

In a chromatography experiment, the solvent moved 4.2 cm and a spot of substance moved 1.4 cm. The R_f value of the substance is:

$$R_f = \frac{1.4}{4.2} = 0.33 \text{ (or } \frac{1}{3}\text{)}$$

Percentages

A percentage is a way of comparing one number to another as a fraction of 100. No matter what you're calculating the percentage of, the method is always the same:

1. Work out the number you're comparing to. Sometimes this may be given to you, but other times you'll have to work it out.
2. Divide your value by the number you're comparing to.
3. Multiply by 100 to get the percentage.

Tip: 'Percent' means 'out of 100'. So, for example, 62% means 62 out of 100. This can also be written as a fraction: $62\% = \frac{62}{100}$

Example

A recycling company receives 250 kg of waste each day. Only 150 kg is suitable for recycling. What percentage of the daily waste is suitable for recycling?

Here, you want to find what the mass of recyclable waste is as a percentage of the total mass of waste. So the number you're comparing to is 250 kg.

Divide your value by the number you're comparing to: $150 \div 250 = 0.60$

Multiply by 100 to get the percentage: $0.60 \times 100 =$ **60%**

Ratios

Ratios are a way of comparing quantities. Ratios are usually written like this:

A colon separates one quantity from the other.

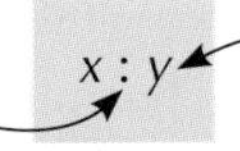

x and y stand for the quantities of each thing.

To write a ratio, first write down the numbers you have of each thing, separated by a colon. Then divide the numbers by the same amount until they're the smallest they can be whilst still being whole numbers.

Tip: Working out the ratio of substances in equations can be really useful for working out the amount of product formed from a given amount of reactant, or vice versa (see pages 82-83).

Example

Give the ratio of oxygen to water in the following reaction in its simplest form: $C_5H_{12} + 8O_2 \rightarrow 5CO_2 + 6H_2O$.

From the equation, there are 8 molecules of oxygen for every 6 molecules of water. So the ratio can be written as 8 : 6.

Both numbers are divisible by 2, so the simplest form of the ratio is **4 : 3**.

Standard form

You might need to use or understand numbers written in standard form. Standard form must always look like this:

$$A \times 10^n$$

This number must always be between 1 and 10. (A)

This number is the number of places the decimal point moves. (n)

Tip: 'A' can be 1 or any number up to 10 but it can't be 10.

Standard form is used for writing very big or very small numbers in a more convenient way.

Tip: If the power that 10 is raised to is a positive number, the number is bigger than 10. If it's a negative number, the number is smaller than 1.

Examples

- There are 602 000 000 000 000 000 000 000 particles in a mole. It's much quicker to write this as 6.02×10^{23}.
- A nanoparticle has a diameter of 0.000000025 m. In standard form, that's 2.5×10^{-8} m.

You can write numbers out in full rather than in standard form by moving the decimal point. Which direction to move the decimal point, and how many places to move it depends on '*n*'. If '*n*' is positive, the decimal point moves to the right. If '*n*' is negative, the decimal point moves to the left.

Examples

Here's how to write out 9.3×10^4 in full.

- The decimal point needs to move to the right because '*n*' is a positive number (4).
- Then count the number of places the decimal point has to move to the right. In this example it's four:

1 2 3 4

$$9.3 \times 10^4 = 93000.$$

- So 9.3×10^4 is the same as 93 000.

Here's how to write out 5.6×10^{-5} in full.

- '*n*' is a negative number (–5) so the decimal point needs to move to the left.
- Count five places to the left.

5 4 3 2 1

$$5.6 \times 10^{-5} = .000056$$

- So 5.6×10^{-5} is the same as 0.000056.

Tip: You can use the 'Exp' button on your calculator to type something in standard form. So if, for example, you wanted to type in 2×10^7, you'd type in: '2' 'Exp' '7'. Some calculators may have a different button that does the same job, for example it could say 'EE' or '$\times 10^x$'.

***Figure 1:** The 'Exp' or '$\times 10^x$' button is used to input standard form on calculators.*

You can do calculations with numbers that are in standard form.

Example

Atoms have a radius of about 1×10^{-10} m. Nuclei have a radius of about 1×10^{-14} m. Approximately how many times bigger than a nucleus is an atom?

To work this out, you just have to divide the approximate radius of an atom by the approximate radius of a nucleus.

$(1 \times 10^{-10}) \div (1 \times 10^{-14}) = \mathbf{1 \times 10^4}$

So the radius of an atom is approximately 1×10^4 (or 10 000) times bigger than the radius of a nucleus.

2. Equations

There are lots of equations to get your head around in GCSE Combined Science. Knowing how to use them properly is really important.

Substituting values into equations

There are a few equations you need to learn for your chemistry exams. They link together certain quantities, such as concentration, mass and volume, or moles, mass and relative mass. To use an equation, substitute the numbers from the question into the correct bit of the equation and calculate the answer.

Exam Tip
You won't necessarily be given equations in the exam, so make sure you learn the ones in this book.

Example

During the first 30 seconds of a reaction, 0.69 g of a gas was produced. Calculate the mean rate of reaction during this time.

The formula to use is: $\text{mean rate of reaction} = \dfrac{\text{quantity of product formed}}{\text{time}}$

In this scenario, the amount of product formed is 0.69 g of gas, and the time is 30 seconds.

So, mean rate of reaction $= \dfrac{0.69}{30} = \mathbf{0.023\ g\ s^{-1}}$

If you're unsure what the units of your final answer should be, you can work them out by substituting the units of the values you did have into the equation. Whatever you've done with the numbers, you do the same with the units.

Tip: The units g s^{-1} are exactly the same as g/s. It's just a different way of writing it.

Example

In the example above, the quantity of product formed was in g, and time was in s.

The units of rate $= \dfrac{\text{units of quantity of product formed}}{\text{units of time}} = \dfrac{\text{g}}{\text{s}} = \mathbf{g\ s^{-1}}$

When you're substituting values into an equation, always double check that they've got the right units. Sometimes the values you need to put into an equation may have different units to the values you're given, so you may need to convert between units (see pages 18-19 for more on this).

Tip: The subject of an equation is the thing that's on its own on one side of the equals sign. It should be the thing you want to calculate.

Rearranging formulas

You'll often need to change the subject of an equation. To do this, you'll need to rearrange it. The crucial thing to remember here is that whatever you do to one side of the equation you need to do exactly the same to the other side.

Example

Rearrange the following equation to make the mass of solute the subject:

$$\text{concentration (g dm}^{-3}\text{)} = \frac{\text{mass of solute (g)}}{\text{volume of solution (dm}^3\text{)}}$$

1. Multiply both sides by the volume of solution:

$$\text{concentration} \times \text{volume of solution} = \frac{\text{mass of solute}}{\text{volume of solution}} \times \text{volume of solution}$$

2. You can cancel out 'volume of solution' on the right hand side:

$$\text{concentration} \times \text{volume of solution} = \frac{\text{mass of solute}}{\cancel{\text{volume of solution}}} \times \cancel{\text{volume of solution}}$$

3. Which leaves: **concentration × volume of solution = mass of solute**

Exam Tip
Write down all the steps if you're rearranging an equation, so that you can check that your method is correct.

Formula triangles

Formula triangles are really useful tools for changing the subject of an equation. If three things are related by an equation like this:

$a = b \times c$ or like this: $b = \frac{a}{c}$

...then you can put them into a formula triangle. The components that are multiplied together go on the bottom of the triangle. Any components that are divided go on the top. To use the formula triangle to write out a formula just cover up the component that you want to make the subject, and write down what's left.

Example

The equation 'number of moles = mass ÷ M_r' can be put into this formula triangle:

MATHS SKILLS

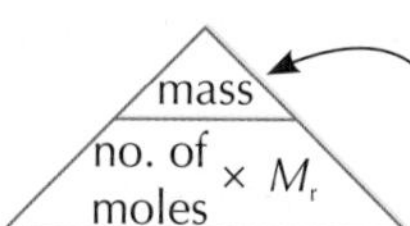

Mass is divided by M_r in the equation, so it must go on the top of the formula triangle.

If you want to make 'mass' the subject of the equation, just cover it up in the triangle and you're left with 'number of moles' next to 'M_r'. This means the number of moles needs to be multiplied by M_r. So mass = number of moles × M_r.

Exam Tip
If you're struggling to rearrange an equation in the exam, it might be useful to work out the formula triangle and use that to help you.

Symbols

You need to know the symbols used to show mathematical relationships. You'll have seen many of these before but here's a quick refresher:

Symbol	Meaning
<	less than
<<	much less than
>	greater than
>>	much greater than

Symbol	Meaning
=	equal to
∝	proportional to
~	approximately

Tip: For the greater than or less than symbols, remember that the wider end always points to the bigger number.

3. Handling Data and Graphs

How to process data from experiments is covered on pages 14-15, but here's a quick round-up of the key points.

Significant figures

The first significant figure of a number is the first digit that isn't zero. Every digit after that is significant (even if it's zero). When doing calculations, you should always round your answer to the lowest number of significant figures of the data you used to calculate your answer. When you're carrying out long calculations, try not to round until you get your final answer, or it might be less accurate.

Tip: The mean is the average of your data, whilst the range tells you how spread out the data is. There's more about calculating these values on page 14.

Tables, graphs and charts

The easiest way to collect data is in a table. Tables should have clearly labelled headers, and you should always make sure you've drawn enough columns for the number of measurements you're going to take. It can also be useful to include columns for calculating the **mean** or **range** of repeated experiments.

Tip: Data can also be shown in bar charts, histograms, frequency tables and frequency diagrams. There's more on these in the Working Scientifically section.

Whilst tables are great for collecting data, they're not great for spotting trends in data. To do this, you'll need to draw a graph or chart. The type of graph you draw will depend on the type of data you have. If it's split into categories, a bar chart may be the way to go. If both the variables you're plotting are continuous, then you should plot a graph. There's lots more about drawing graphs and charts on pages 16-17.

The straight line equation

If you draw a graph and the line of best fit is a straight line, then the line can be represented by the equation:

$$y = mx + c$$

y = *y-axis value*
m = *gradient*
c = *y-intercept*
x = *x-axis value*

The y-intercept is the point at which the line crosses the y-axis. If the straight line passes through the origin of the graph, then the y-intercept is just zero.

Gradients

Tip: The units of the gradient are '(units of y)/(units of x)'.

The **gradient** (slope) of a graph tells you how quickly the dependent variable changes as you change the independent variable. It is calculated using:

$$\text{gradient} = \frac{\text{change in } y}{\text{change in } x}$$

Tip: There's lots more about finding the gradients of lines on graphs on p.194-195.

Finding the gradient of a straight line graph is fairly simple. You just pick two points on the line that are easy to read and a good distance apart. Draw a line down from one of the points and a line across from the other to make a triangle. The line drawn down the side of the triangle is the change in y and the line across the bottom is the change in x.

For a curved graph, the gradient is always changing. So it's a bit more complicated to calculate the gradient at a single point.

To find the gradient of a curve at a point, you need to draw a **tangent** to the curve at that point. A tangent is a straight line that touches the curve at that point, but doesn't cross it. Then you just find the gradient of the tangent in the same way as before.

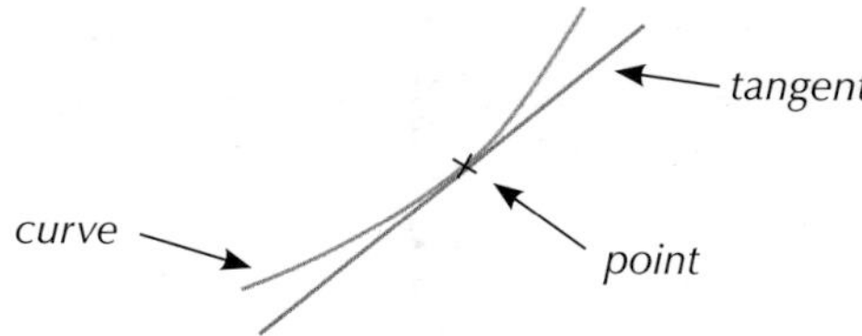

Figure 1: *Finding the tangent to a curve.*

Figure 2: *The rate of a reaction where a gas is produced is equal to the gradient of a graph of mass against time.*

Finding the intercept of a graph

The *y*-intercept of a graph is the point at which the line of best fit crosses the *y*-axis. The *x*-intercept is the point at which the line of best fit crosses the *x*-axis.

Example

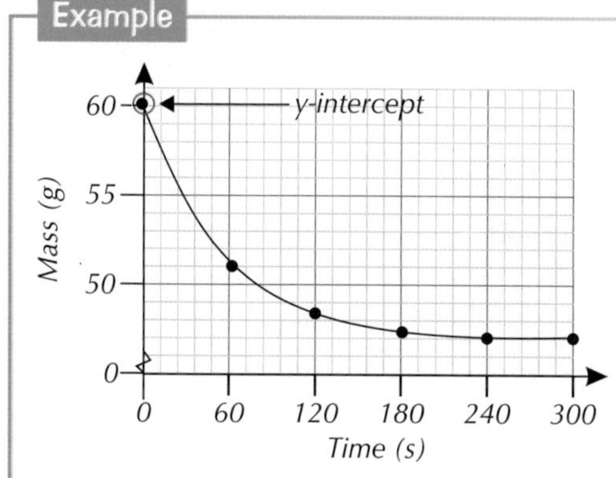

MATHS SKILLS

On a graph showing how the mass of a reaction flask changes over the course of a reaction that produces a gas, the *y*-intercept is equal to the initial mass of the flask.

The initial mass of the reaction flask was **60 g**.

4. Geometry

Time for a look at some 2D and 3D shapes now. They may not be the most obvious things you need to learn about for a chemistry exam, but need to learn them you do — you never know when this information could be useful.

2D shapes

Make sure you remember how to calculate the areas of triangles and squares.

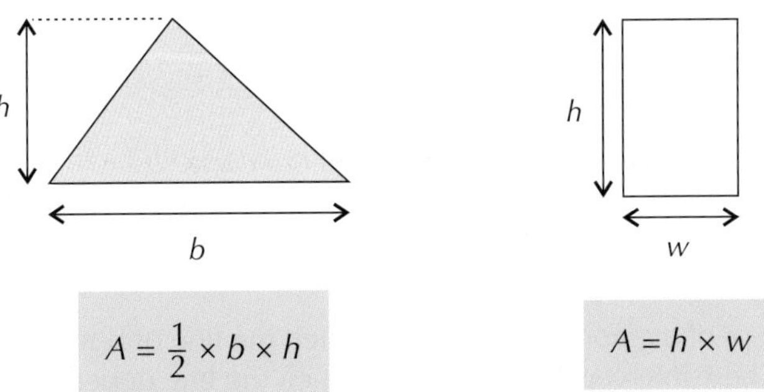

Figure 1: *The equations used to calculate the areas of triangles and rectangles.*

3D shapes

Tip: Make sure you add <u>all six</u> sides together when finding the surface area of a cube or cuboid.

If you need to work out the surface area of a 3D shape, you just need to add up the areas of all the 2D faces of the shape. So, for example, if you need to work out the surface area of a cuboid, you just find the area of all the rectangular faces of the cuboid and then add them together.

Make sure you remember how to calculate the volume of a cuboid:

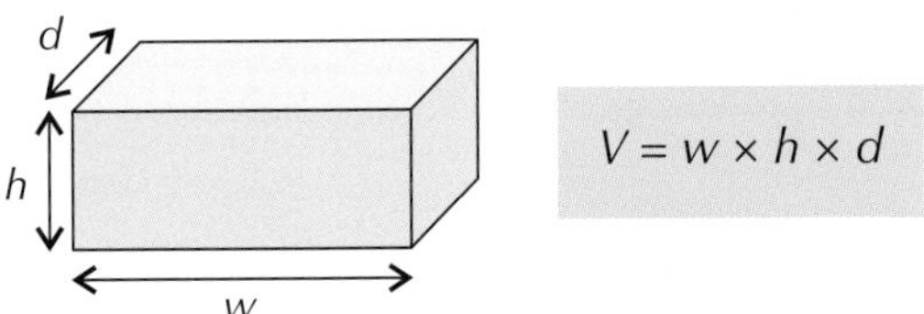

Figure 2: *The equation used to calculate the volume of a cuboid.*

Tip: If the lengths were in m, then the volume would have been in m^3.

Example

MATHS SKILLS

A block of copper is shown. Calculate the volume of the copper.

8 cm

16 cm

5 cm

Volume = $w \times h \times d = 16 \times 8 \times 5 =$ **640 cm³**.

Exam Help

1. The Exams

Unfortunately, to get your GCSE you'll need to sit some exams. And that's what these pages are about — what to expect in your exams.

Exam Tip
Make sure you have a good read through these pages. It might not seem all that important now but you don't want to get any surprises just before an exam.

Assessment for GCSE Combined Science

To get your GCSE Combined Science qualification you'll have to do some exams that test your science knowledge, your understanding of the Core Practical experiments and how comfortable you are with Working Scientifically. You'll also be tested on your maths skills.

All the chemistry content that you need to know is in this book — the chemistry Core Practicals are all covered in detail and clearly labelled, examples that use maths skills are marked up, and there are even dedicated sections on Working Scientifically (p.2-21), Practical Skills (p.241-248) and Maths Skills (p.249-256). You'll also need to know all the biology and physics content, which isn't covered in this book.

Exam Tip
You're allowed to use a calculator in all of your GCSE Science exams, so make sure you've got one. You should also have a pen, spare pen, pencil and a ruler.

Exam structure

You'll sit six separate exams at the end of your course — two for each of biology, chemistry and physics.

In the chemistry exams, you'll be tested on maths skills in at least 20% of the marks, and could be asked questions on the Core Practicals and Working Scientifically requirements in either exam.

The structure of the chemistry exams is shown below.

Exam Tip
You're expected to know the basic concepts of chemistry in both of the chemistry papers.

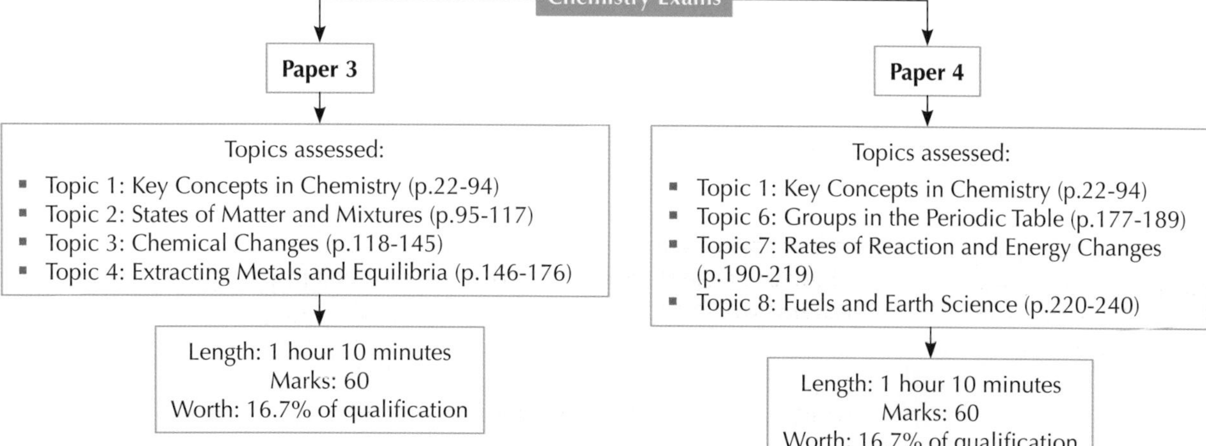

Figure 1: An exam hall of doom... It's really just a hall with some chairs and tables in it. Not so scary, after all.

2. Exam Technique

Knowing the science is vitally important when it comes to passing your exams. But having good exam technique will also help. So here are some handy hints on how to squeeze every mark you possibly can out of those examiners.

Time management

Good time management is one of the most important exam skills to have — you need to think about how much time to spend on each question. Check out the length of your exams (you'll find them on page 257 and on the front of your exam papers). These timings give you about 1 minute per mark. Try to stick to this to give yourself the best chance to get as many marks as possible.

Don't spend ages struggling with a question if you're finding it hard to answer — move on. You can come back to it later when you've bagged loads of other marks elsewhere. Also, you might find that some questions need a lot of work for only a few marks, while others are much quicker — so if you're short of time, answer the quick and easy questions first.

Exam Tip
You shouldn't really be spending more time on a 1 mark question than on a 4 mark question. Use the marks available as a rough guide for how long each question should take to answer.

Example

The questions below are both worth the same number of marks but require different amounts of work.

1 Give the names of **two** fractions of crude oil.

(2 marks)

2 Balance the equation shown below for the reaction between aluminium and hydrochloric acid.

......Al + ...HCl → ......$AlCl_3$ + ...H_2

(2 marks)

Question 1 only asks you to write down the names of two fractions of crude oil — if you can remember them, this shouldn't take you too long.

Question 2 asks you to balance an equation — this may take you longer than writing down a couple of names, especially if you have to have a few goes at it before finding the answer.

So, if you're running out of time it makes sense to do questions like 1 first and come back to 2 if you've got time at the end.

Exam Tip
Don't forget to go back and do any questions that you left the first time round — you don't want to miss out on marks because you forgot to do the question.

Reading the question

You've probably heard it a million times before, but make sure you always read the whole question carefully. It can be easy to look at a question and read what you're expecting to see rather than what it's actually asking you. Read it through before you start answering, and read it again when you've finished, to make sure your answer is sensible and matches up to what the question is asking.

Remember to pay attention to the marks available too. They can often give you a sense of how much work is needed to answer the question. If it's just a 1 mark question, it'll often only need a single word or phrase as an answer, or a very simple calculation. Questions worth 4 or 6 marks are likely to be longer questions, which need to be clearly structured and may involve writing a short paragraph or a more complicated calculation.

Making educated guesses

Make sure you answer all the questions that you can — don't leave any blank if you can avoid it. If a question asks you to cross a box, circle a word or draw lines between boxes, you should never, ever leave it blank, even if you're short on time. It only takes a second or two to answer these questions, and even if you're not absolutely sure what the answer is you can have a good guess.

Example

Look at the question below.

1 (a) Which **two** elements below are metals?

A Iron ☐ **C** Carbon ☐

B Selenium ☐ **D** Cadmium ☐ *(2 marks)*

Say you knew that iron was a metal, and carbon was a non-metal, but weren't sure about the other two elements.

You can choose iron — you know it's a metal. You know carbon is a non-metal, so leave that box blank. That leaves you with selenium and cadmium. If you're not absolutely sure which is a metal and which isn't, just have a guess. You won't lose any marks if you get it wrong and there's a 50% chance that you'll get it right.

Exam Tip
If you're asked, for example, to tick two boxes, make sure you only tick two. If you tick more than two, you won't get the marks even if some of your answers are correct.

Calculations

Questions that involve a calculation can seem a bit scary. But they're really not that bad. You're bound to be asked questions that test your maths, so make sure you've brushed up on them before the exam.

When you're doing calculations the most important thing to remember is to show your working. It only takes a few seconds more to write down what's in your head and it'll stop you from making silly errors and losing out on easy marks. You won't get a mark for a wrong answer but you could get marks for the method you used to work out the answer.

Diagrams

You may be asked to draw a diagram or a graph in your exams. Whatever the diagram is, make sure it's really clear, and draw it large enough to show all the details (but make sure that you stay within the space given for that answer).

If you've drawn a diagram incorrectly, don't scribble part of it out and try to fix it — it'll look messy and be hard for the examiner to figure out what you're trying to show. Cross the whole thing out and start again. And always double check that you've included all the things that you should have done.

Exam Tip
Take a sharp pencil with you into the exams to draw diagrams with. Also take a rubber, a ruler and a pencil sharpener.

Periodic table

You'll be given a copy of the periodic table in the chemistry exams. It contains lots of information about the different elements. For example, it tells you what group elements are in, as well as their relative atomic masses and atomic numbers. If you're unsure about some data for an element, check the periodic table, just in case it has the information you need.

3. Question Types

If all questions were the same, exams would be mightily boring. So really, it's quite handy that there are lots of different question types. Here are just a few...

Command words

Command words are just the bits of a question that tell you what to do. You'll find answering exam questions much easier if you understand exactly what they mean, so here's a brief summary of some of the most common ones:

Exam Tip
When you're reading an exam question, you might find it helpful to underline the command words. It can help you work out what type of answer to give.

Command word:	What to do:
Give / Name / Identify / State / Write down	Give a brief one or two word answer, or a short sentence. This may involve recalling information or selecting information given in the question.
Devise	Plan a procedure or experiment from existing ideas.
Complete / Add / Label	Write your answer in the space given. This could be a gap in a sentence or table, or you might have to finish a diagram.
Describe	Write about what something's like, e.g. describe the trend in a set of results.
Suggest / Predict	Use your scientific knowledge to work out what the answer might be.
Determine	Use the data or information you've been given to reach your answer.
Explain	Clarify a point, or give the reasons why something happens. The points in your answer need to be linked together, so you should include words like because, so, therefore, due to, etc.
Calculate	Use the numbers in the question to work out a numerical answer.
Show that	Give clear evidence that supports a statement.
Compare	Give the similarities or differences between two (or more) things.
Contrast	Give the similarities and differences between two (or more) things.
Evaluate	Give the arguments both for and against an issue, or the advantages and disadvantages of something. You also need to give an overall conclusion.
Sketch	Draw without a lot of detail, e.g. for a graph you just need the general shape and correct axes.
Deduce	Reach conclusions from information provided.

Exam Tip
It's easy to get describe and explain mixed up, but they're quite different. For example, if you're asked to describe some data, just state the overall pattern or trend. If you're asked to explain data, you'll need to give reasons for the trend.

Some questions will ask you to answer using the information provided in the question, (e.g. a graph, table or passage of text) — if so, you must refer to the information you've been given or you won't get the marks. You'll often need to use information or diagrams that are provided for you when answering questions with command words such as 'measure' or 'plot'.

Levels of response questions

Some questions are designed to assess your ability to present and explain scientific ideas in a logical and coherent way, as well as your scientific knowledge. These questions often link together different topics, and are worth more marks than most other question types. These questions will be marked with an asterisk (*) in the exam papers.

This type of question is marked using a 'levels of response' mark scheme. Your answer is given a level depending on the number of marks available and its overall quality and scientific content. Here's an idea of how the levels may work out for a 6 mark question:

Example

Level 0

A Level 0 answer has no relevant information, and makes no attempt to answer the question. It receives no marks.

Level 1

A Level 1 answer usually makes one or two correct statements, but does not fully answer the question. For instance, when asked to describe and explain the differences between two materials, it might state one or two correct properties of the materials, but not explain them or attempt to compare the two. These answers receive 1 or 2 marks.

Level 2

A Level 2 answer usually makes a number of correct statements, with explanation, but falls short of fully answering the question. It may miss a step, omit an important fact, or not be organised as logically as it should be. These answers receive 3 or 4 marks.

Level 3

A Level 3 answer will answer the question fully, in a logical fashion. It will make a number of points that are explained and related back to the question. Any conclusions it makes will be supported by evidence in the answer. These answers receive 5 or 6 marks.

Make sure you answer the question fully, and cover all points indicated in the question. You also need to organise your answer clearly — the points you make need to be in a logical order. Use specialist scientific vocabulary whenever you can. For example, if you're talking about electrolysis, you need to use scientific terms like 'electrodes' and 'oxidation'. Obviously you need to use these terms correctly — it's no good using the words if you don't know what they actually mean.

There are some exam-style questions that use this type of mark scheme in this book (marked up with an asterisk, *). You can use them to practise writing logical and coherent answers. Use the worked answers given at the back of this book to mark what you've written. The answers will tell you the relevant points you could've included, but it'll be down to you to put everything together into a full, well-structured answer.

Exam Tip
It might be useful to write a quick plan of your answer in the spare space of your paper. This can help you get your thoughts in order, so you can write a logical, coherent answer. But remember to cross your plan out after you've written your answer so it doesn't get marked.

Exam Tip
Make sure your writing is legible — you don't want to lose marks just because the examiner couldn't read your handwriting.

Exam Tip
Make sure your writing style is appropriate for an exam. You need to write in full sentences and use fairly formal language.

Core Practicals

The chemistry Core Practicals are five experiments that you need to carry out during your lessons which cover a range of specific techniques. You'll be asked about some of these experiments in your exams. Some questions might cover a slightly different experiment to the one you've done in class, but the techniques will be the same, and any extra information you need will be given to you in the question. There are a lot of different types of question you could be asked on these experiments. Here are some basic areas they might ask you about:

- Carrying out the experiment — e.g. planning or describing a method, describing how to take measurements or use apparatus.
- Risk assessment — e.g. identifying or explaining hazards associated with the experiment, or safety precautions which should be taken.
- Understanding variables — e.g. identifying control, dependent and independent variables.
- Data handling — e.g. plotting graphs or doing calculations using some sample results provided.
- Analysing results — e.g. making conclusions based on sample results.
- Evaluating the experiment — e.g. making judgements on the quality of results, identifying where mistakes may have been made in the method, suggesting improvements to the experiment.

Exam Tip
The Core Practical questions are likely to have some overlap with Working Scientifically, so make sure you've brushed up on pages 2-21.

Answers

Topic 1 — Key Concepts in Chemistry

Topic 1a — Formulae, Equations and Hazards

1. Chemical Equations

Page 24 — Application Questions

Q1 a) Iron sulfate and copper.
b) Copper sulfate and iron.
c) copper sulfate + iron → iron sulfate + copper

Q2 sodium hydroxide + hydrochloric acid → sodium chloride + water

Q3 a) $Cl_2 + \mathbf{2}KBr \rightarrow Br_2 + \mathbf{2}KCl$
b) $\mathbf{2}HCl + Mg \rightarrow MgCl_2 + H_2$
c) $C_3H_8 + \mathbf{5}O_2 \rightarrow \mathbf{3}CO_2 + \mathbf{4}H_2O$
d) $Fe_2O_3 + \mathbf{3}CO \rightarrow \mathbf{2}Fe + \mathbf{3}CO_2$

2. More on Equations

Page 27 — Fact Recall Questions

Q1 (s) = solid, (l) = liquid, (g) = gas, (aq) = aqueous

Q2 a) H_2O
b) CO_2
c) CO_3^{2-}
d) SO_4^{2-}

Q3 a) ammonia
b) nitrate (ion)
c) chlorine
d) oxygen
e) ammonium (ion)

Page 27 — Application Questions

Q1 a) (s)
b) (g)
c) (aq)

Q2 $Fe_{(s)} + 2HCl_{(aq)} \rightarrow FeCl_{2(aq)} + H_{2(g)}$

Q3 a) $Mg_{(s)} + Zn^{2+}_{(aq)} \rightarrow Mg^{2+}_{(aq)} + Zn_{(s)}$
b) $Ba^{2+}_{(aq)} + SO_4^{2-}_{(aq)} \rightarrow BaSO_{4(s)}$
The state symbols show you that $BaSO_4$ is a solid, so you shouldn't split it up into ions when writing your ionic equation.
c) $CO_3^{2-}_{(aq)} + 2H^+_{(aq)} \rightarrow H_2O_{(l)} + CO_{2(g)}$

3. Hazards and Risk

Page 29 — Fact Recall Questions

Q1 a) A hazard is anything that has the potential to cause harm or damage.
b) The risk in an experiment is the probabilty that any hazards will cause harm.

Q2 a) The chemical provides oxygen, and so allows other materials to burn more fiercely.
b) The chemical destroys other materials, including living tissues.
c) The chemical catches fire/ignites very easily.

Page 29 — Application Question

Q1 E.g. the scientist should wear gloves, a lab coat and goggles when handling potassium permanganate. They should keep the potassium permanganate away from any flammable materials. They should dispose of any substances or mixtures that contain potassium permanganate properly. If possible, the scientist should only use low concentrations of potassium permanganate.

Page 31 — Formulae, Equations and Hazards Exam-style Questions

1 a) (i) sulfuric acid + magnesium → magnesium sulfate + hydrogen ***(1 mark)***
(ii) $Mg + H_2SO_4 \rightarrow MgSO_4 + H_2$ ***(1 mark)***
b) (i) $\mathbf{2}HCl_{(aq)} + ZnCO_{3(s)} \rightarrow ZnCl_{2(aq)} + CO_{2(g)} + H_2O_{(l)}$ ***(1 mark)***
(ii) Carbon dioxide gas is produced ***(1 mark)***.
In the equation, CO_2 has the gas state symbol. Whenever a reaction fizzes, it's because a gas is being made.

2 $C_3H_8 + 5O_2 \rightarrow 3CO_2 + 4H_2O$
(1 mark for all reactants correct, 1 mark for all products correct, 1 mark for correct balancing.)

3 a) Rewrite the equation to show all of the ions in the reaction mixture:
$Mg^{2+}_{(aq)} + 2I^-_{(aq)} + 2Na^+_{(aq)} + 2OH^-_{(aq)} \rightarrow Mg(OH)_{2(s)} + 2Na^+_{(aq)} + 2I^-_{(aq)}$
Cross out any ions that appear on both sides:
$Mg^{2+}_{(aq)} + \cancel{2I^-}_{(aq)} + \cancel{2Na^+}_{(aq)} + 2OH^-_{(aq)} \rightarrow Mg(OH)_{2(s)} + \cancel{2Na^+}_{(aq)} + \cancel{2I^-}_{(aq)}$
So, the ionic equation for the reaction is:
$Mg^{2+}_{(aq)} + 2OH^-_{(aq)} \rightarrow Mg(OH)_{2(s)}$
(1 mark for all reactants correct, 1 mark for all products correct, 1 mark for correct balancing.)
b) i) magnesium iodide, sodium hydroxide, sodium iodide ***(1 mark)***
ii) magnesium hydroxide ***(1 mark)***
c) Any two from: e.g. wear gloves to protect your skin / wear safety goggles to protect your eyes / wear a lab coat to protect your clothes and skin / use low concentrations of the sodium hydroxide solution.
(1 mark for each sensible suggestion, up to a maximum of two marks.)

Answers

Topic 1b — Atomic Structure and the Periodic Table

1. The History of the Atom

Page 33 — Fact Recall Questions

Q1 Dalton thought that atoms were solid spheres and that different spheres made up the different elements.

Q2 the electron

Q3 a) Positively charged alpha particles were fired at an extremely thin sheet of gold. Most of the particles passed straight through the sheet, but a small number were deflected backwards.

b) If the plum pudding model was right, all of the alpha particles would have passed straight through the sheet or only been slightly deflected. None of the particles would have been deflected backwards.

Q4 He suggested that the electrons can only orbit the nucleus in fixed shells and aren't found anywhere in between.

2. The Atom

Page 36 — Fact Recall Questions

Q1 a) +1 b) 0 c) –1

Q2 1

Q3 E.g. atoms have a small nucleus surrounded by electrons. The nucleus is in the middle of the atom and contains protons and neutrons. The electrons occupy shells around the nucleus.

Q4 They have the same number of protons as electrons. Protons and electrons have opposite charges of the same size, so the charges cancel each other out.

Q5 a) The number of protons in the atom.

b) The total number of neutrons and protons in the atom.

Page 36 — Application Questions

Q1 Number of neutrons = mass number – atomic number = 19 – 9 = **10**

Q2 Number of protons = atomic number = **79**
Number of neutrons = mass number – atomic number = 197 – 79 = **118**
Number of electrons = number of protons = **79**

Q3 $^{63}_{29}Cu$

Q4 a) **8** protons, 16 – 8 = **8** neutrons

b) **13** protons, 27 – 13 = **14** neutrons

c) **23** protons, 51 – 23 = **28** neutrons

d) **47** protons, 108 – 47 = **61** neutrons

3. Isotopes and Relative Atomic Mass

Page 38 — Fact Recall Questions

Q1 Isotopes are different forms of the same element, which have the same number of protons but a different number of neutrons.

Q2 The average mass of one atom of an element, compared to 1/12 of the mass of one atom of carbon-12.

Page 38 — Application Questions

Q1 A

Q2 Zinc has more than one isotope and the relative atomic mass is an average that takes into account the different masses of these isotopes and how much there is of each one.

Q3 relative atomic mass = $\frac{(92.5 \times 7) + (7.5 \times 6)}{92.5 + 7.5}$

$= \frac{647.5 + 45}{100} = \frac{692.5}{100} = 6.925 = \mathbf{6.9}$

4. Development of the Periodic Table

Page 39 — Fact Recall Questions

Q1 Mendeleev sorted the elements into groups, based on their properties. He realised that if he put the elements in order of atomic mass, he could put elements with similar chemical properties into the same columns.

Q2 When the elements were discovered that fitted the gaps Mendeleev had left, their properties matched the properties that he had predicted.

5. The Modern Periodic Table

Page 41 — Fact Recall Questions

Q1 The number of electron shells.

Q2 The number of electrons in the outer shell.

Q3 1

Page 41 — Application Questions

Q1 3

Q2 Any three from: sodium / magnesium / aluminium / silicon / phosphorus / sulfur / chlorine / argon.

6. Electronic Configurations

Page 43 — Fact Recall Questions

Q1 The one closest to the nucleus. / The one with the lowest energy level.

Q2

Shell	Maximum number of electrons
1st	**2**
2nd	**8**
3rd	**8**

Page 44 — Application Questions

Q1 Neon
Q2 Carbon
Q3 Sulfur
Q4 Calcium
Q5

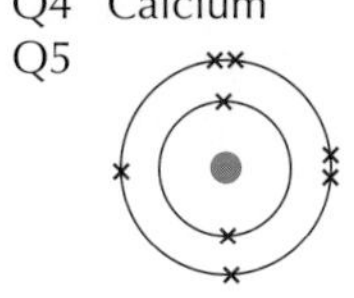

Q6

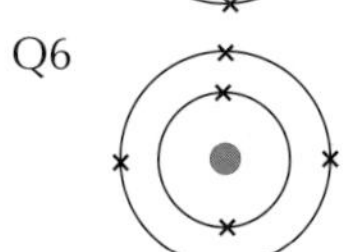

Q7

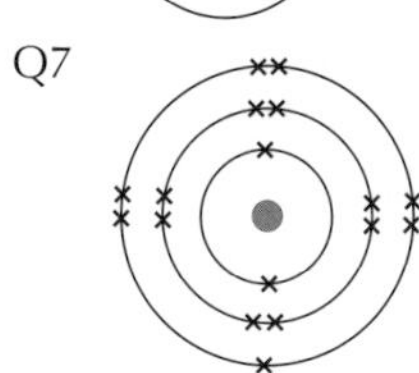

Q8 2.8.5
Q9 2.8.2
Q10 2.8.4

Pages 46-47 — Atomic Structure and the Periodic Table Exam-style Questions

1 a)

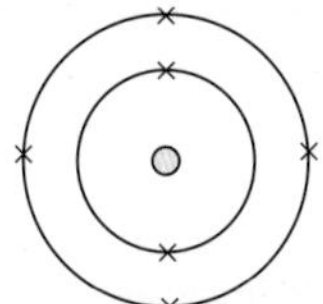

(1 mark for drawing six electrons, 1 mark for placing two in the first shell and four in the second shell.)

It doesn't matter if the electrons in your diagram are in pairs or not — you get the marks either way.

b) +6 ***(1 mark)***. This is because it contains 6 protons which each have a charge of +1 ***(1 mark)***.

2 a) Mendeleev left some gaps in order to keep elements with similar properties in the same groups ***(1 mark)***.

b) The elements are arranged in order of atomic number ***(1 mark)***.

3 a) i) Group 6 ***(1 mark)***

The number of electrons in the outer shell of an element is the same as its group number in the periodic table.

ii) Period 3 ***(1 mark)***

The number of occupied shells in an element is the same as its period number in the periodic table.

b) No, because all atoms of the same element contain the same number of protons/all atoms of element X must contain 16 protons ***(1 mark)***.

4 a) A small nucleus with a positive charge ***(1 mark)*** surrounded by a 'cloud' of negative electrons ***(1 mark)***.

b) E.g. the neutrons and protons are found in the nucleus, whilst the electrons are outside the nucleus ***(1 mark)***. Protons and neutrons have a much greater mass than electrons ***(1 mark)***.

5 a)

Atomic number	**17**
Mass number	37
Number of protons	17
Number of electrons	**17**
Number of neutrons	**20**

(1 mark for each correct answer)

b) i) isotopes ***(1 mark)***

ii) relative atomic mass

$$= \frac{\text{sum of}\left(\text{isotope abundance} \times \text{isotope mass number}\right)}{\text{sum of abundances of all the isotopes}}$$

$$= \frac{(25 \times 37) + (75 \times 35)}{25 + 75} = \frac{925 + 2625}{100} = \frac{3550}{100}$$

$= \mathbf{35.5}$

(2 marks for correct answer, otherwise 1 mark for correctly substituting the numbers into the formula.)

c) 2.8.7 ***(1 mark)***

d)

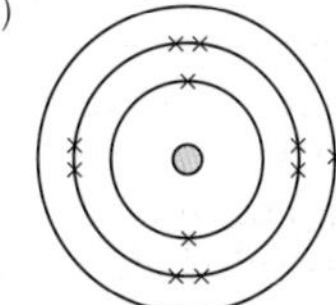

(1 mark for drawing 11 electrons, 1 mark for placing two in the first shell, eight in the second shell and one in the third.)

It doesn't matter if the electrons are paired in your diagram or not, you would still get the marks.

Topic 1c — Bonding and Types of Substance

1. Ions

Page 50 — Fact Recall Questions

Q1 A positive ion is formed when an atom loses one or more electrons.
Q2 +2
Q3 That the ion is a negative ion containing oxygen and at least one other element.
Q4 That the ion is a negative ion containing only one element (unless it's hydroxide).

Answers

Page 50 — Application Questions

Q1 a) Number of protons = **35**
Number of neutrons = 80 – 35 = **45**
Br^- has a 1– charge, so it must have one more electron than protons.
Number of electrons = 35 + 1 = **36**

b) Number of protons = **20**
Number of neutrons = 40 – 20 = **20**
Ca^{2+} has a 2+ charge, so it must have two more protons than electrons.
Number of electrons = 20 – 2 = **18**

c) Number of protons = **11**
Number of neutrons = 23 – 11 = **12**
Na^+ has a 1+ charge, so it must have one more proton than electrons.
Number of electrons = 11 – 1 = **10**

d) Number of protons = **34**
Number of neutrons = 79 – 34 = **45**
Se^{2-} has a 2– charge, so it must have two more electrons than protons.
Number of electrons = 34 + 2 = **36**

Q2 a) NaCl
b) MgI_2
c) CaO
d) K_2O

Q3 $(NH_4)_2CO_3$

2. Ionic Bonding

Page 53 — Fact Recall Questions

Q1 Ionic bonding is the strong electrostatic attraction that holds oppositely charged ions together in an ionic compound.

Q2 Metals and non-metals.

Q3 a)

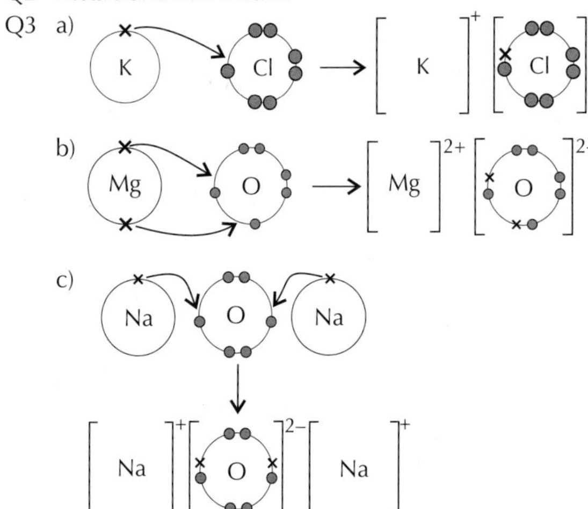

b)

c)

You may have shown all the inner shells of electrons in your answer — that's fine.

Page 53 — Application Questions

Q1 a) E.g. potassium has one electron in its outer shell and iodine has seven electrons in its outer shell. When they react, the electron in the outer shell of the potassium atom is transferred to the iodine atom. A positively charged potassium ion and a negatively charged iodide ion are formed. They both have full outer shells of electrons.

b) Like iodine, fluorine is in Group 7 of the periodic table. This means they both have seven electrons in their outer shell and need one more to get a full outer shell, which they can take from a potassium atom.

Q2

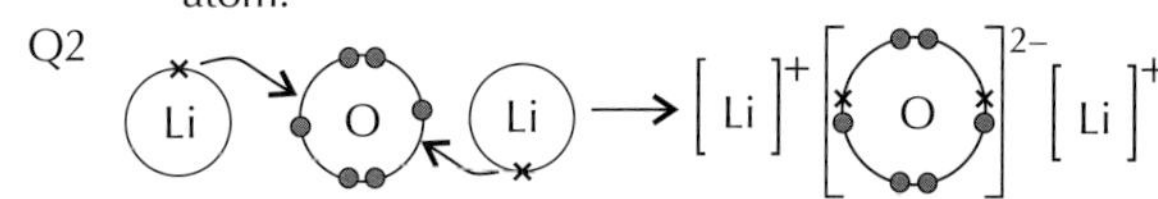

Again, it's fine if you've included the inner shells in your diagram too.

3. Ionic Compounds

Page 55 — Fact Recall Questions

Q1 A giant ionic lattice structure.

Q2 a) Advantage: any one of e.g. dot and cross diagrams show how compounds form / where the electrons in each ion come from.
Disadvantage: any one of e.g. they don't show the lattice structure of the compound / the relative sizes of the ions / how the ions are arranged.

b) Advantage: any one of e.g. ball and stick models show the regular pattern of the ions in the lattice / how the ions are arranged / that the crystal extends beyond what is shown in the diagram.
Disadvantage: any one of e.g. they suggest that there are gaps between the ions / sometimes ions are not shown to scale.

Q3

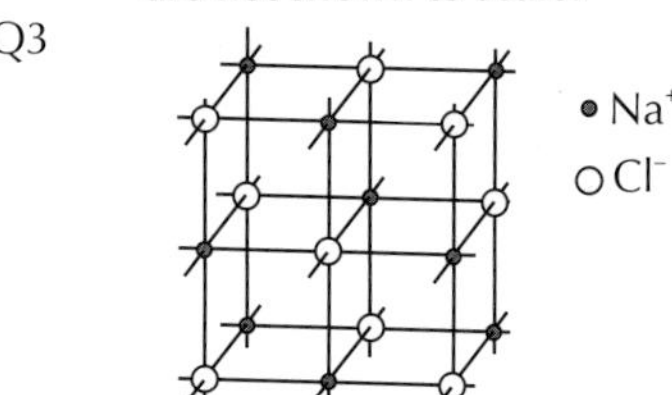

Q4 Ionic compounds tend to have high melting and boiling points, are usually soluble in water and conduct electricity when molten or dissolved, but not when solid.

Page 55 — Application Question

Q1 Substance B, e.g. because potassium chloride is ionic, so it should have a high melting point, be soluble in water and not conduct electricity when solid. Substance B is the only substance in the table that has all of these properties.

4. Covalent Bonding

Page 57 — Fact Recall Questions

Q1 In order to obtain a full outer shell of electrons.

Q2 1

Q3 a) i) E.g. they show which atoms the electrons in a covalent bond come from.

ii) Any one of e.g. they show how the atoms are arranged in space / the shape of the molecule.

b) i) Any one of e.g. they can be confusing when representing large molecules / they make it look like there are gaps between the atoms / they don't show which atoms the electrons come from / they may not show the correct sizes of the atoms.

ii) Any one of e.g. they don't show the 3D structure of the molecule / which atoms the electrons come from / the correct sizes of the atoms.

5. Simple Molecular Substances

Page 61 — Fact Recall Questions

Q1 A molecule made up of only a few atoms held together by covalent bonds.

Q2 a) hydrogen chloride

b) water

Q3 a)

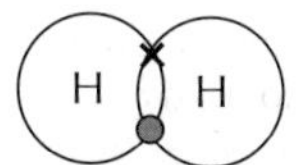

b)

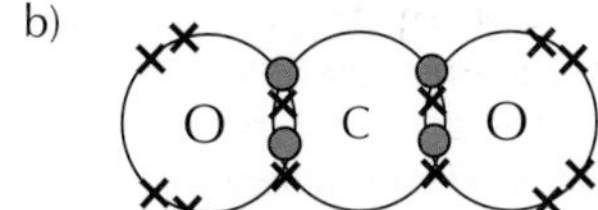

c)

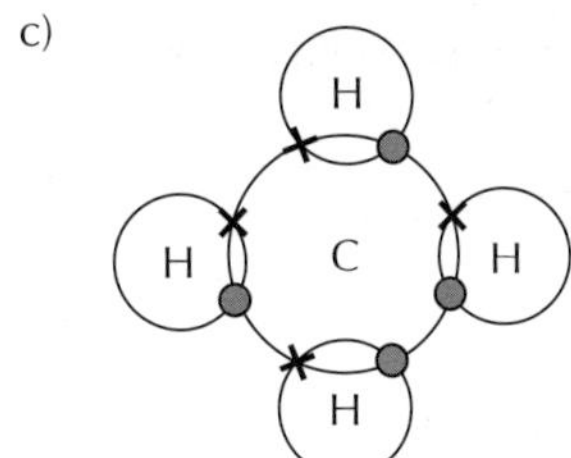

Q4 Only the weak intermolecular forces that exist between the molecules need to be overcome in order to melt the substance. This doesn't take much energy, so the melting points are low.

Q5 Simple molecules do not contain any free electrons or ions, so they do not conduct electricity.

Q6 poly(ethene)

Page 61 — Application Question

Q1 Since nitrogen has five electrons in its second shell, it needs three more to have a full outer shell. Hydrogen needs one more electron to have a full outer shell. Three hydrogen atoms each share one electron with nitrogen so that each atom has a full outer shell. A molecule containing three covalent bonds with the formula NH_3 is formed.

6. Giant Covalent Structures

Page 64 — Fact Recall Questions

Q1 B and C

Q2 In diamond, each carbon atom forms four covalent bonds with other carbon atoms. To melt diamond you have to break all these strong covalent bonds. This requires a lot of energy, so diamond has a very high melting point.

Q3 Graphene is a sheet of carbon atoms joined together in hexagons. It's basically a single layer of graphite.

Q4 Fullerenes are hollow molecules of carbon atoms shaped like balls or tubes.

Q5 C_{60}

Q6 Any two from e.g. in medicine to deliver drugs / as industrial catalysts / in strengthening materials/sports equipment.

Page 64 — Application Question

Q1 Carbon dioxide — Doesn't conduct electricity.
Melting point = –57 °C

Graphite — Conducts electricity.
Melting point = 3500 °C

Diamond — Doesn't conduct electricity.
Melting point = 3500 °C

7. Metallic Bonding

Page 66 — Fact Recall Questions

Q1 A giant structure with the atoms held in a regular arrangement by a sea of delocalised electrons.

Q2 electrostatic

Q3 The layers of atoms are able to easily slide over each other.

Q4 The delocalised electrons are free to move so carry thermal energy through the structure.

Q5 E.g. the atoms in a metal are more tightly packed than in a non-metal.

Q6 a) Metals are good electrical conductors whilst non-metals are generally poor conductors.

b) Metals generally have higher boiling points than non-metals.

Pages 69-70 — Bonding and Types of Substance Exam-style Questions

1 The structure of substance A is **simple molecular** ***(1 mark)***.
The structure of substance B is **metallic** ***(1 mark)***.
The structure of substance C is **giant covalent** ***(1 mark)***.
The structure of substance D is **ionic** ***(1 mark)***.

2 a) i) O^{2-} has a 2– charge, so it must have two more electrons than protons.
Number of protons = atomic number = 8
Number of electrons = 8 + 2 = **10**
(2 marks for correct answer, otherwise 1 mark for correctly stating the number of protons in an oxide ion.)

You might have used a different method here (e.g. you may have used the atomic number of oxygen to work out how many electrons are in an oxygen atom, then worked out that you'd need to add two electrons to get a 2– ion with a full outer shell). Any sensible method gets you the marks.

ii) Na_2O ***(1 mark)***

b)

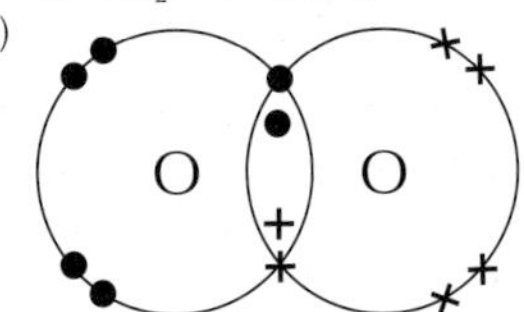

(1 mark for showing two shared electron pairs. 1 mark for showing four other electrons in the outer shell of each oxygen atom.)

You could have drawn this diagram without the circles representing the shells, or with the dots and crosses the other way round — either of these would be fine.

3 a) i) covalent bond ***(1 mark)***
ii) Chlorine is made up of simple molecules ***(1 mark)***. The intermolecular forces between the molecules are weak ***(1 mark)***. Not much energy is needed to overcome them ***(1 mark)***, so chlorine has a low melting point ***(1 mark)***.

b) i)

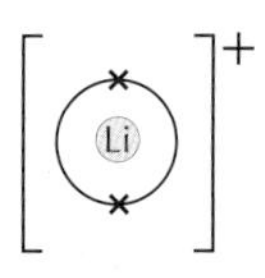

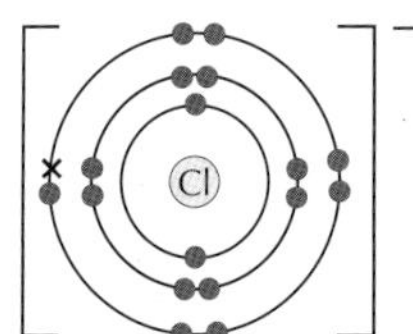

(1 mark for correct electron configuration for a lithium ion, 1 mark for correct electron configuration for a chloride ion and 1 mark for both charges correct.)

ii) The ions in lithium chloride are held together by strong electrostatic forces ***(1 mark)***. A lot of energy is required to overcome these forces and melt the compound ***(1 mark)***.

4 a) How to grade your answer:
Level 0: There is no relevant information. ***[No marks]***
Level 1: There is a very brief explanation of the structure of either diamond or graphite. Some attempt is made to explain how the structure of the substances relates to the property given. ***[1 to 2 marks]***
Level 2: There is some description of the arrangement of atoms and the bonding in both substances. A good attempt is made to explain how the structure of both substances relate to the properties given. ***[3 to 4 marks]***
Level 3: There is a full, detailed description of the arrangement of atoms and the bonding in both substances. There is a clear explanation how the structure of both substances relate to the properties given. ***[5 to 6 marks]***

Here are some points your answer may include:
In diamond, each carbon atom forms four strong covalent bonds.
This forms a very rigid structure of carbon atoms.
This makes diamond very hard.
In graphite, each carbon atom only forms three covalent bonds.
This results in flat layers of carbon atoms.
The layers are held together by weak intermolecular forces/aren't covalently bonded to each other.
The layers are easy to break apart and can slide over each other.
This makes graphite soft and slippery.

b) graphene ***(1 mark)***

c) In graphene, each carbon atom only forms three bonds with other atoms ***(1 mark)***. This means that graphene contains free/delocalised electrons ***(1 mark)***, which can move freely through the structure and conduct electricity ***(1 mark)***.

Topic 1d — Calculations Involving Masses

1. Relative Mass

Page 73 — Fact Recall Questions

Q1 By adding together the relative atomic masses of all the atoms in the compound.

Q2 The simplest possible whole number ratio of atoms of each element within a compound.

Page 73 — Application Questions

Q1 a) 2 × 16 = **32**
b) 39 + 16 + 1 = **56**
c) 1 + 14 + (3 × 16) = **63**
d) 40 + 12 + (3 × 16) = **100**

Q2 a) Al_2O_3 (cannot simplify any further).
b) CH_2 (C: 25 ÷ 25 = 1; H: 50 ÷ 25 = 2)
c) C_2H_2O (C: 6 ÷ 3 = 2; H: 6 ÷ 3 = 2; O: 3 ÷ 3 = 1)

Q3 a) M_r (C_4H_9)= (4 × 12) + (9 × 1) = 57
114 ÷ 57 = 2, so molecular formula = $\mathbf{C_8H_{18}}$
b) M_r ($C_3H_5O_2$) = (3 × 12) + (5 × 1) + (2 × 16) = 73
146 ÷ 73 = 2, so molecular formula = $\mathbf{C_6H_{10}O_4}$
c) M_r ($C_4H_6Cl_2O$) = (4 × 12) + (6 × 1) + (2 × 35.5) + (1 × 16) = 141
423 ÷ 141 = 3, so molecular formula = $\mathbf{C_{12}H_{18}Cl_6O_3}$

2. Conservation of Mass

Page 76 — Fact Recall Questions

Q1 During a reaction, no atoms are destroyed or created, so there are the same number and types of atoms on each side of a reaction equation.
Q2 The masses will be the same.
Q3 E.g. the reaction between a metal and oxygen in an unsealed container.

Page 76 — Application Questions

Q1 127 + 32 = **159 g**
Q2 68 – 56 = **12 g**
Q3 The mass will decrease.
Metal carbonates thermally decompose to form a metal oxide and carbon dioxide gas. So the carbon dioxide gas will expand out of the unsealed reaction vessel, causing the mass of stuff inside the reaction vessel to decrease.
Q4 Total M_r of reactants = (2 × 35.5) + (2 × (23 + 80)) = 71 + 206 = 277
Total M_r of products = (2 × 80) + (2 × (23 + 35.5) = 160 + 117 = 277
The total M_r on the left-hand side of the equation is equal to the total M_r on the right-hand side, so mass is conserved.
Q5 Before the reaction, calcium is in the reaction vessel, but oxygen is in the air, so the mass of oxygen isn't accounted for. When the oxygen reacts with calcium to form calcium oxide, it becomes contained inside the reaction vessel — so the total mass of the stuff inside the reaction vessel increases.

3. Calculating Empirical Formulae

Page 79 — Application Questions

Q1 a) A_r of C = 12
A_r of H = 1
relative amount of C = 72 ÷ 12 = 6
relative amount of H = 6 ÷ 1 = 6
ratio of C:H = 6:6
Divide by the smallest number (6):
ratio of C:H = 1:1
empirical formula = **CH**

b) A_r of C = 12
A_r of H = 1
A_r of Cl = 35.5
relative amount of C = 96 ÷ 12 = 8
relative amount of H = 16 ÷ 1 = 16
relative amount of Cl = 142 ÷ 35.5 = 4
ratio of C:H:Cl = 8:16:4
Divide by the smallest number (4):
ratio of C:H:Cl = 2:4:1
empirical formula = $\mathbf{C_2H_4Cl}$

c) A_r of C = 12
A_r of H = 1
A_r of N = 14
A_r of O = 16
relative amount of C = 192 ÷ 12 = 16
relative amount of H = 10 ÷ 1 = 10
relative amount of N = 28 ÷ 14 = 2
relative amount of O = 64 ÷ 16 = 4
ratio of C:H:N:O = 16:10:2:4
Divide by the smallest number (2):
ratio of C:H:N:O = 8:5:1:2
empirical formula = $\mathbf{C_8H_5NO_2}$

Q2 a) mass of metal oxide = mass of crucible and oxide – mass of crucible = 27.818 – 24.898 = 2.920 g
mass of metal = mass of crucible and metal – mass of crucible = 26.650 – 24.898 = 1.752 g
mass of O = mass of metal oxide – mass of metal = 2.920 – 1.752 = **1.168 g**

b) mass of metal oxide = mass of crucible and oxide – mass of crucible = 26.616 – 23.491 = 3.125 g
mass of metal = mass of crucible and metal – mass of crucible = 24.616 – 23.491 = 1.125 g
mass of O = mass of metal oxide – mass of metal = 3.125 – 1.125 = 2.000 g
relative amount of Be = 1.125 ÷ 9 = 0.125
relative amount of O = 2.000 ÷ 16 = 0.125
Divide by the smallest number (0.125) to give the ratio of Be:O = 1:1
So, the empirical formula is **BeO**.

c) mass of metal oxide = mass of crucible and oxide – mass of crucible = 25.920 – 25.230 = 0.690 g
mass of metal = mass of crucible and metal – mass of crucible = 25.552 – 25.230 = 0.322 g
mass of O = mass of metal oxide – mass of metal = 0.690 – 0.322 = 0.368 g
relative amount of Li = 0.322 ÷ 7 = 0.046
relative amount of O = 0.368 ÷ 16 = 0.023
Divide by the smallest number (0.023) to give the ratio of Li:O = 2:1
So, the empirical formula is $\mathbf{Li_2O}$.

Answers

4. Concentration

Page 81 — Fact Recall Questions

Q1 The amount of a substance in a certain volume of a solution.

Q2 concentration (g dm^{-3}) = mass (g) ÷ volume (dm^3)

Page 81 — Application Questions

Q1 a) concentration = 150 ÷ 3 = **50 g dm^{-3}**

b) concentration = 48 ÷ 0.4 = **120 g dm^{-3}**

Q2 a) volume = 120 ÷ 1000 = 0.120 dm^3
concentration = 60 ÷ 0.120 = **500 g dm^{-3}**

b) volume = 8 ÷ 1000 = 0.008 dm^3
concentration = 2.4 ÷ 0.008 = **300 g dm^{-3}**

Q3 a) mass = 2.5 × 32 = **80 g**

b) mass = 0.35 × 60 = **21 g**

Q4 a) volume = 80 ÷ 1000 = 0.080 dm^3
mass = 0.080 × 200 = **16 g**

b) volume = 15 ÷ 1000 = 0.015 dm^3
mass = 0.015 × 120 = **1.8 g**

5. Calculating Masses from Equations

Page 84 — Fact Recall Question

Q1 A reactant that's used up completely in a reaction / the reactant that limits the amount of product that's formed.

Pages 84 — Application Questions

Q1 a) sodium
The sodium all gets used up, so you know it's the limiting reactant.

b) water

Q2 a) The amount of zinc chloride produced would double.

b) 1.36 ÷ 6.80 = 0.200
So the amount of zinc that reacts = 0.200 × 3.25 = **0.650 g**

Q3 $2KBr + Cl_2 \rightarrow 2KCl + Br_2$
M_r of KBr = 39 + 80 = 119
M_r of KCl = 39 + 35.5 = 74.5
relative amount of KBr = 36.2 ÷ 119 = 0.304...
2 molecules of KBr react to form 2 molecules of KCl, so their relative amounts in the reaction are the same.
mass of KCl = 0.304... × 74.5 = **22.7 g**

Q4 $6HCl + 2Al \rightarrow 2AlCl_3 + 3H_2$
M_r of HCl = 1 + 35.5 = 36.5
M_r of $AlCl_3$ = 27 + (3 × 35.5) = 133.5
relative amount of HCl = 15.4 ÷ 36.5 = 0.421...
6 molecules of HCl reacts to form 2 molecules of $AlCl_3$, so the relative amount of $AlCl_3$ is one third that of HCl: 0.421... ÷ 3 = 0.140...
mass of $AlCl_3$ = 0.140... × 133.5 = **18.8 g**

6. The Mole

Page 87 — Fact Recall Questions

Q1 6.02×10^{23}

Q2 An amount of a substance that contains 6.02×10^{23} particles.

Q3 number of moles =
$$\frac{\text{mass in g (of element or compound)}}{M_r \text{ (of element or compound) or } A_r \text{ (of element)}}$$

Page 87 — Application Questions

Q1 a) 23 g

b) 4 g

c) 2 × 80 = **160 g**

d) (2 × 39) + 16 = **94 g**

Q2 a) A_r of K = 39
moles = mass ÷ A_r = 19.5 ÷ 39 = **0.50 moles**

b) M_r of SO_2 = 32 + (2 × 16) = 64
moles = mass ÷ M_r = 76.8 ÷ 64 = **1.2 moles**

Q3 a) M_r of MgO = 24 + 16 = 40
mass = moles × M_r = 0.50 × 40 = **20 g**

b) M_r $Ca(OH)_2$ = 40 + (2 × (16 + 1)) = 74
mass = moles × M_r = 1.40 × 74 = **104 g**

Q4 a) number of particles = Avogadro's constant × moles
= $6.02 \times 10^{23} \times 0.8$ = **4.8×10^{23} atoms**

b) number of particles = Avogadro's constant × moles
= $6.02 \times 10^{23} \times 2 = 1.2 \times 10^{24}$.
There are two atoms in NaCl, so the number of atoms = $1.2 \times 10^{24} \times 2$ = **2.4×10^{24} atoms**

Q5 M_r of NH_3 = 14 + (3 × 1) = 17
moles = mass ÷ M_r = 27.2 ÷ 17 = 1.6 moles
number of molecules = Avogadro's constant × moles
= $6.02 \times 10^{23} \times 1.6$ = **9.6×10^{23}**

7. The Mole and Equations

Page 90 — Application Questions

Q1 a) 2

b) 1

Q2 3 mol
The molar ratio of magnesium to magnesium oxide is 1:1, so the number of moles of magnesium that react is the same as the number of moles of magnesium oxide that form.

Q3 0.4 ÷ 2 = **0.2 mol**
The molar ratio of sodium bromide to bromine is 2:1, so half as many moles of bromine will form compared to the moles of sodium bromide that reacted.

Q4 M_r of O_2 = 2 × 16 = 32
M_r of Na_2O = (2 × 23) + 16 = 62
Number of moles of each substance:
Na: $\frac{4.6}{23} = 0.20$ O_2: $\frac{1.6}{32} = 0.050$ Na_2O: $\frac{6.2}{62} = 0.10$
Divide by the smallest number (0.050):
Na: $\frac{0.20}{0.050} = 4.0$ O_2: $\frac{0.050}{0.050} = 1.0$ Na_2O: $\frac{0.10}{0.050} = 2.0$
Balanced equation: $\mathbf{4Na + O_2 \rightarrow 2Na_2O}$

Q5 M_r of HCl = 1 + 35.5 = 36.5
M_r of KCl = 39 + 35.5 = 74.5
M_r of H_2 = 2 × 1 = 2
Number of moles of each substance:
K: $\frac{2.34}{39} = 0.060$ HCl: $\frac{2.19}{36.5} = 0.060$
KCl: $\frac{4.47}{74.5} = 0.060$ H_2: $\frac{0.06}{2} = 0.03$
Divide by the smallest number (0.03):
K: $\frac{0.060}{0.03} = 2$ HCl: $\frac{0.060}{0.03} = 2$
KCl: $\frac{0.060}{0.03} = 2$ H_2: $\frac{0.03}{0.03} = 1$
Balanced equation: $\mathbf{2K + 2HCl \rightarrow 2KCl + H_2}$

Q6 Number of moles of each substance:
Z: $\frac{1.20}{30} = 0.040$ O_2: $\frac{4.48}{32} = 0.14$
CO_2: $\frac{3.52}{44} = 0.080$ H_2O: $\frac{2.16}{18} = 0.12$
Divide by the smallest number (0.040):
Z: $\frac{0.040}{0.040} = 1.0$ O_2: $\frac{0.14}{0.040} = 3.5$
CO_2: $\frac{0.080}{0.040} = 2.0$ H_2O: $\frac{0.12}{0.040} = 3.0$
Multiply all the values by 2:
Z: 1.0 × 2 = 2 O_2: 3.5 × 2 = 7
CO_2: 2.0 × 2 = 4 H_2O: 3.0 × 2 = 6
Balanced equation: $2Z + 7O_2 \rightarrow 4CO_2 + 6H_2O$
From the equation, you can see that 2 units of Z contain 4 atoms of C and 12 atoms of H. So 1 unit of Z contains 2 atoms of C and 6 atoms of H, making the chemical formula of Z C_2H_6.
Balanced equation: $\mathbf{2C_2H_6 + 7O_2 \rightarrow 4CO_2 + 6H_2O}$

Pages 93-94 — Calculations Involving Masses Exam-style Questions

1 a) M_r = 63.5 + 16 = **79.5** ***(1 mark)***
b) E.g. there are two copper atoms and two oxygen atoms on both the left-hand side and the right-hand side of the equation ***(1 mark)***.
c) 0.64 g ***(1 mark)***
d) Before the reaction, the oxygen gas wasn't contained inside the reaction container, so its mass wasn't accounted for in the initial mass ***(1 mark)***. After the reaction, the oxygen was contained within the copper oxide inside the reaction vessel, so its mass was included in the total mass of the reaction vessel ***(1 mark)***.

2 a) 7.0 + 5.5 = **12.5 g** ***(1 mark)***
b) 3 × 7.0 = **21 g** ***(1 mark)***
c) $M_r(CaCO_3)$ = 40 + 12 + (3 × 16) = **100** ***(1 mark)***
M_r(CaO) = 40 + 16 = **56** ***(1 mark)***
$M_r(CO_2)$ = 12 + (2 × 16) = **44** ***(1 mark)***
d) Total M_r of reactants = 100
Total M_r of products = 56 + 44 = 100 ***(1 mark)***
Total M_r of reactants = Total M_r of reactants, so mass is conserved ***(1 mark)***.

3 a) volume in dm³ = 30 ÷ 1000 = 0.030 dm³ ***(1 mark)***
mass = concentration × volume = 150 × 0.030
= **4.5 g** ***(1 mark)***
b) volume of new solution = 30 + 60 = 90 cm³
volume in dm³ = 90 ÷ 1000 = 0.090 dm³ ***(1 mark)***
concentration = mass ÷ volume = 4.5 ÷ 0.090
= **50 g dm⁻³** ***(1 mark)***
The mass of $MgCl_2$ in the diluted solution is the same as the mass in the 150 g/dm³ solution.

4 a) M_r of H_2 = 2, M_r of O_2 = 32, M_r of H_2O = 18 ***(1 mark)***
Number of moles of each substance:
H_2: $\frac{0.50}{2} = 0.25$ O_2: $\frac{4.0}{32} = 0.125$
H_2O: $\frac{4.5}{18} = 0.25$ ***(1 mark)***
Divide by the smallest number (0.125):
H_2: $\frac{0.25}{0.125} = 2.0$ O_2: $\frac{0.125}{0.125} = 1.0$
H_2O: $\frac{0.25}{0.125} = 2.0$ ***(1 mark)***
Balanced equation: $\mathbf{2H_2 + O_2 \rightarrow 2H_2O}$ ***(1 mark)***
b) E.g. it will be used up first ***(1 mark)***.

5 a) moles = 4.8 ÷ 24 = **0.20 mol** ***(1 mark)***
b) relative amount of Mg = mass ÷ A_r = 4.8 ÷ 24 = 0.20 ***(1 mark)***.
M_r of magnesium chloride = 24 + (2 × 35.5) = 95 ***(1 mark)***
mass of magnesium chloride = 0.20 × 95 = **19 g** ***(1 mark)***
The equation shows that 1 molecule of Mg reacts to give 1 molecule of $MgCl_2$. So the relative amount of $MgCl_2$ in the reaction is the same as that of Mg (0.20).
c) relative amount of Mg = mass ÷ A_r = 4.8 ÷ 24 = 0.20 ***(1 mark)***.
M_r of zinc chloride = 65 + (2 × 35.5) = 136 ***(1 mark)***
mass of zinc chloride to react = 0.20 × 136 = 27.2 g ***(1 mark)***
mass of zinc chloride remaining = 35 – 27.2 = **7.8 g** ***(1 mark)***
d) The zinc chloride is no longer in excess ***(1 mark)*** because 4.8 g of magnesium requires 27.2 g of zinc chloride to react completely / 0.20 mol of magnesium needs 0.20 mol of zinc chloride to react completely, and only 0.15 mol are available ***(1 mark)***.

6 a) In 30 g of the mixture there will be 30 × (8 ÷ 100) = 2.4 g of bromine ***(1 mark)***.
$M_r(CaBr_2)$ = 40 + (2 × 80) = 200 ***(1 mark)***
% mass of bromine in $CaBr_2$ = ((2 × 80) ÷ 200) × 100 = (160 ÷ 200) × 100 = 80% ***(1 mark)***
Mass of $CaBr_2$ containing 2.4 g of Br = 2.4 ÷ (80 ÷ 100) = **3.0 g** ***(1 mark)***
b) moles of $CaBr_2$ = mass ÷ M_r = 1.5 ÷ 200 = 0.0075 mol ***(1 mark)***
molecules of $CaBr_2$ = Avogadro's constant × moles = $6.02 \times 10^{23} \times 0.0075 = 4.5 \times 10^{21}$ ***(1 mark)***
There are 2 Br atoms in 1 molecule of $CaBr_2$, so the number of Br atoms = $4.5 \times 10^{21} \times 2$
= $\mathbf{9.0 \times 10^{21}}$ ***(1 mark)***

Answers

Topic 2 — States of Matter and Mixtures

1. States of Matter

Page 97 — Fact Recall Questions

Q1 solid, liquid, gas

Q2 a) solid, liquid
b) solid

Q3 As the temperature increases, the particles making up the solid vibrate more. This causes the solid to expand.

Q4 The gas particles have only weak forces of attraction between them, so they move randomly, filling the whole container. They move in straight lines, continuing until they hit another particle or the walls of the container.

Q5 Particles in a substance in the solid state don't have much energy. Particles in a substance in the liquid state have more energy than in the solid state, but less than in the gas state. Particles in the gas state have more energy than either the solid or liquid states.

Page 97 — Application Question

Q1 In solids, there are strong forces of attraction between particles. This holds the particles together in fixed positions. The forces of attraction between particles in a liquid are weak enough that the particles can flow past each other and fill the bottom of the beaker.

2. Changes of State

Page 99 — Fact Recall Questions

Q1 melting

Q2 a) When a solid is heated, the particles' energy increases and they vibrate more, which weakens the forces that hold the solid together. Eventually, the particles have enough energy to break free from their positions, forming a liquid.
b) When a gas is cooled, the particles no longer have enough energy to overcome the forces of attraction between them. Eventually, the forces between the particles are strong enough that the gas becomes a liquid.

Page 99 — Application Question

Q1 a) solid b) liquid
c) liquid d) gas

3. Purity

Page 101 — Fact Recall Question

Q1 A pure substance is completely made up of a single element or compound. A mixture contains more than one compound, or different elements that don't make up a single compound.

Page 101 — Application Question

Q1 a) X, as it melted at a specific temperature whilst Y and Z melted over a range.
b) Z, as it melted over the widest range.

4. Distillation

Page 103 — Application Questions

Q1 a) The boiling points of ethanol and propanol are too close together for simple distillation to separate them successfully.
b) fractional distillation

Q2 Place the mixture in a round-bottomed flask attached to a fractionating column attached to a condenser. Heat the mixture until the thermometer reaches 65 °C. At this point the vapour of the first fraction, methanol, will reach the top of the column, form a liquid in the condenser and can be collected. Increase the temperature to 78 °C. The ethanol fraction will reach the top of the column and can be collected. The final fraction, propanol, can be collected at the end of the condenser when the temperature reaches 97 °C.

5. Filtration and Crystallisation

Page 105 — Fact Recall Questions

Q1 E.g. filtration

Q2 Drying the crystals.

Page 105 — Application Questions

Q1 E.g. fold a filter paper into a cone shape and place it into a filter funnel sitting in a container. Pour the mixture containing water and silver bromide into the funnel lined by the filter paper. The silver bromide will remain on the filter paper and the water will pass through the filter paper into the container below.

Q2 a) lead bromide
b) sodium sulfate

6. Choosing a Separation Method

Page 106 — Application Question

Q1 E.g. use a combination of filtration and crystallisation. Begin by filtering the solution through a filter funnel. This will remove the magnesium carbonate from the mixture. The solution left over from the filtration should contain only sodium chloride and water, so pure sodium chloride could be obtained by crystallisation.

7. Paper Chromatography

Page 110 — Fact Recall Questions

Q1 stationary phase

Q2 Because the ink might be washed away by the solvent.

Q3 To stop the solvent evaporating.

Q4 A chromatogram.
Q5 R_f value = distance travelled by solute ÷ distance travelled by solvent

Page 110 — Application Questions

Q1 6.9 ÷ 12.3 = **0.56**
Q2 a) The red substance.
b) The red substance.
The longer a substance spends in the mobile phase the further it will travel up the paper.
Q3 a) It is likely to be pure.
b) E.g. the substance is likely to have different levels of solubility in the solvents. So it will spend different amounts of time in the mobile phase / will travel further in the mobile phase.
Q4 a) red: 3.5 ÷ 8.3 = **0.42**
purple: 4.7 ÷ 8.3 = **0.57**
yellow: 5.3 ÷ 8.3 = **0.64**
b) E.g. carry out another chromatography experiment using methyl violet as a reference. Repeat the experiment using a number of different solvents. If the purple substance and methyl violet have the same R_f values in all the solvents then it's likely that the substance is methyl violet. If their R_f values are different in any solvents then it's not methyl violet.

8. Analysing the Composition of Inks

Page 111 — Application Question

Q1 The solvent can be identified from the temperature that it evaporates at during the simple distillation, which can be compared to the boiling points of common solvents. The R_f values of the spots on the chromatogram can be compared with R_f values of pure dyes or reference values.

9. Water Treatment

Page 113 — Fact Recall Questions

Q1 Potable water is water that is fit to drink.
Q2 Ground water comes from aquifers (rocks that trap water underground).
Q3 Waste water is water that has been contaminated by a human process.
Q4 A chemical (iron sulfate/aluminium sulfate) is added to the water, which makes fine particles clump together and settle at the bottom.
Q5 Water that has had the ions present in normal tap water removed.

Page 113 — Application Question

Q1 Sea water is made potable by distillation. First, the sea water is boiled to produce steam, which is then condensed. This separates the water from any dissolved salts.

Pages 116-117 — States of Matter and Mixtures Exam-style Questions

1 a) A = liquid ***(1 mark)***, B = solid ***(1 mark)***
b) Freezing ***(1 mark)***. The particles' energy decreases. / They move around less ***(1 mark)***. There's not enough energy to overcome the attraction between them. ***(1 mark)***.
c) In a physical change, only the arrangement or energy of the particles changes ***(1 mark)***. In a chemical change, bonds between atoms break and new substances are formed ***(1 mark)***.
d) solid ***(1 mark)***

2 a) R_f value of A = $\frac{2.0}{6.0}$ = **0.33** ***(1 mark)***
b) E.g. how soluble the compound is in the solvent / how attracted the compound is to the paper ***(1 mark)***.
c) Perform chromatography on a sample of the reference material alongside a sample of the mixture that gave spot A ***(1 mark)*** and compare the R_f of the reference material to that of spot A ***(1 mark)***.

3 a) E.g. to allow crystals to form ***(1 mark)***.
b) e.g. a dessicator/drying oven ***(1 mark)***

4 a) solvent ***(1 mark)***
b) A, as it evaporated from the mixture first ***(1 mark)***.
c) e.g. (paper) chromatography ***(1 mark)***

5 a) The water is filtered by passing through a wire mesh and then gravel and sand beds to remove any solids (this is filtration) ***(1 mark)***. Chemicals (e.g. iron sulfate or aluminium sulfate) are added to the water to make fine particles clump together (this is sedimentation) ***(1 mark)***. Harmful bacteria and other microbes in the water are killed by bubbling chlorine gas through it (this is chlorination) ***(1 mark)***.
b) Distillation of sea water ***(1 mark)***.

Topic 3 — Chemical Changes

1. Acids and Bases

Page 119 — Fact Recall Questions

Q1 E.g. pH is a measure of how acidic or alkaline a solution is.
Q2 pH 7
Q3 pHs greater than 7.
Q4 H^+ ions
Q5 a) OH^- ions
b) The higher the concentration, the higher the pH.

Page 119 — Application Questions

Q1 a) acidic b) alkaline
Q2 a) E.g. pH 2 b) blue
For part a), any pH in the range 1-6 is also acceptable.
Q3 Water/H_2O

2. Neutralisation Reactions

Page 121 — Fact Recall Questions

Q1 Water/H_2O and a salt.

Q2 $H^+_{(aq)} + OH^-_{(aq)} \rightarrow H_2O_{(l)}$

Page 121 — Application Question

Q1 a) hydrochloric acid + calcium hydroxide → calcium chloride + water

b) i) Unreacted calcium hydroxide would start to collect in the bottom of the flask.

ii) E.g. She could use Universal indicator.

iii)

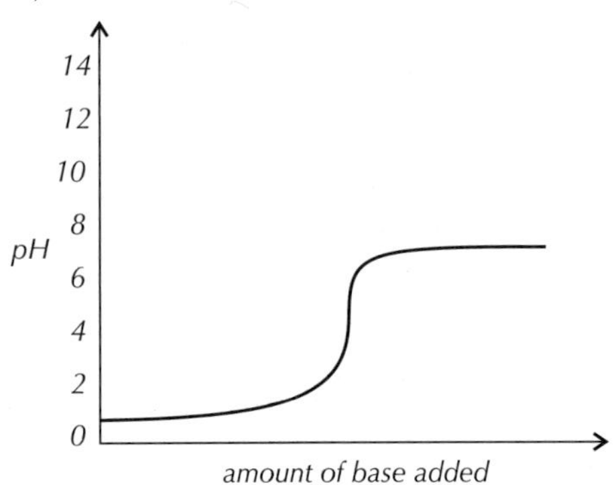

3. Strong and Weak Acids

Page 124 — Fact Recall Questions

Q1 Strong acids fully ionise/dissociate in an aqueous solution.

Q2 Weak acids partially ionise/dissociate in an aqueous solution.

Q3 $CH_3COOH_{(aq)} \rightleftharpoons H^+_{(aq)} + CH_3COO^-_{(aq)}$

Q4 Acid strength tells you what proportion of acid molecules ionise in water whereas the concentration is a measure of the amount of acid molecules in a given volume of water.

Page 124 — Application Questions

Q1 A strong acid fully dissociates in water meaning there is a high concentration of H^+ ions in solution leading to a low pH. A weak acid only partially dissociates, so there is a lower concentration of H^+ ions than in a solution of a strong acid of the same concentration. This leads to a higher pH.

Q2 H^+ concentration increased by a factor of 100, which is 10 × 10. So the pH would have decreased by 2.

Q3 The H^+ ion concentration decreased by a factor of 10, so the pH would have increased by 1. The new pH would be 1.7 + 1 = **2.7**

Q4 For every pH change of 1, the H^+ ion concentration changes by a factor of 10.
Difference in pH = 7 – 4 = 3, so the H^+ concentration has changed by: 10 × 10 × 10 = **1000**

4. Reactions of Acids

Page 127 — Fact Recall Question

Q1 a) E.g. Hydrogen gas will cause a 'squeaky pop' when it comes into contact with a lit splint.

b) E.g. Carbon dioxide, when bubbled through a solution of limewater, will cause the solution to go cloudy.

Page 127 — Application Questions

Q1 a) magnesium chloride

b) potassium nitrate

c) sodium sulfate

Q2 carbon dioxide/CO_2

5. Making Insoluble Salts

Page 129 — Fact Recall Questions

Q1 a) soluble

b) soluble

c) soluble

d) soluble

Q2 precipitation reaction

Page 129 — Application Questions

Q1 There are no carbonate ions present in the solution.

Q2 a) barium chloride + sodium sulfate → barium sulfate + sodium chloride

b) E.g. Add a spatula of barium chloride to a test tube containing deionised water and shake the test tube thoroughly to dissolve it. Repeat this process in a separate test tube for a spatula of sodium sulfate. Tip the two solutions into a beaker and stir thoroughly. Filter the solution through a filter funnel lined with filter paper. Swill the beaker out with some deionised water and pour this into the funnel. Rinse the contents of the filter paper with more deionised water. Scrape off the barium sulfate onto a fresh piece of filter paper and leave to dry in an oven/dessicator.

6. Making Soluble Salts

Page 132 — Application Questions

Q1 a) zinc oxide + hydrochloric acid → zinc chloride + water

b) To ensure that all the hydrochloric acid has reacted.

c) i) By filtering the solution using filter paper and a filter funnel.

ii) To avoid contaminating the zinc chloride salt when it's dried.

Q2 a) E.g. Measure a set amount of the acid into a conical flask using a pipette, and add a few drops of indicator. Add the alkali to a burette. Using the burette, slowly add alkali to the acid, while swirling the flask, until the indicator changes colour. Record how much alkali was used during the titration.

b) E.g. To ensure that the product isn't contaminated with unreacted potassium hydroxide or nitric acid.

7. Electrolysis

Page 133 — Fact Recall Questions

Q1 They contain free ions which can carry a charge.

Q2 cations/positive ions

Page 135 — Application Questions

Q1 a) (molten) zinc chloride
b) the positive electrode/the anode
c) The chloride ions lose one electron each (they are oxidised) and form chlorine molecules.
d) They are reduced.

Q2 a) $2Br^- \rightarrow Br_2 + 2e^-$ / $2Br^- - 2e^- \rightarrow Br_2$
$2H^+ + 2e^- \rightarrow H_2$
b) $Cu^{2+} + 2e^- \rightarrow Cu$
$2O^{2-} \rightarrow O_2 + 4e^-$ / $2O^{2-} - 4e^- \rightarrow O_2$

8. Predicting Products of Electrolysis

Page 138 — Fact Recall Questions

Q1 The reactivity of the metal ions compared to hydrogen and whether halide ions are present.

Q2 no

Q3 bromine

Page 138 — Application Questions

Q1 Sodium is more reactive than hydrogen so the sodium ions will stay in solution.

Q2 a) H^+, OH^- and SO_4^{2-}
b) anode: oxygen and water
cathode: hydrogen

Q3 Hydrogen/H_2, oxygen/O_2 and water/H_2O. Hydrogen is produced at the cathode (negative electrode) because sodium is more reactive than hydrogen. Oxygen and water are produced at the anode (positive electrode) because the solution doesn't contain any halide ions.

Q4 Yes the student is correct. Copper metal is less reactive than hydrogen so will be discharged at the negative electrode. As chloride ions are present, chlorine will be discharged at the positive electrode.

Q5 anode: $4OH^- \rightarrow O_2 + 2H_2O + 4e^-$
cathode: $2H^+ + 2e^- \rightarrow H_2$

9. Electrolysis of Copper Sulfate

Page 141 — Fact Recall Question

Q1 The anode is a lump of impure copper. The cathode is a thin piece of pure copper.

Page 141 — Application Questions

Q1 As copper metal is less reactive than hydrogen, copper metal is produced at the cathode. There are no halide ions present in the solution, so oxygen and water are produced at the anode.

Q2 a) The mass of the anode decreases as copper leaves the copper anode. The mass of the cathode increases as copper ions from the anode are deposited on the surface of the cathode.
b) E.g. Clean the surface of two copper electrodes using a piece of sandpaper. Place the electrodes into a beaker filled with copper sulfate solution. Connect the electrodes to a d.c. power supply using crocodile clips and wires. Turn on the power supply.

Pages 144-145 — Chemical Changes Exam-style Questions

1 a) acid + metal oxide → salt + water ***(1 mark for each correct product).***
b) A neutralisation reaction ***(1 mark).***

2 a) burette ***(1 mark)***
b) The indicator will change colour when all the sodium hydroxide solution has reacted ***(1 mark),*** so the student will be able to see the end-point of the reaction ***(1 mark).***
c) Phenolphthalein ***(1 mark),*** because it would give a clear colour change at the end-point (it would change from pink to colourless) and Universal indicator would not ***(1 mark).***
d) So that the product is not contaminated with indicator ***(1 mark).***
e) E.g. slowly evaporate off some of the water ***(1 mark)*** and leave the solution to crystallise ***(1 mark).*** Filter off the solid and dry it in a drying oven ***(1 mark).***

3 a) Ethanoic acid partially ionises in solution ***(1 mark).***
b) hydrochloric acid ***(1 mark)***
c) sulfuric acid ***(1 mark)***
sulfuric acid + magnesium → magnesium sulfate + hydrogen ***(1 mark)***

4 a) $Pb(NO_3)_{2(aq)} + MgSO_{4(aq)} \rightarrow PbSO_{4(s)} + Mg(NO_3)_{2(aq)}$
(2 marks — 1 mark for correct balancing, 1 mark for correct state symbols.)
b) E.g. copper sulfate ***(1 mark).***
Any soluble sulfate salt would get you the mark for this question. Lead sulfate, barium sulfate or calcium sulfate would not get you the mark, as these are insoluble.
c) silver chloride ***(1 mark)***

5 a) Copper chloride solution ***(1 mark).***
b) water ***(1 mark)***
c) Each copper ion gains two electrons/is reduced ***(1 mark)*** and becomes a neutral copper atom ***(1 mark).***
d) $2Cl^- \rightarrow Cl_2 + 2e^-$ ***(1 mark)***
e) $Cu^{2+} + 2e^- \rightarrow Cu$ ***(1 mark for the correct species on the left and right hand side of the equation, 1 mark for balancing.)***

Answers

Topic 4 — Extracting Metals and Equilibria

Topic 4a — Obtaining and Using Metals

1. Oxidation and Reduction

Page 147 — Fact Recall Questions

Q1 Oxidation is the gain of oxygen by a substance.

Q2 Reduction is the loss of oxygen by a substance.

Page 147 — Application Questions

Q1 a) $CuO + H_2 \rightarrow Cu + H_2O$

b) Copper has been reduced in this reaction because it has lost oxygen.

Q2 a) Cu

b) Mn

Q3 a) H

b) C and H

2. Reactivity of Metals

Page 151 — Fact Recall Questions

Q1 A reactivity series shows a list of metals in order of how reactive they are.

Q2 more reactive

Q3 calcium

Q4 silver

Q5 metal + acid → salt + hydrogen

Q6 Iron is more reactive / is oxidised more easily than copper.

Page 152 — Application Questions

Q1 $Fe + 2HCl \rightarrow FeCl_2 + H_2$

Q2 a) hydrogen

b) Any two from, e.g. the starting temperature of the reaction / the volume of acid / the concentration of the acid / the mass of metal used / the surface area of the metal.

c) Aluminium would produce a larger volume of gas as it is more reactive / higher in the reactivity series / more easily oxidised than iron.

Q3 B, C, A

Q4 a) zinc + iron(II) sulfate → zinc sulfate + iron

b) Copper is less reactive than iron and therefore will not displace it in a compound.

3. Displacement Reactions and Redox

Page 154 — Fact Recall Questions

Q1 Oxidation is the loss of electrons by a substance.

Q2 Reduction is the gain of electrons by a substance.

Q3 The more reactive metal will displace the less reactive metal in the salt solution / the more reactive metal will be oxidised and the less reactive metal will be reduced.

Page 154 — Application Questions

Q1 a) $3Zn_{(s)} + Fe_2(SO_4)_{3(aq)} \rightarrow 2Fe_{(s)} + 3ZnSO_{4(aq)}$

b) oxidised

c) zinc

During a displacement reaction, a more reactive metal displaces a less reactive metal in a salt solution. Since zinc displaces iron, zinc must be more reactive.

Q2 In the reaction between magnesium and hydrochloric acid, magnesium is oxidised — it loses two electrons to become an Mg^{2+} ion. Hydrogen is reduced — it gains electrons to become hydrogen atoms. The oxidation of magnesium and the reduction of hydrogen happen simultaneously, so the reaction is a redox reaction.

4. Extracting Metals from their Ores

Page 156 — Fact Recall Questions

Q1 E.g. gold/platinum/silver

Q2 A rock that contains enough metal to make it profitable to extract the metal from it.

Q3 false

Page 156 — Application Questions

Q1 a) reduction with carbon

b) electrolysis

c) reduction with carbon

d) electrolysis

Q2 Lithium is more reactive than carbon and therefore cannot be reduced by it.

5. Electrolysis of Metal Ores

Page 158 — Fact Recall Questions

Q1 The positive metal ions gain electrons and become metal atoms.

Q2 $2O^{2-} \rightarrow O_2 + 4e^-$

Page 158 — Application Question

Q1 a) i) reduction with carbon, electrolysis

ii) electrolysis

b) The manufacturer should use zinc to make the component. Aluminium requires electrolysis to be extracted from its ore. Electrolysis requires lots of electricity and there are costs associated with melting and dissolving the aluminium ore. This makes it an expensive process. Zinc can be extracted from its ore by reduction with carbon, which is a comparatively cheap process.

6. Alternative Methods of Extracting Metals

Page 160 — Fact Recall Questions

Q1 E.g. the supply of some metals is limited.

Q2 E.g. scrap iron is very cheap / it reduces the amount of scrap metal going to landfill.

Q3 a) E.g. during phytoextraction, plants are grown in soil that contains copper. The copper builds up in the leaves of the plants. The plants are harvested, dried and burned in a furnace, and copper extracted from the ash by electrolysis / displacement with a more reactive metal.
b) Advantage: e.g. less damaging to the environment / uses less energy than traditional mining and extraction methods.
Disadvantage: e.g. the process is slow / it takes a long time for plants to grow.

7. Recycling

Page 162 — Fact Recall Questions

Q1 Any two from, e.g. conserves fossil fuels / conserves resources / preserves habitats as fewer mines are needed / reduces material sent to landfill.

Q2 Any one from, e.g. increases jobs / reduces energy costs.

Page 162 — Application Question

Q1 a) aluminium
b) E.g. zinc is less abundant in the Earth's crust.

8. Life Cycle Assessments

Page 165 — Fact Recall Questions

Q1 Life cycle assessments assess the environmental impact of a product over its entire life.

Q2 E.g. getting the raw materials, manufacturing and packaging the product, using the product, disposal of the product.

Page 165 — Application Question

Q1 a) The wooden table as it is made out of a renewable resource and uses less energy to manufacture.
b) E.g. how long the table lasts / whether the material can be recycled at the end of the life time of the table.

Pages 167-168 — Obtaining and Using Metals Exam-style Questions

1 a) D ***(1 mark)***
b) Attach a gas syringe to the test tube ***(1 mark)***, and measure the volume of gas given off at regular intervals ***(1 mark)***.

2 a) Any one from: zinc / iron / silver ***(1 mark)***
b) Any one from: sodium / magnesium / aluminium ***(1 mark)***
c) i) magnesium + zinc sulfate →
zinc + magnesium sulfate
(1 mark for each correct product with the correct reactants)
ii) Magnesium has been oxidised. Zinc has been reduced ***(1 mark)***.
iii) A reaction wouldn't occur ***(1 mark)*** as silver is less reactive than zinc, so wouldn't displace the zinc from the solution ***(1 mark)***.
iv) When magnesium reacts with sulfuric acid, magnesium is oxidised to form magnesium ions (Mg^{2+}) ***(1 mark)***. The hydrogen ions from the acid are reduced to form hydrogen gas ***(1 mark)***.

3 a) How to grade your answer:

Level 0: There is no relevant information. ***[0 marks]***

Level 1: One or two of the environmental factors in Figure 3 have been discussed. No attempt has been made to compare the different types of bag. The points made are basic and not linked together. ***[1 to 2 marks]***

Level 2: Three or four of the environmental factors in Figure 3 have been discussed. A brief attempt has been made to compare the different types of bag. Some of the points made are linked together. ***[3 to 4 marks]***

Level 3: All of the environmental factors in Figure 3 have been discussed. There is a detailed comparison of the different types of bag. The points made are well-linked and the answer has a clear and logical structure. ***[5 to 6 marks]***

Here are some points your answer may include:
Bag A uses the second highest mass of materials and produces the second highest mass of waste.
Bag A produces the most greenhouse emissions and uses by far the most energy.
Therefore, bag A has a comparatively large environmental impact.
Bag B uses the most materials and produces the most waste.
Bag B uses the lowest amount of energy to produce, but produces the second highest level of greenhouse gases.
On balance, bag B has a similar environmental impact to bag A.
Bag C uses the least material, produces the least waste and has the smallest greenhouse emissions.
Bag C uses the second highest amount of energy.
On balance, bag C seems to have the smallest environmental impact.

b) E.g. If the product is disposed of in landfill, it will take up space and can pollute the water and land ***(1 mark)***. The product could be incinerated, but this could cause air pollution ***(1 mark)***.

4 a) E.g. $CuO + C \rightarrow Cu + CO$ ***(1 mark for the correct reactants and products, 1 mark for correctly balanced)***

You would also get the marks if you balanced the equation to show the reaction producing carbon dioxide:
E.g. $2CuO + C \rightarrow 2Cu + CO_2$

b) It would increase the cost of extracting copper ***(1 mark)*** as electrolysis is an expensive process ***(1 mark)***.

c) i) E.g. During bioleaching, bacteria converts copper compounds in the ore into soluble copper compounds ***(1 mark)***. This separates the copper from the ore. The leachate contains copper ions ***(1 mark)*** which can then be extracted by electrolysis or displacement (with a more reactive metal) ***(1 mark)***.

ii) E.g it's slow ***(1 mark)***.

Topic 4b — Reversible Reactions and Equilibria

1. Reversible Reactions

Page 170 — Fact Recall Questions

Q1 A reaction where the products of the reaction can themselves react to produce the original reactants.

Q2 $A + B \rightleftharpoons C + D$

Q3 temperature = 450 °C
pressure = 200 atmospheres

Q4 The rates of the forward and reverse reactions are the same.

Q5 temperature, pressure, concentrations (of reactants or products)

Page 171 — Application Questions

Q1 $N_{2(g)} + 3H_{2(g)} \rightleftharpoons 2NH_{3(g)}$

Q2 a) E.g. dynamic equilibrium is when the forward and backwards reactions are occurring at the same rate.

b) Changing the pressure only affects the position of equilibrium in reactions involving gases. Since this reaction doesn't contain any gases, it will be unaffected by changes in pressure.

Q3 The carbon dioxide gas will escape as it is not a closed system, so the backward reaction will not balance the forward reaction.

2. Le Chatelier's Principle

Page 174 — Fact Recall Questions

Q1 Le Chatelier's principle

Q2 the exothermic reaction

Q3 E.g. raising the pressure favours the reaction which produces less volume (the fewest number of gas molecules).

Q4 E.g. the system tries to increase the concentration of products by reducing the amount of reactants.

Page 174 — Application Questions

Q1 a) i) It would move to the left/towards the reactants.

ii) NH_4Cl/ammonium chloride

b) Decreasing the pressure would favour the production of NH_3.

Q2 If the pressure was decreased, the equilibrium position would move to the left since there are more moles of gas on the left-hand side/with the reactants. This would cause the yield of sulfur trioxide (SO_3) to decrease.

Page 176 — Reversible Reactions and Equilibria Exam-style Questions

1 a) E.g. natural gas ***(1 mark)***

b) an iron catalyst ***(1 mark)***

c) E.g. increase the pressure / decrease the temperature ***(1 mark)***.

2 a) The reaction is reversible ***(1 mark)***.

b) The reverse reaction is an endothermic reaction ***(1 mark)*** so the energy from heating converts the solid sodium acetate trihydrate back to sodium acetate trihydrate solution ***(1 mark)***.

3 a) This would decrease the yield of ethanol ***(1 mark)*** because increased temperature favours the reverse (endothermic) reaction ***(1 mark)***.

b) This would increase the yield of ethanol ***(1 mark)*** because increased pressure favours the reaction that produces fewer molecules of gas (the right-hand side of the equation) ***(1 mark)***.

Answers

Topic 6 — Groups in the Periodic Table

1. Group 1 — The Alkali Metals

Page 179 — Fact Recall Questions

Q1 Group 1

Q2 They have low melting points.

Q3 Reactivity increases as you move down Group 1.

Q4 Group 1 metals react by losing their outermost electron. As you move down Group 1, the atomic radius gets larger. This means that the outermost electron becomes less strongly attracted to the nucleus because it is further away. So, less energy is required to remove the outer electron from elements at the bottom of the group and it is more easily lost.

Q5 a) alkali metal + water → metal hydroxide + hydrogen

b) alkaline

Q6 a) Lithium would move quickly around the surface of the water, and fizz vigorously.

b) Potassium would move quickly around the surface of the water and fizz violently. The potassium would also melt, and the hydrogen gas produced during the reaction may catch fire.

Page 179 — Application Questions

Q1 a) potassium b) rubidium

Q2 a) lithium b) potassium

Q3 ionic compound

Q4 $2Rb_{(s)} + 2H_2O_{(l)} \rightarrow 2RbOH_{(aq)} + H_{2(g)}$

2. Group 7 — The Halogens

Page 182 — Fact Recall Questions

Q1 The melting points of the halogens increase as you move down Group 7.

Q2 A red-brown liquid which gives off an orange vapour.

Q3 Chlorine gas will bleach damp litmus paper, turning it white.

Q4 The most reactive halogens are found at the top of Group 7.

Q5 1– / –1

Q6 As you go down Group 7, the halogens become less reactive. This is because the atomic radius gets larger as you go down Group 7, which makes it harder to attract the extra electron to fill the outer shell as it's further away from the nucleus.

Page 182 — Application Questions

Q1 a) chlorine b) fluorine

Q2 a) iodine b) bromine

Q3 a) $I_2 + 2K \rightarrow 2KI$

b) $Cl_2 + 2Li \rightarrow 2LiCl$

Q4 hydrobromic acid

3. Halogen Displacement Reactions

Page 185 — Fact Recall Questions

Q1 The reaction that occurs when a more reactive halogen displaces (kicks out) a less reactive halogen from an aqueous solution of its halide salt.

Q2 a) chloride

b) bromide

Q3 a) no reaction would occur/nothing

b) The halogen would not be able to displace the halide from its salt, as it is less reactive.

Q4 E.g. Measure a small amount of halide salt solution in to a test tube. Add a few drops of a halogen solution to the test tube and shake the tube gently. A colour change indicates a successful reaction.

Page 185 — Application Questions

Q1 a) yes b) no

c) no d) yes

Q2 a) $Cl_{2(g)} + 2KI_{(aq)} \rightarrow I_{2(aq)} + 2KCl_{(aq)}$

b) $Br_{2(g)} + 2NaI_{(aq)} \rightarrow I_{2(aq)} + 2NaBr_{(aq)}$

Q3 a) Chlorine is reduced and bromine/bromide is oxidised.

b) Bromine is reduced and iodine/iodide is oxidised.

4. Group 0 — The Noble Gases

Page 187 — Fact Recall Questions

Q1 the noble gases

Q2 Any one from: e.g. to provide an inert atmosphere in filament lamps/in flash bulbs/when welding / to make airships/balloons float.

Page 187 — Application Questions

Q1 a) 8

b) Argon has a full outer shell of electrons so doesn't need to gain or lose electrons to become more stable. This means that it's inert.

Q2 Estimated boiling point of helium = boiling point of argon – gap between xenon and argon

Gap between xenon and argon: (–108) – (–186) = 78 °C

Estimated boiling point of helium:

(–186) – 78 = **–264 °C**

The experimentally determined boiling point of helium is actually –269 °C.

Answers

Page 189 — Groups in the Periodic Table

Exam-style Questions

1 a) hydrogen ***(1 mark)***

b) A metal hydroxide is formed in the reaction ***(1 mark)***, which dissolves in the water to give an alkaline solution ***(1 mark)***.

c) E.g. boiling point of potassium = (boiling point of sodium + boiling point of rubidium) ÷ 2 = (883 + 688) ÷ 2 = 785.5 = **786 °C** ***(1 mark)***

Any answer within the range of 700-850 °C would get the mark.

E.g. melting point of rudbidium = (melting point of potassium + melting point of caesium) ÷ 2 = (63 + 28) ÷ 2 = 45.5 = **46 °C** ***(1 mark)***

Any answer in the range between 35-55 would get the mark.

d) How to grade your answer:

Level 0: There is no relevant information. ***[0 marks]***

Level 1: The answer includes a basic description of the relative reactivities of the elements. No attempt has been made to explain the trend in the reactivities. The points made are basic and not linked together. ***[1 to 2 marks]***

Level 2: A comparison of the relative reactivities of the elements has been given. The answer includes a basic explanation for the trend. Some of the points made are linked together. ***[3 to 4 marks]***

Level 3: A comparison of the relative reactivities of the elements has been given, along with a full explanation for the trend. The points made are well-linked and the answer has a clear and logical structure. ***[5 to 6 marks]***

Here are some points your answer may include:
Atoms get larger as you go down Group 1.
So the outer electron is further from the nucleus in atoms of elements that are further down Group 1.
This means the outer electrons are less strongly attracted to the nucleus as you go down the group.
This makes it easier for the outermost electrons to be removed.
Atoms in Group 1 react by losing their outermost electron.
As the electron is more easily lost from large atoms, reactivity increases as you move down the group.
Sodium is the highest up the group of the metals, followed by potassium and then rubidium. So Sodium is the least reactive, then potassium, and rubidium is the most reactive.

2 a) Group 7 ***(1 mark)***

b) Chlorine and bromine both have the same number of electrons in their outer shell / both have 7 electrons in their outer shell ***(1 mark)***.

c) E.g. add chlorine water to a test tube containing a solution of magnesium bromide and shake the test tube ***(1 mark)***. The chlorine will displace the bromide to form magnesium chloride (and bromine) ***(1 mark)***.

d) Argon has a full outer shell of electrons / a stable arrangement of electrons ***(1 mark)*** so is inert ***(1 mark)***.

Topic 7 — Rates of Reaction and Energy Changes

Topic 7a — Rates of Reaction

1. Measuring Rates of Reaction

Page 192 — Fact Recall Questions

Q1 mean rate = $\frac{\text{quantity of reactant used or product formed}}{\text{time}}$

Q2 E.g. observe a mark through the solution and time how long it takes for the mark to disappear. The quicker the mark disappears, the quicker the reaction.

Q3 a) E.g. gas syringes are usually quite sensitive and they don't release the gas into the room, which is useful if the gas produced is harmful. But you can only use this technique to measure the rate if the reaction produces a gas. Also, if the reaction is too vigorous the plunger could blow out of the end of the syringe.

b) E.g. the student could measure the change in mass of the reaction using a mass balance.

Page 192 — Application Questions

Q1 E.g. by directly measuring the amount of carbon dioxide produced over time using a gas syringe. / By measuring the decrease in mass of the reactants over time as carbon dioxide is given off using a mass balance.

You can use either of these methods for this reaction because one of the products of the reaction is a gas — carbon dioxide. You can tell this from the equation for the reaction that you're given in the question.

Q2 E.g. by putting a mark behind the solution and timing how long it takes for the mark to disappear.

One of the products of this reaction is a solid ($Mg(OH)_2$), which means it will form as a precipitate in the solution.

Q3 4.3 cm^3 ÷ 5.0 s = **0.86 cm^3/s**

Q4 34.31 g – 32.63 g = 1.68 g
1.68 g ÷ 8.0 s = **0.21 g/s**

2. Rate of Reaction Graphs

Pages 196-197 — Application Questions

Q1 a) C

Graph C shows that gas is forming over time and the curve levels off at 200 s, showing that this is the time when the reaction is complete. At this point, 24 cm³ of gas have been produced.

b) steeper

Both reactions produce the same amount of gas but the second reaction finishes sooner, so will have a faster rate of reaction to begin with.

Q2 Reaction A — reaction A has the steepest curve at the beginning of the reaction, which means this reaction was the fastest.

Q3

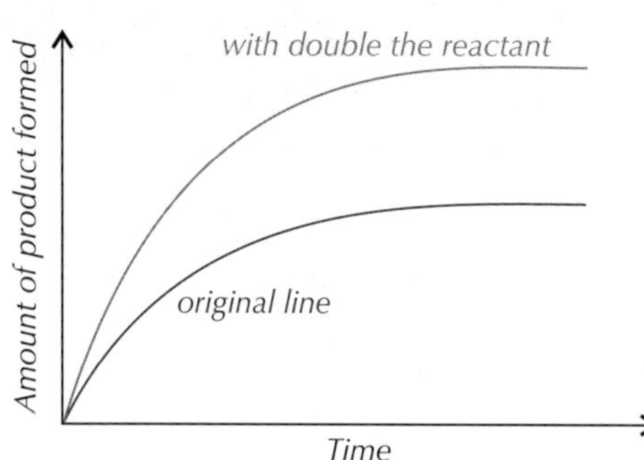

Q4 a) Change in conc. = 0.27 – 0.02 = 0.25 g/dm³
Mean rate = 0.25 ÷ 60 = **0.0042 g/dm³/s**

b)

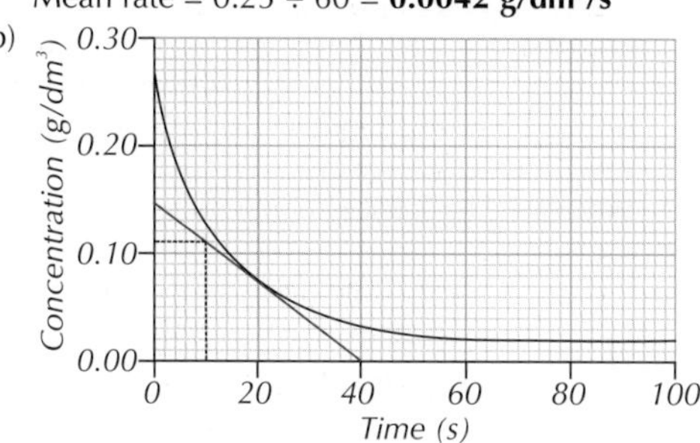

E.g. change in x = 40 – 10 = 30 s
change in y = 0 – 0.11 = –0.11 g/dm³
Gradient = change in y ÷ change in x = –0.11 ÷ 30 = –0.0037
Rate = **0.0037 g/dm³/s**

Depending on how you drew your gradient, you may end up with a slightly different value for the rate. But as long as your value is similar, you can still mark it as correct.

3. Rate Experiments Involving Gases

Page 199 — Fact Recall Question

Q1 E.g. Add a known volume and concentration of hydrochloric acid to a conical flask. Add a known mass of marble chips to the flask and quickly attach an empty gas syringe. Record the volume of gas produced at regular intervals and plot the results on a graph with time on the x-axis and volume of gas produced on the y-axis. Repeat the experiment at least twice more, using a different concentration of acid for each repeat, but keeping all other conditions (mass of chips, size of chips, volume of acid, etc.) the same.

4. Rate Experiments Involving Precipitation

Page 201 — Fact Recall Question

Q1 E.g. the reaction between sodium thiosulfate and hydrochloric acid produces a yellow sulfur precipitate. To determine how temperature affects the rate of the reaction, you could repeat the reaction at different temperatures and watch a mark on a piece of paper through the solution and time how long it takes for the mark to disappear.

Page 201 — Application Question

Q1 a) Independent variable: temperature.
Dependent variable: time taken for the reaction mixture to change colour.

b) Any two from: e.g. the concentrations of the reactants / the volume of the solution / the depth of the solution / the person who decides when the colour change is complete.

c) In order to calculate a mean, which will be more accurate than an individual result.

d) The different scientists might think the colour change is complete at slightly different times, so to make the results precise, the same person should judge each time as their opinion should be consistent.

5. Collision Theory

Page 204 — Fact Recall Questions

Q1 The two particles must collide with sufficient energy.

Q2 Increasing the temperature increases the frequency of collisions because the particles are moving faster. It also increases the energy of the collisions, so more particles collide with enough energy to react.

Q3 If you increase the concentration of the reactants, the particles will be closer together and so collisions between the particles will be more likely. More frequent collisions means a faster rate of reaction.

Q4 The minimum energy that particles must have when they collide in order to react.

Page 204 — Application Question

Q1 a) E.g. going from marble chips to crushed chips to powdered chalk, the surface area of the marble increases and the rate of the reaction also increases. The larger surface area means that there are more frequent collisions between the reacting particles and so the rate of reaction is faster.

b) The frequency of successful collisions in the reaction with crushed marble chips is double the frequency of sucessful collisions in the reaction with marble chips.

6. Catalysts

Page 206 — Fact Recall Questions

Q1 A catalyst is a substance that can increase the rate of a reaction without being chemically changed or used up during the reaction, and without changing the reaction products.

Q2 A biological catalyst.

Q3 E.g. Enzymes are used in the fermentation reaction that produces alcoholic drinks.

Pages 208-209 — Rates of Reaction Exam-style Questions

1 a) E.g. measuring the decrease in mass as the CO_2 is given off using a mass balance ***(1 mark)***.

b) 14 minutes ***(1 mark)***

You can tell that the reaction finished after 14 minutes because this is how long it took for the graph to level off.

c) 12 cm^3 of CO_2 was produced in the first 2 minutes, so the rate of reaction was 12 ÷ 2 = **6 cm^3/min**.
(2 marks for correct answer, otherwise 1 mark for dividing a volume read from the graph by a time read from the graph).

d) As the volume of product/CO_2 increases, the reactants get used up, so the concentration of the reactants decreases ***(1 mark)***. This means there are fewer collisions between the reacting particles ***(1 mark)***.

e)
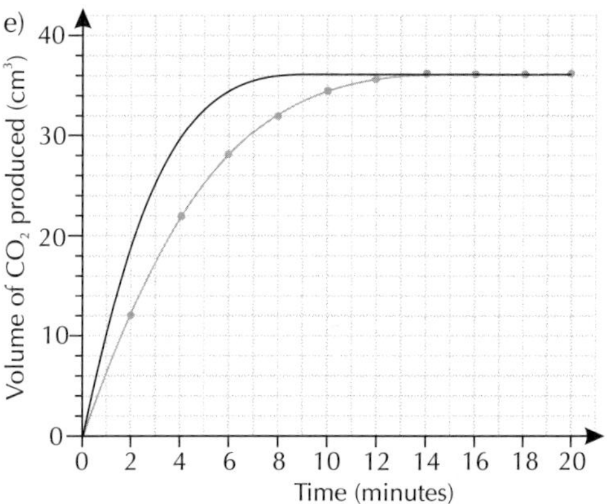

(1 mark for the curve being steeper than the original curve, 1 mark for the curve ending at the same level as the original curve).

The question asked for a sketch, so if you didn't put in the values on the axes, you still get the marks. The important thing here is that the shapes of both curves are correct.

2 a) E.g. Hydrochloric acid increases the rate of reaction ***(1 mark)*** but doesn't appear in the reaction equation/alter the products of the reaction ***(1 mark)***.

b) They provide an alternative reaction pathway ***(1 mark)*** with a lower activation energy ***(1 mark)***.

c) E.g increase the temperature / increase the concentration of ethanol/ethanoic acid ***(1 mark)***

3 a) a gas syringe ***(1 mark)***

b)
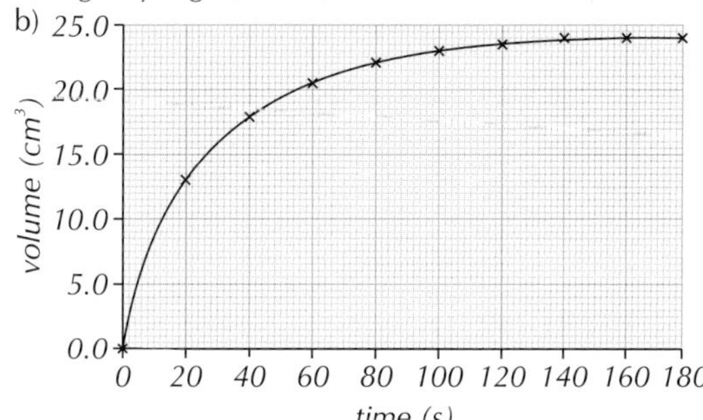

(3 marks — 1 mark for correctly labelled axes (including units from the table) with sensible scales, 1 mark for points plotted correctly, 1 mark for a line of best fit.)

c) E.g. cm^3/s / $cm^3\ s^{-1}$ ***(1 mark)***

d)

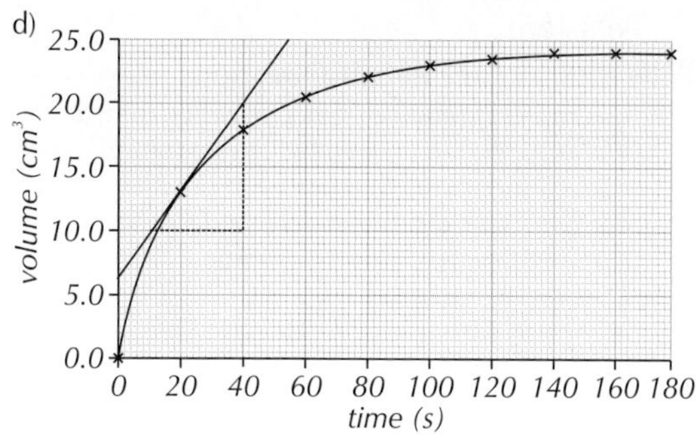

E.g. gradient = change in y ÷ change in x
= (20.0 – 10.0) ÷ (40 – 10) = 10.0 ÷ 30 =
0.33 cm^3/s

(3 marks for rate between 0.25 cm^3/s and 0.40 cm^3/s, otherwise 1 mark for tangent to curve drawn at 20 s, 1 mark for correct equation used to calculate gradient.)

e) It halved ***(1 mark)***.

Topic 7b — Energy Changes in Reactions

1. Endothermic and Exothermic Reactions

Page 212 — Fact Recall Questions

Q1 A reaction which gives out heat energy to the surroundings.

Q2 Because endothermic reactions absorb energy from the surroundings.

Q3 E.g.

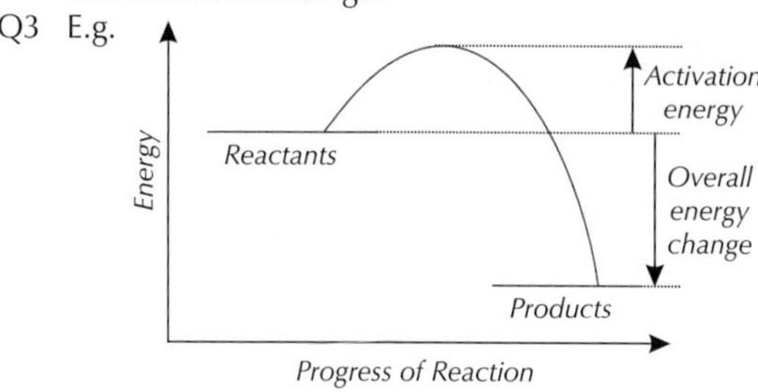

Page 212 — Application Question

Q1 C

2. Measuring Temperature Changes

Page 214 — Fact Recall Question

Q1 E.g. salt dissolving in water / neutralisation reaction / displacement reaction / precipitation reaction

Page 214 — Application Question

Q1 a) E.g. measure out both solutions and record their temperature. Check that they are the same temperature. Pour both solutions into a polystyrene cup and stir well. Observe the temperature of the mixture and record the highest temperature it reaches. Calculate the temperature change.

b) The temperature will increase.

3. Bond Energies

Page 217 — Fact Recall Questions

Q1 a) endothermic

b) exothermic

Q2 During an exothermic reaction, the energy released in bond formation is greater than the energy used in breaking old bonds. The energy that is left over is released into the surroundings.

Page 217 — Application Questions

Q1 Energy used in bond breaking =
(2 × 436) + 498 = 1370 kJ mol^{-1}
Energy released in bond making =
(4 × 464) = 1856 kJ mol^{-1}
Energy change = 1370 – 1856 = **–486 kJ mol^{-1}**

Q2 Energy used in bond breaking =
(2 × ((3 × 413) + 358 + 464)) + (3 × 498)
= 5616 kJ mol^{-1}
Energy released in bond making =
(2 × (2 × 805)) + (4 × (2 × 464)) = 6932 kJ mol^{-1}
Energy change = 5616 – 6932 = **–1316 kJ mol^{-1}**

Page 219 — Energy Changes in Reactions Exam-style Questions

1 a)

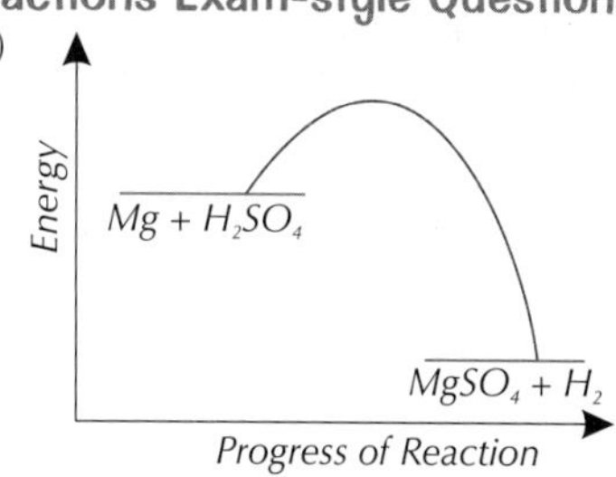

(1 mark for labelling the axes correctly, 1 mark for having the energy of the reactants higher than the energy of the products, 1 mark for drawing a correctly shaped curve)

Instead of writing out the chemical formulae, you could simply label the energy levels as 'reactants' (on the left) and 'products' (on the right).

b) To reduce energy loss from the reaction ***(1 mark)***.

c) To make sure the investigation is valid/a fair test ***(1 mark)***.

2 a) The formation of ammonia is exothermic ***(1 mark)*** because the reactants are at a higher energy on the reaction profile than the products ***(1 mark)***.

b) Energy used in bond breaking =
945 + (3 × 436) = 2253 kJ mol^{-1} ***(1 mark)***
Energy released in bond making =
2 × (3 × 391) = 2346 kJ mol^{-1} ***(1 mark)***
Energy change = 2253 – 2346 = **–93 kJ mol^{-1}**
(1 mark)

c)

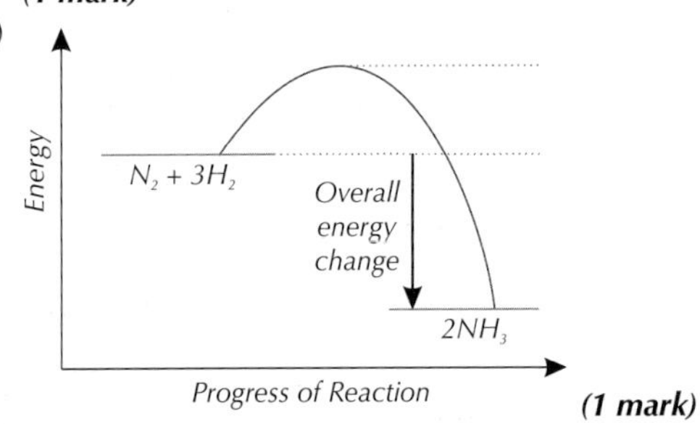

(1 mark)

Topic 8 — Fuels and Earth Science

1. Fractional Distillation of Crude Oil

Page 222 — Fact Recall Questions

Q1 A resource that cannot be replaced once it has been used up.

Q2 a) E.g. as a fuel in cars.
b) E.g. as a fuel for large ships/in some power stations.

Page 222 — Application Questions

Q1 a) diesel
The fractionating column is hottest at the bottom and coolest at the top, so the fraction with the highest boiling temperature range will be removed at the bottom. This is diesel.
b) 68 °C, petrol

Q2 Tetracontane

2. Hydrocarbons

Page 225 — Fact Recall Questions

Q1 A hydrocarbon is any molecule that is formed from hydrogen and carbon atoms only.

Q2 hydrocarbon + oxygen → carbon dioxide + water

Page 225 — Application Question

Q1 a) decane
b) Butane is a larger molecule than ethane. This means that there are stronger intermolecular forces between butane molecules than between ethane molecules, so more energy is required to break these forces.
c) decane

3. Pollutants

Page 228 — Fact Recall Questions

Q1 Incomplete combustion occurs when (a hydrocarbon) fuel is burned in an insufficient amount of oxygen.

Q2 Carbon monoxide that has been breathed in can combine with red blood cells and stop the blood from carrying oxygen around the body.

Q3 a) E.g. sulfur dioxide
b) Any two from: e.g. it can cause lakes to become acidic and many plants and animals may die as a result. / It can kill trees. / It can damage limestone buildings or stone statues.

Q4 A high temperature.

Page 228 — Application Questions

Q1 Advantage: any one from: e.g. the only waste product is water. / No harmful pollutants are formed. / Hydrogen is obtained from water, which is renewable.
Disadvantage: any one from: e.g. a special, expensive engine is required. / Hydrogen gas is expensive to manufacture. / Hydrogen gas production requires energy which often comes from burning fossil fuels. / Hydrogen is highly flammable so is hard to store safely. / Hydrogen is not widely available, which can make it more expensive than other fuels.

Q2 Fuel A, as it contains less sulfur, so will release less sulfur dioxide, a cause of acid rain, when it's burnt.

4. Cracking Crude Oil

Page 230 — Fact Recall Questions

Q1 Cracking is a process where long-chain, saturated hydrocarbons are broken down into smaller, more useful ones.

Q2 alkanes and alkenes

Q3 It allows the supply of petrochemicals to match demand. / There is a greater demand for short chain hydrocarbons than for long-chain hydrocarbons.

5. Evolution of the Atmosphere

Page 232 — Fact Recall Questions

Q1 The early atmosphere was probably mostly carbon dioxide with virtually no oxygen. There may also have been water vapour, nitrogen and small amounts of methane and ammonia.

Q2 Carbon dioxide was removed from the atmosphere as it dissolved in the oceans. Marine animal shells formed, containing carbonates using the dissolved carbon dioxide. These formed sedimentary rocks after they died, locking the carbon dioxde away.

Page 232 — Application Question

Q1 a) The concentration of water vapour in the atmosphere decreased because 4.5 billion years ago the Earth began to cool and the water vapour in the atmosphere condensed to form the Earth's oceans.

b) E.g. oxygen, because the concentration of oxygen in the early atmosphere was initially low but increased due to plants and algae producing oxygen during photosynthesis.

6. Greenhouse Gases & Climate Change

Page 236 — Fact Recall Questions

Q1 They absorb long wavelength IR radiation that gets reflected back off Earth. They then re-radiate this in all directions, including back towards the Earth. This radiation is thermal radiation, so it keeps Earth warm.

Q2 E.g. more food production/farming.

Q3 Different areas may have varying carbon dioxide levels so may be unrepresentative of the global level.

Q4 a) An increase in Earth's temperature.

b) Any one from: e.g. polar ice caps melting / sea levels rising / more flooding / a change in the ability of certain regions to produce food / an increase in the frequency and severity of storms / changes in the distribution of certain wild species / changes in rainfall patterns.

Q5 E.g. reduce carbon dioxide emissions by limiting our use of fossil fuels.

Pages 239-240 — Fuels and Earth Science Exam-style Questions

1 a) Fractions are simpler, more useful mixtures than crude oil ***(1 mark)***.

b) They have short carbon chains. / They have low boiling points. ***(1 mark)***

c) heptane + oxygen → carbon dioxide + water ***(2 marks for correct answer, otherwise 1 mark for correct reactants, 1 mark for correct products)***.

2 a) CH_2 ***(1 mark)***.

b) Decane ***(1 mark)*** because it has the longest carbon chain ***(1 mark)***.

c) Propane ***(1 mark)*** because it has the shortest carbon chain ***(1 mark)*** so has the lowest boiling point ***(1 mark)***.

d) i) At high temperatures ***(1 mark)***, nitrogen and oxygen react together to form nitrogen oxides ***(1 mark)***.

ii) e.g. (photochemical) smog ***(1 mark)***

3 a) cracking ***(1 mark)***

b) E.g. as a fuel in some vehicles/cars/trains ***(1 mark)***

4 a) volcanoes ***(1 mark)***

b) Any two from: e.g. lots of the carbon dioxide was dissolved in the oceans. / Some carbon dioxide was absorbed by plants and algae when they photosynthesised. / The carbon dioxide was locked away in sedimentary rocks/fossil fuels ***(1 mark for each correct answer, up to a maximum of 2 marks)***.

c) E.g. the increased concentration of carbon dioxide contributes to global warming ***(1 mark)***.

5 a) Cows produce lots of methane gas ***(1 mark)***.

b) i) The soot may have formed from incomplete combustion ***(1 mark)***.

ii) E.g. soot may cause respiratory problems ***(1 mark)*** and make buildings look dirty ***(1 mark)***.

iii) Carbon monoxide ***(1 mark)*** can cause fainting/coma/death ***(1 mark)***.

c) The only product of the reaction in a hydrogen fuel cell is water/no harmful pollutants are produced ***(1 mark)***. Hydrogen fuel cells don't release carbon dioxide into the atmosphere ***(1 mark)***.

Glossary

Accurate result
A result that is close to the true answer.

Acid
A substance with a pH of less than 7 that forms H^+ ions in water.

Acid rain
Acidic rainwater that forms when sulfur dioxide dissolve in rain droplets.

Activation energy
The minimum amount of energy that reactant particles must have when they collide in order to react.

Alkali
A substance with a pH of more than 7 that forms OH^- ions in solution.

Alkali metal
An element in Group 1 of the periodic table. E.g. sodium, potassium etc.

Alkane
A saturated hydrocarbon with the general formula C_nH_{2n+2}. E.g. methane, ethane, propane etc.

Alkene
An unsaturated hydrocarbon that contains a carbon-carbon double bond and has the general formula C_nH_{2n}. E.g. ethene, propene etc.

Anion
An ion with a negative charge, formed when an atom gains one or more electrons.

Anode
A positively charged electrode. Anions move towards the anode during electrolysis.

Anomalous result
A result that doesn't fit with the rest of the data.

Aqueous solution
A solution in which a solute is dissolved in water.

Atom
A neutral particle made up of protons and neutrons in the nucleus, with electrons surrounding the nucleus.

Atomic number
The number of protons in the nucleus of an atom.

Atomic radius
A measure of the size of atoms. The distance from the nucleus to the outermost shell.

Avogadro constant
The number of particles in one mole of a substance, which is 6.02×10^{23}.

Base
A substance that reacts with acids in neutralisation reactions.

Bias
Unfairness in the way data is presented, possibly because the presenter is trying to make a particular point (sometimes without knowing they're doing it).

Bioleaching
The process by which a metal is separated from its ore using bacteria.

Boiling
The transition of a substance from a liquid to a gas.

Bond energy
The amount of energy required to break a bond (or the amount of energy released when a bond is made).

Calibrate
Measure something with a known quantity and set the instrument being used to that quantity.

Catalyst
A substance that can speed up a reaction without being chemically changed or used up in the reaction, and without changing the reaction products.

Categoric data
Data that comes in distinct categories, e.g. blood type (A+, B–, etc.) or metals (copper, zinc, etc.).

Cathode
A negatively charged electrode. Cations move towards the cathode during electrolysis.

Cation
A particle with a positive charge, formed when one or more electrons are lost.

Chemical change
A change that occurs during a chemical reaction, where bonds between atoms break and new substances are formed.

Chromatogram
The pattern of spots formed as a result of separating a mixture using chromatography.

Chromatography
An analytical method used to separate the substances in a mixture based on how the components interact with a mobile phase and a stationary phase.

Climate change
A change in the Earth's climate. E.g. global warming, changing rainfall patterns etc.

Collision theory
The theory that in order for a reaction to occur, particles must collide with sufficient energy.

Combustion
An exothermic reaction between a fuel and oxygen.

Combustion reaction
An exothermic reaction between a fuel and oxygen.

Complete combustion
When a fuel burns in plenty of oxygen. The only products are carbon dioxide and water.

Concentration
The amount of a substance in a certain volume of solution.

Condensing
The transition of a substance from a gas to a liquid.

Continuous data
Numerical data that can have any value within a range (e.g. length, volume or temperature).

Control group
A group that matches the one being studied, but where the independent variable isn't altered. The group is kept under the same conditions as the group in the experiment.

Control variable
A variable in an experiment that is kept the same.

Conversion factor
A number which you must multiply or divide a unit by to convert it to a different unit.

Correlation
A relationship between two variables.

Covalent bond
A chemical bond formed when atoms share a pair of electrons.

Covalent substance
A substance where the atoms are held together by covalent bonds.

Cracking
The process of breaking down long-chain hydrocarbons into shorter ones.

Crystallisation
The formation of solid crystals as water evaporates from a solution.

Deforestation
The removal of forests, usually to make room for crops or housing.

Delocalised electron
An electron that isn't associated with a particular atom or bond and is free to move within a structure.

Density
The mass of a substance in a given volume.

Dependent variable
The variable in an experiment that is measured.

Discrete data
Numerical data that can only take a certain value, with no in-between value (e.g. number of people).

Displacement reaction
A reaction where a more reactive element replaces a less reactive element in a compound.

Distillation
A way of separating out a liquid from a mixture. You heat the mixture until the bit you want evaporates, then cool the vapour to turn it back into a liquid.

Dot and cross diagram
A way of representing an ionic compound or a molecule that shows the electronic configuration of the atoms or ions it's made up of.

Dynamic equilibrium
The point at which the rates of the forward and backward reactions in a reversible reaction are the same, and so the amounts of reactants and products in the reaction container don't change.

Electrode
An electrical conductor which is submerged in the electrolyte during electrolysis.

Electrolysis
The process of breaking down a substance using electrical energy from a direct current supply.

Electrolyte
An ionic compound in a solution or liquid state that is used in electrolysis to conduct electricity between the two electrodes.

Electron
A subatomic particle with a relative charge of –1. In atoms, electrons are found in shells around the nucleus.

Electron shell
A region of an atom that contains electrons. It's also known as an energy level.

Electronic configuration
The number of electrons in an atom (or ion) of an element and how they are arranged.

Empirical formula
A chemical formula showing the simplest possible whole number ratio of atoms in a compound.

End-point
The point at which an acid or alkali is completely neutralised during a titration.

Endothermic reaction
A reaction which takes in heat energy from the surroundings.

Enzyme
A biological catalyst.

Evaporation
The transition of a substance from a liquid to a gas.

Exothermic reaction
A reaction which transfers heat energy to the surroundings.

Fair test
A controlled experiment where the only thing that changes is the independent variable.

Feedstock
A raw material that can be used to create useful substances.
E.g. crude oil.

Filtration
A physical method used to separate an insoluble solid from a liquid.

Finite resource
A resource that isn't replaced at a quick enough rate to be considered replaceable.

Fraction
A group of hydrocarbons that condense together when crude oil is separated using fractional distillation.
E.g. petrol, diesel oil, kerosene etc.

Fractional distillation
A process that can be used to separate the substances in a mixture according to their boiling points.

Freezing
The transition of a substance from a liquid to a solid.

Frequency density
The height of a bar on a histogram. It is found by the frequency divided by the class width.

Gas
A state of matter where particles have weak forces of attraction and are therefore free to move with random motion filling the container they are held in. Gases have no fixed volume and no fixed shape.

General formula
A formula that can be used to find the molecular formula of any member of a homologous series.

Giant covalent structure
A structure made up of lots of atoms that are all bonded to each other by strong covalent bonds.

Global warming
The increase in the average temperature of the Earth.

Greenhouse effect
When greenhouse gases in the atmosphere absorb long wavelength radiation and re-radiate it in all directions, including back towards Earth, helping to keep the Earth warm.

Greenhouse gas
A gas that can absorb and re-radiate long wavelength radiation.

Ground water
Water stored in rocks underground.

Group
A column in the periodic table.

Haber process
A process used to make ammonia by reacting nitrogen with hydrogen.

Half equation
An equation which shows how electrons are transferred when a substance is reduced or oxidised. E.g. at an electrode during electrolysis.

Halide ion
An ion with a 1– charge formed when a halogen atom gains an electron. E.g. Cl–, Br– etc.

Halogen
An element in Group 7 of the periodic table. E.g. chlorine, bromine etc.

Hazard
Something that has the potential to cause harm.

Homologous series
A group of compounds that have the same general formula and have similar chemical properties because they have the same functional group.

Hydrocarbon
A compound that is made from only hydrogen and carbon.

Hydrogen halide
A compound that forms between hydrogen and a halogen, e.g. hydrogen chloride.

Hypothesis
A possible explanation for a scientific observation.

Incomplete combustion
When a fuel burns but there isn't enough oxygen for it to burn completely. Products can include carbon monoxide and carbon.

Independent variable
The variable in an experiment that is changed.

Indicator
A substance that changes colour above or below a certain pH.

Inert
Chemically unreactive.

Insoluble
A substance is insoluble if it does not dissolve in a particular solvent.

Intermolecular force
A force of attraction that exists between molecules.

Ion
A charged particle formed when one or more electrons are lost or gained from an atom or molecule.

Ionic bond
A strong electrostatic attraction between oppositely charged ions.

Ionic compound
A compound that contains positive and negative ions held together in a regular arrangement (a lattice) by electrostatic forces of attraction.

Ionic equation
An equation that shows only the reacting particles and the products they form.

Ionic lattice
A closely-packed regular arrangement of particles held together by electrostatic forces of attraction.

Isotope
A different atomic form of the same element, which has the same number of protons, but a different number of neutrons.

Joules
The standard unit of energy.

L

Law of conservation of mass
A law that states that during a reaction no atoms are destroyed or created, so there are the same number and types of atoms on each side of a reaction equation.

Le Chatelier's principle
The idea that if the conditions of a reaction are changed when a reversible reaction is at equilibrium, the system will try to counteract the change.

Life cycle assessment
An assessment of the environmental impact of a product over the course of its life.

Limiting reactant
A reactant that gets completely used up in a reaction, so limits the amount of product that's formed.

Liquid
A state of matter where randomly arranged particles tend to stick closely together but are free to move past each other. Liquids have a fixed volume but no fixed shape.

Litmus
A single indicator that's blue in alkalis and red in acids.

Malleable
A malleable material can be easily hammered or rolled into flat sheets.

Mass number
The total number of protons and neutrons in an atom.

Mean (average)
A measure of average found by adding up all the data and dividing by the number of values there are.

Melting
The transition of a substance from a solid to a liquid.

Metal
An element that can form positive ions when it reacts.

Metal halide
A compound that forms between a metal and a halogen, e.g. potassium chloride.

Metal ore
Rocks that are found naturally in the Earth's crust containing enough metal to make the metal profitable to extract.

Metallic bond
The attraction between metal ions and delocalised electrons in a metal.

Methyl orange
A single indicator that's yellow in alkalis and red in acids.

Mixture
A substance made from two or more elements or compounds that aren't chemically bonded to each other.

Mobile phase
In chromatography, the mobile phase is a gas or liquid where the molecules are able to move.

Model
Something used to describe or display how an object or system behaves in reality.

Mole
A unit of amount of substance — the mass of one mole of a substance is equal to the value of the relative particle mass (A_r or M_r) of that substance in grams, and contains 6.02×10^{23} particles of the substance.

Molecular formula
A chemical formula showing the actual number of atoms of each element in a compound.

Neutral substance
A substance with a pH of 7.

Neutralisation reaction
The reaction between acids and bases that leads to the formation of neutral products — usually a salt and water.

Neutron
A subatomic particle with a relative charge of 0 and a relative mass of 1. Neutrons are found in the nucleus of an atom.

Noble gas
An element in Group 0 of the periodic table. E.g. helium, neon etc.

Nucleus
The central part of an atom, made up of protons and neutrons.

Oxidation
A reaction where electrons are lost or oxygen is gained by a species.

Paper chromatography
An analytical technique that can be used to separate and analyse coloured substances.

Peer-review
The process in which other scientists check the results and explanations of an investigation before they are published.

Period
A row in the periodic table.

Periodic table
A table of all the known elements, arranged in order of atomic number so that elements with similar chemical properties are in groups.

pH scale
A scale from 0 to 14 that is used to measure how acidic or alkaline a solution is.

Phenolphthalein
A single indicator that's pink in alkalis and colourless in acids.

Physical change
A change in the arrangement or the energy of particles in a substance that doesn't change what the substance is.

Phytoextraction
The process by which a metal is extracted from soil by using plants.

Plum pudding model
A disproved theory of the atom as a ball of positive charge with electrons inside it.

Potable water
Water that is safe for drinking.

Precipitate
A solid that is formed in a solution during a chemical reaction.

Precise result
When all the data is close to the mean.

Prediction
A statement based on a hypothesis that can be tested.

Product
A substance that is formed in a chemical reaction.

Proton
A subatomic particle with a relative charge of +1 and a relative mass of 1. Protons are found in the nucleus of an atom.

Pure substance
A substance that only contains one compound or element throughout.

Random error
A difference in the results of an experiment caused by things like human error in measuring.

Range
The difference between the smallest and largest values in a set of data.

Rate of reaction
How fast the reactants in a reaction are changed into products.

Reactant
A substance that reacts in a chemical reaction.

Reaction profile
A graph that shows how the energy in a reaction changes as the reaction progresses.

Reactivity series
A list of elements arranged in order of their reactivity. The most reactive elements are at the top and the least reactive are at the bottom.

Redox reaction
A reaction where one substance is reduced and another is oxidised.

Reduction
A reaction where electrons are gained or oxygen is lost.

Relative atomic mass (A_r)
The average mass of one atom of an element measured relative to the mass of one atom of carbon-12.

Relative formula mass (M_r)
All the relative atomic masses (A_r) of the atoms in a compound added together.

Reliable result
A result that is repeatable and reproducible.

Repeatable result
A result that will come out the same if the experiment is repeated by the same person using the same method and equipment.

Reproducible result
A result that will come out the same if someone different does the experiment, or a slightly different method or piece of equipment is used.

Resolution
The smallest change a measuring instrument can detect.

Reversible reaction
A reaction where the products of the reaction can themselves react to produce the original reactants.

R_f value
In chromatography, the ratio between the distance travelled by a dissolved substance and the distance travelled by a solvent.

Risk
The chance that a hazard will cause harm to someone.

Rough titration
A titration carried out to find the approximate value of the end-point, but not used in any calculations of the mean titre.

S

S.I. unit
A standard unit of measurement, recognised by scientists all over the world.

Salt
An ionic compound that is produced during the neutralisation reaction between an acid and a base.

Saturated
A molecule that contains only single bonds.

Scaling prefix
A word or symbol which goes before a unit to indicate a multiplying factor (e.g. 1 km = 1000 m).

Significant figure
The first significant figure of a number is the first non-zero digit. The second, third and fourth significant figures follow on immediately after it.

Simple distillation
A way of separating out a liquid from a mixture if there are large differences in the boiling points of the substances. You heat the mixture until the bit you want evaporates, then cool the vapour to turn it back into a liquid.

Simple molecule
A molecule made up of only a few atoms held together by covalent bonds.

Solid
A state of matter where particles are held close together with strong forces of attraction to form a regular lattice arrangement. Solids have a fixed volume and a fixed shape.

Soluble
A substance is soluble if it can be dissolved in a solvent.

Solvent front
The point the solvent has reached up the filter paper during paper chromatography.

Stationary phase
In chromatography, the stationary phase is a solid or really thick liquid where molecules are unable to move.

Strong acid
An acid which fully ionises in an aqueous solution.

Subliming
The transition of a substance from a solid to a gas.

Successful collision
A collision between particles that results in a chemical reaction.

Surface area to volume ratio
The amount of surface area per unit volume of a particle.

Surface water
Water from lakes, rivers and reservoirs.

Systematic error
An error that is consistently made throughout an experiment.

Tangent
A straight line that touches a curve at a particular point without crossing it.

Theory
A hypothesis which has been accepted by the scientific community because there is good evidence to back it up.

Titration
A type of experiment that you can use to find the concentration of a solution.

Titre
The minimum volume of acid needed to neutralise an alkali (or vice versa).

Trial run
A quick version of an experiment that can be used to work out the range of variables and the interval between the variables that will be used in the proper experiment.

Uncertainty
The amount by which a given result may differ from the true value.

Universal indicator
A wide range indicator that changes colour depending on the pH of the solution that it's in.

Unsaturated hydrocarbon
A molecule that contains two fewer hydrogen atoms than the equivalent alkane due to the presence of a double bond.

Valid result
A result that is repeatable, reproducible and answers the original question.

Waste water
Water that has been contaminated by a human process.

Weak acid
An acid which partially ionises in an aqueous solution.

Zero error
A type of systematic error caused by using a piece of equipment that isn't zeroed properly.

Acknowledgements

Photograph acknowledgements

Cover photo: **Laguna Design**/Science Photo Library

p 6 **Tony Craddock**/Science Photo Library, p 8 **Tony McConnell**/Science Photo Library, p 9 **Tek Image**/Science Photo Library, p 12 istock.com/**tunart**, p 13 **Martyn F. Chillmaid**/Science Photo Library, p 21 **Pr. M. Brauner**/Science Photo Library, p 23 **Martyn F. Chillmaid**/Science Photo Library, p 26 **GIPhotoStock**/Science Photo Library, p 33 Science Photo Library, p 39 **Sputnik**/Science Photo Library, p 40 **Andrew Lambert Photography**/Science Photo Library, p 54 **Charles D. Winters**/Science Photo Library, p 55 **Charles D. Winters**/Science Photo Library, p 62 **Lawrence Lawry**/ Science Photo Library, p 63 **Science Stock Photography**/Science Photo Library, p 64 **Victor Habbick Visions**/Science Photo Library, p 75 **Andrew Lambert Photography**/Science Photo Library, p 76 **Andrew Lambert Photography**/ Science Photo Library, p 78 **Andrew Lambert Photography**/Science Photo Library, p 81 **GiPhotoStock**/Science Photo Library, p 83 **Andrew Lambert Photography**/Science Photo Library, p 87 **Andrew Lambert Photography**/ Science Photo Library, p 96 **Andrew Lambert Photography**/Science Photo Library, p 101 **Andrew Lambert Photography**/Science Photo Library, p 102 **Andrew Lambert Photography**/Science Photo Library, p 103 **Andrew Lambert Photography**/Science Photo Library, p 104 **Martyn F. Chillmaid**/Science Photo Library, p 105 Science Photo Library, p 108 Science Photo Library, p 119 **Andrew Lambert Photography**/Science Photo Library, p 120 **Martyn F. Chillmaid**/Science Photo Library, p 121 **GiPhotoStock**/Science Photo Library, p 126 **Martyn F. Chillmaid**/ Science Photo Library, p 129 **GiPhotoStock**/Science Photo Library, p 131 **Alexandre Dotta**/Science Photo Library, p 136 **Trevor Clifford Photography**/Science Photo Library, p 140 **Sputnik**/Science Photo Library, p 147 **Martyn F. Chillmaid**/Science Photo Library, p 150 **Charles D. Winters**/Science Photo Library, p 152 **Martyn F. Chillmaid**/ Science Photo Library, p 153 **Charles D. Winters**/Science Photo Library, p 154 **Charles D. Winters**/Science Photo Library, p 157 **Sputnik**/Science Photo Library, p 160 **Dirk Wiersma**/Science Photo Library, p 170 **Martyn F. Chillmaid**/Science Photo Library, p 171 Science Photo Library, p 174 **Andrew Lambert Photography**/Science Photo Library, p 178 **Martyn F. Chillmaid**/Science Photo Library, p 181 **Andrew Lambert Photography**/Science Photo Library, p 184 **Andrew Lambert Photography**/Science Photo Library, p 191 **Martyn F. Chillmaid**/Science Photo Library, p 192 (top) **Andrew Lambert Photography**/Science Photo Library, p 192 (bottom) **Andrew Lambert Photography**/Science Photo Library, p 198 **Martyn F. Chillmaid**/Science Photo Library, p 203 **GiPhotoStock**/Science Photo Library, p 203 **Trevor Clifford Photography**/Science Photo Library, p 206 **Laguna Design**/Science Photo Library, p 210 **Martyn F. Chillmaid**/Science Photo Library, p 213 **Martyn F. Chillmaid**/Science Photo Library, p 217 **Charles D. Winters**/Science Photo Library, p 221 **Paul Rapson**/Science Photo Library, p 224 **Martyn F. Chillmaid**/ Science Photo Library, p 227 (top) **Simon Fraser**/Science Photo Library, p 227 (bottom) **Adam Hart-Davis**/Science Photo Library, p 229 **Paul Rapson**/Science Photo Library, p 243 Science Photo Library, p 244 (top) **Andrew Lambert Photography**/Science Photo Library, p 244 (bottom) **Andrew Lambert Photography**/Science Photo Library, p 245 **Charles D. Winters**/Science Photo Library, p 246 **GiPhotoStock**/Science Photo Library, p 248 **Martyn F. Chillmaid**/ Science Photo Library, p 248 **Martyn F. Chillmaid**/Science Photo Library, p 251 David Maliphant, p 255 **Andrew Lambert Photography**/Science Photo Library

Index